COLLINS GUIDE TO THE

INSECTS

OF BRITAIN AND WESTERN EUROPE

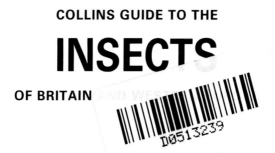

Michael Chinery

HarperCollins Publishers
London

This book owes much to the devoted care and skill of its various artists.

Principally, **Denys Ovenden** contributed the whole initial design, all the line-drawings, and the paintings of Odonata, Orthoptera, Hemiptera, the bees and many of the minor groups; **Richard Lewington** the Lepidoptera, Coleoptera and much of the Hymenoptera; and **Stephen Falk** (while still a student at London University) the Diptera. **Réné Préchac** painted the Trichoptera, **Anthony Hopkins** the wasps, and **John Wilkinson** the plates of stoneflies, larvae and other arthropods. **Hermann Heinzel**, throughout the book, made many invaluable contributions to conception and design.

We are extremely grateful to them all.

First edition, 1986
Reprinted, 1991
Reprinted, 1993
Reprinted, 1997

ISBN 000 219137-7

Printed in Hong Kong

Introduction

About a million different kinds of insects have so far been described and named, and many more certainly remain to be discovered. This is more than all the other known animal species put together. They occupy almost every known habitat outside the polar regions and the deep sea. They are represented by immense populations – perhaps 10 million in a single termite colony, and 60,000 springtails in a square metre of turf. In this they are certainly exceeded by nematode worms, with 20 million or more to the square metre in some soils, while over 90,000 individuals of various species have been extracted from a single rotting apple; but nematodes do not exhibit anything like the fantastic variety of insect life.

The European insect fauna numbers nearly 100,000 known species, with a great range of form and size. Candidates for the largest of them include the Giant Peacock Moth (p. 138), *Saga pedo* (p. 54), *Ephippiger provincialis* (p. 56) and various chafer beetles (p. 265–6). This book is an introduction and general guide to their identification. With it, the reader ought to be able to place those he finds at least in their correct family.

The **geographical** area covered by this book is essentially western Europe – west of a line from Finland to the northern shores of the Adriatic. Many Mediterranean species are included, but generally not those found only in Italy or in the Iberian Peninsula.

All orders are covered and all the major families. The selection of insects to illustrate these, from a total of nearly 100,000 species so far discovered in Europe, was not always easy. We have chosen those *most likely to be noticed*, whether from their size, colour, habits, frequency, or association with human habitation. Many small and dull-coloured species are omitted because, though common, only the specialist would give them a second glance – or be able to identify them with any certainty. But sometimes quite rare or local insects are included because they are so striking that they cannot be overlooked, e.g. the Spanish Moon Moth (p. 139) and the longhorn beetle *Rosalia alpina* (p. 281).

Closely related species can often be distinguished only by microscopic examination of the genitalia and other minute features, description of which are beyond the scope of this book. In such instances the commonest species is normally illustrated and the text indicates that there are several similar species without trying to distinguish them.

The **illustrations** show most of the insects in their natural resting positions, just as you might find them in the wild. Many can be identified perfectly well from this. Others need a closer examination of the venation or perhaps of the hind-wings, and these are shown in the set position so that the relevant features can be seen. **Sexes** are indicated ($\circlearrowleft$ = male, $\circlearrowleft$ = female) only where they are conspicuously different. **Sizes** are shown by magnifications printed beside the illustrations: '× 2½' would mean that the picture is roughly 2½ times life-size. Sizes do vary a good deal, however, and these are no more than rough guides. Where no magnification is given, the insect is approximately life-size.

The **text** complements the illustrations, sometimes drawing attention to important diagnostic features or those which are not visible (undersides, for example), and colour variation or sexual differences. Aspects of behaviour, habitat and food are mentioned when these are useful in identifying the insect. There are brief introductions to each insect order and to the larger families. These give the basic features of the groups and the species texts should be read in conjunction with them. Many families are represented here by a single species, in which case the name of the new family follows that of the species. Where no family name is given, the insect belongs to the same family as the preceding species. **English names** for the insects are used where possible, but most of the smaller and less familiar species do not have them.

Time of appearance is indicated in figures for the months in which the adults may be seen: e.g. '5–8' = May–August. These periods apply to the species' whole geographical range, and the time of appearance may be much more restricted in northern or montane areas. Only a single annual brood may be produced there, while in warmer parts there may be two or even three broods in a year, with adults in evidence for many months. Where no figures are given, the adults may be found throughout the year, though they may go into hibernation in the cooler regions.

Distribution. *European* distribution is given in a simple form:

N = Scandinavia and Finland

C = central – north of a line from Bordeaux to Venice, to include Denmark and the British Isles

S = southern – the whole area south of that line

SW= south-western – west of Nice

SE = south-eastern – east of Nice

Distribution for *Britain and Ireland* is given by the following symbols:

▲ = fairly common in suitable habitats throughout the British Isles.

▲ = fairly common but confined to the northern half of Britain.

▲ = fairly common but confined to the southern half of Britain.

△ = a scattered or local distribution, though possibly common where it does occur, △s = southern; △n = northern.

△ = rare in Britain, △s = southern; △n = northern.

Southern Britain is taken as roughly south of the the Tees, but many species listed as southern will obviously have a more restricted distribution than this. However, there are no hard and fast dividing lines for insect distributions, many of which are imperfectly known, and individual specimens may often be found outside the indicated areas.

Early stages. Distinctive larvae of butterflies and moths (caterpillars) have been illustrated in the main descriptive part of the book beside the adult insects. The nymphs and larvae of other groups are often very similar – hard or impossible to distinguish in the field, and their study a specialist affair. We have illustrated a range of them on pp. 294–5 (terrestrial) and 296–7 (aquatic), to provide a representative survey of the different forms, cross-referenced to and from the main text.

Other creepy-crawlies. Insects belong to the phylum Arthropoda ('jointed feet'), which also includes centipedes, millipedes, woodlice, mites, spiders and other quite separate classes of animal. Beginners can easily confuse some of these with insects, so to make the distinction clear we have included on pp. 298–307 a brief illustrated survey of them, with examples drawn from common or conspicuous species of the region.

Insect Anatomy

Technical terms are kept to a minimum in this book, but some are unavoidable when referring to various parts of insects' bodies, and a basic knowledge of insect anatomy is necessary for identifying many species.

The insect body consists of three main parts: the **head, thorax** and **abdomen**.

THE HEAD. The **vertex** is the area on top of the head, above and between the eyes. The **cheeks** (or **genae**) are the areas below and behind the eyes, and their lower portions are sometimes differentiated as the **jowls**. The head carries a pair of **antennae** or feelers, which are mainly concerned with the senses of smell and touch. Their shape varies a great deal, but in their simplest form they are a chain of more or less identical segments, each well supplied with nerve-endings. The number of segments, ranging from one to over a hundred, is sometimes of value in identifying the insects. The first or basal segment is the **scape**, and is often longer than the others. The second, usually very short, is the **pedicel**, while the rest together form the **flagellum**. In some insects, such as the ants, the scape is particularly long and the rest of the antenna hinges upon it. Such an antenna is called **elbowed** or **geniculate**.

The head also has a pair of **compound eyes**, their surfaces clothed with a number of tiny lenses called facets. Dragonflies and other active fliers have several thousand of these lenses in each eye, enabling them to detect very small movements, but some of the ants and other soil-dwellers have very few lenses or none at all. Many insects also possess some very simple eyes called **ocelli** – usually three, forming a little triangle on the vertex or sometimes on the front of the head, and looking like tiny glass beads. It seems unlikely that ocelli can produce true images, and they may be used simply for detecting variations in light intensity.

The **mouth** is surrounded by a number of greatly modified limbs, collectively known as the **mouth-parts**. The form of these appendages varies enormously with the insect's diet, but the basic set consists of a pair of **mandibles** or **jaws**, a pair of **maxillae** (sometimes called secondary jaws), and a **labium** or lower lip, formed by the fusion of two maxilla-like appendages. The maxillae and labium help first to catch and hold food while it is cut up by the mandibles, then to shovel it into the mouth. They also have sensory arms known as **palps**, which examine and taste the food first. Several other structures may be associated with these mouth-parts, notably the **labrum** or upper lip. This is an outgrowth from the front of the head and forms a roof over the jaw area, where the food is cut and chewed before entering the true mouth.

The head of a cockroach, seen from the front and the side, to show the major regions

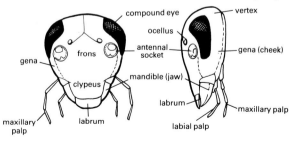

The above arrangement is designed for coping with a solid diet, and is found in a wide range of insects, including grasshoppers, mantids, dragonflies, beetles and wasps. Among the liquid-feeders we find some remarkable modifications. The mandibles are virtually absent in butterflies and moths, and the maxillae have become long and slender and linked together to form a nectar-sucking **proboscis**. Mandibles are also absent in house-flies, but among mosquitoes and horse-flies they are long and needle-like, forming part of the hypodermic syringe with which they draw blood from their victims. The true bugs also have piercing mouth-parts for sucking juices from plants or animals.

THORAX. The insect thorax consists of three segments – **prothorax**, **mesothorax** and **metathorax** – each of which carries a pair of legs. Wings, when present, are borne on the second two, or if there is only one pair, on the middle one. The prothorax never carries wings and is often reduced to a narrow collar, though it is large in bugs and beetles where its dorsal surface, the **pronotum**, is a conspicuous feature. The meso- and metathorax are generally fused into a single unit and the two component sections are not easy to distinguish: the mesothorax is the larger and its dorsal covering, the **mesonotum**, commonly terminates in a prominent triangular or shield-shaped plate called the **scutellum**.

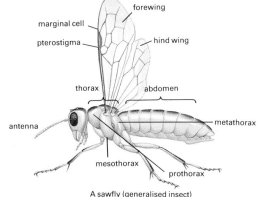

A sawfly (generalised insect)

LEGS. With the exception of a few aberrant forms – notably some female scale insects – all adult insects have three pairs of legs. One can usually recognise four main regions in each. The **coxa** is the basal segment, joining the rest of the leg to the thorax. Then come the **femur** (plural femora), which is usually the largest segment and beyond it the **tibia** - often as long as or even longer than the femur, but generally much more slender. Finally the **tarsus** or foot, which consists of one to five segments and normally bears one or two claws at the tip. The **trochanter** is usually a very small segment between the femur and the coxa: it is firmly fused to the femur and usually hard to detect. The shapes and relative lengths of the different leg segments vary a great deal according to the insects' habits. Many predatory species, including the mantids, have **prehensile** or **raptorial** front legs, in which the tibia can fold back against the femur to trap and grip the prey.

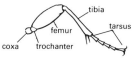

A typical insect leg

WINGS are present in most insects, but not in the most primitive groups – the springtails and bristletails (p. 16). They are also missing from a number of highly specialised parasites such as lice and fleas (pp. 98–101), and many high-altitude insects are wingless or virtually so. The 'typical' insect, however, has two pairs of wings. Both pairs may be membranous, as in dragonflies or butterflies, or the front pair may be rather tough and function largely as protection for the more delicate hind wings at rest. Toughened forewings of this kind are called **tegmina** if they are leathery but still winglike, as in the grasshoppers and cockroaches. The forewings of beetles are known as **elytra**. They are generally very hard and horny and completely cover the flimsy hind wings at rest, making the insects look as if they have no wings at all. Hind wings are absent in all true flies (pp. 190–217), where they have been converted into minute pin-like structures called **halteres**. These are also known as balancers, for they act like gyroscopes and help to stabilise the insects in flight. Hind wings are also missing from some mayfly species and from a number of flightless beetles and grasshoppers.

Membranous wings may be covered with scales as in butterflies and moths, or with hairs as in caddis flies, but otherwise the most obvious feature is the **venation**. This varies enormously and is very important in classifying insect groups, but there is an underlying pattern based on longitudinal veins. Their full pattern, worked out from anatomical and fossil studies, is shown in the hypothetical forewing below. No living insect has the complete set and the number of branches is often greatly reduced, but the main longitudinal veins can usually be recognised in most winged species. Only two **cross-veins** are shown in the diagram. These are present in most insects, but there are often many minor cross-veins as well, especially among the dragonflies and lacewings. The areas of membrane between veins are called **cells**, and the major ones are named according to the vein in front of them: thus the costal cell is just behind the costa, the radial cell behind the radius, the 1st anal cell behind the 1st anal vein, and so on. A **discal cell** occurs in the wings of many insects and is commonly used in classification; but it does not refer to any particular cell and is merely a rather conspicuous cell near the middle of the wing. The discal cell of one insect group is not necessarily bounded by the same veins as the discal cell of another group. Cells bounded by veins on all sides are called **closed cells**, while those bounded on one side by the wing-margin are called **open cells**.

Several systems have been used for naming veins, and care must be taken when referring to the older literature: a given vein then might not refer to the vein of the same name today. Dipterists and lepidopterists, whose charges often have a reduced venation, commonly use a system of numbering for dealing with the longitudinal veins (p. 190).

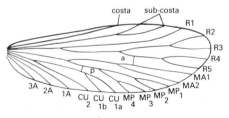

A hypothetical insect wing, showing the full ancestral venation. Living insects all show some reduction of these major veins. R1 is the radius, while R2–R5 are branches from a division of the radius known as the radial sector. MA and MP are the anterior and posterior divisions of the media. Cu is the cubitus, while 1A to 3A are the anal veins. a is the anterior cross vein, always linking the radius to the media, and p is the posterior cross vein which links the media to the cubitus.

ABDOMEN. The adult abdomen has up to 11 segments, although not all are visible, each with a dorsal plate called a **tergite** and a ventral one called a **sternite**. The abdomen has no real limbs but the hind end commonly carries a pair of appendages called **cerci**. These are most obvious in the mayflies (p. 18), where they are long and thread-like, and in the earwigs (p. 68), forming the familiar pincers. Male dragonflies and bush-crickets (p. 48) use their prominent cerci to grasp the females while mating. The **genitalia** are carried on the 8th and 9th abdominal segments. They are usually concealed inside the body though some females have a permanently exposed, often very conspicuous **ovipositor**. Blade- or needle-like, this is used for laying eggs in the ground or plant or animal tissues and is well seen in bush-crickets and some ichneumons (p. 230). The detailed structure of cerci and male/female genitalia is often crucial for separating species, but needs a specialised microscopic technique.

Insect life cycles

Nearly all insects begin life as eggs. Protected by tough, waterproof, often elegantly patterned shells, these can survive a wide range of adverse conditions, from drought to severe frost. Many species pass the winter as eggs, often exposed on the bare twigs of what will be their food-plants. Apart from some primitive wingless insects (p. 16), the hatchlings rarely resemble their parents. They never have wings and often have quite different feeding habits. The considerable change these insects undergo as they develop is called **metamorphosis**.

Like all other arthropods (see p. 298), insects have a tough outer skeleton which does not grow with the rest of the body, so has to be changed periodically for a larger one. The change is called **moulting** or **ecdysis**. When about to moult, the insect stops feeding and becomes quiescent for several hours or even days while the inner layers of its coat or skeleton are dissolved away. A soft new skin is secreted under the old outer layers which, now very thin and fragile, split open as the insect puffs itself up by muscular action and by swallowing air or water. The insect then slowly drags itself out of its old skin and the new one gradually hardens. At this stage, the insect is especially vulnerable: most species therefore try to conceal themselves when about to moult.

When the new skin has become firm, the insect gets rid of excess air or water and makes room for further growth. There is some elasticity in the skin, especially in caterpillars, but there comes a time when further stretching is impossible and another moult must take place. Some insects moult as many as 50 times, but most less than 10 – most butterflies and moths only 4 or 5. The stages between moults are called **instars**: a '2nd-instar larva' would mean a larva (see below) between the first and second moult. The adult insect is the **imago**. Springtails and bristletails go on moulting throughout their lives; the others stop when they have reached maturity. No insect grows any more once it has fully developed wings, though mayflies (p. 18) do undergo one further moult in the winged state.

Winged insects are classified in two divisions, according to the way in which their wings develop. Among the dragonflies, grasshoppers, bugs and several other groups, the wings develop gradually on the outside of the body. These are the EXOPTERYGOTA (= outside wings). The young resemble the adults in general appearance and often live in the same places and have similar feeding habits. The resemblance increases as the wing-buds get larger with each moult. There is thus a gradual change from young to adult form and the insects are said to show **partial** or **incomplete metamorphosis**. The young are known as **nymphs**.

But in the butterflies and moths, beetles, flies, ants, bees, wasps and a few other groups, the young look nothing like the adults, never show any sign of wings, and often have completely different homes and habits. They are known as **larvae**. At each moult until the last, they simply emerge as larger larvae. On reaching full size, the larva splits its skin again and reveals the **pupa** or **chrysalis**, a non-feeding and generally inactive stage as far as external appearance goes. Internally, however, great changes take place as the larval body is broken down and rebuilt in the adult form. Outlines of the wings and other adult features can be seen on the pupal skin, but these organs all develop inside the pupa and this division is therefore called the ENDOPTERYGOTA. Transformation takes anything from a few days to months, and the imago finally breaks out of its pupal skin. This type of development is called complete metamorphosis.

Some insects can fly as soon as they emerge from the nymphal or pupal skin, but most of the larger species need to harden their wings before taking to the air. Most of the endopterygotes emerge with very small and crumpled wings, and their first action is to find a perch where the wings can be unfurled without damage. Blood is gradually pumped into the wing veins, and the wings normally swell to full size within a few minutes. They take much longer to harden, and flight is not usually possible for at least an hour.

Collecting and studying

Many of the larger and more colourful insects, notably butterflies and moths and some of the beetles, can be identified quite easily in the field without catching them. Accurate identification of most of the smaller species, however, involves catching them and taking a closer look at the venation or other details.

Nets. The traditional butterfly net is the best tool for catching free-flying insects. Good nets can be bought from entomological suppliers, but satisfactory ones are not difficult to make at home. The frame should be light, but strong enough to keep its shape when the net is swept through the air. It can be circular or kite-shaped, but must be at least 30 cm across – big enough to get your hands in to manipulate the catch. The bag must be strong enough to resist brambles, but the mesh not so dense that you cannot see the trapped insects. It must be at least twice as deep as the diameter of the frame, so that it can be folded around the frame to trap the captured insects. Dark colours are best for collecting dragonflies and butterflies, but smaller insects show up better against a light-coloured net. A short handle – up to 30 cm – is good for general use. Nets with longer ones are more difficult to control, though certainly useful when trying to catch dragonflies over water or moths gyrating around streetlamps. A short permanent handle with a detachable extension is ideal.

Catching. Night-flying moths are nearly all attracted to light, and many can be caught simply by hanging a electric light bulb over a white sheet in the garden, and standing by with a net. A moth trap will do the same job with less effort and can be left on to sample the moth population throughout the night. Some are truly portable and can be run from a car battery out in the wilds. The heart of the trap is a mercury-vapour lamp. Attracted by its ultra-violet light, the moths crash into baffles around the lamp and fall into a box below. Egg-packing material in the box provides snug resting-places and they settle down quietly until the trap is emptied in the morning. Traps should not be positioned so that they are in full sun early in the morning; the warmth agitates the moths and they damage themselves before they can be examined. One should also take care when emptying the trap to ensure that its contents are not eaten by birds; this particularly when a trap is regularly used in one place, such as a garden, since birds quickly learn that the trap is a source of food. The moths should be released into dense vegetation if possible, with the birds kept away till the insects have settled down. Or the trap can be covered and kept in a cool place till nightfall, when the moths can safely be released.

Crawling insects which spend much of their time on the vegetation can often be spotted and picked up individually, but sweeping is a more productive method and essential for any serious survey of insect life in the herbage. A very sturdy net is needed, reinforced around the rim, for sweeping to and fro through the vegetation. Huge numbers of insects can be collected in this way and the net must be examined and emptied at frequent intervals to prevent their getting damaged. White is the best colour for a sweep net since the smaller insects in the herbage are mainly green or brown.

Insects living in the foliage of **trees** and **bushes** can easily be collected with a beating tray and a stout stick. The 'tray' consists of a sheet of fairly tough material stretched over a collapsible frame about 1 metre square. A long handle makes it easier to hold the tray under a branch. Hitting the branch sharply with a stick usually causes an assortment of caterpillars and other insects to fall from the leaves on to the tray.

Small insects roaming the ground or sitting on leaves or trunks are not always easy to pick up, and are best collected with the aid of a **pooter** – a simple suction device incorporating a holding cage for the insects.

When they have been caught, most insects are easily transferred to plastic tubes or boxes. Entomological dealers market these in a range of convenient sizes: 7.5×2.5 cm is the ideal tube size, and circular boxes about 5 cm $\times$ 2 cm deep can cope with most insects. Insects will travel well in these containers for several hours, providing they are not exposed to the sun. A small piece of leaf or moss gives them something to cling to and also provides essential moisture on a journey.

A good **hand-lens** magnifying about 10× is all that is needed to identify most of the insects in this book, but a low-power microscope (magnifying about 30×) is certainly very useful and can reveal a lot of fascinating detail, especially when used to examine living specimens.

Most insects can be released unharmed after identification, but some of the smaller species cannot be properly identified, at least by the beginner, unless they are killed and examined in detail. Ethyl acetate is one of the most useful killing agents for the amateur entomologist – though it must not be used in plastic containers – but laurel leaves (*Prunus laurocerasus*) are a very good standby, especially for anyone who does not do much collecting. The crushed young shoots and leaves give off a weak cyanide vapour and, when enclosed in an air-tight jar and covered with blotting paper or tissue, make a very convenient killing bottle. But don't be in too much of a hurry to kill your insects: watch their behaviour and look at their natural resting attitudes, for these will help you to identify the insects in the field on another occasion. And don't kill any more insects than you really need for study.

Insect conservation

A small reference collection is necessary for the serious student of insects and will do no harm to the populations of most species, but conservation must always be kept in mind. It is unlikely that collecting alone has caused the extinction of any insect species, but when combined with the alarming rates at which habitats are currently being destroyed it could certainly hasten the end of some of our rarer species. So British conservationists, anxious to minimise the risks to our insect fauna, have issued a **Code for Insect Collecting**, of which the main points may be summarised as follows:

> Take and kill no more specimens than are strictly required: a pair of each species should be enough for normal purposes.
>
> Do not take a species year after year from the same locality. Local forms and species known to be rare should be collected with the utmost restraint, and preferably not at all.*
>
> Leave the environment as you find it: replace logs and stones after searching beneath them, and replace bark removed from dead timber.
>
> Breeding from a fertilised female is better than taking specimens from the wild: unwanted specimens that have been reared should be released in the original locality.
>
> Never collect more larvae or other insects for breeding than can be supported by readily available supplies of food plant.

*Several butterfly species – including the Apollo, Purple Emperor, Large Blue and Large Copper – are already protected by law in some parts of Europe, often with a complete ban on collecting.

The orders of insects

The insects are split into a number of **orders**, based largely on the structure of the wings and the mouth-parts. The names of the orders generally end in *-ptera*, meaning wings: Lepidoptera = scale wings, Coleoptera = sheath wings, Diptera = two wings, and so on. The 28 orders recognised in this book are listed below, with page references. Some entomologists prefer to split several of them and make a total of more than 30 orders. There is much variation in the size of the orders: some contain only a handful of species, while the Coleoptera (beetles) are represented by more than 300,000 different kinds.

Apterygotes: primitive wingless insects which have never had wings at any stage of their evolutionary history

Thysanura	Bristletails (silverfish and allies), p. 16
Diplura	Two-tailed bristletails, p. 16
Protura	Minute soil-dwelling insects, p. 16
Collembola	Springtails, p. 16

Pterygotes: essentially winged insects, although some orders have lost their wings during their evolution. There are also wingless species or forms scattered through most of the other orders.

Exopterygotes: insects with only partial metamorphosis and no pupal stage. Young are nymphs.

Ephemeroptera	Mayflies, p. 18
Odonata	Dragonflies, p. 22
Plecoptera	Stoneflies, p. 36
Orthoptera	Crickets and Grasshoppers, p. 38
Phasmida	Stick and Leaf Insects, p. 64
Dermaptera	Earwigs, p. 68
Embioptera	Web-spinners, p. 66
Dictyoptera	Cockroaches and Mantids, pp. 60, 62
Isoptera	Termites, p. 66
Psocoptera	Booklice and Barklice (Psocids), p. 98
Mallophaga	Biting Lice (all wingless), p. 100
Anoplura	Sucking Lice (all wingless), p. 100
Hemiptera	True Bugs, p. 70
Thysanoptera	Thrips, p. 99

Endopterygotes: insects with complete metamorphosis and a pupal stage. Young are larvae.

Neuroptera	Lacewings, Alder flies, and Snake flies, p. 102
Mecoptera	Scorpion flies, p. 108
Lepidoptera	Butterflies and Moths, p. 110
Trichoptera	Caddis flies, p. 183
Diptera	True Flies, p. 190
Siphonaptera	Fleas (all wingless), p. 100
Hymenoptera	Bees, Wasps, Ants, Sawflies, Ichneumons and others, p. 218
Coleoptera	Beetles, p. 254

THE KEY

This key is designed so that adult insects of all but a few aberrant species can be assigned to their correct group. It is based on wing structure, but also makes use of the feet and antennae and a few other features, all of which are easily seen with the aid of a lens. Winged specimens will always be adults, but wingless ones can be adults or young. Nymphs of exopterygote insects, such as bugs and grasshoppers, can usually be tracked down through the key because they resemble the adults, but the larvae of beetles and other endopterygote insects are not included. If you suspect that your specimen is a larva (other than a caterpillar, for which see pp. 110–82), turn to the range of larvae illustrated on pp. 294–7. Some aquatic nymphs are also illustrated on these pages. Some insect orders occur more than once in the key, because they contain both winged and wingless species or because they cover two or more rather distinct groups: groundhoppers and grasshoppers, for example, are fairly distinct groups within the order Orthoptera.

[1] INSECTS WITH WINGS
(This includes the beetles and other insects with hard and smooth front wings, although these might appear wingless at first sight.)

[2] All wings membranous

One pair of wings

Grasshopper-like, with long back legs; pronotum extending back over abdomen. **Groundhoppers** p. 46

2 or 3 long 'tails' at end of abdomen; wings held vertically at rest; very small antennae. **Mayflies** (some families) p. 18

Minute insects (< 5 mm long) with only one forked vein in the wing; one or more short 'tails'; antennae much longer than head; rare.
Scale Insects (males) p. 96

Large fan-shaped hind wings; front wings in form of twisted clubs (halteres). **Stylopids** (males) p. 255
Front wings normal; hind wings in the form of tiny, pin-shaped structures (halteres), although these may be hidden under flaps in the stouter species; antennae often short and bristle-like. **True Flies** pp. 190–217

Two pairs of membranous wings

Minute insects with feathery wings, which are usually folded tightly over body. **Thrips** p. 98

**Wing membrane clothed with minute scales or hairs*

Wings clothed with scales, often very colourful: usually a coiled proboscis for sipping nectar.
Butterflies and Moths pp. 110–182

Wings hairy, usually yellow, brown or black; held roofwise over body at rest, with antennae pointing forward; few cross-veins; hind wing normally broader than front; no coiled proboscis. **Caddis Flies** pp. 183–9

Wings hairy and all alike; front tarsi swollen: **Web-spinners** p. 66 (more often seen in wingless form)

Tiny insects clothed with white powder.
With wings ± flat at rest.
White Flies p. 97

Wings held roofwise at rest.
Lacewings (Family Coniopterygidae) p. 107

**Wing membrane without a noticeable coating of hairs or scales, although veins may be hairy: usually colourless and transparent, but may be coloured

All wings alike and very flimsy; ± veinless: usually in swarms: southern Europe. **Termites** p. 66

Head extended downwards to form a stout beak: wings usually mottled and ± alike; males mostly with up-turned, scorpion-like abdomen.
Scorpion Flies p. 109

Hind wings similar to or broader than front; folded flat or rolled round body at rest; often 2 fairly stout 'tails', no longer than body and usually much shorter. **Stoneflies** p. 36

***Wings with many cross-veins forming a dense network

2 or 3 'tails', as long as or longer than body; antennae minute; wings held vertically at rest; hind wing much smaller than front.

Mayflies (some families) p. 18

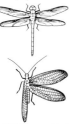

Antennae short and bristle-like (shorter than width of head); body at least 25 mm long, often very slender; wings never held roofwise over body. **Dragonflies** pp. 28–37

Antennae relatively long, sometimes clubbed; wing veins usually forking at margin; wings held roofwise over body at rest; flight slow in most species.
Ant-lions, Lacewings, Alder Flies etc pp. 102–9

***Wings with few cross-veins

Very small insects, often with hairy wing veins and sometimes with a few scales on the wing membrane; venation characteristic; wings held roofwise at rest; relatively long antennae, with at least 12 segments.
Psocids (booklice and barklice) pp. 98

Very small insects, often pear-shaped, with a slender, needle-like beak; wings normally held roofwise at rest, but sometimes flat; antenna never with more than 10 segments: often in masses on plants. **Aphids** p. 94

Stout-bodied insects with clear, shining wing membrane (quite stiff); wings held roofwise at rest; a long, slender beak for sucking sap from trees and shrubs; antennae short and bristle-like. **Cicadas** p. 88

Minute to quite large insects with hind wing very much smaller than front and linked to it by a row of microscopic hooks; wings typically with a small number of large cells, but venation much reduced in some of the smaller species; wings never held roofwise.

With a distinct 'waist' **Bees, Wasps, Ants, Ichneumons** etc pp. 226–53

Without a 'waist' **Sawflies** pp. 222–5

13

[2] Front wings at least partly horny or leathery; hind wings membranous (sometimes absent)

Front wings veinless and meeting in mid-line without overlap

Front wings short and square, leaving most of abdomen uncovered; pincers at hind end. **Earwigs** p. 68

Front wings often very hard and usually covering all of abdomen, but sometimes leaving abdomen partly exposed. **Beetles** pp. 254–91

Front wings with veins and normally overlapping to some extent at rest or else held distinctly roofwise

Front wings with membranous tips; folded flat over body at rest; a slender, piercing beak for sucking plant and animal fluids. **Heteropteran Bugs** pp. 72–87

Front wings of uniform texture and usually opaque, although not always much tougher than hind wings; held roofwise at rest; slender beak for sucking plant juices; insects often leap when disturbed. **Homopteran Bugs: Leaf Hoppers:** p. 92 and **Psyllids** p. 96

Body bullet-shaped, with wings wrapped tightly around it at rest; hind legs enlarged for jumping. **Grasshoppers and Crickets** pp. 38–59

All 3 pairs of legs long and spiky; fast-running; wings folded flat over body at rest; pronotum broad and almost covering head. **Cockroaches** p. 60

Front legs enlarged and very spiny for catching prey; head very mobile on end of long neck. **Mantids** p. 62

[1] INSECTS WITHOUT WINGS OR WITH JUST VERY SMALL FLAPS

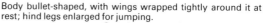
Body long and stick-like. **Stick Insects** p. 64

Body bullet-like, often with small wing flaps just behind head; hind legs enlarged for jumping. **Grasshoppers and Crickets** pp. 38–59

Insects with long, slender 'tails' at hind end

2 'tails'; small soil-dwelling insects. **Diplurans (Family Campodeidae)** p 16

3 'tails'; body usually clothed with shining scales: some species found indoors. **Bristletails** p. 16

Insects with pincers at hind end

Slender, pale soil-dwelling insects with just one tarsal segment. **Diplurans (Family Japygidae)** p. 16

Stouter, often dark brown insects with 3 tarsal segments: often under stones. **Earwigs** p. 68

Insects with short 'tails' or none at all

 Slender, soft-bodied soil-dwellers with 2 short tails: front tarsi swollen. **Webspinners** p. 66

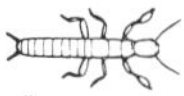

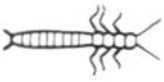

 Pale, slender soil-dwellers with 2 short tails; front tarsi not swollen. **Diplurans (Family Projapygidae)** p. 16

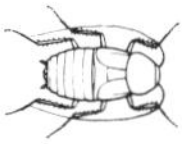

 Flattened insects with spiky legs and a broad pronotum almost covering head; 2 stumpy tails usually visible. **Cockroaches** p. 60

 Elongated insects with enlarged, spiny front legs for catching prey; long neck; 2 short tails usually visible. **Mantids** pp. 62–5

 Small leaping insects with vestigial wings and head extending downwards to form a stout beak. **Snow Fleas** p. 108

 Small leaping insects with no sign of wings; a forked 'spring' at hind end (usually tucked under body); in soil and leaf litter mainly. **Springtails** p. 16

 Body clothed with scales or flattened hairs; wing vestiges present. **Moths** (some females) pp. 124–82

 Body with a marked 'waist', often bearing small lobes or scales, at front of abdomen; antennae often elbowed. **Ants** p. 234 and some other **Hymenoptera** p. 220

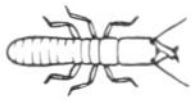

 Slender, soft-bodied and pale insects, normally with 4 tarsal segments; usually in colonies in dead wood: southern Europe. **Termites** p. 66

 Small, pear-shaped insects with head much narrower than body; a needle-like beak under head; often a pair of tubular outgrowths near end of abdomen: found on growing plants. **Aphids** p. 94

 Flattened insects with relatively broad head; antennae long and slender: hind femur often broad; commonly found indoors among dried materials. **Psocids** (booklice) p. 98

*Parasitic insects living on birds and mammals
**Insects flattened laterally

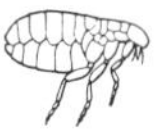

 Jumping insects with long back legs; flattened from side to side; usually brown. **Fleas** p. 101

**Insects flattened dorso-ventrally
***Head partly sunk into thorax

 Antennae more or less concealed in grooves; legs relatively stout, usually with 2 strong claws to grip host: piercing beak (not always obvious). **True Flies** (some families) p. 214

Antennae clearly visible; legs more slender and claws less prominent; slender piercing beak. **Heteropteran Bugs** (some families) p. 80

***Head not sunk into thorax

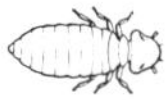

Very small, oval or elongate insects; head nearly as wide as body; prothorax distinct; tarsi with 1 or 2 claws; biting mouths. **Biting Lice** p. 100

Very small, pear-shaped insects; head much narrower than body; thoracic segments fused into one unit; tarsi each with 1 large claw; sucking mouths. **Sucking Lice** p. 100

15

 A proturan

The insects on this page are all primitive, wingless species belonging to the sub-class Apterygota (= without wings). Virtually no metamorphosis during the life cycle. The microscopic proturans (Order Protura) are soil-living insects with neither eyes nor antennae.

BRISTLETAILS   Order Thysanura

Shuttle-shaped insects with 2 long cerci and a central 'tail' known as the epiproct, making 3 'tails' in all, each fringed with minute bristles. Bristletails have biting jaws and are clothed with scales.

▲ **Petrobius maritimus** Machilidae. Antennae as long as or longer than body. Eyes large, with angular outer margin. Ocelli long and slit-like. Lives as scavenger among coastal rocks in splash zone. ▲ *P. brevistylis* is almost identical.

△ **Dilta hibernica**. Antennae shorter than body. Eyes rectangular. Commonest of several similar species on ground in densely vegetated places.

▲ **Silverfish** *Lepisma saccharina* Lepismatidae. Body flattened. Eyes small and separated. Abundant in houses: mainly nocturnal, feeding on starchy materials including spilled flour, paper, etc. Prefers a slightly moist environment.

Ctenolepisma lineata. Less shiny than *Lepisma* and with antennae as long as body. 'Tails' also very long. Indoors and outside. S & C.

▲ **Firebrat** *Thermobia domestica*. Browner and more bristly than *Lepisma* and with longer appendages. Body hairs in distinct patches. Prefers warmer places: always indoors and very common in bakeries and heating ducts.

TWO-TAILED BRISTLETAILS   Order Diplura

Two cerci, of variable form, but no epiproct. Thoracic segments clearly separated, unlike Thysanura. Mostly very small soil-dwelling scavengers and carnivores. Eyes absent.

▲ **Campodea fragilis** Campodeidae. One of several very similar species abundant in compost heaps and other decaying vegetation.

Japyx solifugus Japygidae. Tunnels under stones and among fallen leaves, catching prey with pincer-like cerci. S & C, but rarely seen.

Anajapyx vesiculosus Anajapygidae. Relatively stout cerci are tubular and discharge secretions from abdominal glands. A scavenger. Known only from Italy.

SPRINGTAILS   Order Collembola

The largest group of apterygotes, with about 1,500 species. Body has fewer segments than other insects. Named for the springing organ (furcula) at rear of most species. Like a minute tuning fork, it is clipped under abdomen at rest, but released on disturbance to shoot the insect forward through the air. All species are very small and often clothed with scales or hairs. No compound eyes. Most live in leaf litter, feeding on fungi and decaying plant matter. The ventral tube on underside of abdomen is characteristic of this order.

▲ **Podura aquatica** Poduridae. Abundant on and around still water, especially where there is a good covering of duckweed. Spring reaches ventral tube when folded.

▲ **Neanura muscorum** Hypogastruridae. Grey or purplish black with very short limbs. Spring does not reach ventral tube. Insect hardly jumps. Abundant in woodland.

▲ **Isotoma viridis** Isotomidae. Spring white. Abundant in damp leaf litter and mosses.

▲ **Entomobrya nivalis** Entomobryidae. A distinctive pattern Abundant in mosses.

▲ **Orchesella cincta**. Pale orange to deep brown or black, but 3rd abdominal segment always black. Very hairy, but no scales. Common under woodland mosses.

▲ **Tomocerus vulgaris** Tomoceridae. Body with clear silvery reflections: ciliated at hind end. One of the largest European springtails and a good jumper. Under stones and rotten wood. △ *T. longicornis* is identified by very long antennae. Pale yellow body colour shows through if scales rubbed off. Legs very hairy.

▲ **Lucerne Flea** *Sminthurus viridis* Sminthuridae. Prefers living plants: often abundant on legumes, including garden peas. Mainly on mosses in winter.

▲ **Dicyrtoma fusca**. Brick red to deep brown: very hairy. One of the smallest springtails (1 mm long). Abundant in woodland leaf litter and under loose bark.

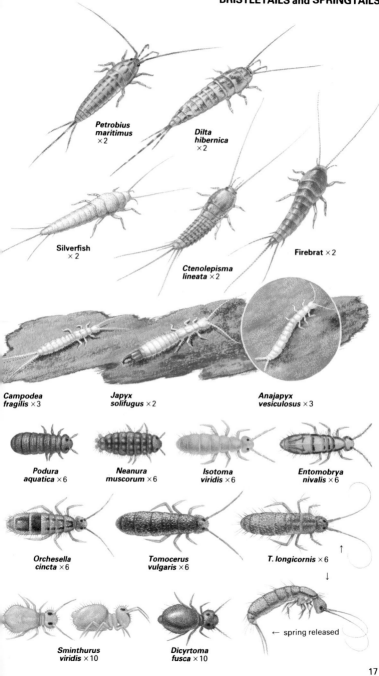

Petrobius maritimus × 2

Dilta hibernica × 2

Silverfish × 2

Ctenolepisma lineata × 2

Firebrat × 2

Campodea fragilis × 3

Japyx solifugus × 2

Anajapyx vesiculosus × 3

Podura aquatica × 6

Neanura muscorum × 6

Isotoma viridis × 6

Entomobrya nivalis × 6

Orchesella cincta × 6

Tomocerus vulgaris × 6

T. longicornis × 6

← spring released

Sminthurus viridis × 10

Dicyrtoma fusca × 10

17

MAYFLIES   Order Ephemeroptera

Delicate, weak-flying insects with 2 or 3 long 'tails' at hind end. Front legs very long, especially in males, which can be recognised by a pair of claspers at the hind end. Usually 2 pairs of wings with complex venation: hind pair always much smaller than forewings and sometimes missing. Wings held vertically above body at rest or partly open: cannot be folded back along the body. Antennae minute. Eyes larger in male than in female and sometimes much expanded to form turrets well above the rest of the head (turbinate condition). Adults do not feed. Mainly crepuscular or nocturnal and rarely found far from the water in which they grow up.

Nymphs (p. 296) include burrowing, crawling, and free-swimming forms and feed mainly on organic debris: some are partly carnivorous. Mayflies are unique in moulting again after attaining the fully-winged state. Adults emerging from nymphal skins are rather dull and hairy and are called duns or sub-imagines, but within hours (sometimes within minutes) they shed another very fine skin and emerge as shiny imagines, generally known as spinners. Females can sometimes be seen with egg masses protruding from their bodies, ready to be dropped or washed into the water.

There are about 2500 known species, with some 200 in Europe. Colours fade after death and identification depends largely on venation: a good lens is essential.

> **Palingenia longicauda** Palingeniidae. 2 tails. Wings smoky brown throughout: hardly transparent. The largest European mayfly. Female does not shed sub-imaginal skin. Breeds in large rivers. C (mainly eastern).
>
> **Oligoneuriella rhenana** Oligoneuriidae. 3 tails. Venation greatly reduced in both wings. Breeds mainly in large, clear rivers. Adults form enormous swarms over the water 7–8; usually late afternoon and evening. S & C (mainly eastern).
>
> **Metrotopus norvegicus** Ametropodidae. 2 tails. Hind wing markedly oval. Forewing with 2 short (intercalary) veins between the last 2 long veins. Nymph swims freely in clear but well-vegetated streams. N.
>
> **Ephoron virgo** Polymitarcidae. 2 tails. Readily identified by the milky wings. Females do not shed sub-imaginal skin. 8–9. Swarms in huge numbers over large, slow-moving rivers and lakes in which it breeds. Strongly attracted to light. S & C.
>
> ▲ **Ephemera danica** Ephemeridae. 3 tails. Wings always spotted. Veins in basal area of forewing run sharply backwards. Abdomen cream or greyish above with darker markings towards rear. 4–9. Nymph (p. 296) lives in lakes and rivers with muddy or sandy bottoms. There are several similar species with darker abdomens.
>
> ▲ **Siphlonurus lacustris** Siphlonuridae. 2 tails. Several wavy veinlets run back from last prominent long vein to the hind margin of forewing. Hind tarsus longer than tibia: femora unbanded. 5–9, mainly in upland areas. Breeds at edges of hill streams. There are several similar species.
>
> △s **Potamanthus luteus** Potamanthidae. 3 tails. Venation as in *Ephemera* but wings yellowish and never spotted with brown. 6–7. Strongly nocturnal. Breeds in large, swift rivers. S & C.

Siphlonurus wing

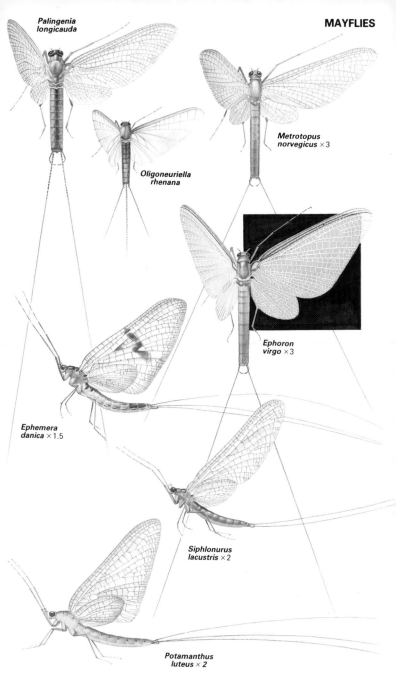

Palingenia longicauda

Oligoneuriella rhenana

Metrotopus norvegicus × 3

Ephoron virgo × 3

Ephemera danica × 1.5

Siphlonurus lacustris × 2

Potamanthus luteus × 2

▲ **Ecdyonurus dispar** Heptageniidae. 2 tails. Venation dark brown. Forewing has 2 pairs of short (intercalary) veins between the last 2 long veins. 6–10. Nymph (p. 296) lives in stony streams and lakes. There are several similar species.

▲ **Rhithrogena semicolorata**. 2 tails. Basal half of forewing commonly bronze or golden brown: often appearing yellow in flight. Femur has brown streak in centre. 4–9. Breeds in fast, stony streams.

▲ **Caenis horaria** Caenidae. A very small mayfly with 3 tails and no hind wings. Forewings milky and fringed with minute hairs (lens!). First 5 or 6 abdominal segments grey on top. Female has lighter thorax. 6–9. Breeds in large lakes and rivers with plenty of vegetation and debris. There are several similar species.

▲ **Ephemerella ignita** Ephemerellidae. 3 tails. Veins Cu$_1$ and Cu$_2$ are very close at the base (lens!). 4–9. Breeds in fast streams. △ **E. notata** is similar but somewhat paler and with small black marks on underside of abdomen.

Isonychia ignota Isonychidae. 2 tails. Last long vein (Cu$_2$) of forewing runs almost parallel to hind margin. Breeds in rivers. S & C (southern). Sometimes placed in Siphlonuridae.

▲ **Baetis rhodani** Baetidae. 2 tails. Hind wing very small. Intercalary veins in forewing always paired. Male with large turbinate eyes. as in all this family. Adult most of the year but mainly spring and autumn. Breeds in small fast streams. One of several very similar species, very difficult to separate.

▲ **Chloeon dipterum**. 2 tails. Hind wing absent. 3–5 cross veins in pterostigma near wing tip. Front margin of wing yellowish brown in female. Male eyes turbinate. 5–10. Breeds in ponds and ditches and even water butts. ▲ **C. simile** is similar but has 9–11 cross veins in pterostigma.

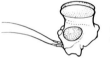

head of *Centroptilum* ♂
showing large eye

▲ **Centroptilum luteolum**. 2 tails. Hind wing very small: strap-like, with pointed tip. Intercalary veins around edge of forewing single (not paired as in *Baetis*). Male eyes turbinate. 4–11. Breeds in stony streams and lake margins.

▲ **Leptophlebia vespertina** Leptophlebiidae. 3 tails. Rather similar to *Ephemerella* but lens shows base of vein Cu$_2$ midway between Cu$_1$ and 1A. Front edge of hind wing without a projection. 4–8. Breeds in lakes and streams, mainly in acidic regions. ▲ **L. marginata** is similar but forewing is smoky brown towards tip.

▲ **Paraleptophlebia cincta**. 3 tails. Base of vein Cu$_2$ is nearer to 1A than to Cu$_1$. Hind wing without a projection on front margin. Male abdomen whitish and translucent at front. 5–8. Breeds in small fast streams in alkaline areas.

▲ **Habrophlebia fusca**. 3 tails. Hind wing with strong projection about half way along front margin. Forewing venation like *Paraleptophlebia* but with virtually no intercalary veins. 5–9. Breeds in slow, well vegetated streams and ditches.

Ecdyonurus intercalary veins

Isonychia Cu$_2$

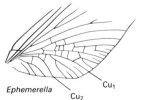

Ephemerella Cu$_1$ Cu$_2$

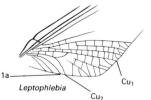

1a *Leptophlebia* Cu$_1$ Cu$_2$

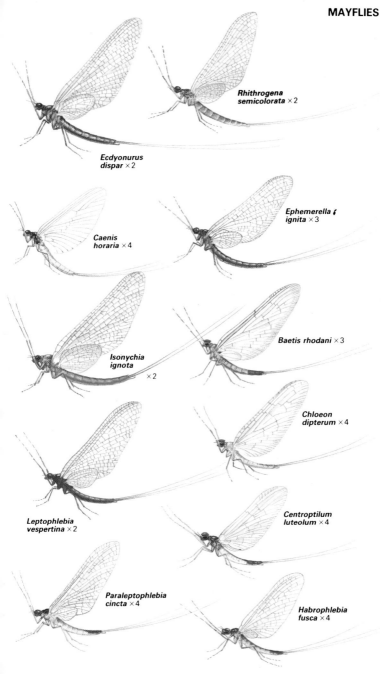

Rhithrogena semicolorata × 2

Ecdyonurus dispar × 2

Caenis horaria × 4

Ephemerella ♀ ignita × 3

Isonychia ignota × 2

Baetis rhodani × 3

Chloeon dipterum × 4

Leptophlebia vespertina × 2

Centroptilum luteolum × 4

Paraleptophlebia cincta × 4

Habrophlebia fusca × 4

21

DRAGONFLIES   Order Odonata

Relatively long-bodied, predatory insects with large eyes and tiny, bristle-like antennae. Wings stiff and often rustling in flight, with a dense network of veins and usually a dark spot, known as the pterostigma, on the front margin near the tip. The wings are not linked and each pair moves independently. Flight is often very fast and many of the insects are amazingly agile. They can hover and even fly backwards, which with their superb eyesight can make them very difficult to catch. Dragonflies feed on other insects, especially flies, which they normally catch in mid-air, swooping about to scoop them up in their spiky legs which are held like a net under the head. Some prey is also plucked from vegetation, particularly by the smaller dragonflies.

There are over 5,000 known species, mainly in tropical regions. About 100 species occur in Europe, falling into two distinct sub-orders. The **Zygoptera** contains the damselflies, mostly delicate insects with very slender bodies and rather weak flight. Front and hind wings are roughly alike and are held above the body when at rest. Eyes well separated on the sides of the head.

The sub-order **Anisoptera** has larger insects, sometimes called true dragonflies to distinguish them from the damselflies. Hind wings are usually broader than forewings (Anisoptera means "unequal wings"), and the wings are always held out to the sides of the body at rest. The eyes are very large and usually meet on the top of the head. Two distinct type of feeding behaviour are found among the true dragonflies. The HAWKERS remain airborne for long periods, often hawking to and fro along a particular beat, such as a stream or hedgerow. The DARTERS, on the other hand, spend much of their time on a perch – on either ground or vegetation – and dart out from it when prey approaches. They usually return to the same perch and an individual may remain on station for a whole day. European dragonflies are essentially sun-loving insects, although some may fly at dusk, especially if food is abundant.

Life-cycle. The dragonflies have a unique system of mating, involving accessory reproductive organs at the front of the male's abdomen. These can be seen as small swellings under the 2nd abdominal segment, and are one way to distinguish the sexes. The hind end of the male abdomen bears a pair of modified cerci, technically known as superior anal appendages but more

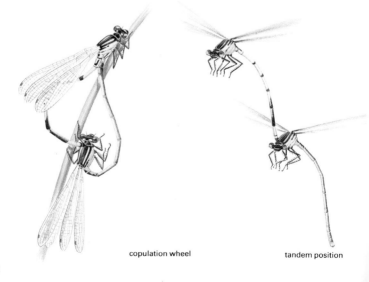

copulation wheel   tandem position

conveniently called claspers. They are usually curved, often very long and conspicuous in the anisopterans but usually less obvious in the damselflies. Male anisopterans usually have a third (inferior) anal appendage, just below the claspers and appearing between them when seen from above. Male damselflies have a pair of inferior anal appendages, just below the claspers and usually much smaller. Female anisopterans may have prominent cerci – usually straighter and more slender than those of the males – but they lack the other anal appendages. Some females have a visible ovipositor just under the tip of the abdomen.

Before courtship, the male transfers sperm from the true reproductive openings at his hind end to his accessory reproductive organs. Finding an agreeable female, he then grasps her by the neck or back of the head with his claspers – which are just the right shape for each species. The insects can fly in this tandem position. They soon settle and the female curves the tip of her abdomen round to collect the sperm from the male's accessory organs. This position is known as the copulation wheel. When sperm transfer is complete, the insects may separate, but many species – particularly among the damselflies and the smaller dragonflies – remain in the tandem position until the female has laid her eggs. These may be simply dropped into the water, or washed off as the female dips her abdomen into it in flight. Some eggs are laid in silt, or placed in slits cut in plant stems. Some female damselflies go right down into the water to lay their eggs in plant stems.

The **nymphs** (p. 296) grow up in water. They eat a wide range of other aquatic creatures, which they impale on spines at the end of a remarkably extensile lower jaw known as the mask. Most damselflies complete their life-cycle in one year, but the anisopterans take anything up to five years, especially in cooler regions. A few species in southern Europe have two generations in a year. When fully grown, the nymph crawls out of the water, usually climbing up a plant stem, and the adult soon emerges. Empty skins are commonly found on the vegetation beside ponds and streams in summer.

Freshly emerged dragonflies are very pale and are called tenerals. The full colours do not develop for several days or even weeks. Many species, especially the males, develop a powdery blue coating on many parts of their bodies when mature. This is called pruinescence. Many lose their colours soon after death, however, and colour cannot always be relied on for identifying dead specimens.

Dragonfly **classification** is based largely on wing venation, and the main features used are shown in the illustrations below.

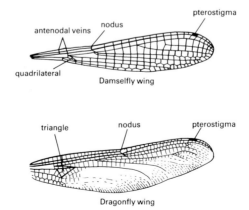

Damselfly wing

Dragonfly wing

DAMSELFLIES   Sub-order Zygoptera

Slender-bodied insects with all wings more or less the same shape and size. Eyes well separated at sides of head, which resembles a tiny hammer head. Generally weak-flying, resting with wings partly open or closed vertically above body.

Family Platycnemididae A fairly small family, identified by the almost rectangular quadrilateral (p. 26). The middle and hind tibiae are expanded and often feather-like in males, and also in females of some species, but extent of expansion varies even within a species.

△ **White-legged Damselfly** *Platycnemis pennipes*. Middle and hind tibiae expanded in both sexes; white with a black line down the middle. Female abdomen pale green with black markings, sometimes almost white. Frequents slow-flowing rivers, canals, and large lakes without too much vegetation. 5–8. Absent from Iberia and far north. *P. latipes* is similar, but expanded tibiae without black line. Front half of abdomen often very pale in both sexes. Slow-flowing water. 6–8. France and Iberia. *P. acutipennis* has orange and black body and tibiae are expanded only in male – and even then not very much. Eyes are clear blue when mature. 5–7. S & C.

Family Coenagriidae A large family in which the quadrilateral (p. 26) is acutely pointed. Pterostigma diamond-shaped.

▲ **Large Red Damselfly** *Pyrrhosoma nymphula*. Black legs and red stripes on thorax distinguish this from the next species. Female abdomen usually more heavily marked with black; thoracic stripes sometimes yellow. Slow-moving streams and still water, including peat bogs. 4–8. Absent from extrene N & S.

△s **Small Red Damselfly** *Ceriagrion tenellum*. Red legs and no coloured stripes on thorax. Female with largely black abdomen. Restricted to acidic bogs and marshes. 5–8. S & C.

▲ **Blue-tailed Damselfly** *Ischnura elegans*. Abdomen usually black with 8th segment bright blue in both sexes, but female sometimes lacks blue. Pterostigma bicoloured. Around still waters of all kinds, including polluted ponds: often abundant. 3–10, with 2 generations in south. Rapid development allows it to breed in rice fields of S in summer. Absent from much of Spain, where replaced by *I. graellsi*.

△ **Red-eyed Damselfly** *Erythromma najas*. More robust than other members of the family, with prominent red eyes. No coloured spots on head. Female lacks blue tip to abdomen. Venation at tip of hind wing distinctly denser than in forewing. Shallow ponds, canals, and slow-moving rivers. Flies close to water and often settles on floating leaves. Relatively fast. 4–9. N & C.

▲ **Common Blue Damselfly** *Enallagma cyathigerum*. Resembles *Coenagrion* spp, but hind wing-tip somewhat more densely veined than front. Male usually identified by 'ace-of-spades' mark at front of abdomen. (*Coenagrion hastulatum* has similar marks but with dark lines alongside – see below.) Female green and black with prominent spine under 8th abdominal segment. Very common over still water with plenty of floating vegetation: often settles on lily leaves. 4–8.

▲ *Coenagrion puella*. One of 11 very similar species in Europe. Male has U-shaped mark at front of abdomen. Female largely black with some green on thorax and blue at tip of abdomen. No spine under abdomen. 4–9. One of the commonest damselflies, abundant by still water almost everywhere, but rare in N.

Males of *Coenagrion* spp can often be distinguished by the black marks on 2nd abdominal segment, although these do vary. Females are more difficult as markings, different from those of males, are often indistinct.

▲ *puella*   ▲ *pulchellum*   △ *mercuriale*   △ *hastulatum*

2nd abdominal segments of *Coenagrion* males

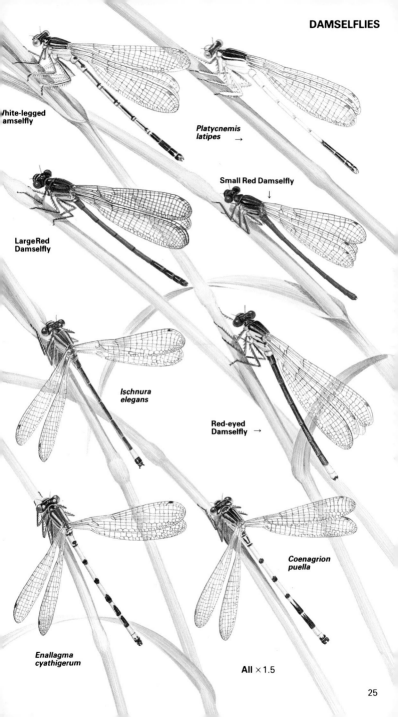

DAMSELFLIES

White-legged Damselfly

Platycnemis latipes →

Large Red Damselfly

Small Red Damselfly ↓

Ischnura elegans

Red-eyed Damselfly →

Enallagma cyathigerum

Coenagrion puella

All ×1.5

Nehalennia speciosa. Europe's smallest damselfly, easily recognised by size alone. Abdomen largely black with blue or green spots. Only 1 or 2 cross veins beyond stigma. Still waters with plenty of emergent vegetation. 5–7. Local and usually uncommon in N & C.

Family Lestidae
A relatively small family in which pterostigma is distinctly elongated. Quadrilateral is acutely pointed at outer end. Body is generally metallic and mostly green. Males have long and strongly curved claspers.

Platycnemis(p.24)   Coenagrion(p.24)   Lestes

Forewings with quadrilaterals
blacked in to emphasise different shapes

▲ **Lestes sponsa**. Pale blue patches develop only on mature male. Female entirely bronzy green with reddish-green eyes. Still waters, including drainage ditches and acidic heathland pools as well as large lakes, but always with plenty of fringing vegetation. Insects usually keep close to the edge. Habitually rest with wings half open. 6–10. Mainly N & C: rare in S. There are several similar species. **L. barbarus** of S is a little larger, with outer third of pterostigma white. Its body never becomes blue.

Sympecma fusca. Body dull brown. Pterostigma of forewing clearly nearer to wing tip than that of hind wing. Over still water, even where polluted. All year S & C. This and its close relative **S. paedisca** of C are the only European dragonflies which hibernate as adults. They hide among dead leaves or in dense shrubs, but often take to the wing on sunny days, even in the middle of winter.

Family Agriidae
A large family, found mainly in the tropics but with three handsome species in Europe. These are our largest damselflies and are sometimes called demoiselles. Body is strongly metallic. Wings have numerous antenodal veins. There is no pterostigma, although females have a small white patch (false pterostigma). Male wings are at least partly clothed with a patch of dense colour – smoky brown at first but becoming darker as insects mature and eventually assuming a deep blue or purplish sheen. The males, more agile than other damselflies, display these colours to females during fluttering courtship dances.

⊿ **Banded Agrion** Agrion splendens. Male body brilliant green or blue: colour patch on wing does not start before nodus, but otherwise varies in extent and may reach wing-tip in southern races. Female body always greenish: wings colourless at first, greenish-yellow when mature. False pterostigma near wing-tip. Canals and quiet river stretches with muddy bottoms, usually by open fields. 4–9. Absent from far north.

▲ **Agrion virgo**. Male body like splendens, but wing colour starts well before nodus. Female body always green: wings clear at first and then brownish – never greenish. False pterostigma well away from wing-tip. Prefers faster-flowing streams with sandy or gravelly bottoms: often among trees. 5–9.

Agrion haemorrhoidalis. Body shining bright, that of male distinctly pink at hind end of abdomen. Male wings dark nearly all over but with a clear base. Female wings like those of virgo but tip of hind wing clouded with brown. 5–8. Clear running water. S.

A. haemorrhoidalis
hind wing of female

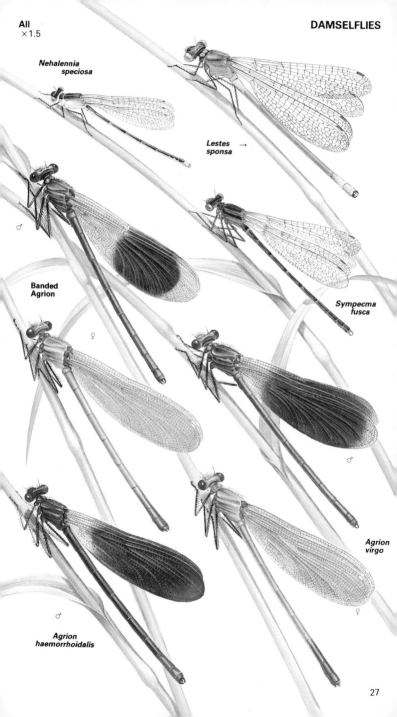

Nehalennia speciosa

Lestes sponsa →

♂

Banded Agrion

Sympecma fusca

♀

♂

Agrion virgo

♂

Agrion haemorrhoidalis

♀

27

TRUE DRAGONFLIES   Sub-order Anisoptera

Stouter than damselflies and with hind wings broader than front. Eyes usually meet on top of head. Wings held more or less flat at rest: never brought together above body (except when first emerged from nymphal skin). Mostly strong fliers, either hawking up and down for long periods (hawkers) or perching for long periods and periodically darting off to snatch prey (darters).

Family Gomphidae   Hawker dragonflies with widely separated eyes: ocelli more or less in a straight line. Abdomen swollen at end, especially in males. Triangles similar in front and hind wing. Base of hind wing angular in male, rounded in female.

△s ***Gomphus vulgatissimus***. The only European gomphid appearing more black than yellow, and the only British species. Legs black. Relatively slow-flying, with a short beat along streams, although often flies far from water. Rests on rocks and bare ground as well as on vegetation. Mainly swift rivers, but also lakes. Eggs are laid at water surface and nymphs burrow in silt or mud. 4–8. Absent from Iberia, but otherwise widely distributed.

Gomphus pulchellus. Legs almost entirely yellow. Abdomen less swollen than in other *Gomphus* spp. Much less black on sides of thorax than in *vulgatissimus*, and altogether paler. Yellow never very bright, and dark markings often grey. Rests on paths and other bare ground and also on trees – a rare habit in *Gomphus*. Still waters, the nymphs burrowing in mud. 5–7. Spain and south-west France.

Onychogomphus uncatus. General body colour is clear, bright yellow, but older insects may become greenish around thorax. Eyes greyish-blue. Male claspers are not forked at apex, but are bent sharply inwards to give abdomen a distinctly blunt tip. Rests on ground. Very clear, fast-flowing streams. Nymphs crawl on to waterside rocks and stones ready for adult emergence. 6–9. S.W. Europe, north to the Rhine. ***O. forcipatus*** is similar, but smaller and paler yellow with forked male claspers. Much of Europe.

Family Cordulegasteridae   Large hawkers in which the eyes just meet at a point in both sexes. Triangles similar in front and hind wing. Base of hind wing angular in male, rounded in female. Female has long ovipositor, reaching beyond tip of abdomen, which she digs into stream bed to lay eggs.

▲   **Gold-ringed Dragonfly** *Cordulegaster boltonii*. Occipital triangle, just behind eyes, is yellow. Male claspers strongly divergent when seen from above. Hind wing of male usually with 5-celled anal triangle. Flies strongly at low levels along streams, but often far from water. Rests on ground or vegetation. Clear, shallow streams with silty bottoms. Nymph burrows in the silt. 5–8. Widely distributed, especially in upland areas.

Cordulegaster bidentatus. Occipital triangle, just behind eye, is black. Male claspers more or less parallel when seen from above. Hind wing of male with 3-celled anal triangle. Habits similar to *boltonii*, but breeds in still water of bogs and marshes as well as in streams. 5–8. S & C: mainly mountains in S.

Gold-ringed Dragonfly laying eggs in the silt of a shallow heathland stream.

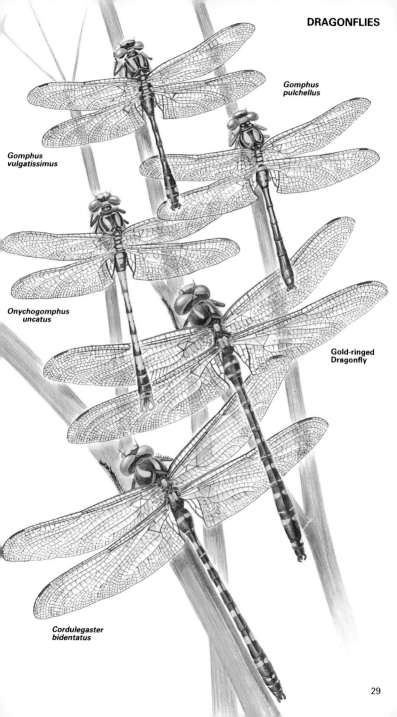

Gomphus
pulchellus

Gomphus
vulgatissimus

Onychogomphus
uncatus

Gold-ringed
Dragonfly

Cordulegaster
bidentatus

Family Aeshnidae A family of relatively large hawker dragonflies in which the eyes touch for an appreciable distance in the mid-line. The triangles are similar in front and hind wings. Claspers are well developed in both sexes, although often straighter and narrower in female. Males are usually easily distinguished by inferior anal appendage below the claspers. Most of the European species belong to the genus *Aeshna*, in which the base of the male hind wing is very angular and possesses a well-marked anal triangle. The number of cells in this triangle is useful in identifying the species (see below).

△s **Brachytron pratense**. Extremely hairy and with very long, slender pterostigma. Female lacks conspicuous green stripes of thorax and her abdominal spots are green or yellow: base of wings yellow. Still and slow-moving water: enjoys sunbathing. 3–6: one of the earliest dragonflies. S & C, but local in S.

▲ **Emperor Dragonfly** *Anax imperator*. Male, easily identified by deep blue abdomen with black line, is one of the largest European dragonflies. Base of hind wing is rounded, instead of pointed as in *Aeshna* spp., and has no anal triangle. No inferior anal appendage. Female has greenish-blue abdomen. Neither sex has stripes on top of thorax. A very fast-flying species, usually keeping over still water and often breeding in very small ponds and ditches. 5–10. S & C.

▲ **Aeshna grandis**. Easily distinguished by amber wing membrane. Female lacks blue spots at front of abdomen. Still waters of lakes, canals, gravel pits, etc: often flies close to the edge, but sometimes far from water. 4–9. Most Europe, but mainly mountains in S.

▲ **Aeshna cyanea**. One of the commonest species. Broad green stripes on thorax in both sexes. Anal triangle of male with 3 cells (sometimes more). Female has all spots green or yellow. In both sexes, last two abdominal segments carry complete bands of colour, not broken into spots. Mainly still waters, from marshes to large lakes: often flies far from water and commonly hawks along hedgerows and in woodland clearings. 6–10. Mainly S & C: just creeps into N.

▲ **Aeshna juncea**. Narrow thoracic stripes, blue spotting throughout abdomen, and 2-celled anal triangle distinguish male from *A. cyanea*. Female very like that of *cyanea*, but without stripes on top of thorax, although she has bright yellow stripes on sides of thorax. Colour spots on last 2 abdominal segments clearly divided. Well-vegetated ponds and other still waters. 6–10. All Europe, but mainly on mountains in S.

▲ **Aeshna mixta**. Very like *A. juncea*, but smaller and top of thorax virtually without stripes. Male with 3-celled anal triangle. Abdominal pattern quite different at the front: female has small yellow triangular or T-shaped mark at front of abdomen. Mainly still waters. Often migrates in swarms. 6–10. S & C and just reaching southern Scandinavia. Has spread northwards a good deal in recent years.

Hind wing bases
showing anal
triangles

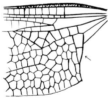 

　　　　A. juncea　　　　　　　　　　*A. mixta*

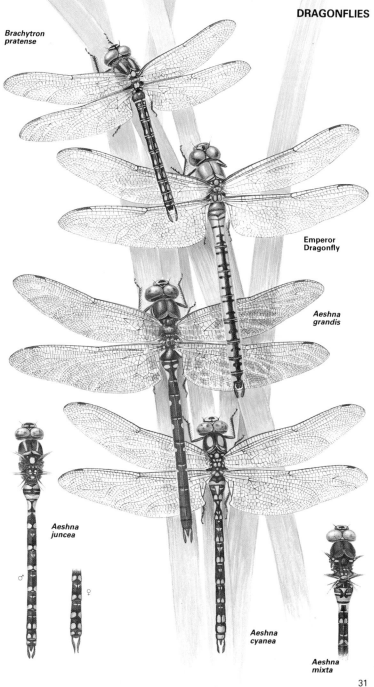

*Brachytron
pratense*

Emperor
Dragonfly

*Aeshna
grandis*

*Aeshna
juncea*

♂

♀

*Aeshna
cyanea*

*Aeshna
mixta*

Family Corduliidae Medium-sized hawkers with distinctly metallic bodies – usually bronze or green. Triangles of front and hind wings differ in shape. That of forewing has front and basal sides about equal. Claspers usually well developed in both sexes. Male abdomen distinctly narrowed in front half.

△s **Cordulia linaenea**. Shiny green thorax, densely clothed with golden hair: abdomen dark bronze, with sides of 2nd segment clear yellow in male. Inferior anal appendage of male deeply forked and resembling an extra pair of claspers. Hind wing triangle undivided. Female stouter than male. Flies swiftly over lakes and ponds and rarely settles. 4–8. Most of Europe, but rare in S.

△ **Somatochlora metallica**. Thorax much less hairy than *Cordulia* and abdomen much brighter green – detectable even in flight. Claspers much longer than in *Cordulia*, especially in female. Inferior anal appendage of male unforked. Triangle of hind wing 2-celled. Female stouter than male and easily identified by a sharp spine projecting from underside of abdomen just before the tip. Still and slow-moving water in lowlands and mountains. Flies rapidly. 6–9. Most Europe, but not Iberia. Two distinct populations in B: one in south-east England, the other in north-west Scotland.
△n **S. arctica**, a similar but more northerly species, has strongly curved claspers in male and no sharp spine in female.

———————

Family Libellulidae A large family of darters in which triangles are of different shapes in front and hind wings. That of forewing has front side very much shorter than basal side. Body not metallic in European species. Mature males often with pale blue pruinescence. Claspers sometimes prominent in females. Often perch on exposed twig or reed and rest with body horizontal. In hot weather the wings may be lowered to shade thorax (see below). Most of the European species belong to the genus *Sympetrum*, in which the last antenodal vein (see p. 22) is usually incomplete.

▲ **Orthetrum cancellatum**. Wing bases completely clear: pterostigma black. Only mature male is blue: young male resembles female. Marshes, ponds, and lakes. 5–9. Absent from far north.

△ **Orthetrum coerulescens**. Wing bases clear. Shorter and more slender than *cancellatum*: pterostigma yellowish brown. Only mature male is blue: young male resembles female. Mainly on bogs and marshes. Male commonly rests on ground. 6–9. Absent from far north. Several similar species in S.

▲ **Libellula quadrimaculata**. Named for the prominent spot on each nodus (*quadrimaculata* means 4-spotted). Sometimes has a brown patch near each wing-tip. Always a triangular brown patch at base of hind wing: amber shading at base of forewing. Sexes alike: female claspers about as long as those of male. Male never becomes blue. Bogs and marshes, often high in mountains: often by the sea. 4–9. All Europe, often migrating in swarms.

▲ **Libellula depressa**. All wings brown at base. Very broad abdomen. Blue only in mature males: young males resemble females. A very fast darter, often perching on tops of bushes. Frequents ponds and slow-moving streams, often breeding in garden ponds and similar small bodies of water. 4–8. The much rarer △s **L. fulva** is similar, but lacks yellow spots and has much less dark shading on wing bases, especially on front wing. Abdomen is marked with black towards the tip.

Libellula depressa in typical warm-weather pose, with wings lowered slightly to shade thorax. Wings are horizontal in cooler weather, when the insects often choose to rest on the ground.

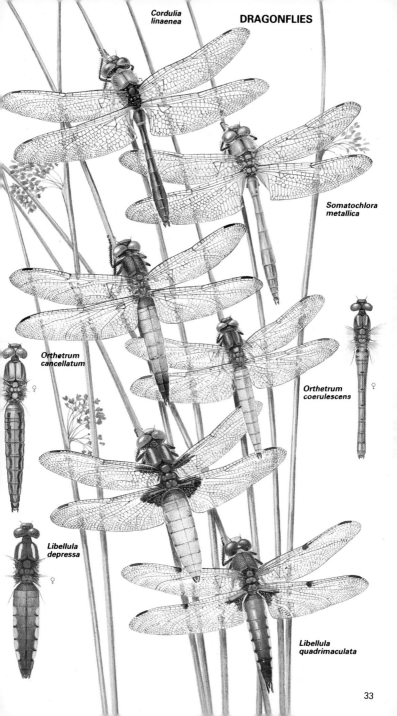

DRAGONFLIES

Cordulia linaenea

Somatochlora metallica

Orthetrum cancellatum
♀

Orthetrum coerulescens
♀

Libellula depressa
♀

Libellula quadrimaculata

33

Crocothemis erythraea. Resembles *Sympetrum*, but broader: last antenodal vein may or may not be complete. Body yellow or brown at first, becoming red with age: especially vivid in male. No trace of black on upper surface (but dead specimens may show black line along abdomen). Costa and radius red: other veins black. Patch on hind wing orange or red in male, yellow in female. Likes to perch on bare twig or reed. Still water, including Mediterranean rice fields. 5–10. Mainly S. occasionally C. Two generations per year in southernmost areas.

▲ ***Sympetrum striolatum***. Commonest member of genus. Legs dark with yellow stripe. Black band across head just in front of eyes does not continue down side of each eye. Thoracic sutures well marked with black. Female is orange-brown with dark marks on end of abdomen. Still waters. 6–10. All Europe: a great migrant. There are several similar species. △s **S. vulgatum** has black line on head running down side of each eye. **S. meridionale** has no black sutures on sides of thorax: legs almost entirely yellow. ▲ **S. sanguineum** has entirely black legs: male abdomen deep red. △n **S. nigrescens** has a very broad dark stripe on side of thorax.

△ ***Sympetrum fonscolombei***. Distinguished from *striolatum* by yellowish pterostigma sharply edged with black. Many veins are red or yellow, especially near base. Female body is sand coloured. Still waters, including Mediterranean rice fields. 5–11. Resident in S with two generations per year: migrates to C each spring.

Sympetrum pedemontanum. The only European *Sympetrum* species with clouding in outer part of wing. Marshland. 7–10. S & C.

△ ***Sympetrum scoticum***. Black triangle on top of thorax clearly identifies female and teneral male. Mature male is jet black. Mainly on peat bogs. 7–9. N & C.

△ ***Sympetrum flaveolum***. Extensive yellow patch at base of wings identifies this species. Pterostigma red. Bogs and marshes. 7–9. All Europe. A strong migrant.

△ **White-faced Dragonfly** *Leucorrhinia dubia*. White face. Pterostigma short and broad: reddish-brown in male, black in female. Female has yellow markings instead of red and dark wing bases are surrounded by a yellow cloud. Teneral males also have yellow body markings. Rarely far from peat bogs or wet heaths. 5–8. Most of Europe: mainly mountains in S.

Leucorrhinia caudalis. Pterostigma short and broad: pale in male, brown in female. Abdominal segments 6–9 enlarged. Female and immature male lack blue in middle of abdomen. Bogs and marshes. 5–7. C.

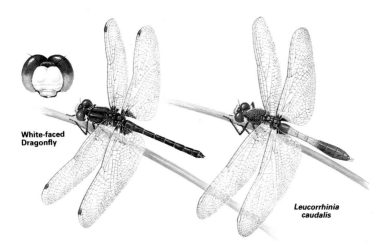

White-faced Dragonfly

Leucorrhinia caudalis

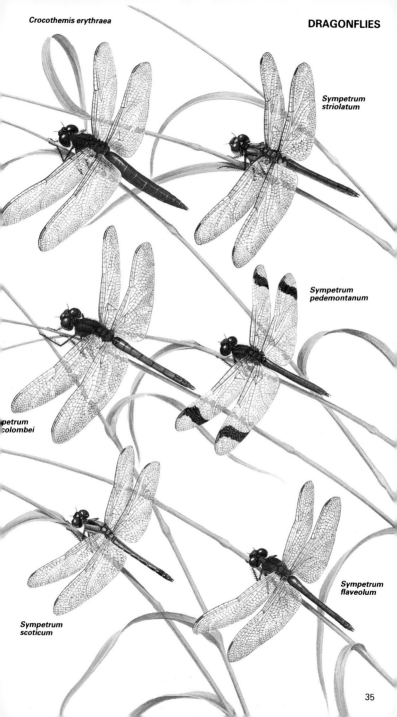

Crocothemis erythraea

*Sympetrum
striolatum*

*Sympetrum
pedemontanum*

*...petrum
...colombei*

*Sympetrum
scoticum*

*Sympetrum
flaveolum*

35

STONEFLIES   Order Plecoptera

Weak-flying or flightless insects with rather soft and flattened bodies: often with two long cerci. Never brightly coloured. Wings folded flat over body or wrapped around it at rest. Forewings often with two prominent rows of cross-veins forming a 'double ladder'. Hind wings usually much broader than front ones. Venation very variable, even within a species. Males commonly smaller than females and often with very short wings. Nymphs (p. 296) are aquatic and usually prefer cool, running water. They crawl on to waterside stones ready for adult emergence. Adults rarely move far from water, usually crawling on stones and tree trunks close to the streams. Some scrape algae or nibble pollen, but many do not feed at all. There are about 3000 known species, but less than 150 occur in Europe.

▲ **Leuctra fusca** Leuctridae. One of many similar species known as needle flies because wings are wrapped tightly round body at rest. Cerci very short. Stony streams and lake shores, including chalk streams. Lowlands and uplands. 4–11, but most commonly 7–9; probably all year in S.

  Members of the family Nemouridae are similar but they have an oblique vein in apical cell of wing and wings are less tightly rolled around body. Members of the Taeniopterygidae are also similar, but their tarsal segments are all about equal: Leuctridae and Nemouridae have 2nd tarsal segment very short.

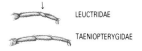

LEUCTRIDAE

TAENIOPTERYGIDAE

hind tarsi

▲ **Isoperla grammatica** Perlodidae. Anal region of hind wing much enlarged, with 2 prominently forked veins. One of several very similar species, but the only large yellow species in B (commonly called yellow sally by anglers). Stony and gravelly streams: very common in limestone regions. 4–9.

▲ **Perlodes microcephala**. Distinguished from most other large species by the irregular network of veins near wing-tips. Male normally with very short wings. Stony streams and rivers: the only large stonefly commonly found in chalk streams. 3–7. Several similar species in Alps and Pyrenees.

▲ **Capnia bifrons** Capniidae. Forewing has no 'double ladder' of cross-veins. A single cross-vein in apical space. Hind wing distinctly shorter than forewing and more rounded. Male has very short wings – no more than 2.5 mm long and often just minute stumps. Basal tarsal segment about as long as 3rd segment – this distinguishes the Capniidae from other families with long cerci, in which basal tarsal segment is always shorter. Common by stony rivers and lake shores. 2–5. Mainly S & C. A few similar species occur mainly in N and on mountains.

▲ **Chloroperla torrentium** Chloroperlidae. Anal area of hind wing small, with no forked veins. Lake shores and sandy or gravelly streams, mainly in upland areas. 4–8. Called small yellow sally by anglers. One of several similar species.

▲ **Dinocras cephalotes** Perlidae. One of the largest stoneflies. No network of veins near wing-tip. Three long cells are prominent near middle of hind wing, and hindmost of these has 1–3 cross-veins (often very faint: occasionally absent). Pronotum black. Male no more than half size of female. Common on stony rivers with firm beds and fixed, moss-covered stones, especially in upland regions: may reach 2000m. 5–8.

▲ **Perla bipunctata** resembles *D. cephalotes* but has a paler body. Pronotum yellowish with dark central stripe and dark borders. Hind wing lacks cross-veins in hindmost long cell. Cerci extend well beyond wings at rest. Male ½–¾ size of female. A very common species, preferring rivers with loose stones on bed. Mainly uplands, but not as high as *Dinocras*. 5–7.

cross vein

front wing of NEMOURIDAE showing cross-vein in apical space

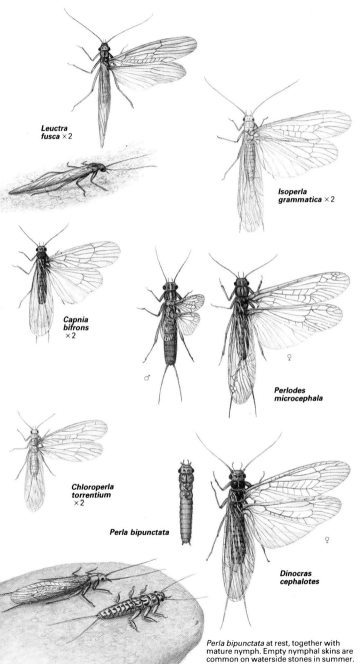

Leuctra fusca × 2

Isoperla grammatica × 2

Capnia bifrons × 2

♂

Perlodes microcephala

♀

Chloroperla torrentium × 2

Perla bipunctata

Dinocras cephalotes

♀

Perla bipunctata at rest, together with mature nymph. Empty nymphal skins are common on waterside stones in summer.

37

GRASSHOPPERS and CRICKETS   Order Orthoptera

There are some 17,000 known members of the order, of which more than half are grasshoppers. Over 600 species occur in Europe, but the great majority of these are confined to the south – notably in Iberia and Greece – and only about 250 species extend into central Europe. Only 30 occur in Britain. The main groups of European Orthoptera may be distinguished with the table opposite.

They are mostly rather stout insects, with hind legs enlarged for jumping. There is a prominent, saddle-shaped pronotum, the top (known as the disc) often with a central keel. There may also be side keels where the disc joins the side flaps of the pronotum. A transverse groove, known as the sulcus, normally runs across the centre of the disc, and there may be other grooves in front of it. The forewings (tegmina) are thicker and tougher than the hind wings and usually quite narrow. They may completely cover the abdomen at rest, but many species have very short forewings and some have none at all. The hind wings are similarly variable, but when fully developed they are broad and membranous. Flight is normally weak, though some species fly very well. The jaws are of the biting type.

The males of most species 'sing' by rubbing one part of the body against another. This is known as stridulation and serves to bring the sexes together. Allowing for differences in pitch and volume, the sounds may be likened to sewing machines and other machinery. In the presence of females, many males produce special courtship songs.

The orthopterans all begin life as eggs, and the great majority of European species pass the winter in the egg stage. There is no pupal stage and the youngsters pass through several nymphal stages before reaching maturity. Older nymphs can easily be distinguished from adults of short-winged species because their wing-buds are twisted so that the front edge is uppermost: in adults the front edge of the forewing lies along the side of the body.

Grasshoppers (Family Acrididae) are almost entirely vegetarian and the majority are active only in sunshine. The males usually stridulate by rubbing the hind legs against the forewings. One of these surfaces bears a row of tiny pegs and the other a hard ridge. The effect of moving one over the other is just like running a finger-nail over the teeth of a comb, producing a buzzing sound. The pitch varies with the number of pegs and also with the rate at which the legs are moved. Each species has its own characteristic song. In one major group of grasshoppers the stridulatory pegs are carried on the inner face of each hind femur, and the ridge runs along the centre of the forewing.

In the other major group the pegs are borne on the forewing and the ridge is on the femur. The songs of this last group are usually rather weak and their heads tend to be blunter than those of the first group, although there are some exceptions. Some female grasshoppers can stridulate, but their pegs are smaller and their songs usually very soft. Hearing organs are on the sides of the body. Some species do not stridulate at all.

Colours are very variable and cannot always be relied on for identification. The shape of the pronotum and the arrangement of the keels are often of greater use.

male

The sexes are easily distinguished because the hind of the male turns up like the prow of a boat.

female

Locusts are large grasshoppers which assume gregarious habits from time to time and build up huge populations. Insects of the gregarious phase differ in several anatomical features from the solitary insects.

Bush-crickets (Family Tettigoniidae) are mostly omnivorous, eating other insects as well as plant material. A few are entirely carnivorous. Long antennae easily distinguish them from the grasshoppers, and females are further distinguished by the blade-like ovipositor. Species with very short, curved ovipositors normally lay their eggs in plants, cutting slits for them with the saw-like teeth at the tip of the ovipositor. Other species lay eggs in the ground. During mating the male produces a large, jelly-like spermatophore, which is then attached to the hind end of the female. Sperms enter her body from it, but she eats most of the jelly. Bush-crickets are largely crepuscular or nocturnal. They sing by raising the forewings and rubbing their bases together. The songs are often much higher-pitched than those of the grasshoppers and often more prolonged. Both sexes sing in some species. The hearing organs are on both sides of the front tibiae.

True Crickets (Family Gryllidae) resemble bush-crickets in many ways but the forewings are usually broader across the top and the females have needle-like ovipositors. The songs are produced in the same way, except that the right fore-wing overlaps the left one – the reverse of the bush-cricket condition. True crickets are either vegetarians or omnivores.

Key

Front legs greatly enlarged for digging

Mole Crickets, p. 58

Front legs normal
  Antennae shorter than body
    Pronotum extended back over abdomen

Groundhoppers, p. 46

    Pronotum not extended back over abdomen

Grasshoppers, pp. 38–47

Antennae longer than body
  Palps very long; always wingless

Cave-crickets, p. 56

Palps not particularly long: usually with at least traces of wings
  Tarsi 4-segmented

    Bush-crickets, pp. 48–57

  Tarsi 3-segmented   **True Crickets**, p. 58

GRASSHOPPERS Acrididae Essentially diurnal, sun-loving insects with short antennae. Shape of pronotum and arrangement of keels often help to identify species. Female usually larger than male: sometimes much larger. Songs described are those of isolated males (p. 38). Unless otherwise stated, the stridulatory pegs are on the hind femur.

Arcyptera fusca. Female heavy and flightless. Song up to 8 short, croaky notes followed by harsh rustle which becomes very loud for 2–3 secs and then dies away with 2 or 3 more short notes. 7–9. Montane grassland, mainly in Alps and Pyrenees.

Pyrgomorpha conica. Head conical with rather stout antennae. Male grey or brown, often tinged with green: female green. Hind wings slightly pink at base. No stridulation. Dry grassy places. 3–9. S.

△s **Large Marsh Grasshopper** *Stethophyma grossum.* Stridulatory pegs on forewing, but male's normal call is a soft ticking sound made by tapping tip of forewing with hind tibia. Marshy areas, especially peat bogs with extensive sphagnum cover. 7–10. N & C: very local.

 ▲ **Mottled Grasshopper** *Myrmeleotettix maculatus.* Brown, green, or black: always mottled. Tip of antenna less swollen in female. Song a series of 10–30 short chirps, increasing in volume over 10–15 secs and rather like the sound of winding a clock: repeated at irregular intervals. 6–10. Heathland and other dry places.

 △ **Rufous Grasshopper** *Gomphocerippus rufus.* Normally brown: female sometimes purple. Antenna less strongly clubbed in female. A small bulge on front edge of forewing. Song a soft chirp, fluctuating in volume like a sewing machine and lasting about 5 secs. 7–11. Mainly on limestone.

 ▲ **Common Field Grasshopper** *Chorthippus brunneus.* One of many similar species. Grey, green, brown, purple, or black. A small bulge on front edge of forewing. Very hairy below thorax. Song 6–10 short chirps, like time-signal pips at a lower pitch: sequence repeated irregularly. Female sings before mating. Mostly dry and often sparse grassland 6–10. *C.biguttulus* is very similar, but front edge of forewing is strongly curved, especially in male. Song loud and metallic, like old-fashioned dentist's drill, in chirps of 1–1.5 secs: chirps often in threes. Most Europe, but not B.

▲ **Meadow Grasshopper** *C.parallelus.* Green, brown, or purple. A small bulge on front edge of forewing. Hind wings absent (the only flightless grasshopper in B). Song like a sewing machine in bursts of up to 3 secs, getting louder: repeated every 5–15 secs. All kinds of grassland., but especially where moist. 6–10.

△ **Lesser Marsh Grasshopper** *C.albomarginatus.* Green and/or brown. A small bulge on front edge of forewing. Side keels of pronotum virtually straight. Song like *brunneus* but softer and slower: 2–6 chirps, each under 1 sec and separated by about 2 secs: series repeated at irregular intervals. Dense grassland, both dry and moist: mainly low-lying. 7–10.

▲ **Common Green Grasshopper** *Omocestus viridulus.* Distinguished from several similar species by short keel on top of head. Grey, green, or brown in any combination, but female always green on top. Forewing often dark towards tip. Abdomen yellowish-green below. Song a fluctuating hiss lasting 10–20 secs and getting louder – rather like an approaching moped – before ending abruptly. Full volume is reached about half-way through song. 7–10. Mainly on the lusher grasslands. Absent from far south.

△ **Woodland Grasshopper** *O.rufipes.* Usually brown: female may be green above. Palps very white at tip. Abdomen red at hind end. Song like *viridulus* but only 5–10 secs and stops as soon as full volume is reached. Heaths and woodland clearings. 6–10.

brunneus forewing

biguttulus forewing

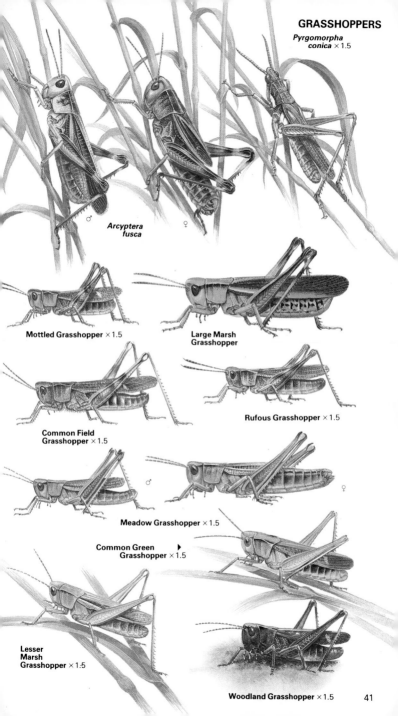

GRASSHOPPERS

Pyrgomorpha conica × 1.5

Arcyptera fusca

♂ ♀

Mottled Grasshopper × 1.5

Large Marsh Grasshopper

Common Field Grasshopper × 1.5

Rufous Grasshopper × 1.5

♂ ♀

Meadow Grasshopper × 1.5

Common Green Grasshopper × 1.5 ▶

Lesser Marsh Grasshopper × 1.5

Woodland Grasshopper × 1.5

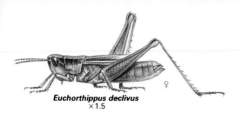

Euchorthippus declivus
×1.5 ♀

Euchorthippus declivus. Forewings short in both sexes, usually with a clear white stripe. Flightless. Side keels of pronotum almost straight. Song a prolonged succession of short croaks, each consisting of a few distinct pulses. Abundant in both dry and damp grassland, including woodland clearings and montane pastures. 6–10. S & C.

Gomphocerus sibiricus. Male immediately identified by swollen front tibiae. Female has no swelling and less strongly clubbed antennae. Pronotum usually clearly humped in front half and often with a clear X-shaped mark on top. Song begins with well-separated chirps, getting quicker, rather like the rapid winding of a watch, and then becomes a constant loud call reminiscent of a small cicada: this lasts for up to a minute and then dies away with a few more short chirps. 7–9. Montane pastures, mainly in Alps and Pyrenees.

Chorthippus scalaris. Usually dark brown: sometimes green. Male has greatly enlarged front region of forewing. Median area of forewing enlarged in both sexes, with prominent parallel cross veins in male and irregular cross veins in female. Hind wings dark. Song starts with slow build-up of short croaks, getting quicker and louder until it becomes a constant rattle like a free-wheeling bicycle. This lasts about 10 secs and is punctuated by short, higher-pitched notes. Both sexes rustle loudly in flight. 7–9. Montane pastures from southern Sweden southwards.

Dociostaurus maroccanus. Pale to dark brown. Side keels of pronotum form a cross with pale outer edges. Central keel clearly cut by transverse sulcus. Female up to 37 mm long. Song a soft staccato croak, not unlike a clock ticking. 4–10 in a wide range of habitats. Becomes gregarious and develops into a serious pest in some years, especially in Corsica and Italy and other parts of the far south. The gregarious form has less strongly marked forewings and a less clear white cross on the thorax. S & C.

Euthystira brachyptera. Flightless, with forewings very short in both sexes – mere lateral flaps in female. Body with bright silky lustre. Song repeated short buzzing sounds, rather like striking matches. 7–9. Short turf and stony places in the mountains. S & C.

E. dispar. Sharply angled forehead. Male forewing distinctly oval. Flightless, with greatly reduced hind wings. Song a very harsh, ratchet-like chirp lasting about 1 sec and repeated at short intervals. Heathland, woodland clearings, hedgerows, and damp grassland. 6–9.

▲ **Stripe-winged Grasshopper** *Stenobothrus lineatus*. Mainly green, sometimes with brown forewings and legs. Median area of forewings enlarged, with prominent parallel cross-veins. Female usually with white stripe near front edge of forewing. End of abdomen orange-red when mature. Song a rather high-pitched whine lasting 10–20 secs and with a marked rhythmic rise and fall in volume. The male's legs move remarkably slowly during stridulation, but he has up to 450 pegs on each hind femur and so the pitch remains high. Warm, dry grassland, especially on limestone. 6–10. S & C.

Paracinema tricolor. Stridulatory pegs on forewing. Pronotum with a straight dark stripe on each 'shoulder'. Forewings become clear towards tip. Hind tibiae red with black-tipped white spines. Female 30–40 mm, male only 25 mm. Rustles in flight. Moist grassland. Quite rare in most places, but not uncommon in the rice fields of the Camargue, where it causes some damage. 7–10. S.

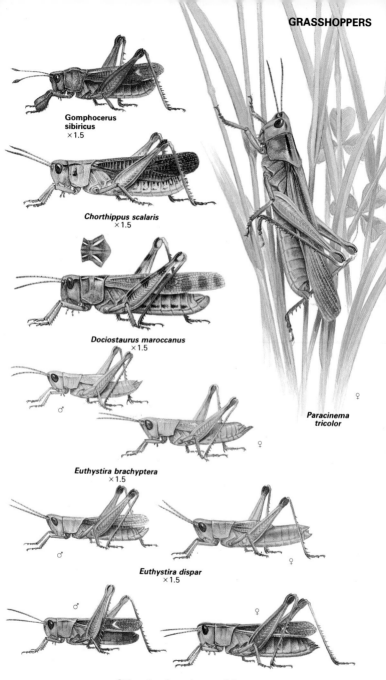

Gomphocerus sibiricus ×1.5

Chorthippus scalaris ×1.5

Dociostaurus maroccanus ×1.5

Euthystira brachyptera ×1.5

♂   ♀

Euthystira dispar ×1.5

♂   ♀

♀

Paracinema tricolor

Stripe-winged grasshopper ×1.5

43

FLASH COLOURS. Several grasshoppers have brightly coloured hind wings. When disturbed, they fly on an erratic course and flash their colours. A bird chasing one of these insects latches on to the colourful 'hunting image', but then the grasshopper drops to the ground, covers its hind wings, and 'disappears', leaving the bird searching in vain for a colourful object. Human observers are often deceived by this flash coloration and even mistake the grasshoppers for butterflies. Most of the colourful species, including all those on this page, have stridulatory pegs on the forewings, but stridulation is at best very weak.

Psophus stridulus. Central keel of pronotum quite pronounced and not crossed by the sulcus. Hind femur smoothly curved on upper edge. Female forewings only just reach tip of abdomen. Both sexes produce a grating sound. They also produce a rustling noise in flight, especially loud in male. Rough grassy places, mainly in upland areas. 7–10. Southern Scandinavia southwards.

Acrotylus insubricus. Hairy. Large head standing above pronotum, especially in male. Pronotum knobbly in front half: hind margin ± rounded, not sharply pointed. Brown to black. Dry places, especially on sandy soils: common on sand dunes. All year in warmest regions: hibernates elsewhere and active mainly 3–11. S.

Oedipoda germanica. Superficially like *Psophus*, but central keel clearly interrupted by sulcus. Upper edge of hind femur has distinct notch just beyond middle. Light or dark brown. Rough ground in dry, sunny places – including roadsides and cultivated land. 7–11. Locally common in S & C.

O. caerulescens is similar but has blue hind wings. Forewings and body grey or brown. Commoner and more widely distributed than *germanica* in warm, dry places: often on sand dunes. 7–11. S & C.

Oedaleus decorus. Head large and rounded. Strong central keel on pronotum, hardly or not at all interrupted by sulcus. Usually a distinct white cross on top of pronotum. Body and forewings green or brown. Hot, dry places. 6–10. S & C.

Sphingonotus caerulans. Central keel of pronotum very weak and present only in hind region. Forewings clear and distinctly membranous towards tip. Hind wing with no trace of black band. Hind femur with just one complete pale band on inner surface. Warm, sandy places. 6–10. S & C.

Aiolopus thalassinus. Pronotum with weak central keel and no side keels. Proportion of green and brown very variable. Hind wings colourless. Stridulatory pegs on forewing. Grassland and woodland clearings, especially where damp: also cultivated land. 3–10, but may be all year in far south. S & C.

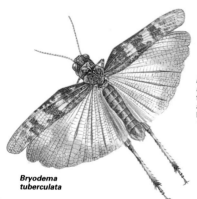

Bryodema tuberculata. Side keels virtually absent: central keel prominent only at front. Disc very flat: hind end ± right-angled or obtuse. Surface markedly rough. Rustles in flight. Mainly sandy places. 7–10. N & C.

Bryodema tuberculata

GRASSHOPPERS

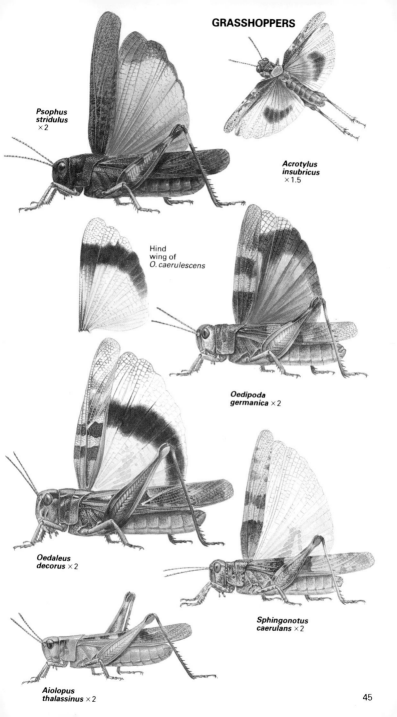

Psophus stridulus ×2

Acrotylus insubricus ×1.5

Hind wing of *O. caerulescens*

Oedipoda germanica ×2

Oedaleus decorus ×2

Sphingonotus caerulans ×2

Aiolopus thalassinus ×2

△ **Migratory Locust** *Locusta migratoria*. Solitary phase has swollen pronotum with arched central keel. Male averages only 35 mm long: often brown. Female usually green. Flies rapidly. Stridulatory pegs on forewing. Male screeches loudly in presence of female. Dense vegetation, including cultivated land: but not a serious pest in Europe. 7–11: sometimes through winter in far south. S & C: rare visitor to B. Gregarious phase, more rarely seen in Europe, is greyish-brown or yellowish: sexes ± alike.

Nymph of Egyptian grasshopper

showing reversal of wing buds

△ **Egyptian Grasshopper** *Anacridium aegyptium*. Like gregarious phase of *Locusta*, but clearly distinguished by indented pronotal keel, striped eyes, and a blunt peg on underside of thorax between front legs. Male about 35 mm long: female 50–65 mm. Flies well. On shrubs and trees in warm dry areas. Causes little damage. Silent. All year. S: sometimes carried north in produce. Nymphs are green or orange-brown.

Underside of
Podisma thorax
showing peg

Podisma pedestris. A peg between front legs. Pronotum with straight or smoothly curved hind edge. Forewings flap-like in both sexes. Male quite sprightly: heavy female drags herself over the ground. Stony, sparsely vegetated places in mountains, usually above 1000 m, but lower in north: often near snow-line. 7–10.

Pezotettix giornai. Hairy. Peg between front legs tongue-like and bent backwards. Central keel runs length of pronotum: side keels in front half. Forewings very short in both sexes. Grey to reddish-brown or almost black. Dry scrubby places and cultivated land. Silent. All year in S: 6–10 in southern C.

Calliptamus italicus. Peg between front legs. Very blunt forehead. Central and side keels well developed: pale stripes on side keels and forewings not always present. Hind femur reddish-pink internally, with 3 dark spots: middle and posterior spots of equal size. Male 14–25 mm long: female 22–40 mm. Male cerci very long and curved. No stridulation, but male can 'sing' by rubbing jaws together. Common and often abundant on grassland and cultivated areas: sometimes a pest. 7–11. S & C. (*C. barbarus* is very similar but middle spot on hind femur is much larger than others.)

Acrida ungarica. Unmistakable shape. Green or brown. Female 50–70 mm long and often mottled. Damp grassy places, including coastal marshes. No stridulation. 7–10. S.

GROUNDHOPPERS Tetrigidae

Superficially like grasshoppers, but pronotum extends back over whole top of abdomen. Forewings reduced to small scales, but hind wings usually well-developed. Active all year in sunshine, preferring bare and sparsely-vegetated ground. Eat mosses and other small plants. Silent. Several species in Europe: 3 in Britain.

▲ **Common Groundhopper** *Tetrix undulata* is pale brown to black. Hind wings do not reach tip of pronotum. Heaths, open woods, and other dry places. ▲ **Slender Groundhopper** *T. subulata* has a relatively longer pronotum: hind wings reach its tip. Pale brown to black. Flies and also swims well. Damp places.

T. depressa has central keel only in front half of pronotum, and two dark depressions near centre. Damp places, including seashore. S & C.

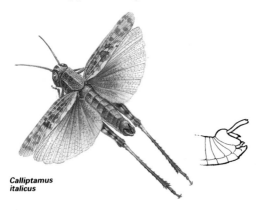

Calliptamus italicus

Hind end of male, showing large *cercus*

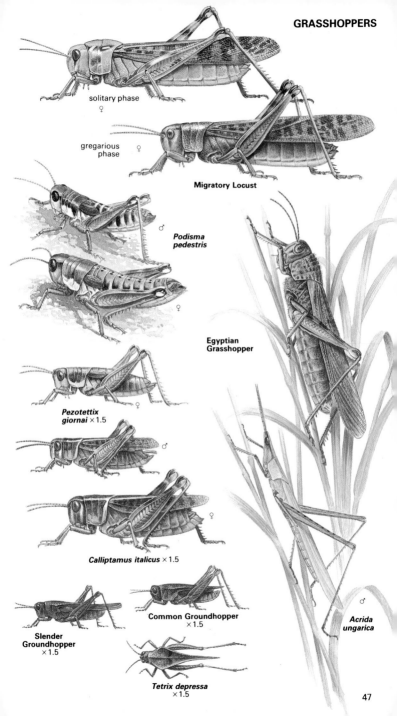

GRASSHOPPERS

solitary phase ♀

gregarious phase ♀

Migratory Locust

Podisma pedestris ♂

♀

Pezotettix giornai ×1.5 ♀

♂

Calliptamus italicus ×1.5 ♀

Egyptian Grasshopper

Acrida ungarica ♂

Slender Groundhopper ×1.5

Common Groundhopper ×1.5

Tetrix depressa ×1.5

47

BUSH-CRICKETS Tettigoniidae Orthoptera with long, slender antennae and 4-segmented tarsi. Female has blade-like ovipositor, either short and strongly curved like a sickle or long and sabre-like. Mated female often seen with gelatinous spermatophore attached to base of ovipositor (p. 38). Wings often short and sometimes virtually absent, but male retains enough of the forewings to produce his song. An 'ear' on each face of front tibiae. Mostly crepuscular or nocturnal insects.

'ear'

front leg of
Phaneroptera

Phaneroptera nana. 'Ear' on front tibia oval. Hind wings extend well beyond forewings at rest. Side lobes of pronotum rounded, especially on hind margin. Whole insect covered with tiny rust-coloured dots. Ovipositor short and strongly curved. Song: a high-pitched staccato ticking, mostly at night. On a wide range of bushes. 8–10. S & C.

Tylopsis liliifolia. Like *Phaneroptera* but 'ear' slit-like. Green or brown. Antennae up to 5 times length of body. Side lobes of pronotum rectangular. Ovipositor short and curved. Song: 2–4 weak chirps, like striking a match, repeated irregularly: mainly at night. Scrubby places (brown form) and grassy areas (green form). 7–10. S & C.

'ear'

front leg of
Tylopsis

Isophya pyrenea. Stout, with many tiny red dots on back. Forewings very small in both sexes, those of female half covered by pronotum. Song: a very weak squeak, like a cork turning in a bottle. Grassy places in mountains: mainly ground-living. 5–8. S & C. Many similar species in SE.

Barbitistes fischeri. Bright green when young, becoming heavily speckled and then almost black as it matures: shiny. Forewings very short in both sexes, those of male inflated and perched on back as in *Leptophyes*. Song a series of 20–40 feeble grinding sounds, produced over a period of 10–20 secs and repeated at irregular intervals: mainly at night, although insect often active by day and enjoys sunbathing. On trees and shrubs: often abundant and sometimes damaging vines. 5–8. SW.

ovipositor of
I. pyrenea

Polysarcus denticauda. Heavy-bodied. Forewings very short in both sexes, almost entirely hidden in female. Ovipositor 15–25 mm long, curved towards apex and toothed at tip. Male cerci very large. Song a prolonged series of soft but monotonous metallic chirps, produced in sunshine. Montane pastures. 6–9. S & C.

▲ **Speckled Bush-cricket** *Leptophyes punctatissima*. Densely speckled with very short forewings in both sexes. Female has only very thin brown line along the back. Song a very short and feeble scratching sound repeated every few seconds; interval gets shorter as temperature rises; day and night. Superbly camouflaged on nettles, brambles, and other scrubby vegetation, including garden plants. 7–11. S & C.

▲ **Oak Bush-cricket** *Meconema thalassinum*. Fully winged in both sexes: often flying to lights at night, although flight rather weak. Male has long, curved claspers. Ovipositor about 9 mm long and gently curved. No stridulation, but male drums gently on leaf surface with hind foot. Forewings are raised while doing this and sound can be heard several metres away. Inhabits a wide range of deciduous trees, including garden apples. Rarely seen by day. 7–11.

Cyrtaspis scutata. Readily identified by enlarged pronotum completely covering forewings in both sexes; hind end of pronotum raised in male. Pale green to pinkish grey. Song very feeble, rather like the ticking of a watch. On trees and shrubs. 8–12: sometimes surviving until spring in mild years. S: mainly western.

Speckled
Bush-cricket ♀ × 1.5

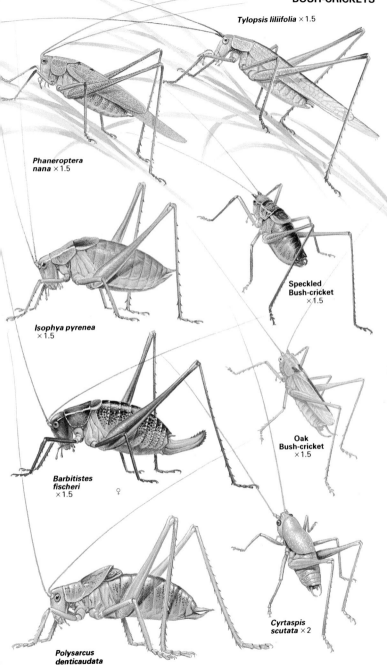

Tylopsis liliifolia ×1.5

Phaneroptera nana ×1.5

Isophya pyrenea ×1.5

Speckled Bush-cricket ×1.5

Oak Bush-cricket ×1.5

Barbitistes fischeri ×1.5 ♀

Cyrtaspis scutata ×2

Polysarcus denticaudata

49

Short-winged Conehead

△s **Short-winged Conehead** *Conocephalus dorsalis*. Forewings short in both sexes, hind wings vestigial. Ovipositor 8–11 mm long. Song long bursts of faint, high-pitched sound consisting of alternating periods of hissing and ticking – like a knife-grinding machine when the blade is alternately pressed firmly and lightly against the wheel. Marshes, river banks, and other moist grassland. More active by day than by night, but hard to see when stretched along reed stems and leaves. 7–10. Mainly coastal.

Long-winged Conehead

△s **Long-winged Conehead** *C. discolor* resembles *dorsalis* but is fully-winged and ovipositor longer and less strongly curved. Both species occasionally all brown. Song long bursts of high-pitched, quiet sound of constant tone – rather like a distant knife-grinder. Mainly diurnal in areas of tall grass; dry and moist habitats. 7–10. S & C. South coast only in B.

Ruspolia nitidula. Green or brown. Fully winged. Head acutely pointed. Ovipositor longer than abdomen and almost straight. Song: a prolonged and rather strident sound: very loud, like a knife-grinder or even an alarm clock ringing at a lower pitch. River banks and other damp places with tall grass: sits more or less vertically on leaves and stems. Strictly nocturnal. 7–10. S & C.

△ **Great Green Bush-cricket** *Tettigonia viridissima*. Fully winged, but not a strong flier. The largest British bush-cricket. Stridulatory area of male forewings always brown and about 1/6th of total length. Ovipositor about 20 mm long and just reaching tip of forewings: slightly down-curved. Song: loud and harsh, like a sewing machine, continuing for long periods with short breaks every few seconds. Becomes active in afternoon and carries on for much of the night, but peak of activity in evening. In trees, shrubs, and rough vegetation in general. Can deliver painful bite if handled, as can most other large species. 7–10. *T. cantans* is similar but forewings much shorter and more rounded, with stridulatory area occupying about ¼ of total length. Ovipositor straight and reaching well beyond tip of forewings. Song: more rasping than *viridissima*, starting slowly and then increasing in speed and volume: continuous for long periods. 7–10, mainly in upland areas.

△s **Wart-Biter** *Decticus verrucivorus*. Green or brown, always heavily mottled. Pronotum flat with central keel running its whole length. Fully winged. Ovipositor about 20 mm long, with very gentle upward curve. Named because once used in Sweden to bite warts from the skin. Song long bursts of clicking sounds, starting slowly and then speeding up to resemble the sound of a free-wheeling bicycle: continues for several minutes. Mainly diurnal, usually singing only in sunshine. Open grassy places, including marshy habitats and montane pastures. 7–10. Most Europe: south coast only in B.

D. albifrons Similar to *verrucivorus*, but larger and never green: face very pale. Song: very high pitched, beginning with isolated chirps more like a bird than an insect but then speeding up and becoming louder and finishing with a strident ratchet-like sound. Diurnal. Dry, scrubby habitats: sometimes a pest in cereals and fruit crops. 7–11. S.

nymph of *viridissima* showing characteristic bright green colour with brown dorsal stripe, together with reversed wing-buds typical of young orthopterans.

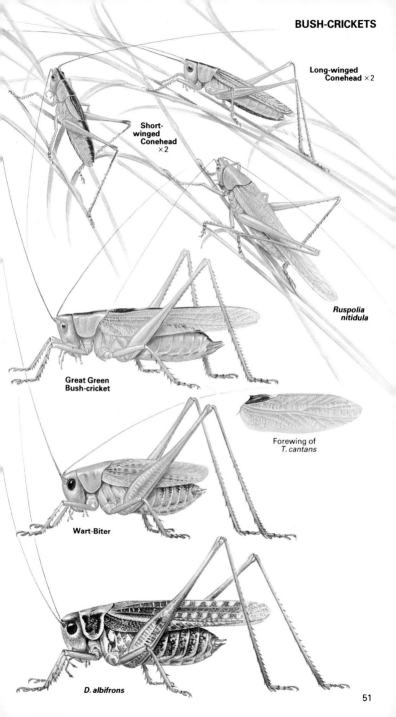

Long-winged
Conehead × 2

Short-
winged
Conehead
× 2

*Ruspolia
nitidula*

Great Green
Bush-cricket

Forewing of
T. cantans

Wart-Biter

D. albifrons

Grey Bush-cricket

P. tessellata

P. affinis

△s **Grey Bush-cricket** *Platycleis albopunctata*. Fully winged and flies readily. Sometimes green on top. Central keel in posterior half of pronotum: side keels converge towards the front. Ovipositor (left) 8–11mm long. Song a prolonged series of short (½ sec) buzzing sounds like winding a watch. Active mainly afternoon and evening. Dry, scrubby places. 7–10. S & C: mainly coastal in B. One of several very similar species, often difficult to separate.

P. tessellata is smaller and distinguished by heavy markings in centre of forewing: female easily recognised by 4–6mm ovipositor (left). Song: a harsh scratching sound like drawing comb over finger nail: a few well-spaced chirps, followed by several rapid ones and then a few more well-spaced ones. 7–10. Dry places. S (and most of France).

P. affinis is like a large *albopunctata* (20–25mm long) but vein running along sharp fold of forewing, just behind pronotum, is distinctly yellow. Ovipositor (left) 13–16mm. 6–10. Rough and cultivated land. S.

P. sepium differs from above in being short-winged and having no side keels on pronotum. Pinkish-brown, sometimes reddish, with very long hind feet. Ovipositor 11–15mm. Song a prolonged strident hiss, mainly at night: shorter bursts by day. Rough vegetation, especially where damp. 7–9. S.

△ **Bog Bush-cricket** *Metrioptera brachyptera*. Forewings normally short in both sexes, hind wings vestigial. A short central keel in posterior half of pronotum. Pale band normally only on hind margin of pronotal flaps. Green may be absent from upper parts, but always green underneath. Ovipositor 8–10mm long, moderately curved. Song a prolonged series of short, shrill chirps – 2–6 per sec and resembling the rapid ticking of a clock. Mainly diurnal. Peat bogs and damp heaths. 7–11. N & C. One of several similar species.

△s **Roesel's Bush-cricket** *M. roeselii*. Pale yellow or green stripe all round pronotal flaps. Head and body brown or green, but forewings always brown. Ovipositor 5–6mm long: strongly curved. Song long bursts of high-pitched sound, like high-speed drill. Active day and night. Lush vegetation in moist areas. 6–11. Mainly coastal marshes in B.

M. abbreviata differs from the above in its slightly longer forewings (about 10mm) and in the much shorter male cerci, which are very stout at the base and largely covered by the last abdominal segment. Ovipositor 6–7mm long. Moist mountain slopes with lush grass. 6–9. SW (mainly Pyrenees).

▲ **Dark Bush-cricket** *Pholidoptera griseoaptera*. No central keel on pronotum. Light brown, through chestnut, to almost black: but top of head and pronotum always brown and underside of body always greenish-yellow. Female usually paler than male. Forewings vestigial in female. Song a single very short high-pitched chirp repeated irregularly. Will sing in daytime, especially in afternoon, and likes sunbathing, but becomes most active in evening and sings well into the night. 7–11. Rough vegetation in hedgerows and woodland clearings and on roadsides. Also in garden shrubberies. Absent from heathland and other open habitats. Several similar species in southern Europe, especially SE.

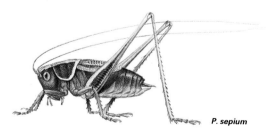

P. sepium

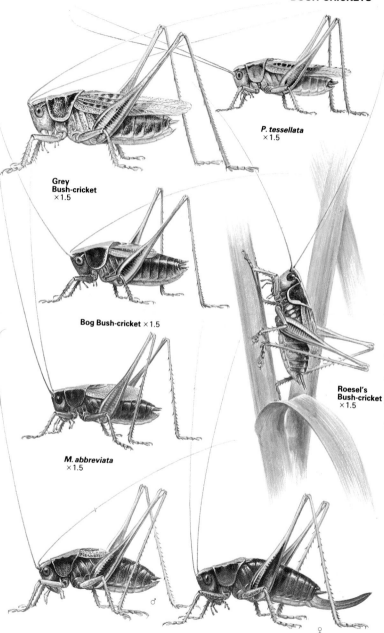

P. tessellata
×1.5

**Grey
Bush-cricket**
×1.5

Bog Bush-cricket ×1.5

**Roesel's
Bush-cricket**
×1.5

M. abbreviata
×1.5

Dark Bush-cricket ×1.5

Eupholidoptera chabrieri. One of the most beautiful bush-crickets, easily identified by bright green top of pronotum, which is strongly rounded at back. Rest of body generally green or yellowish-green above and often orange below: abdomen sometimes largely brown. Face lime-green with black spots. Female forewings almost completely hidden under pronotum. Ovipositor 18–24 mm long: very slightly curved. Song a series of shrill staccato chirps, about 2 per sec., rather like striking matches but higher pitched: mainly after dusk. On bushes and low vegetation, mostly in upland areas. 7–10. S & C (southern).

Anonconotus alpinus. Upper surface generally dark brown or black, often heavily mottled with olive-green: sometimes chestnut coloured. Cream or pale grey below. Female forewings only 1 mm long and carried at sides. Front tibia with 3 spines on outer edge. Ovipositor 11–16 mm long: slightly curved. Song short bursts of rather soft warbling sound, like a sewing machine: produced only in sunshine. Insect enjoys sunbathing. Often infested with red mites. Stony ground and low-growing plants in mountains, usually above 600 m. 7–10. S & C. **A. apenninigenus**, a rare species from the mountains of S. France and Italy, is similar but has only one or two spines on front tibia.

Rhacocleis germanica. Basically brown with darker markings: sometimes marbled with grey or yellow. Pronotum elongate and lightly rounded behind, with a pale stripe in mid-line. Stripe often extends along abdomen. Female forewings are minute flaps. Ovipositor 14–19 mm: very slightly curved. Long flaps under hind tarsi. Dry habitats, especially woodland margins and olive groves. Mainly crepuscular. 7–10. S & C (southern). Several similar species in SE.

Antaxius pedestris. Grey or light brown above, generally with darker markings: sometimes entirely greyish, relieved only by pale border of pronotum and dark spot above it. Often pinkish below. Male forewings black at base and pale at apex: female forewings hardly visible beyond pronotum. Ovipositor 13–19 mm long: almost straight. Song a low-pitched scratching sound, ratchet-like with fluctuating volume: in bursts of 1–2 secs. Active largely by day. Shrubby habitats, mainly in uplands. Usually falls to ground when disturbed. 8–9. S & C (southern). Several similar species.

Gampsocleis glabra. Mainly light green as a rule, but sometimes brown: top of pronotum always brownish. Fully winged in both sexes. Forewings heavily spotted with brown. Ovipositor 15–23 mm long, curving gently downwards towards tip. Song a rather weak, but continuous warble lasting for as much as a minute: produced mainly by day. Lush vegetation in moist habitats. 7–9. S & C.

Yersinella raymondi. Like a small *Rhacocleis* but no large flaps under hind tarsi. Shiny, with a smoothly rounded pronotum. Sometimes chestnut: more often light brown with dense speckling. A dark stripe along each side of the body. Forewings minute in both sexes. Ovipositor 10 mm long, quite strongly curved. Rough areas and shrubby habitats, especially near water. Attracted to lights at night. 7–9. S & C (southern).

Saga pedo. Unmistakable: one of Europe's largest insects. Occasionally grey with pale yellow stripe on side, but stripe may be absent from both green and grey specimens. Wings completely absent. Male unknown: female reproduces by laying parthenogenetic eggs. Grassy and shrubby habitats, especially on limestone: lives on ground on the vegetation and feeds almost exclusively on other bush-crickets and grasshoppers, which are held down by the spiky front legs. Quite rare. 7–9. S (rarely far from Mediterranean coasts).

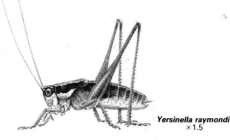

Yersinella raymondi
× 1.5

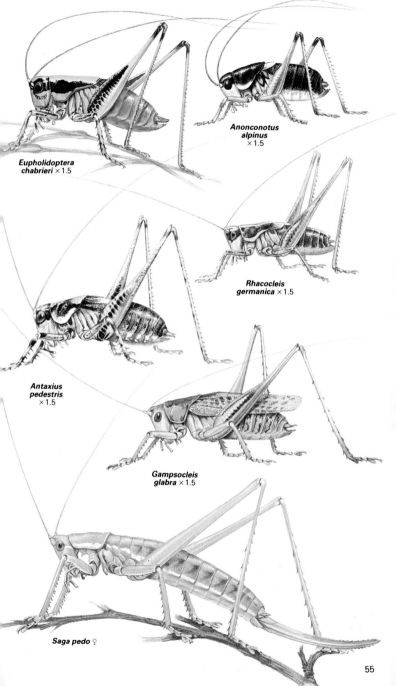

Eupholidoptera chabrieri × 1.5

Anonconotus alpinus × 1.5

Rhacocleis germanica × 1.5

Antaxius pedestris × 1.5

Gampsocleis glabra × 1.5

Saga pedo ♀

Ephippiger provincialis. Pronotum strongly raised in posterior half, producing a very distinctive saddle-shape: top of pronotum joining side in a smooth curve. Forewings very short and with stridulatory apparatus in both sexes. Antennae attached below eyes. These features are shared by all *Ephippiger* species, but *provincialis* is easily distinguished by its size. Ovipositor about 30 mm long: gently curved. 6–9. On a wide range of shrubs, including vines. Populations fluctuate markedly from year to year, sometimes becoming very high and causing severe damage to vineyards. Confined to southern France.

Ephippiger ephippiger. One of several very similar species. Green or brown, often with clearly banded abdomen. Ovipositor up to 25 mm long: gently curved. Known as 'le tizi' in France, for the characteristic song – a short, high-pitched, rasping, double chirp sounding like *ti-zi* and repeated irregularly, sometimes in quick succession. Female also chirps, as in all *Ephippiger* species, but less readily than male. Rough ground and scrubby habitats, often damaging vines when abundant. 7–11. S & C.
E. cruciger resembles *E. ephippiger* but is generally a little larger and usually has a dark cross on the top of the pronotum, which is shinier and less wrinkled than in *ephippiger*. The species appears to be confined to southern France.

Uromenus rugosicollis. Resembles *Ephippiger*, but pronotum has side keels in posterior half, forming a distinct angle between top and sides. Ovipositor 10–12 mm long: quite strongly curved towards tip. Occasionally greyish-green. Song rather like a slowed-down 'tizi' song, each chirp lasting about ⅔rd sec. and repeated about 20 times a minute: not unlike winding a watch or running a comb over a finger nail. Female chirp is shorter, more like typical 'tizi'. Scrubby places. 7–10. SW. Several similar species, mainly in Iberia.

Pycnogaster inermis. Greenish or reddish-brown. Pronotum virtually flat on top with a shallow V-shaped notch at hind end: side keels run all along it, interrupted by two transverse grooves. Forewings almost covered by pronotum, especially in female. Antennae attached near base of eyes (attached between the eyes in most other bush-crickets). Ovipositor 30–35 mm long. Scrubby places. 5–8. Spain.

CAVE-CRICKETS Rhaphidophoridae

Completely wingless insects with very long antennae: legs, palps, and cerci are also unusually long and slender. Tarsi 4-segmented. Ovipositor blade-like, as in bush-crickets. Most species inhabit caves and scavenge on dead animal matter. They are also called wingless camel-crickets. About 30 species live in Europe, mostly in SE.

Dolichopoda azami. One of several very similar species. Plain or mottled coloration. Ovipositor about 14 mm long, almost straight and lightly toothed near tip. Cave-dwelling, but often seen on vegetation outside in summer. Strictly nocturnal. Adult all year, but most common in late autumn, when most mating occurs. Confined to SE France & N Italy, often high in the hills.

⚠ **Greenhouse Camel-cricket** *Tachycines asynamorus.* Very similar to *Dolichopoda* but with much spinier hind tibia (50–80 closely-packed spines, compared with less than 30 in *Dolichopoda*). Usually mottled. Ovipositor 11–12 mm: very gently curved. A native of eastern Asia, but now established in heated greenhouses throughout Europe. Strictly nocturnal. May nibble plants, but probably compensates by eating insect pests, although feeds mainly on dead animal matter.

Ephippiger eggs are laid in the ground. Raising herself up on her long legs, the female drives her ovipositor into the soil to its full length.

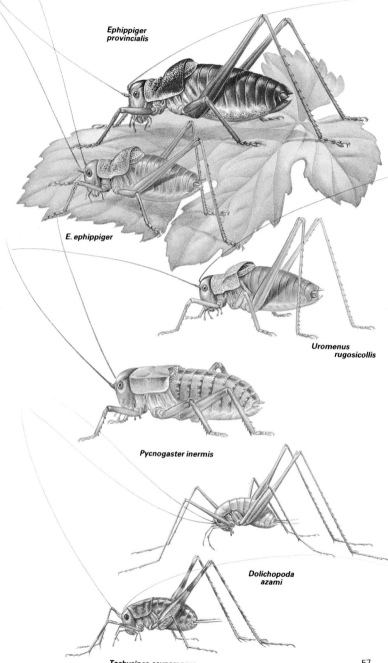

Ephippiger provincialis

E. ephippiger

Uromenus rugosicollis

Pycnogaster inermis

Dolichopoda azami

Tachycines asynamorus

57

TRUE CRICKETS Gryllidae Orthoptera with long slender antennae, globular head, 3-segmented tarsi, and long cerci. More flattened than bush-crickets, with forewings (when present) fitted over body like a lid. Hind wings (when present) rolled up and protruding beyond abdomen like tails. Ovipositor straight and needlelike. Front tibiae usually with an 'ear' on inner and outer faces, although inner one often very small.

▲ **House Cricket** *Acheta domestica*. Fully winged. Song a bird-like warble: 2–3 chirps per second and continued for long periods. Mainly nocturnal. Native of SW Asia and N Africa but well established in houses, bakeries, etc in Europe. Often on rubbish dumps and in gardens in summer.

△s **Field Cricket** *Gryllus campestris*. Pale yellow at base of forewing often obscure, especially in female. Her forewings less shiny, with denser venation. Hind wings vestigial in both sexes. Hind femur orange below. Song like *Acheta* but usually 3–4 chirps per second: very musical. Active day and night. Grassland. Lives in burrow and male sings at entrance. 4–9. Absent from far north.

Eugryllodes pipiens. Front tibia has 'ear' only on outside. Female forewings hardly longer than pronotum: obliquely truncated. Song: shrill musical chirps, like cheeping chick with occasional trills. Mainly nocturnal. Dry, stony places, including old walls and buildings. 7–10. SW.

Gryllomorpha dalmatina. Wingless. A pale cross on pronotum. No 'ears'. Damp rocky places, often in and around buildings. Mostly nocturnal. Mainly 9–12. S.

Melanogryllus desertus. Forewings may reach end of abdomen. Hind wings short or fully developed. All legs entirely black. Song short shrill chirps: 30–40 per minute. Among stones and turf, often on cultivated land. 5–8. S & C.

Modicogryllus frontalis. Wings vary from very short to fully developed. Front tibia has 'ear' on outer face only. Pale band between eyes. Hind tibia with short spines. Sunny woodland edges and scrub: also vineyards. 5–8. S & C.

△s **Wood Cricket** *Nemobius sylvestris*. Front tibia has 'ear' on outer face only. Forewings shorter in female, not or only just meeting in centre. No hind wings. Hind tibia with long spines (distinctly longer than width of tibia). Song: a soft prolonged warble with brief pauses every second or two. On ground in woodland and scrub. Active day and night. 6–11. S & C.

Pteronemobius heydeni. Like *Nemobius* but smaller. Forewings cover at least half abdomen. Hind wings rudimentary or fully developed. Song shrill, but soft, in bursts of about 3 secs: repeated every 2–3 secs. Damp grassland. 5–8. S & C.

Arachnocephalus vestitus. Wingless: clothed with fine scales. No 'ears'. Male drums by tapping end of abdomen on leaves. On shrubs in dry places. 7–10. S.

Italian Cricket *Oecanthus pellucens*. Very delicate. Female forewings much narrower. Song a beautiful soft warble, *griii-griii-griii*, produced mainly at night and continued for long periods. On trees, shrubs and tall herbage. (Sometimes called Tree Cricket). 7–10. S & C.

Italian Cricket

♂

△s **Mole Cricket** *Gryllotalpa gryllotalpa* Gryllotalpidae. A burrowing insect with much enlarged front legs. Body furry. Forewings short but hind wings fully developed. Flies on warm evenings. Song: long periods of quiet churring, usually produced at mouth of burrow in the evening. Moist meadows, especially near rivers. Adult all year, but dormant in winter.

Mole Cricket

House Cricket ×1.25

Field Cricket ×1.25

Eugryllodes pipiens ×1.25

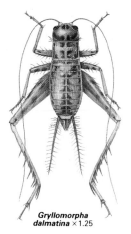

Gryllomorpha dalmatina ×1.25

Melanogryllus desertus ×1.25

Modicogryllus frontalis ×1.25

Wood Cricket ×2

Pteronemobius heydeni ×3

Arachnocephalus vestitus ×3

COCKROACHES   Order Dictyoptera:
Sub-order Blattodea

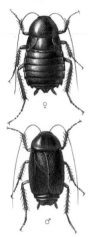

♀

♂

Common Cockroach

Rather flat jnsects with long antennae and long, spiky legs. Mostly fast-running, ground-living scavengers, feeding largely on dead plant matter. Broad pronotum almost completely covers head: central area of pronotum is called the disc. Forewings (tegmina) leathery: often shorter in female than in male but sexes otherwise alike. Hind wings membranous, but often absent. Eggs laid in horny cases (oothecae), which female may carry protruding from her hind end. Nymphs very like adults without wings. There are about 3500 known species, mostly in the warmer parts of the world. Several tropical species have become cosmopolitan pests in houses and other buildings. Native European species are all rather small.

▲ **Common Cockroach** *Blatta orientalis* Blattidae. Commonly called the black beetle. Wings vestigial in female: both sexes flightless. Introduced from Africa or Asia. Usually found indoors in Europe – in houses, bakeries, etc. Sometimes on rubbish dumps in summer, and may survive there in winter in warmer regions.

▲ **American Cockroach** *Periplaneta americana.* Introduced from Africa, despite this name. Rarely out of doors in Europe: inhabits bakeries, warehouses, greenhouses, sewers, etc: rarely in dwelling houses. Usually near ports. Common on ships. Flies well in warm conditions.

▲ **Australian Cockroach** *P. australasiae* is also probably African. Slightly smaller than *americana*, with distinct yellow margin to pronotum. Habits and distribution like *americana.*

▲ **German Cockroach** *Blattella germanica* Blattellidae. Introduced from N. Africa. Mostly in bakeries and other buildings in Europe, but also on rubbish dumps in summer. Pronotal stripes vary. Both sexes can fly, but reluctant to do so.

▲ **Brown-banded Cockroach** *Supella longipalpa.* An African species only recently established in houses in Europe. Ground colour yellowish to deep brown. Female darker and with shorter wings, leaving part of broad abdomen exposed. Male can fly.

Loboptera decipiens. Wings form minute flaps on sides of thorax. Pale margin of pronotum may extend round abdomen. Under stones and debris, often by sea. 4–8. S.

△s **Tawny Cockroach** *Ectobius pallidus* Ectobiidae. Fully winged in both sexes and flies in warm weather. Like the other *Ectobius* species, it inhabits woodlands, heaths, and rough grassland: mostly in turf and leaf litter but sometimes in trees. 4–10. S & C.

E. sylvestris. Pronotal disc entirely black, sharply angled behind. Male forewings cover only about half of black abdomen. Male can fly. 5–9. *E. vittiventris* Body and forewings unspotted. Pronotal disc rounded. Fully winged in both sexes. 7–10. SE & C.

△s **Dusky Cockroach** *E. lapponicus.* Like *sylvestris* but pronotal disc rounded. Male often very pale. Female shorter, broader, and browner, with forewings not usually reaching tip of abdomen. Male flies. 4–10.

△s **Lesser Cockroach** *E. panzeri.* Always under 9 mm long. Pale to dark brown, sometimes greyish: heavily speckled. Male forewings narrow and pointed: female short and truncated. Mainly coastal areas and sandy ground. 6–10. S & C.

Phyllodromica subaptera. Forewings minute, not wider than pale margin of pronotum. Female cerci brownish. Under leaves and stones: rare. 5–9. S.

P. maculata. Female forewings roundly truncated, but more or less meet in centre. In debris. 5–9. C. The forewings of *Phyllodromica* spp are stiffer than in *Ectobius* and less distinctly veined.

P. marginata has unmistakable pattern. In leaves and debris. 4–7. SE.

**German Cockroach
with ootheca** ×2

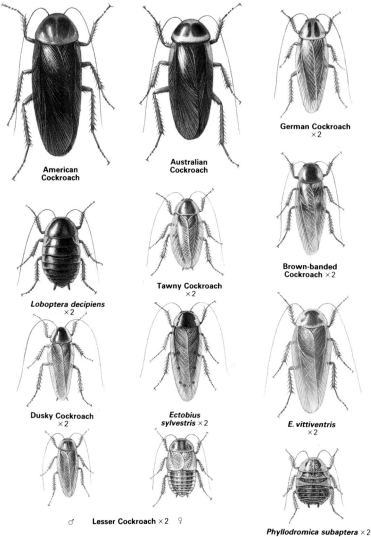

American Cockroach

Australian Cockroach

German Cockroach ×2

Loboptera decipiens ×2

Tawny Cockroach ×2

Brown-banded Cockroach ×2

Dusky Cockroach ×2

Ectobius sylvestris ×2

E. vittiventris ×2

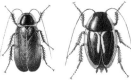

♂ **Lesser Cockroach** ×2 ♀

Phyllodromica subaptera ×2

P. maculata ×2

P. marginata ×2

MANTIDS   Order Dictyoptera: Sub-order Mantodea

Predatory insects related to cockroaches, with thickened, leathery forewings (tegmina) and a long neck. They usually lie in wait for their prey with the front legs folded in front of the face. The highly mobile head turns to face any movement, and when prey comes within reach the spiky front legs shoot out to impale it. Females of the larger species often eat the males during copulation, starting with the head – quite an efficient arrangement, for the male then helps to nourish the eggs as well as fertilising them. Eggs are laid in frothy 'soufflés' which harden into horny cases. There may be several hundred eggs in each case. Most species pass the winter in the egg stage. There are some 2000 known species. Most are tropical, but about 18 reach S & C Europe. They feed on a variety of other insects, including grasshoppers. None lives in B.

female *Mantis*
laying her eggs

hind wing of *R. baetica*

head of
A. spallanziana

head of
A. decolor

Praying Mantis *Mantis religiosa* Mantidae. The commonest European species: green or sometimes brown. Male much more slender than female. Both sexes fly well in warm weather. When disturbed, it puts on a threat display, raising front legs to reveal dark eye-spots on their insides and making a hissing sound by rubbing abdomen against the partly-raised wings. Rough grassland and scrub. 7–11. S & C.

Rivetina baetica. Truncated forewings immediately identify female: male forewings reach end of abdomen. Edges of pronotum strongly toothed, especially in female: usually a dark stripe down the centre. Hind wing with large apical eye-spot. Hot, dry places. 6–9. Far south.

Ameles spallanziana. A small mantid that scuttles over low vegetation in warm, dry places. Male flies when disturbed, but female is almost wingless. Eyes moderately pointed, especially in male. Not a cannibalistic species. 6–9. S.

A. decolor inhabits the same dry, scrubby habitats as *spallanziana* and is more common. Generally a little larger, but female lacks the swollen abdomen. Eyes rounded. 7–10. S. Several similar species occur in far south.

Geomantis larvoides. Because of its small size and lack of wings, this species may be mistaken for a young *Ameles*. The *Geomantis* prothorax, however, is widest near the front and finely toothed along the margins, whereas the *Ameles* prothorax is widest in the middle and smooth-edged. Runs rapidly on the ground in dry, sunny places. 7–9. S.

Iris oratoria. May be green or brown, sometimes with a rosy tinge. Forewings of male completely cover abdomen. Smaller size and coloured hind wings distinguish it from *M. religiosa*. Male often comes to light at night. Common on bushes in warm places. 6–10. S.

A male *Mantis* has already lost his head, but continues to pump sperm into the female as she devours him.

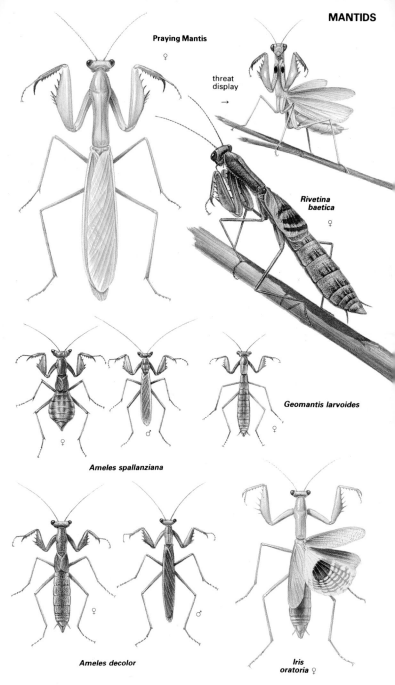

Praying Mantis ♀

threat
display
→

*Rivetina
baetica* ♀

Geomantis larvoides ♀

Ameles spallanziana ♀ ♂

Ameles decolor ♀ ♂

*Iris
oratoria* ♀

Empusa pennata Empusidae. Identified by tall crest on the head, this species may be green or brown. Male antennae rather feathery. Flies well in warm weather, especially the male, which regularly comes to lights at night. Eats relatively small prey – mainly small flies. Female never eats male. Rough grassy places. 5–9. Unlike other European mantids, nymphs hatch in summer, feeding through autumn and spasmodically in winter. Growth is completed late spring. SW. ***E. fasciata*** of SE is similar.

Perlamantis alliberti Amorphoscelididae. Wings well developed in both sexes: forewings almost transparent with a distinct network of veins. Pronotum very short and not dilated in middle, thus separating this small mantid from *Ameles* spp. Front tibia has no spines apart from terminal spur. Rough vegetation, the males readily flying to lights at night. 6–9. SW.

STICK INSECTS   Order Phasmida

Leaf-eating insects with stick-like bodies. Extremely well camouflaged on shrubs and grasses, but can be found by careful searching, especially at night when they do most of their feeding. Males of *Bacillus* and *Clonopsis* are extremely rare. The females reproduce parthenogenetically, laying unfertilised but viable eggs for generation after generation. The eggs are simply dropped to the ground. They remain there throughout the winter, looking just like seeds, and hatch in the spring. The sausage-shaped eggs of *Leptynia* are readily identified. Those of *Bacillus* and *Clonopsis* are best distinguished by using a lens to examine the micropylar plate – an elongate area on one side of the egg enclosing the microscopic pores through which the egg is fertilised. Young stick insects resemble the adults in all but size. The half dozen species living in southern Europe are completely wingless, but many tropical species are winged and able to fly. There are about 2,500 known species, including the very flat leaf insects. The majority live in S.E. Asia.

Bacillus rossius. Phylliidae. Green or brown, the surface of green specimens being smooth while that of brown ones is rather granular. Female 65–100 mm long: antennae with 20–25 segments. Eggs oval and very dark: micropylar plate runs full length of egg. Common on many kinds of shrubs in warm, dry places. 6–12. S.

Clonopsis gallica. Very similar to *B. rossius*, but female rarely over 75 mm long and antennae with only 12–13 segments. Green or brown, the green specimens being rather smoother. Eggs are mottled brown and usually a little larger than those of *rossius*: micropylar plate much shorter than the egg. More common than *rossius* on shrubs in warm, dry places. 5–10. S, but extending well up into central France.

Leptynia hispanica. Phasmatidae. Green or yellowish-brown. Male up to 46 mm: female to 58 mm. Male cerci extend beyond tip of abdomen. Male antennae usually 16-segmented: female antennae usually 11-segmented. Although still heavily outnumbered by females, males are more common than among the last two species. Egg is sausage-shaped. Local in grassy places. 5–9. SW.

Carausius morosus. Known as the laboratory stick insect because it is widely bred in schools and laboratories, this oriental species sometimes escapes and becomes temporarily established in gardens. Completely wingless: female green or brown and up to 80 mm long. Base of front leg pink. Male very rare.

Bacillus rossius   Clonopsis gallica

stick insect heads, showing different lengths of antennae

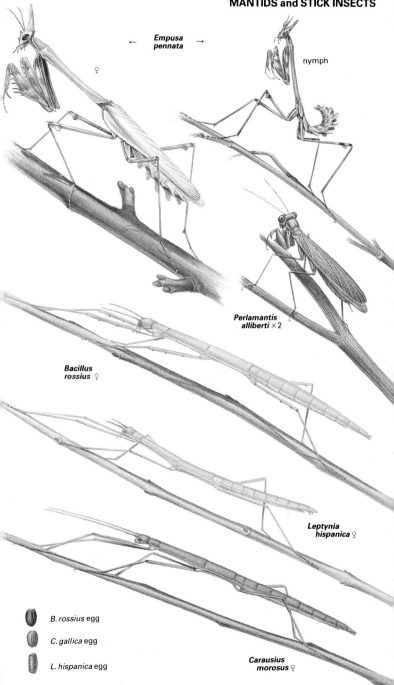

MANTIDS and STICK INSECTS

Empusa pennata ♀ ← →

nymph

Perlamantis alliberti × 2

Bacillus rossius ♀

Leptynia hispanica ♀

B. rossius egg

C. gallica egg

L. hispanica egg

Carausius morosus ♀

TERMITES   Order Isoptera

Soft-bodied social insects, forming long-living colonies headed by a king and a queen. Most individuals are juvenile workers: large-jawed soldiers, which defend the colony, form about 5% of population. Only the young reproductive forms have wings. These are very flimsy, with front and hind ones almost identical (Isoptera means 'equal wings'). There are over 2000 known species, with just two native to southern Europe. Both live in tree stumps and other dead wood, chewing out their living quarters and digesting the timber with the aid of hordes of protozoans in their digestive canals. Swarms of reproductive forms periodically emerge, but they lose their wings after a short flight and, after mating, some become kings and queens of new colonies.

Kalotermes flavicollis Kalotermitidae. Small colonies of a few hundred individuals in dry wood. Workers all youngsters, many of which later grow into soldiers or reproductives. Pronotum rectangular in all castes. Soldiers with toothed jaws. Winged insects emerge mainly in early spring. Widespread in S: mainly near coast.

Reticulitermes lucifugus Rhinotermitidae. Colonies of several thousand insects, usually in damper wood, including building timbers at or below ground level. Workers are juveniles and remain so all their lives, never turning into other forms. Pronotum of all castes rounded at back and often heart-shaped. Soldiers' jaws not toothed. Swarms appear mainly 4–6, usually in the morning. Throughout S: slightly hardier than *Kalotermes* and extends further from coast.

WEB-SPINNERS   Order Embioptera

Slender insects with first tarsal segment of front leg conspicuously swollen. Male may be winged in some species: female always wingless and somewhat larger than male. Female cerci slender and symmetrical: male cerci strongly asymmetrical. Live among leaf litter and turf, usually under stones or logs, inhabiting silken tunnels which they make with silk from glands in the swollen front legs. Wriggle rapidly along tunnels, moving backwards and forwards with equal ease. Feed mainly on dead leaves, with some animal matter. Adult females can be found all year, but they go deeper into ground to avoid desiccation in summer. Adult males occur in spring, but are rarely found. Many females can reproduce parthenogenetically. Nymphs resemble adult females and remain in mother's tunnel for some time: often build their own tunnels under the same stone, but they do not co-operate in the way that the termites do. Most of the 300 or so known species are tropical, but a few live in S. Europe. Males can usually be identified by the shape of their cerci; females are much harder to separate.

Haploembia solieri Oligotomidae. Very like *Embia ramburi* but often paler. Best distinguished by 1st segment of hind tarsus, which has two tubercles on lower surface compared with one in *Embia* (but microscope needed to see this feature!). Fairly common throughout S, often living with *E. ramburi*.

Embia amadorae Embiidae. One of the few European species with winged male. Female paler, Iberia only. *E. ramburi* is wingless in both sexes: male jet black, female brownish, often with purplish tinge, and with pale intersegmental membranes. Head more rounded than in *amadorae*. SW: one of the commonest species in Europe.

part of a *Reticulitermes* colony with developing winged forms

a web-spinner emerging from its tunnel

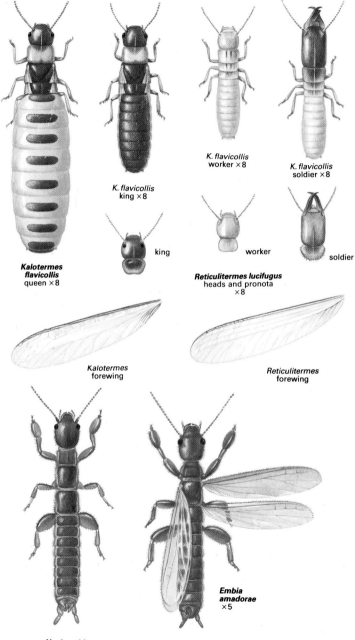

K. flavicollis
worker ×8

K. flavicollis
soldier ×8

K. flavicollis
king ×8

**Kalotermes
flavicollis**
queen ×8

king

worker

soldier

Reticulitermes lucifugus
heads and pronota
×8

Kalotermes
forewing

Reticulitermes
forewing

**Embia
amadorae**
×5

**Haploembia
solieri** ×5

67

EARWIGS   Order Dermaptera

Elongate insects with pincer-like cerci – usually strongly curved in male, slimmer and straighter in female and often meeting or just crossing at the tip. Forewings (elytra), when present, short and horny. Hind wings, when present, very thin: elaborately folded under elytra and often projecting beyond them at rest. Many species lack hind wings and some lack elytra as well. Even fully-winged species generally reluctant to fly. Essentially ground-living, nocturnal scavengers of both plant and animal matter. Hide under stones and in crevices by day. Many species can be found as adults all year, although they hibernate in the coldest months. Females of most species guard their eggs, and some prolong this parental care until young are well grown. Nymphs resemble adults, but have very slender cerci. Newly-moulted individuals are white or cream. About 34 of the 1300 known species occur in Europe: only 4 are British.

Anisolabis maritima Carcinophoridae. Elytra and hind wings absent. Body reddish-brown below. Male cerci asymmetrical. Among debris on seashore and stream banks: also in damp woodlands. 3–9. S: occasionally carried elsewhere by ships.

Euborellia moesta. Elytra reduced to minute flaps at sides of thorax. Male cerci asymmetrical: female cerci stout and usually held together. Antennae usually 18-segmented. Leaf litter. S. *E. annulipes* Paler than *moesta*, with no trace of elytra. Antennae usually 16-segmented. Under stones in damp places. 6–10. S: sometimes carried north in produce.

▲ **Labia minor** Labiidae. Smallest European earwig. Flies readily. Common near human habitation, especially on compost heaps and rubbish dumps.

Marava arachides. Hind wings usually very small or absent. Tropical, but sometimes temporarily established in bakeries and other buildings in Europe, mainly in S.

Labidura riparia Labiduridae. Largest European earwig. Sandy places, especially seashores and river banks: makes long tunnels in sand or hides under debris. Also on rubbish dumps. Partly predatory. Mainly S; local in C.

Nala lividipes. Slightly downy and rather flattened. Elytra with markedly parallel margins and abdomen usually parallel-sided. Pronotum rounded at back. In debris of various kinds. 6–9. SW.

Family Forficulidae The largest family. 2nd tarsal segment expanded and heart-shaped (see below). Mostly fully-winged, although hind wings often concealed under elytra at rest. *Forficula* spp are primarily vegetarians and often found quite high in trees and shrubs during the summer.

Chelidura aptera. Elytra form collar-like flaps: no hind wings. Male cerci very long, with no teeth. Female generally much lighter. Under stones on north-facing slopes of Alps. 7–10. *C. pyrenaica* is similar, but male cerci short and strongly curved: female usually dark. 6–10. Pyrenees.

Chelidurella acanthopygia. Elytra collar-like: no hind wings. Cerci very thin in both sexes. On woodland shrubs and in leaf litter.

Anechura bipunctata. Elytra distinctly longer than pronotum. Male cerci not flat at base: curve downwards at tip. Female cerci distinctly crossed at tip. Under stones in uplands. 6–10. S & C.

Pseudochelidura sinuata. Elytra equal to or shorter than pronotum: hind margin very oblique. Mountains of SW, under stones and in turf.

▲ **Apterygida media**. Hind wings vestigial. Regularly climbs vegetation and, like *Forficula* spp, commonly rests in flowers and chews petals.

▲ **Forficula auricularia**. Commonest European earwig: only one commonly seen in B. Male cerci broad and flat at base, with a tooth at end of the flat part. Hind wings project beyond elytra.

F. decipiens is similar, but hind wings concealed. Flat part of male cerci about ⅓ of length. S & C.

F. pubescens is downy: flat part of male cerci over ½ length. Damp places. S.

△ **F. lesnei** is slightly larger. Flat part of male cerci about ½ length. S & C.

Female *Forficula auricularia* tending her eggs. Constant licking keeps them free of fungal spores.

swollen 2nd tarsal segment.

All paintings are of ♂: ♀ pincers alongside

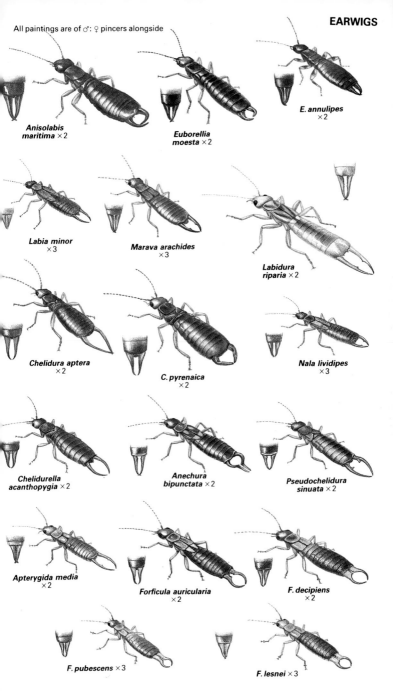

Anisolabis maritima ×2

Euborellia moesta ×2

E. annulipes ×2

Labia minor ×3

Marava arachides ×3

Labidura riparia ×2

Chelidura aptera ×2

C. pyrenaica ×2

Nala lividipes ×3

Chelidurella acanthopygia ×2

Anechura bipunctata ×2

Pseudochelidura sinuata ×2

Apterygida media ×2

Forficula auricularia ×2

F. decipiens ×2

F. pubescens ×3

F. lesnei ×3

69

BUGS   Order Hemiptera

An order of some 75,000 known species of hemimetabolous insects, of which some 8,000 occur in Europe and about 1,700 in Britain. The range of form within the order is very great, but all species possess a piercing beak (the rostrum) like a minute hypodermic needle, with which they suck juices from plants or other animals. Many are serious crop pests, including the aphids, reducing yields through mechanical damage to the plants and also transmitting an assortment of virus diseases. Two pairs of wings are normally present, the front ones usually hardened to some extent, but there are many wingless species. There is also great variation within many species, with fully-winged (macropterous), short-winged (brachypterous), and wingless (apterous) forms often present in the same population. Males and females often differ in wing-length and other features.

There are two very distinct sub-orders – the Heteroptera (p. 72) and the Homoptera (p. 88) – with no obvious connection apart from the beak or rostrum: the two are often treated as entirely separate orders.

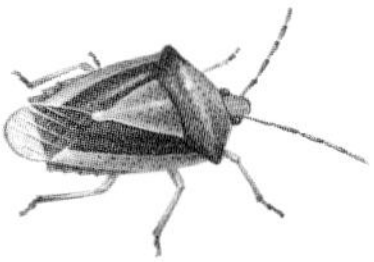

A heteropteran bug, showing the membranous tips of the forewings.

In the **Heteroptera** the forewing, when fully developed, is clearly divided into two regions – a horny or leathery basal area and a membranous tip. The hind wings are always membranous, and all the wings are folded flat over the body at rest. The head is more or less horizontal; and clearly visible from above. The antennae never have more than five segments and the beak clearly arises from the front of the head. The pronotum is very large and the scutellum is generally very conspicuous too, sometime extending back to cover the whole body – making the insect appear wingless.

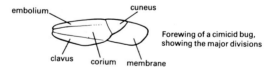

Forewing of a cimicid bug, showing the major divisions

Family classification of the Heteroptera depends on various features, including the number of segments in the antennae, tarsi and rostrum, and the structure of the forewing (when present), whose main regions are shown below. All winged species have a claval suture, dividing the toughened area of the forewing into the clavus – which is next to the scutellum when the wings are folded – and the corium. The corium may be further divided by sutures marking off the embolium along the front edge and the cuneus at the tip. The membrane commonly contains visible veins, whose number and shape are useful in identification.

The heteropterans include both plant and animal feeders, and all the water bugs, both surface-dwelling and submerged. The latter generally breathe in the same ways as the water beetles (p. 255), but the water scorpion and its relatives have solved the problem with a long breathing-tube which conducts air down from the surface.

In the **Homoptera** the forewings, when present, are generally of uniform texture throughout, though they may be either horny or membranous. They are usually held roof-wise over the body at rest. The head is commonly deflected backwards and the rostrum appears to spring from its rear – almost between the front legs in some species.

A homopteran bug, showing the roof-like resting position of the wings.

The Homopterans are entirely vegetarian and generally far less active than the heteropteran bugs. Many spend virtually their whole lives sucking sap from the host plant. The sap has a relatively low protein content but is very rich in sugars. In order to get enough protein, therefore, the bugs have to take in a large excess of sugar, but most of this passes straight through the gut and is exuded through the anus as honeydew. The aphids and psyllids are the most prolific producers of this sticky material and infested trees and other plants become covered with it in summer. Bees, ants and many other insects feed on it, but much remains on the leaves and is later colonised by a black fungus.

Two distinct groups can be recognised within the Homoptera. Members of the **Auchenorrhyncha** generally have short antennae with a terminal bristle, and 3-

The bristle-like antenna of the cicada

Hind wing of a froghopper, showing the peripheral vein

— peripheral vein

segmented tarsi. Forewings are often opaque and brightly coloured, and usually quite stiff. Many jump well, and the group as a whole are often known as hoppers. There are many families and they are not always easy to separate, but the presence of a peripheral vein just inside the margin of the hind wing – at least in the hind part of it – distinguishes the froghoppers (p. 92) and the leafhoppers (p. 90) from other superficially similar groups of plant hoppers.

The other main group within the Homoptera is the **Sternorrhyncha**, in which the antennae are relatively long and thread-like and the tarsi 1- or 2-segmented. This is a very diverse group containing the aphids, psyllids, whiteflies and scale insects (p. 96).

Young. Being hemimetabolous, the bugs do not go through a pupal stage. The young nymphs may or may not resemble the adults, but the beak readily identifies them as bugs. There are usually five instars, during which the young gradually get more like the adults, though the wing-buds are not usually clear until the 4th instar. It is sometimes difficult to decide whether a specimen is a fully grown nymph or a brachypterous adult, but if the wings meet the scutellum with a well-defined junction the specimen is almost certainly an adult. There are often considerable colour changes during development, and this is especially true between the last nymphal instar and the imago. *Nezara viridula*, for example, has a multi-coloured nymph (p. 74) and an almost plain green adult.

HETEROPTERAN BUGS
Sub-order Heteroptera

Bugs in which the forewings, when fully developed, are horny at the base and membranous at the tip.

▲ **Pine Flat-bug** *Aradus cinnamoneus* Aradidae. Very flat, with head narrowing strongly behind eyes. Antennae 4-segmented. Forewings very narrow and lacking membrane: even smaller in female. Feeds on pine sap. Most members of the family are fully winged and feed on fungi under loose bark.

▲ *Aneurus laevis* Aneuridae. One of the bark bugs. Very flat: forewings almost entirely membranous. Antennae 4-segmented. Feeds on fungi under bark.

typical shield bug
showing beak (p. 70)

The following bugs are known as shield bugs, from their general shape. All have 5-segmented antennae. They are also known as stink bugs because many species emit pungent fluids when alarmed. Many hibernate as adults and are seen mainly in autumn and spring. The group contains both herbivorous and carnivorous species. Their colours often fade after death.

▲ **Hawthorn Shield Bug** *Acanthosoma haemorrhoidale*. Acanthosomatidae. Tarsi 2-segmented, as in whole family. Feeds on leaves and fruit of hawthorn and other trees.

▲ **Parent Bug** *Elasmucha grisea*. Named for female's habit of standing guard over eggs and young nymphs, probably protecting them from attack by parasites. Mainly grey or yellow, usually tinged with purplish red. Mainly on birch.

▲ **Pied Shield Bug** *Sehirus bicolor* Cydnidae. Tarsi 3-segmented and tibiae very spiny, as in the whole family. On deadnettles and other labiates. ▲ *S. dubius* is metallic green or violet and sometimes black. It lives on various labiates.

Aethus flavicornis. Reddish brown to black. Legs extremely spiny. On coastal dunes and sea shore, usually buried in sand by day. Feeds on various plants.

▲ **Negro Bug** *Thyreocoris scarabaeoides*. Large rounded scutellum covers most of abdomen. In leaf litter and dry turf, especially on sandy and chalky soils.

△s *Odontoscelis dorsalis* Scutelleridae. As in all members of the family, tarsi are 3-segmented and scutellum covers whole abdomen. Forewings (covered by scutellum) largely membranous. Very hairy. Light bands may be reduced. Mainly on coastal dunes, feeding on storksbill. S & C.

▲ *Eurygaster testudinaria*. Damp grassy places, feeding mainly on rushes and sedges. ▲ **European Tortoise Bug** *E. maura* varies from yellowish to black, with or without brown stripes. Scutellum parallel-sided. Polyphagous. Often damages cereal grains.

Family Pentatomidae The largest shield bug family, with a total of about 3,000 species. Scutellum usually triangular and reaching at least to middle of abdomen. Tarsi 3-segmented. Nymphs usually rounded, often brightly coloured. Abundant on continent, but relatively few in B owing to short, cool summers.

▲ *Eysarcoris fabricii*. Greenish bronze, golden, or brownish violet: always heavily punctured. On hedge woundwort and other labiates.

△s *Eurydema dominulus*. Orange or red. A common pest of brassicas on the continent. △s **Brassica Bug** *E. oleracea*. Metallic green, blue, or violet, often with red, yellow, or cream spots. Mainly on crucifers and often a pest of cultivated brassicas.

▲ *Zicrona caerulea*. Dark green, blue, or violet. A carnivorous species, sucking juices from eggs and young larvae of various beetles, butterflies, and moths – including such pests as the Colorado beetle and cabbage white butterflies.

▲ **European Turtle Bug** *Podops inuncta*. Resembles Scutelleridae in its large scutellum covering most of abdomen, but readily distinguished by 2 small anvil-shaped projections at front of pronotum. Grassy places.

▲ **Bishop's Mitre** *Aelia acuminata*. Rough grassland and cereal fields, occasionally attacking ripening grain. *A. glebana* is similar but larger. S & C (southern).

Graphosoma italicum. Abundant on umbellifer flowers 6–10. Bold colour warns of foul taste. Legs often much blacker than shown here. S & C. *G. semipunctatum* has pronotal stripes broken into dots and tibiae almost entirely red. S.

Ancyrosoma albolineatum. Ground colour yellowish to violet-brown. Shape unmistakable. On various plants in dry habitats. S.

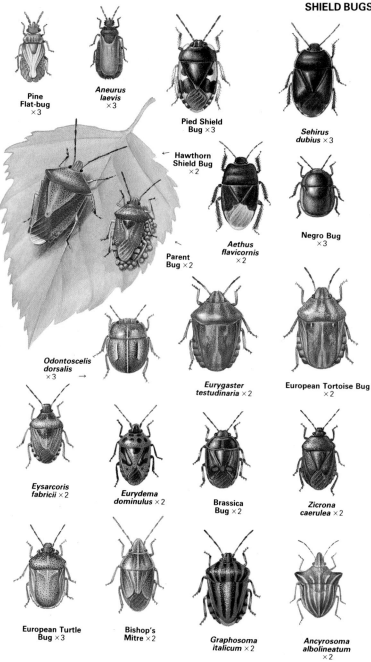

SHIELD BUGS

Pine
Flat-bug
×3

*Aneurus
laevis*
×3

Pied Shield
Bug ×3

*Sehirus
dubius* ×3

← Hawthorn
Shield Bug
×2

*Aethus
flavicornis*
×2

Negro Bug
×3

← Parent
Bug ×2

*Odontoscelis
dorsalis*
×3 →

*Eurygaster
testudinaria* ×2

European Tortoise Bug
×2

*Eysarcoris
fabricii* ×2

*Eurydema
dominulus* ×2

Brassica
Bug ×2

*Zicrona
caerulea* ×2

European Turtle
Bug ×3

Bishop's
Mitre ×2

*Graphosoma
italicum* ×2

*Ancyrosoma
albolineatum*
×2

73

▲ **Forest Bug** *Pentatoma rufipes*. Distinguished from most shield bugs by its very square 'shoulders' and almost rectangular pronotum. 6–10 on a wide range of trees and shrubs, sometimes attacking other insects as well as feeding on sap. Often common in orchards, especially on cherry. Nymphs are yellow with dark spots.

▲ *Picromerus bidens*. Pronotum slopes sharply back from head and then expands to form a sharp 'thorn' on each side. Abundant on bushes and other vegetation, especially in damp habitats, 7–10. Predatory on larvae of butterflies, moths, and beetles.

▲ **Common Green Shield Bug** *Palomena prasina*. Sides of pronotum slightly concave. Abundant on trees and shrubs and in rank herbage in autumn. Becomes bronze coloured in late autumn before going into hibernation: becomes bright green again before re-emerging 4–5. There are several similar species. *P. viridissima* has sides of pronotum slightly convex.

Nezara viridula. Slightly narrower than *Palomena*, with paler membrane at wing-tip and 3–5 pale spots on front margin of the scutellum. Head and front of pronotum may be pale brown. The nymph (left) is beautifully coloured. Abundant on a wide range of herbaceous plants, often causing damage to peas and potatoes. S & C.

▲ **Gorse Shield Bug** *Piezodorus lituratus*. The red colour is present only in young adults 7–10: after hibernation the insects are yellowish green, often with a bronze tinge. Always heavily punctured. Mainly on gorse, but sometimes on broom and other leguminous plants, often in very large numbers. S & C.

Nezara viridula
nymph × 1.5

Carpocoris fuscispinus. Ground colour ranges from yellow to reddish brown. Pronotal angles slightly raised and extending as black points well beyond wing margins. Double-brooded in south, where only mid-summer insects have the sharp pronotal angles: the autumn-spring brood have smaller and blunter angles. Polyphagous, but especially common on composites and umbellifers.

▲ **Sloe Bug** *Dolycoris baccarum*. Very hairy when seen under a lens: often tinged purple or red. On a wide variety of herbaceous plants as well as the blackthorn and other rosaceous shrubs, usually feeding on flower and fruit. Very common on dunes.

△ *Coreus marginatus* Coreidae. Two tiny horns on head between antennae. Latter are 4-segmented in this and all remaining families of land-living heteropterans. On docks and related plants, feeding mainly on the seeds: also feeds on other fruits, especially blackberries, in autumn. Often much darker brown. Like most members of the family, it hibernates as an adult and is most often seen in autumn and spring. There are many rather similar species, nearly all members of the family being dull brown. The family as a whole are known as squash bugs because several are pests of squashes in North America: nearly all are fruit feeders.

Philomorpha laciniata. On silvery paronychia in dry sunny places. Eggs are usually laid on other bugs of the same species and thus carried to fresh food plants. S & C.

△s *Verlusia rhombea*. Abdomen diamond-shaped and extending sideways well beyond wings. In dry habitats, usually on sandy soils, including heaths, grasslands, and open woods. On sandworts and related plants. Mainly coastal in B.

△ *Coriomeris denticulatus*. A rather spiky bug found on trefoils and other leguminous plants. Generally only on light, well-drained soils.

△s *Chorosoma schillingi* Rhopalidae. Straw-coloured to green. Forewings sometimes even shorter. In long grass, mainly on coastal dunes: rarely on inland dunes and heaths. 7–9.

△ *Rhopalus subrufus*. Resembles some coreids but head is broader (almost as wide as pronotum) and pronotum not expanded sideways. Woodland clearings and other lush flowery places, feeding on St John's-wort and many other plants. Flies readily.

△ *Myrmus miriformis*. Males green or brown: females always green. Usually brachypterous. Forewings always with prominent pink veins. 6–10 in all kinds of grassland from dry heath to water meadows. Feeds mainly on ripening grass seeds.

△s *Corizus hyoscyami*. Superficially resembles some of the ground bugs (p. 76) but distinguished by its hairiness and numerous veins in forewing membrane (ground bugs never have more than 5). Sandy areas, feeding on a wide range of plants. Mainly on coastal dunes in B.

Coptosoma scutellata Plataspidae. 2 tarsal segments. Scutellum covering almost whole of abdomen. Hind edge of scutellum strongly indented in male, weakly so in female. On legumes in damp grassland in summer. S and southern C.

Coptosoma scutellata × 3

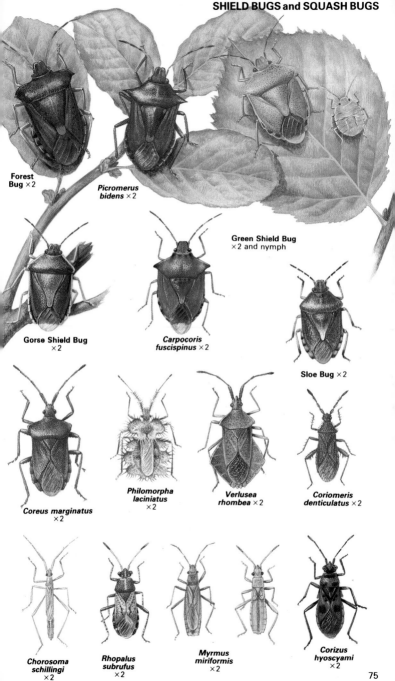

Forest Bug ×2

Picromerus bidens ×2

Green Shield Bug ×2 and nymph

Gorse Shield Bug ×2

Carpocoris fuscispinus ×2

Sloe Bug ×2

Coreus marginatus ×2

Philomorpha laciniatus ×2

Verlusea rhombea ×2

Coriomeris denticulatus ×2

Chorosoma schillingi ×2

Rhopalus subrufus ×2

Myrmus miriformis ×2

Corizus hyoscyami ×2

△ **Alydus calcaratus**. Alydidae 4th antennal segment much longer than 3rd and distinctly curved. Fast-flying in sunshine, with red abdomen exposed in flight. On heathland and other dry habitats, associated with a variety of plants and also partly carnivorous: sometimes feeds at carrion. Nymphs are ant-like and often found in ants' nests.

Camptopus lateralis. Like *Alydus* but pronotum much squarer. 4th antennal segment only slightly curved. Larger than *Alydus* and with yellowish brown underside marked with brown (underside bronzy black in *Alydus*). Dry habitats in S & C.

△s **Fire Bug** *Pyrrhocoris apterus* Pyrrhocoridae. Generally brachypterous: rarely macropterous. On many kinds of vegetation: often swarms on ground and feeds on fallen seeds, especially in early spring after hibernation. Also attacks other insects. S & C.

Fire Bug ×2

GROUND BUGS Lygaeidae A large family of essentially sombre coloured bugs, although some display bright warning colours. Membrane of forewing (when present) has no more than 5 veins (see p. 70). Antennae basically 4-segmented, although some individuals may have only 3 segments. Many species resemble mirid bugs (p. 80) but the forewings are much tougher and lack the distinct cuneus of the mirids. Ground bugs also have ocelli, which are lacking in mirids. Mainly seed-eating, although some are partly predatory, and mostly ground-living – often in sandy areas. Most species hibernate as adults.

△s **Aphanus rolandri**. Pale spot varies from yellow to red. In dry places with plenty of stones or leaf litter: occasionally under loose bark. Mostly nocturnal, feeding on fallen seeds. Mainly coastal counties in B.

△ **Megalonotus chiragra**. Antennae often all black. Forewing membrane may extend beyond abdomen. In moss and leaf litter in sandy places, feeding on various plants. Mainly coastal in B.

▲ **Scoloposthetus decoratus**. One of several rather similar species. Abundant on heathland, often swarming over heather shoots. Active all winter, feeding on shoots and seeds and partly on other insects.

△ **European Chinch-bug** *Ischnodemus sabuleti*. Long and short-winged forms equally common. Swarms on reeds and other tall grasses, including cereals, in damp and dry habitats. Adults and young hibernate in masses in leaf sheaths.

Lygaeus saxatilis. Underside of abdomen red with a black band at base of each segment. Common on a wide range of plants in sunny habitats. S & C. *L. equestris* is similar but forewing membrane is marked with white. Underside of abdomen has 2 black spots on each side of each segment.

▲ **Spruce Cone Bug** *Gastrodes abietum*. Very flat. Usually high up on Norway spruces, hiding in old cones by day and feeding on needles and young seeds at night. Over-winters in cones or bark crevices. ▲ **Pine Cone Bug** *G. grossipes* is readily distinguished by its rich chestnut colour. It lives mainly on pines but is less confined to the cones than *abietum* and commonly found on lower branches.

Trapezonotus ullrichi. Largest of several species with bicoloured pronotum and black scutellum. Among grasses in dry habitats, mainly on coast. S & C (southern). ▲ *T. arenarius* with 2nd and 3rd antennal segments black instead of brown, is common in dry grassland everywhere.

△ **Rhyparochromus pini**. An active runner on dry heathland. Found mainly around the bases of heathers and other plants, but higher up on the vegetation in warm weather. Feeds mainly on seeds.

▲ **Nysius thymi**. Pronotum without a keel. On dry sandy or gravelly areas, especially waste land, with short turf or scattered vegetation. 6–11 (occasionally living through winter). On numerous plants, especially composites such as Canadian fleabane, but also partly carnivorous.

Geocoris grylloides. Short forewings distinguish it from some related species. Mainly on coastal sand dunes. N & C.

Phymata monstrosa Phymatidae. A predatory species with enlarged raptorial front legs. Abdomen angular and toothed. Yellowish brown to black. S. *P. crassipes* is similar but a little larger and without teeth on sides of abdomen. Usually reddish brown. S & C (southern).

Phymata monstrosa ×3

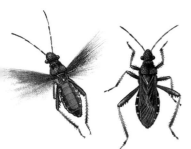

Alydus calcaratus × 2

Camptopus lateralis × 2

Aphanus rolandri × 2

Megalonotus chiragra × 4

Scoloposthetus decoratus × 4

long-winged short-winged
European Chinch-bug × 4

Lygaeus saxatilis × 2

L. equestris × 2

Spruce Cone Bug × 3

Pine Cone Bug × 3

Trapezonotus ullrichi × 3

Rhiparochromus pini × 3

Nysius thymi × 4

Geocoris grylloides × 3

Gampsocoris punctipes ×3

△ **Gampsocoris punctipes** Berytidae. One of the stilt bugs, named for the very long legs and antennae of most members of the family. A spine on the scutellum distinguishes this species. On restharrow, usually in sandy areas: often plentiful on coastal dunes. Nymphs are bright green in this family. S & C.

△ **Neides tipularius**. Superficially like *Empicoris* and other assassins but no distinct neck or enlarged front legs. Rostrum straight. Short-winged form has narrower forewings just reaching tip of abdomen. In dense vegetation in dry places such as heaths, dunes, and weedy arable fields. Feeds on a wide range of plants and 'freezes' when disturbed.

▲ **Berytinus minor**. Commonly short-winged. In dry grassy places, feeding on grasses and various leguminous plants. Absent from far south.

△ **Cymus melanocephalus**. Resembles ground bugs (p. 76), but distinguished by scutellum being much shorter than commisure and by inflated edges of forewings. In rank vegetation in damp places. Feeds on various rushes. Several related species have a pale keel on scutellum. S & C.

ASSASSIN BUGS Reduviidae
Predatory bugs with distinct neck and strong, curved, 3-segmented rostrum (left). Antennae often elbowed after long 1st segment. Some have enlarged, raptorial front legs. All feed on other insects and many show remarkable similarities to their prey (aggressive mimicry).

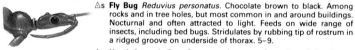

R. iracundus showing beak

△s **Fly Bug** *Reduvius personatus*. Chocolate brown to black. Among rocks and in tree holes, but most common in and around buildings. Nocturnal and often attracted to light. Feeds on wide range of insects, including bed bugs. Stridulates by rubbing tip of rostrum in a ridged groove on underside of thorax. 5–9.

▲ **Heath Assassin Bug** *Coranus subapterus*. Sometimes fully winged, especially in north. 6–10 on heaths and sand dunes, usually on bare patches of ground. Stridulates loudly if touched, like previous species.

Rhinocoris iracundus. Variable red and black pattern: pronotum may be all-black. 1st segment of rostrum red (black in *R. erythropus*). On flowers. 5–9. S & C (southern).

Pirates hybridus. Anterior part of pronotum much longer than posterior part. Waves antennae as it walks over the ground. 4–10. S & C.

▲ **Empicoris vagabundus**. Readily distinguished from stilt bugs by strongly curved rostrum and raptorial front legs. Lives mainly in trees and looks like a gnat at rest. Feeds on aphids and other small insects. Pale sides of abdomen separate it from several similar species.

Ploiaria domestica. Always wingless. Nocturnal, usually in and around buildings. Feeds on mosquitoes and other small flies. S.

DAMSEL BUGS Nabidae
Predatory bugs resembling assassins but with a 4-segmented rostrum. Antennae not clearly elbowed: 2nd segment longer than 1st. Like the assassins, larger species will pierce human skin if handled.

Prostemma guttula. Usually short-winged. Dry sandy places, at the bases of various plants. S & C. Common in Channel Islands.

▲ **Kalmanius flavomarginatus**. Upper surface and sides of abdomen with golden hair. Forewings occasionally reach beyond tip of abdomen. 6–10 in rough, damp grassland.

▲ **Common Damsel Bug** *Nabis rugosus*. Pale to dark brown: one of several very similar species. Forewings long or short. Grassy places everywhere.

▲ **Marsh Damsel Bug** *Dolichonabis limbatus*. Very rarely with longer wings. 7–11 in damp grassy places, feeding on a very wide variety of insects.

△ **Tree Damsel Bug** *Himacerus apterus*. Forewings occasionally reach tip of abdomen. 6–10. One of very few tree-dwelling damsel bugs. S & C. The very similar △ **Ant Damsel Bug** *Aptus mirmicoides* lives on the ground and has much shorter antennae. Its nymphs are extremely ant-like.

♂

▲ **Loricula elegantula** *Microphysidae*. A very tiny bug with fully winged male and short-winged or virtually wingless female. 6–9 among lichens on trees and old walls. Males uncommon: rarely seen after July. Feeds on mites, springtails, etc.

♀

Loricula elegantula ×6

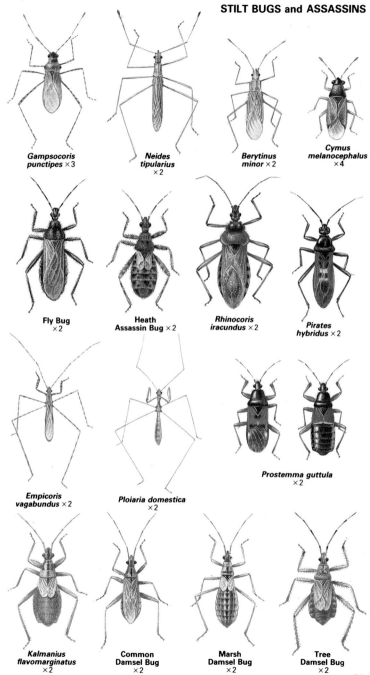

Gampsocoris punctipes ×3

Neides tipularius ×2

Berytinus minor ×2

Cymus melanocephalus ×4

Fly Bug ×2

Heath Assassin Bug ×2

Rhinocoris iracundus ×2

Pirates hybridus ×2

Empicoris vagabundus ×2

Ploiaria domestica ×2

Prostemma guttula ×2

Kalmanius flavomarginatus ×2

Common Damsel Bug ×2

Marsh Damsel Bug ×2

Tree Damsel Bug ×2

79

Common Flower Bug feeding on aphid

▲ **Piesma maculatum** Piesmatidae. Superficially like lacebugs, with strongly punctured forewings and pronotum, but latter does not cover scutellum. Pronotum has 2 keels at front. On sea purslane, orache, goosefoot, and other chenopods on coastal saltmarshes and waste ground. Occasionally on beet. △ **P. quadratum** has 3 keels on pronotum and may be green or brown. Male stridulates by rubbing wings on abdomen. Most of European coastline: inland in parts of C, where it carries virus disease of sugar beet. Both species are known as beet bugs.

▲ **Tingis cardui** Tingidae. One of the lacebugs, so called because of densely punctured and reticulate pronotum and forewings. Pronotum extends back to cover scutellum. Clothed with powdery wax. On spear thistle, nymphs living in dense clusters on underside of flower heads. There are many similar species.

BEDBUGS and FLOWER BUGS Cimicidae
Bedbugs are wingless bloodsuckers attacking birds and mammals. Flower bugs and their relatives are generally fully winged, capturing small insects on flowers or amongst debris. They resemble mirids but have a clear embolium in anterior part of forewing.

▲ **Bedbug** *Cimex lectularius*. Orange to deep brown. In and around houses, hiding in crevices by day and emerging to suck blood from man or other animals at night. Common in zoos.

△ **Oeciacus hirundinis**. Smaller and hairier than bedbug. Feeds on house martins and swallows (occasionally other birds) and over-winters in and around their nests. May enter houses when birds leave in autumn.

▲ **Common Flower Bug** *Anthocoris nemorum*. Forewings shiny throughout – distinguishing this from several similar species. Abundant everywhere on a wide range of trees, shrubs, and herbaceous plants – on leaves as well as flowers. A useful predator of aphids and red spider mites. Will pierce human skin and suck blood if handled.

△ **Orius niger**. One of several similar very small species. Colour varies, but can be identified by black hind tibiae. Male has swollen antennae. On a wide range of plants, especially gorse, heather, and mugwort.

▲ **Hot-bed Bug** *Xylocoris galactinus*. Antennae distinctly hairy (lens!). Named for its liking for compost heaps and similar places. Also in stables, birds' nests, etc., feeding on other insects and also sucking birds' blood.

MIRID or CAPSID BUGS Miridae
The largest family in the Heteroptera, with some 6,000 known species. Body and forewings are relatively soft. Forewings, when present, have a well developed cuneus (p. 70), which distinguishes the family from most other bugs. The embolium is not distinct and the membrane generally contains one or two distinct cells at the base. Most are herbivorous, feeding largely on developing fruits and seeds. Most pass the winter as eggs.

△s **Deraeocoris olivaceus**. 6–8 on hawthorn, feeding on young fruits as well as on various small insects. S & C.

△ **D. ruber** is smaller and shinier: generally brick coloured but ranges from yellow to black: cuneus always red. Tibiae not ringed. On a wide range of plants. 6–9. S & C.

△ **Systellonotus triguttatus**. 5–9, mainly on heathland, feeding on shoots and fruits of many plants and also on aphids. Often associated with ants, which nymphs and females resemble closely, although not in movements.

▲ **Phylus melanocephalus**. Yellow or brick coloured and distinguished from related species by black head. On oak and hazel, feeding partly on the plants and partly on aphids and other small insects. 5–8.

▲ **Psallus varians**. Reddish, yellow, or greyish brown. 5–9 on various deciduous trees, especially oaks. Partly predatory. There are many similar, closely related species.

△ **Amblytylus nasutus**. One of many rather similar mirids. Green at first, often becoming brown with age. 5–8 in dry grassy places. S & C.

▲ **Dicyphus errans**. 5–10 in rough herbage, including stinging nettles. Partly predatory. Most members of genus are entirely herbivorous, with just one food plant.

△ **Macrotylus paykulli**. Tibiae clothed with minute black spines. 6–9 on restharrow in dry grassland and waysides. Usually gregarious.

Fern Bug
(short-winged)
×5

▲ **Fern Bug** *Bryocoris pteridis*. Forewing membrane commonly absent, the shortened wings leaving tip of abdomen exposed: in this form forewings get wider towards the tip, giving a pear-shaped outline. 6–9 in damp woods, on bracken and other ferns. N & C.

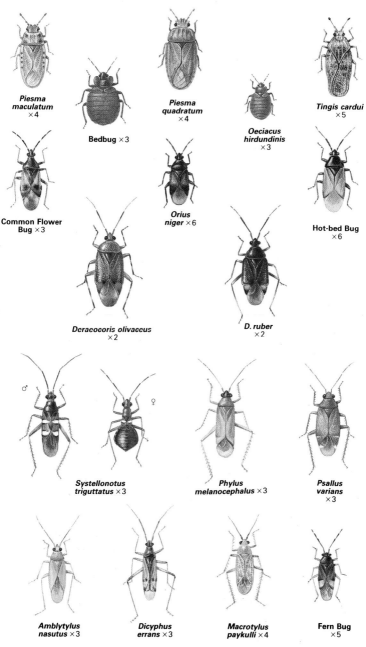

Piesma maculatum ×4

Bedbug ×3

Piesma quadratum ×4

Oeciacus hirdundinis ×3

Tingis cardui ×5

Common Flower Bug ×3

Orius niger ×6

Hot-bed Bug ×6

Deracocoris olivaceus ×2

D. ruber ×2

♂ ♀ *Systellonotus triguttatus* ×3

Phylus melanocephalus ×3

Psallus varians ×3

Amblytylus nasutus ×3

Dicyphus errans ×3

Macrotylus paykulli ×4

Fern Bug ×5

▲ **Orthocephalus saltator**. Rather hairy. Head not noticeably wider than front of pronotum. Antennae black. Tibiae red or brick coloured (black in **O. coriaceus**). Hind femora enlarged for jumping, especially in female. Male always fully winged: female usually brachypterous as illustrated. 6–9 in rough grassland, mainly on composites.

▲ **Orthotylus virescens**..6–9 on broom. Partly predatory. One of many rather similar green bugs in this genus, although rather darker than most. Specific identification is difficult in this genus, although host plant is a good guide. The genus may be confused with some species of *Lygus* and *Lygocoris*, but these genera are generally more robust and they have a distinct collar at the front of the pronotum.

▲ **Black-kneed Capsid** *Blepharidopterus angulatus*. Named for the black patches at the tops of the tibiae – especially prominent in the nymphs. Antennae much shorter in some males. 6–10 on a wide range of trees, especially apple and lime. Partly predatory, destroying large numbers of red spider mites in orchards.

△ **Pilophorus perplexus**. Pale bands are due to silvery hairs. 6–10 on oaks and other deciduous trees, feeding mainly on aphids and sometimes on leaves and young fruits. Rather active and sometimes mistaken for ants. △ **P. cinnamopterus** is similar but found on pines.

▲ **Campyloneura virgula**. Bright yellow cuneus with red apex distinguishes this from several otherwise similar bugs. 6–10 on a wide range of trees, feeding on aphids and other smaller insects and on red spider mites. Nymphs are bright yellow and orange.

▲ **Mecomma ambulans**. Sexes markedly different, but fully winged females occasionally found in north and on mountains. 6–9 among rushes and other vegetation, especially in and around damp woods. Partly predatory.

△ **Halticus apterus**. Head noticeably wider than front of pronotum. Wings occasionally fully developed and covering abdomen. Femora black: tibiae and antennae yellowish brown. Leaps with aid of enlarged hind femora. 6–9 on legumes and bedstraws in grassy places: sometimes a pest of clovers and related crops. Related species have pale head and sometimes pale thorax as well.

△ **Myrmecoris gracilis**. Almost always micropterous and extremely ant-like, running rapidly on ground. 6–9 on heathland and other dry habitats. Largely predatory: sometimes in ant nests, feeding on brood but not on adults. N & C.

▲ **Pithanus maerkeli**. Usually micropterous and ant-like, the pale wing pads giving the illusion of a narrow waist. Female occasionally fully winged. 5–9 in grassy places, especially where damp. Partly predatory.

▲ **Lygus pratensis**. In northern half of Europe and on mountains both sexes are light reddish brown, usually with no marks on pronotum. Elsewhere males are darker red with a yellow scutellum and females are greenish brown, both with dark marks on pronotum. Both forms occur in B. Feeds on a wide range of plants. Hibernates as adult.

▲ **Tarnished Plant Bug** *L. rugulipennis* varies from yellow to brick red or brown. Dense coat of short fine hair distinguishes it from *pratensis*. Abundant on a wide range of plants and often a pest of field and garden crops, causing white spotting on leaves. Often attacks flowers. Very common on stinging nettle. Hibernates as adult.

▲ **Liocoris tripustulatus**. Young adults (late summer) are light brown with yellow spots. After hibernation they are deep reddish brown with bright orange scutellum and cuneus. Mainly on nettles. △ **Capsodes gothicus** is superficially similar but is parallel-sided and has a dark head.

▲ **Common Green Capsid** *Lygocoris pabulinus*. Abundant 5–10 on a very wide range of woody and herbaceous plants: woody plants, on which over-wintering eggs are laid, are infested mainly in spring. Often a pest of soft fruit, potatoes, and several other crops. Pale brown tibial spines distinguish this from several closely related species: narrow pronotal collar distinguishes it from Orthotylus spp.

▲ **Polymerus unifasciatus**. Fine golden pubescence on forewing (strong lens!) Tibiae with strong black spines. 5–9 in rough grassy places, feeding on various bedstraws.

▲ **Phytocoris tiliae**. White or pale green with black markings. 6–10 on a wide range of deciduous trees, largely predatory, taking small caterpillars, aphids, red spider mites, etc. There are several similar species but they lack the pale patch at junction of corium and cuneus.

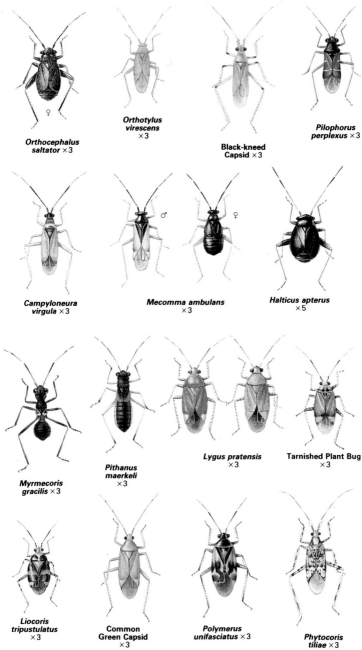

Orthocephalus saltator ×3

Orthotylus virescens ×3

Black-kneed Capsid ×3

Pilophorus perplexus ×3

Campyloneura virgula ×3

Mecomma ambulans ×3

Halticus apterus ×5

Myrmecoris gracilis ×3

Pithanus maerkeli ×3

Lygus pratensis ×3

Tarnished Plant Bug ×3

Liocoris tripustulatus ×3

Common Green Capsid ×3

Polymerus unifasciatus ×3

Phytocoris tiliae ×3

83

△ **Miris striatus**. A very striking bug found mainly on oak and hawthorn in B but on alder, birch, sallow, and many other trees on the continent. 5–8. Partly predatory. ▲ **Calocoris quadripunctatus** has similar colours but is smaller and much more oval in outline.

▲ **Calocoris stysi**. Light areas yellow or pale green: cuneus always orange. 5–8, mainly in wooded areas. Feeds on the flowers and young fruits of stinging nettle: also feeds on aphids. Adults visit umbellifer flowers.

▲ **Lucerne Bug** Adelphocoris lineolatus. Tibial spines at least as long as tibial width distinguish this genus from *Calocoris*, which has very short spines. 6–10 in damp grassland, almost always on legumes although adults may attack composite flowers. A pest of lucerne in parts of C. and in the USA.

△ **Stenotus binotatus**. Both sexes yellow and black at first: with age, male becomes orange and black and female becomes greyish and black. 2 black pronotal spots always present. 5–10 in rough grassland, feeding largely on flower heads of grasses.

▲ **Capsus ater**. Head and pronotum often black. 2nd antennal segment greatly swollen, as in all members of the genus. 6–9 in long grass everywhere, including woodland clearings and gardens. Feeds mainly on lower parts of stems.

▲ **Heterotoma merioptera**. Inhabits dense vegetation, especially nettles and other hedgerow plants, and various trees and shrubs. 6–10. Partly predatory.

▲ **Pantilius tunicatus**. Dull yellowish green at first, becoming reddish later. Mature insects have red patch at tip of abdomen. Clothed with short black hairs. Last 2 antennal segments very short. 9–10 on hazel, alder, and birch.

△ **Miridius quadrivirgatus**. Cuneus not always red. Waste places and rough grassland, on wall barley and other grasses, especially where fairly damp. S & C: coastal in B.

▲ **Stenodema laevigatum**. 1st antennal segment stout and hairy. Pronotum strongly punctate. Young adults (7–8) are pale yellow with reddish brown stripes, but stripes soon fade and bugs become browner. Hibernate as adults and become green in spring (male darker than female) to match fresh grass. Abundant in long grass of all kinds.

△ **Notostira elongata**. Tibiae and 1st antennal segment very hairy. Pronotum smooth. 2 broods per year. Males of both broods largely black, margined with greyish or yellowish green. Summer females mainly green: autumn females pinkish brown, developing a green abdomen after hibernation. Males do not survive winter. Abundant in rough grassland.

▲ **Teratocoris antennatus**. Varies from pale green (mainly females) to deep orange, with varying amounts of black: males generally blacker than females. Wing length variable, usually leaving part of abdomen exposed. 1st antennal segment always reddish brown. 6–10 in marshes and damp grassland. N & C.

▲ **Leptopterna dolabrata**. Legs and antennae very hairy. Black and yellow or black and orange. Males generally fully winged: females mostly brachypterous. Emit a very pungent odour. Abundant 5–9 in grassy places, as long as not too dry. Feeds on cocksfoot and other tall grasses: sometimes a cereal pest in north. The very similiar ▲ **L. ferrugata** inhabits the drier grasslands.

▲ **Common Shore Bug** Saldula saltatoria Saldidae. Rather flat, with very prominent ocelli and eyes. Rostrum 3-segmented. Predatory and like most members of family, living on mud at edges of ponds and ditches: very active in sunshine. Rather variable and not easily separated from its numerous relatives.

△ **Marine Bug** Aepophilus bonnairei. No ocelli. Always short-winged. Lives in rock crevices and among seaweeds on lower part of shore, usually in family groups. Predatory. Atlantic, Irish sea, and Channel coasts.

Leptopus marmoratus Leptopodidae. Resembles shore bugs but has ocelli on stalked platform. Under stones at edges of ponds and streams. S & C.

Isometopus mirificus Isometopidae. On old, lichen-covered trees, feeding on aphids, and psocids. Sometimes placed in Miridae. S & C (southern).

Ochterus marginatus Ochteridae. A semi-aquatic bug living at the edges of rivers. Differs from true water bugs (p. 86) in having ocelli and visible antennae. Flies rapidly. Predatory, feeding mainly on fly larvae. S & C (southern).

Ochterus
marginatus ×3

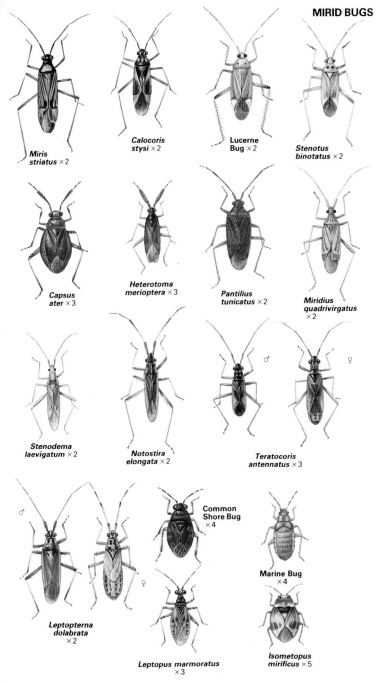

Miris striatus × 2

Calocoris stysi × 2

Lucerne Bug × 2

Stenotus binotatus × 2

Capsus ater × 3

Heterotoma merioptera × 3

Pantilius tunicatus × 2

Miridius quadrivirgatus × 2

Stenodema laevigatum × 2

Notostira elongata × 2

♂ ♀

Teratocoris antennatus × 3

♂ ♀

Leptopterna dolabrata × 2

Common Shore Bug × 4

Leptopus marmoratus × 3

Marine Bug × 4

Isometopus mirificus × 5

85

SURFACE DWELLERS Antennae clearly visible. All are predatory and are clothed, at least on lower surface, with water-repellent hairs which prevent them from becoming wet. Most hibernate as adults.

▲ **Water Measurer** *Hydrometra stagnorum* Hydrometridae. Head very long and thin. Virtually wingless as a rule but sometimes with partly or fully developed wings. Walks slowly over surface, usually among vegetation, at margins of ponds and streams. Spears small prey with beak. △ *H. gracilenta* is slightly smaller and much rarer.

▲ **Common Pond Skater** *Gerris lacustris* Gerridae. Wings range from minute to fully developed. Skates rapidly over surface of still and slow-moving water, using front legs to snatch up other insects that fall on to the surface. Winged individuals often fly far from water to hibernate. There are several similar species.

▲ *Aquarius najas*. Like a large *Gerris* but prefers flowing water. Usually wingless. Sides of 7th abdominal segment produced into long points, but these do not reach tip of abdomen. △ *A. paludum* is similar but usually fully winged.

▲ **Water Cricket** *Velia caprai* Veliidae. Winged or wingless. Underside orange. On still and slow-moving waters with little vegetation, especially in wooded areas and uplands. It feeds like *Gerris*.

△ *Mesovelia furcata* Mesoveliidae (below). Usually wingless. Runs rapidly on floating leaves of pondweeds and other aquatic plants, on which it is well camouflaged. 7–9, feeding on small insects on or just below the surface. S & C.

SUBMERGED BUGS Antennae concealed in pits or grooves on head. Mainly carnivorous. Most hibernate as adults, or at least become quiescent for winter, usually in mud.

▲ **Water Scorpion** *Nepa cinerea* Nepidae. Very flat. Creeps slowly over mud and vegetation in shallow water, drawing air from surface through hollow 'tail'. Catches prey, including small fishes, in raptorial front legs. Fully winged but few individuals ever fly. Active all year.

△s **Water Stick Insect** *Ranatra linearis*. In deep ponds with plenty of vegetation, on which it lies in wait for small prey to pass. Breathes like *Nepa*. Flies by day in warm weather. S & C.

△ **Saucer Bug** *Ilyocoris cimicoides* Naucoridae. Fully winged but flightless. In weedy and muddy ponds, carrying a large air bubble under forewings and on underside of body. Fiercely carnivorous and may pierce skin if handled.

△ *Aphelocheirus aestivalis* Aphelocheiridae. Varies from micropterous to fully winged, but always micropterous in B. Mainly in swift streams with gravelly beds and scattered vegetation. Feeds on various young insects and may stab fingers if handled. Breathes with a plastron (p. 255) and never needs to surface.

▲ **Common Backswimmer** *Notonecta glauca* Notonectidae. Also called water boatman. Swims on its back with a large air bubble attached to ventral surface. Dorsal surface strongly keeled. Still waters. Active all year and flying readily in warm weather. △ *N. maculata* has mottled brick-coloured forewings.

▲ *Plea atomaria* Pleidae (below). A small back-swimming predator living in still and slow-moving water with plenty of weed. Often present in vast numbers.

▲ *Corixa punctata* Corixidae. One of several similar species, often known as lesser water boatmen. Swims right way up: dorsal surface not keeled: middle and hind legs more or less the same length. Feeds largely on unicellular algae and plant debris in weedy ponds and slow-moving water. Active all year and flies well. Like most members of the family, the males stridulate loudly during courtship.

△s *Sigara striata*. In still water. Males stridulate very loudly and can be heard yards away if placed in a shallow dish of water. There are many similar species, some very common in B.

▲ *Cymatia coleoptrata* (below). Distinguished from *Corixa* and *Sigara* by unbanded pronotum and long front tarsi. Usually micropterous. In weedy ponds and ditches, darting out to catch small prey.

Mesovelia furcata
×5

Plea atomaria
×5

Cymatia coleoptrata ×5

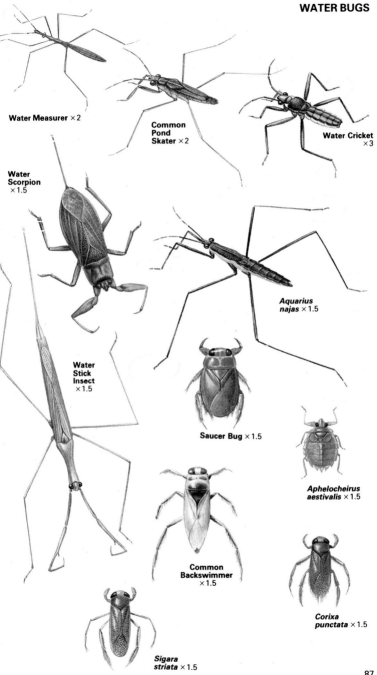

Water Measurer × 2

Common Pond Skater × 2

Water Cricket × 3

Water Scorpion × 1.5

Aquarius najas × 1.5

Water Stick Insect × 1.5

Saucer Bug × 1.5

Aphelocheirus aestivalis × 1.5

Common Backswimmer × 1.5

Corixa punctata × 1.5

Sigara striata × 1.5

Cicada orni freshly emerged from nymphal skin

HOMOPTERAN BUGS
Suborder Homoptera

Bugs in which the forewings, when present, are of uniform texture – either horny or membranous – and usually held roofwise over the body at rest. Antennae are short and bristle-like in the cicadas and hoppers but much longer in the aphids and psyllids (pp. 94–6).

CICADAS Cicadidae Large homopterans with transparent and usually shiny wings. They live mainly on trees and shrubs. Males produce very shrill sounds by vibrating small membranes (tymbals) on each side of the body. Flaps called opercula protect the tymbals on the underside and may act as sounding boards. Female has a long ovipositor with which she lays eggs in bark, but nymphs fall to ground on hatching and burrow down to feed on roots for several years. They have massive front legs for tunnelling. The group is largely tropical, but several species live in southern Europe: one reaches B.

Tibicen plebejus. The largest European cicada, with an extremely loud song. Tymbals completely concealed: opercula very large and overlapping. 6–9, mainly on pines. S.

Cicadi orni. Forewing with 11 small dark spots. Body often covered with dense grey bloom. Rostrum longer than in any other species, reaching back to base of abdomen. Tymbals partly exposed, especially at the sides. Opercula oval and well separated. Abundant on trees, mainly pines, 6–9. Can sometimes be seen in hundreds on fences and telegraph poles when freshly emerged and drying their wings. S.

Tibicina haematodes. Tymbals completely exposed from above. Opercula very small and widely separated, 2 spines on front femur. Extensive reddish colour on pronotum. Costa and basal parts of other veins very red. 6–9 on various trees. S & C (southern).

△s **Cicadetta montana**. Tymbals completely exposed from above. Opercula very small. Pronotal colour and pattern vary, but usually dark. Front femur with 3 spines, the posterior one sloping sharply forward. 5–8 in woodland clearings and scrubby places: on a wide range of shrubs and herbaceous plants. Song is soft and warbling and easily missed. **C. argentata** is very similar but has much more red on the pronotum. Wing veins are also distinctly paler than in *montana*. Scrubby areas 6–9. S. **C. pygmea** is the smallest species. It lives on a wide range of trees and shrubs, especially oaks, pines and junipers. 6–9. SW. **C. tibialis** is similar to *pygmea*, with very bright red banding on abdomen. SE.

Cicadatra atra. Tymbals partly exposed from above and from the sides, as in **C. orni**. 2 dark spots near tip of forewing. Pronotum with extensive yellow mottling. Front femur with 3 or 4 spines, the basal one being the longest. 6–9 on a wide range of trees and shrubs. S.

TREEHOPPERS Membracidae A large family of jumping bugs in which the pronotum extends back over the body. Mainly tropical, with only 4 spp in western Europe. Pronotum often ornate, frequently resembling prickles or thorns in tropical species and thereby affording protection. Nymphs rather spiky and pointed at rear.

△s **Gargara genistae**. Rear extension of pronotum straight, reaching about half way back along the abdomen. 6–10 on broom and other leguminous plants.

▲ **Centrotus cornutus**. Pronotum horned on each side, horns being larger in south than in north. Rear extension of pronotum sinuate on lower edge and reaching back to about tip of abdomen. 4–8 in wooded habitats, on a variety of herbs and shrubs. **Acanthophyes chloroticus** resembles *Centrotus* but is much shorter and pronotum is usually brown or yellowish. 5–8 on various herbs and shrubs. S.

Buffalo Treehopper *Stictocephalus bisonia*. Green fades to dirty yellow after death. Rear extension of pronotum wider than in the other species and completely covering scutellum. 7–9 on a wide range of woody and herbaceous plants: often causes damage to apples and other fruit trees by laying eggs in bark of twigs. Moves to opposite side of twig if disturbed: further disturbance causes it to leap or fly away. An American species now widely distributed in S & C (western).

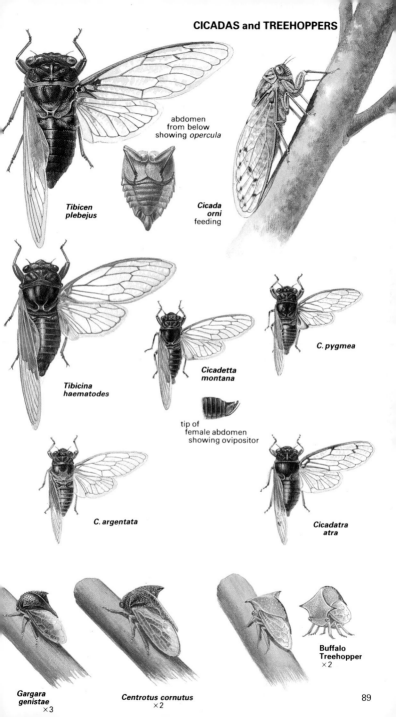

CICADAS and TREEHOPPERS

abdomen from below showing *opercula*

Tibicen plebejus

Cicada orni feeding

Tibicina haematodes

Cicadetta montana

C. pygmea

tip of female abdomen showing ovipositor

C. argentata

Cicadatra atra

Gargara genistae ×3

Centrotus cornutus ×2

Buffalo Treehopper ×2

89

FROGHOPPERS Aphrophoridae Jumping homopterans, mostly brown, in which the hind tibiae are rounded and bear just a few spines. This distinguishes them from the cicadellids (p. 92), which have many spines. Antennae arise from between the eyes. Forewings horny and pitted. Hind wings have a peripheral vein, at least in hind region. Nymphs of most species live in masses of froth, giving rise to their other common names of spittle bugs and cuckoo-spit insects.

▲ **Neophilaenus lineatus**. Forewings light or dark brown, generally with a pale stripe along the costa. Basal half of costa more or less straight, 6–9 on grasses: dark form generally in cooler and damper areas. There are several similar species.

Lepyromia coleoptrata. Yellow to dark brown. Costal margin of forewing very convex. 5–9 on grasses in marshes and damp grassland. N & C.

▲ **Aphrophora alni**. Pronotum has central keel. Forewings may lack one or both pale patches on costal margin: whole wing may be darker. 5–10 on many kinds of trees and shrubs. There are several similar species.

▲ **Common Froghopper** *Philaenus spumarius*. Ground colour basically buff, with a very variable dark pattern: occasionally dark all over. Abundant 6–9 on a wide range of woody and herbaceous plants.

◣ **Cercopis vulnerata** Cercopidae. Anterior margin of pronotum straight, not arching forward between eyes as in Aphrophoridae. Nymphs live communally on roots, surrounded by solidified froth. 4–8 on various plants, mainly in wooded areas. S & C. There are several similar species on the continent.

▲ **Cixius nervosus** Cixiidae. Forewings membranous with well-defined veins. Hind wing without peripheral vein. Pronotum yellowish brown with prominent lateral keels. Scutellum dark brown or black with 3 keels. 5–10 on various trees. There are several similar species.

◬ **Issus coleoptratus** Issidae. Forewings rather horny with a network of cross-veins. Hind wings smoky brown without a peripheral vein. Pronotum bulges strongly forward between eyes: hind margin almost straight. 5–10 on various trees and in moss. Several similar species live on the continent, mainly in S.

△s **Tettigometra impressopunctata** Tettigometridae. Forewings horny and distinctly pitted: veins weak. Hind wings with no peripheral vein. Hind tibia with an apical circlet of spines. On dry grassland, hibernating as adult. S & C: mainly on sand dunes and chalk in B. Many similar species live on continent, mainly in S.

Epiptera europaea Dictyopharidae. Becomes yellowish after death, but easily identified by conical head and network of veins towards tip of forewing. 6–10 on a wide range of herbaceous plants, especially umbellifers. Leaps strongly. S & C.

Bursinia genei. 6–9 on a wide range of herbaceous and shrubby plants. S.

Family Delphacidae A family of small hoppers distinguished from similar groups by a large movable spur at apex of hind tibia. Forewings rather tough: hind wing with no peripheral vein. Antenna arises from a notch in lower margin of eye. Sexes are often very different. Most species have brachypterous and fully-winged individuals.

◬ **Delphax pulchellus**. Female usually brachypterous, with few dark marks on forewing. Latter reaches about half way along abdomen. 6–9 on reeds in marshy places and on river banks.

▲ **Megamelus notula**. Forewings may be almost entirely brown: sometimes fully winged. 4–10 in marshy habitats. Absent from most of S.

▲s **Delphacodes pellucida**. Forewings always reach at least to tip of abdomen in male: long or short in female. Pronotum and scutellum black in male: brown to black in female. 5–9 in grassland nearly everywhere. There are many similar species.

◬ **Asiraca clavicornis**. Front and middle legs broad and flat. 1st antennal segment long and broad. Scutellum with 4 keels. 4–10 in damp grassy places. S & C.

◬ **Stenocranus minutus**. Always fully winged. Forewings transparent and iridescent, with prominent nerves. Dark patch often indistinct but may cover inner half of wing. On grasses in many habitats.

△ **Delphacinus mesomelas**. Lateral keels of pronotum arched round eyes. Long-winged form equally common. 6–8 in wooded and scrubby areas, especially on broom.

Tropidocephala elegans. 1st two antennal segments very short. Head, pronotum, and scutellum green or yellow. Scutellum with 3 keels. 5–10 in well vegetated habitats. S.

hind leg of CERCOPIDAE   hind leg of CICADELLIDAE   hind leg of DELPHACIDAE

spur ↗

Neophilaenus lineatus ×3

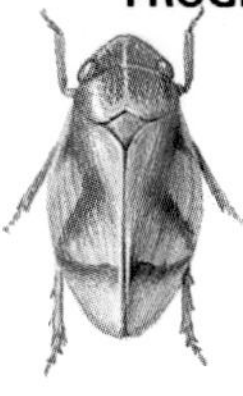

Lepyromia coleoptrata ×3

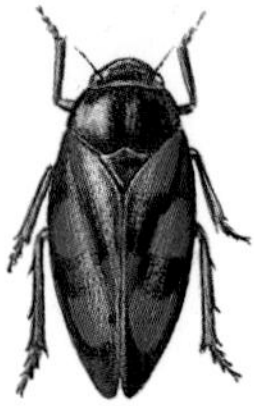

Cercopis vulnerata ×2

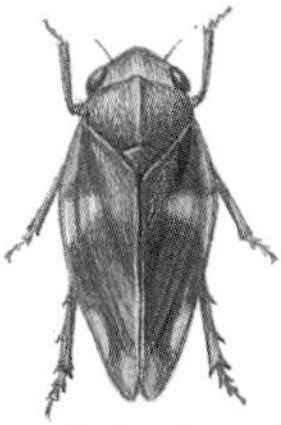

Aphrophora alni ×2

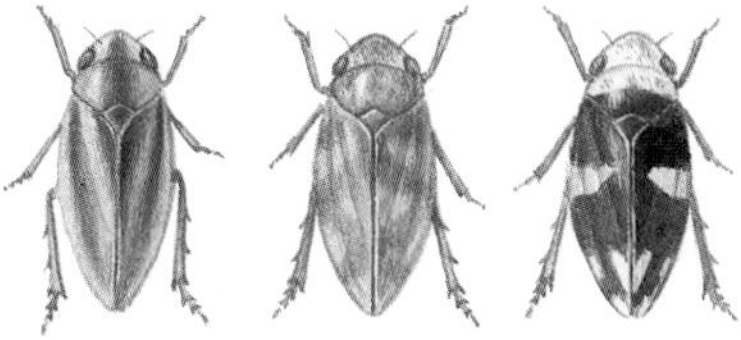

Common Froghopper ×3

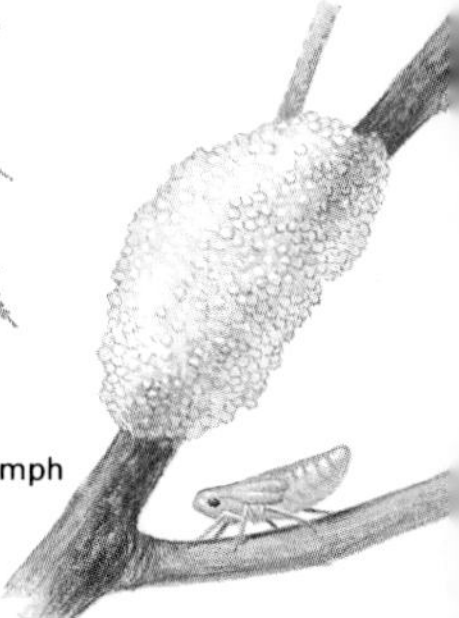

Cuckoo-spit and nymph

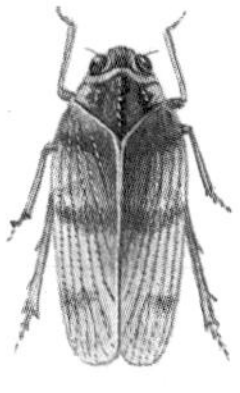

Cixius nervosus ×3

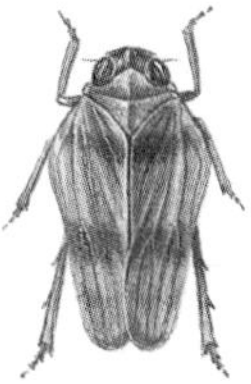

Issus coleoptratus ×3

Tettigometra impressopunctata ×3

Epiptera europaea ×2

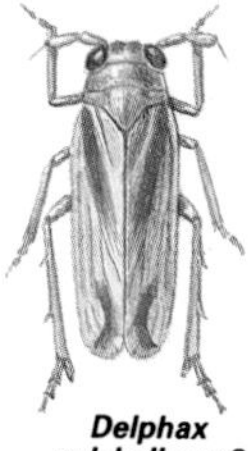

Delphax pulchellus ×3

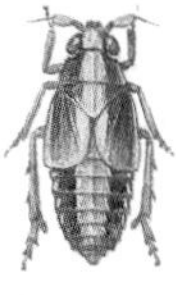

Megamelus notula ×3

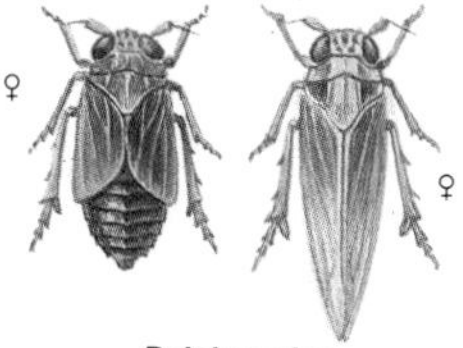

♀

Delphacodes pellucida ×3

♀

Bursinia genei ×3

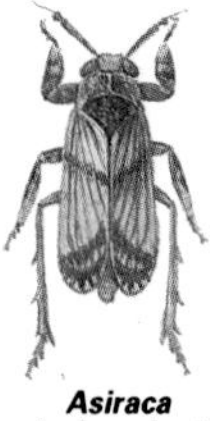

Asiraca clavicornis ×3

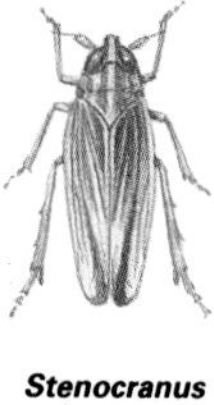

Stenocranus minutus ×3

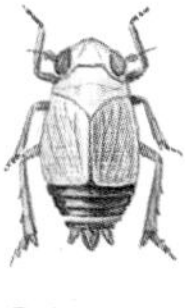

Delphacinus mesomelas ×5

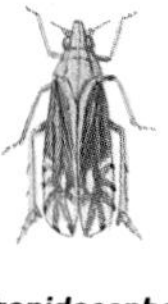

Tropidocephala elegans ×5

Ledra
aurita
×2

LEAFHOPPERS Cicadellidae A large family of jumping homopteran bugs with relatively soft forewings. A peripheral vein in hind wing. Distinguished from froghoppers by numerous spines on hind tibiae (see p. 90). Identification of many species depends on detailed facial features and measurements. Winter is spent in adult or egg stage.

△ *Ledra aurita*. An unmistakable bug – the only European member of its group. 5–10 in woodlands, especially on oaks. Well camouflaged when feeding on lichen-covered branches. S & C.

▲ *Aphrodes bifasciatus*. Very variable: anterior white band on forewing often broken or absent. 6–9 in damp or dry grassland, mainly in lowlands. Males of several related species all have light and dark bands on forewings – a generic character.

▲ *Eupteryx aurata*. Pale areas often tinged with orange. Abundant 5–11 on a wide range of plants, especially nettles and labiates. Often a pest of potatoes. As in all leaf hoppers, its saliva is toxic to plants and destroys chlorophyll: feeding punctures are surrounded by pale spots, and if infestation is severe the spots join up and destroy large areas of leaf.

▲ *Iassus lanio*. Head and thorax yellowish or green, always heavily mottled with brown. Forewings green or reddish brown. 7–10 in woodland, especially on oaks.

Penthimia nigra. Brown or black, with or without red spots on pronotum. Forewings overlap slightly at tip. 5–8 on various trees, especially oak. S & C.

▲ *Elymana sulphurella*. Greenish face with broad black spot around base of each antenna. Sides of thorax with black spots: sometimes a dark patch on top of head. 7–10 among grasses, often in quite dry places.

△ *Idiocerus vitreus*. Head broadly rounded in front. Forewings overlap slightly at apex. Forewings often redder, especially after hibernation. 3–10 on poplars. N & C. Several similar species, not easy to separate.

▲ *Thamnotettix confinis*. Forewings with prominent greenish veins. Pronotum may have darker markings. 5–9 on a wide range of trees, shrubs, and herbage. N & C.

▲ *Eupelix cuspidata*. Dark markings vary in density. Head with sharp keel on top. Pronotum with 3 keels. Forewing with prominent veins. 3–9 in dry grassy places.

△ *Macropsis scutellata*. Top of head largely covered by pronotum. Veins dark brown, with some clear cells in middle of forewing. 6–10 on nettles.

△ *Macrosteles variatus*. Head and thorax yellow or greenish. Dark areas of forewing less distinct in male. 5–9 on nettles and other herbage. Several very similar spp.

△ *Psammotettix sabulicola*. Pronotum and scutellum yellowish brown, often with dark markings. 6–10 among grasses on coastal dunes, often resting on bare sand. N & C.

▲ *Cicadella viridis*. Top of head (vertex) smoothly rounded in front, clearly bi-coloured. Pronotum yellow at front, dark green behind. Forewings generally green in female, purplish brown or black in male. 7–10 in marshy places, generally on grasses.

△ *Anaceratagallia laevis*. Pronotum with fine transverse ridges. Black marks on scutellum meet side margins. 7–9 on sand dunes. S & C.

△ *Arboridia ribauti*. Top of head (vertex) with 2 black spots. Scutellum pale with 2 black triangles at front. All year on various trees. S & C.

△ *Eupterycyba jucunda*. Vertex with 2 black spots. Pronotum with 3 large black spots. Scutellum has 2 black triangles at front. Forewing apex greyish. 7–10 on alder. S & C.

▲ *Evacanthus interruptus*. Pronotum black, with or without pale central stripe. Wings shorter than abdomen in female. 6–10 on a wide variety of herbage, especially in damp places.

▲ *Edwardsiana geometrica*. Apex of forewing greyish. Dark streak on forewing and dark scutellum distinguish this from many related species. 7–10 on alder.

▲ *Balclutha punctata*. Head and thorax green or dirty yellow, often marked with brown. Forewings pale green or yellow to reddish brown, often spotted. All year, mainly on grasses but often passing the winter on conifers.

▲ *Ulopa reticulata*. Vertex very flat in front. Forewings horny, distinctly pitted and strongly convex. No hind wings. All year on heathers.

△ *Graphocephala fennahi*. Red stripes on forewing readily identify this North American bug now established on rhododendrons in southern B. 6–10.

Aphrodes bifasciatus
×4

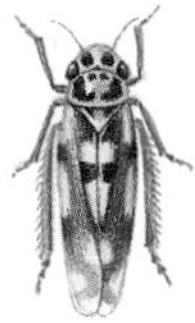

**Eupteryx
aurata**
×4

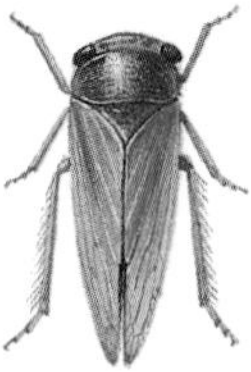

**Iassus
lanio** ×3

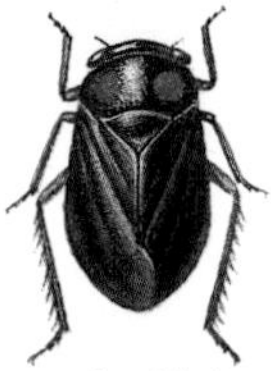

**Penthimia
nigra** ×3

**Elymana
sulphurella** ×4

**Idiocerus
vitreus**
×4

**Thamnotettix
confinis** ×3

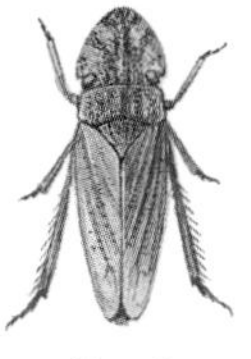

**Eupelix
cuspidata** ×3

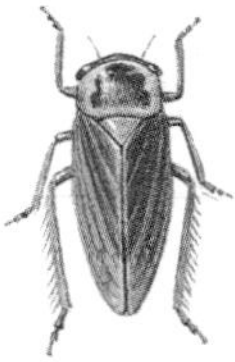

**Macropsis
scutellata** ×4

**Macrosteles
variatus** ×4

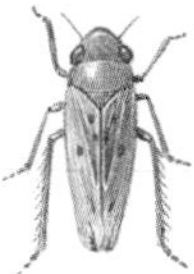

**Psammotettix
sabulicola** ×4

**Cicadella
viridis** ×3

**Anaceratagallia
laevis** ×4

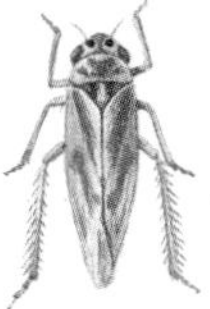

**Arboridia
ribauti** ×4

**Eupterycyba
jucunda** ×4

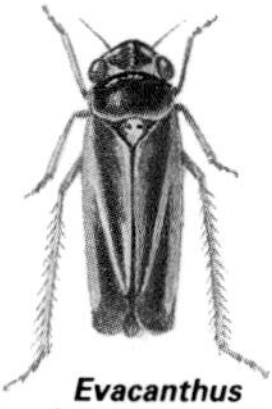

**Evacanthus
interruptus** ×3

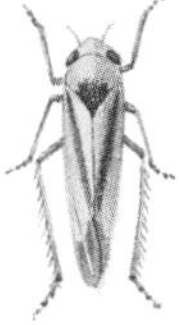

**Edwardsiana
geometrica** ×4

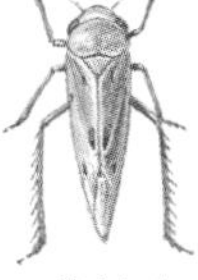

**Balclutha
punctata**
×4

**Ulopa
reticulata**
×4

**Graphocephala
fennahi** ×3

APHIDS Very small, pear-shaped, sap-sucking homopteran bugs. Both wings, when present, are membranous: generally held roofwise at rest. Hind end of abdomen generally has a pair of 'horns', known as cornicles, which exude waxy secretions. Honeydew is produced in abundance (see p. 70). Life cycles are generally complex, with winged and wingless forms in most species. Winter is usually passed in the egg stage, although many species can remain active in mild winters. Spring aphids are generally wingless and all female, building up dense colonies through parthenogenetic reproduction. Most give birth to active young – sometimes several in a day – instead of laying eggs. Winged aphids gradually increase in late spring and summer and spread to other plants. Most species have more than one host plant during the year. The Aphididae is the largest of several families. The wings in this family have at least 4 oblique cross veins. The Pemphigidae is similar but cornicles are very short or absent.

△ **Viteus vitifolii** Phylloxeridae. Wings, when present, held flat at rest. No cornicles. An American vine pest, now well established in Europe. Feeds on leaves and roots. Winged forms, occurring only in late summer, are rare in Europe.

▲ **Phylloxera quercus**. No cornicles. Wingless females abundant under oak leaves in spring, surrounded by eggs (this family of aphids does not give birth to active young). Yellow spots develop around feeding sites on leaves. Winged forms appear in summer.

▲ **Adelges abietis** Adelgidae. Only 3 oblique cross veins. No cornicles. Causes cone-like pineapple galls on spruce. Gall is green at first and opens 6–7 to allow aphids to escape. It then becomes brown and woody. New aphids fly to larch and other conifers, where they produce several generations without galls.

▲ **Woolly Aphid** *Eriosoma lanigerum* Pemphigidae. Purplish brown body densely clothed with waxy fluff. In dense clusters on apple bark in summer, especially where tree has been damaged. Some individuals pass the winter feeding on the roots.

▲ **Tetraneura ulmi**. Causes bladder-like galls on elm leaves in spring. Summer generations are orange or brown and feed on grass roots. Larger, irregular pouch galls are caused by ▲ *Schizoneura lanuginosa*.

▲ **Pemphigus bursarius**. Causes pouch galls on poplar leaf stalks in spring. Summer aphids are cream coloured and very waxy and live on roots of lettuce and other composites, often causing wilting. ▲ *P. spirothecae* is similar and causes spiral galls on poplar leaf stalks, but appears to have no herbaceous host plant.

▲ **Cabbage Aphid** *Brevicoryne brassicae* Aphididae. Cornicles short. Wingless forms green with mealy white coating. Abundant on brassicas in spring and early summer, causing severe damage. May remain active all year if mild.

  ▲ **Black Bean Aphid** *Aphis fabae*. The familiar garden 'blackfly', with black or olive-green body. Passes winter as egg on spindle and a few other shrubs, and spends summer on beans, sugar beet, docks, and many other herbaceous plants. There are several very similar species.

  Peach-Potato Aphid *Myzus persicae*. Yellow or pale green: sometimes pink, especially the nymphs. Winged form with black patch on abdomen. Cornicles swollen in middle (lens!). Curls peach leaves in spring and then moves to a wide range of herbaceous plants, including potato. Does not form large colonies.

  ▲ **Rose-Grain Aphid** *Metopolophium dirhodum*. Shiny green with a darker dorsal stripe. Overwinters as egg on roses. Aphids migrate to grasses, especially cereals, 5–6. Often swarm off the cereals in summer.

    ▲ **Rose Aphid** *Macrosiphum rosae*. The gardener's 'greenfly'. Relatively large: green or pink. Long black cornicles distinguish it from other rose-inhabiting species. On roses in spring: scabious or teasel in summer.

    ▲ **Bird Cherry Aphid** *Rhopalosiphum padi*. Wingless forms darker, with large rust-coloured patch at rear. Rolls leaves of bird cherry in spring, when insects are clothed with white wax. On cereals and other grasses in summer: may remain there through winter if mild.

    Baizongia pistaciae. Causes huge red candle-like galls on leaves of pistachio and related trees. Greyish aphids live in galls all summer, escape in autumn, and fly to grass roots where they spend the winter. S.

gall of
Baizongia pistaciae

half natural size

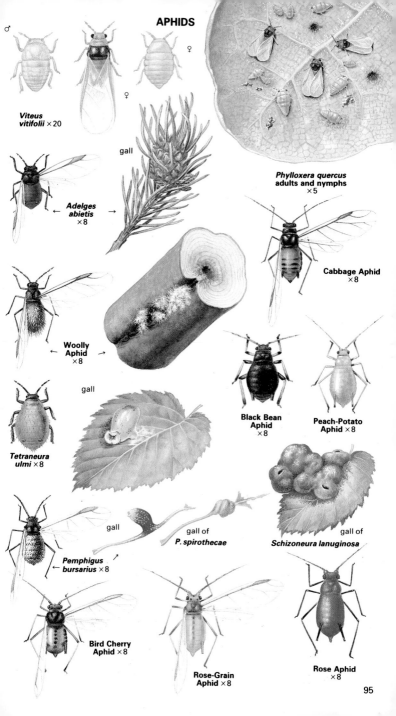

APHIDS

♂ ♀ ♀

Viteus vitifolii ×20

gall

Adelges abietis ×8

Phylloxera quercus adults and nymphs ×5

Cabbage Aphid ×8

Woolly Aphid ×8

Black Bean Aphid ×8

Peach-Potato Aphid ×8

gall

Tetraneura ulmi ×8

gall

gall of *P. spirothecae*

gall of *Schizoneura lanuginosa*

Pemphigus bursarius ×8

Bird Cherry Aphid ×8

Rose-Grain Aphid ×8

Rose Aphid ×8

95

JUMPING PLANT LICE Psyllidae Also known as psyllids, these small homopterans are now often split into several smaller families. Resembling miniature cicadas, they leap well with the aid of their enlarged hind legs. Antennae are much longer than in the superficially similar leafhoppers (p. 92). Forewings relatively tough, with prominent veins: hind wings very flimsy. Nymphs are very flat and usually gregarious, secreting large amounts of honeydew and wax.

△ **Livia juncorum**. Lives on rushes (*Juncus* spp) in damp meadows. Nymphs live in flower heads and induce growth of red tassel-like galls in summer.

▲ **Homatoma ficus**. Very flat, bristly antennae distinctly darker towards tip. Veins hairy. On figs 6–8. S & C: introduced to B.

▲ **Apple Psyllid** *Psylla mali*. Abundant on apple trees 4–10. Green at first, becoming red and brown in late summer. Nymphs damage blossom and stunt young shoots by gregarious feeding. △ *P. buxi* has distinctly yellowish forewings. Body bright green or yellowish. 4–9. Nymphs live in young shoot tips of box, causing leaves to cluster tightly together. The presence of this insect is revealed by abundant white wax.

▲ **Trioza urticae**. Wing membrane pale yellow. Body green to cream with dark markings. On stinging nettles in summer: on evergreen trees in winter. Several similar species.

▲ **Psyllopsis fraxini**. One of several similar species living on ash. Nymphs cause leaves to curl and swell up to form red-veined galls. 5–10.

WHITEFLIES Aleyrodidae Tiny homopterans with waxy white wings spanning about 3 mm. They resemble minute moths. There are numerous species, not easily separated, although many are host-specific. They usually feed on the underside of leaves.

Best known is the ▲ **Cabbage Whitefly** *Aleyrodes proletella*, common on brassicas in spring and summer. △ The **Greenhouse Whitefly** *Trialeurodes vaporariorum* infests various greenhouse plants: especially damaging to cucumbers and tomatoes.

SCALE INSECTS A large group of homopterans, belonging to several families, named for the waxy or horny scales under which most of the females live. Most females are wingless and legless: only the sap-sucking beak reveals their relationship to other bugs. In fact, these female scale insects don't really look like insects at all. A few, such as the mealy bugs, retain their legs and some mobility. Male scale insects have one pair of wings and resemble small midges, but they are rarely seen. Most species reproduce by parthenogenesis, and lifting a female scale may reveal hundreds of eggs. 1st instar nymphs wander freely, but then lose their legs and settle down to feed in one place. Because they exist in vast numbers, the scale insects cause serious damage to crops, although less of a problem in Europe than in tropical areas.

Icerya purchasi and *Planococcus citri* are both citrus pests. ▲ *Lepidosaphes ulmi* is the mussel scale, abundant on the bark of apple and many other fruit trees. The rose scale ▲ *Aulacaspis rosae* should be looked for on wild and cultivated roses, especially on the older parts. △ *Parthenolecanium corni* infests many cultivated trees and shrubs, including vines and currants, while △ *Pseudococcus longispinus* can be found on a wide range of greenhouse plants.

**Icerya
purchasi**
♀ ×2

**Planococcus
citri**
♀ ×2

Mussel Scale ♂
×20

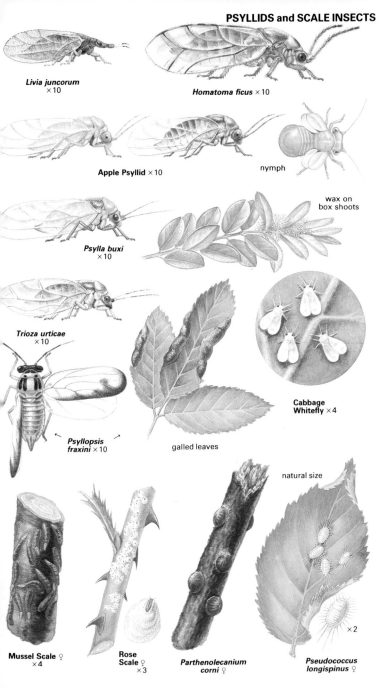

Livia juncorum ×10

Homatoma ficus ×10

Apple Psyllid ×10

nymph

Psylla buxi ×10

wax on box shoots

Trioza urticae ×10

Psyllopsis fraxini ×10

galled leaves

Cabbage Whitefly ×4

natural size

Mussel Scale ♀ ×4

Rose Scale ♀ ×3

Parthenolecanium corni ♀

Pseudococcus longispinus ♀

×2

97

PSOCIDS   Order Psocoptera

Very small, winged or wingless insects also known as booklice, barklice, and dustlice. There are about 2,000 known species, but many thousands more undoubtedly await discovery. All have biting jaws and a rather broad head. Wings, when present, have a rather characteristic venation, although this is occasionally much reduced. Two cells are of particular importance in classifica-

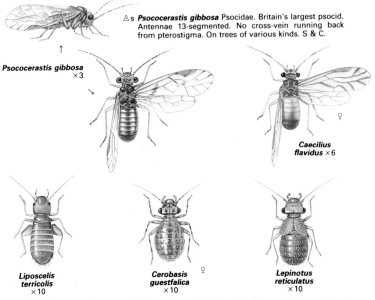

△s **Psococerastis gibbosa** Psocidae. Britain's largest psocid. Antennae 13-segmented. No cross-vein running back from pterostigma. On trees of various kinds. S & C.

Psococerastis gibbosa
×3

Caecilius flavidus ×6   ♀

Liposcelis terricolis
×10

Cerobasis guestfalica ♀
×10

Lepinotus reticulatus
×10

tion: the pterostigma on the front edge of the forewing is generally semi-circular or lens-shaped, and the areola postica is a similar cell on the hind margin of forewing. The areola postica is absent in some families. Wings are held roofwise over the body at rest, the insects then resembling the psyllids (p. 96) although the venation is quite different. Psyllids also have sucking beaks. Psocids are found mainly on shrubs and other vegetation, where they chew pollen, fungal spores, and bark-living algae. Many occur indoors, where they feed on a variety of starchy materials and cause some damage. Parthenogenesis is very common, with males very rare or even absent in some species. Nymphal stages are very similar to adults. Because of their small size, the psocids are not easy to identify, but those shown here are fairly distinct and should be recognised without much trouble.

▲ **Caecilius flavidus** Caeciliidae. One of the commonest outdoor species, easily recognised by its yellow body and bristly wings. Antennae 13-segmented. No cross-vein running back from pterostigma. Males unknown. On broad-leaved trees, mainly on foliage.

▲ **Liposcelis terricolis** Liposcelidae. The commonest domestic booklouse, often damaging books and paper, stored foods, and also insect collections. Occasionally found out of doors. Antennae 15-segmented. One of several similar species with a flat body and broad hind femur with a distinct 'hump' near base. A cosmopolitan pest. Males unknown.

▲ **Cerobasis guestfalica** Trogiidae. A wingless species easily recognised by densely speckled body. Antennae with more than 20 segments. Abundant on tree bark and fences; also in buildings. Males almost unknown.

▲ **Lepinotus reticulatus**. One of several similar species with forewings reduced to small flaps; hind wings absent. Antennae with more than 20 segments. A common domestic species, feeding on debris of all kinds; will destroy insect collections.

THRIPS   Order Thysanoptera

Minute, usually dark insects with very narrow body and usually two pairs of tiny feather-like wings. Some are wingless. Very common in flowers, where many species pierce and scrape cells to get sap. Thousands take to the air in still, thundery weather – hence a common name of thunderflies. Most females have a curved, saw-like ovipositor for laying eggs in plants. Male abdomen usually smoothly rounded. Thrips are exopterygote insects, but nymphal development is complex, with one or more resting stages. Over 3,000 species are known.

 Tip of abdomen of *Phlaeothripidae*

 Down-curving ovipositor of *Thripidae*

▲ **Phlaeothrips annulipes** Phlaeothripidae. Somewhat stouter than most thrips. As in whole family, abdomen is tubular at tip in both sexes and wings overlap strongly at rest. On dead birch twigs and branches (look at fire brooms in forests!), feeding on fungal spores and threads. 5–9.

Phlaeothrips annulipes
×10

Aeolothrips intermedius
×10

Aeolothrips albicinctus ×10

▲ **Aeolothrips intermedius** Aeolothripidae. One of many species with banded wings. 5–9, mainly on yellow crucifer and composite flowers. ▲ *A. albicinctus* is virtually wingless and antlike. Very common at bases of grasses 5–9. Possibly predatory. In this family, wings are more or less parallel at rest, forewings rounded at tip, body not flattened, and ovipositor curved upwards.

△ **Pea Thrips** *Kakothrips pisivorus* Thripidae. Relatively large, with yellow tarsi. Breeds in flowers of peas and related plants and damages young pods. 5–9.

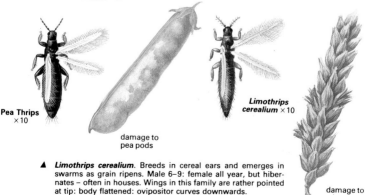

Pea Thrips
×10

Limothrips cerealium ×10

damage to pea pods

damage to wheat ear

▲ **Limothrips cerealium**. Breeds in cereal ears and emerges in swarms as grain ripens. Male 6–9: female all year, but hibernates – often in houses. Wings in this family are rather pointed at tip: body flattened: ovipositor curves downwards.

LICE

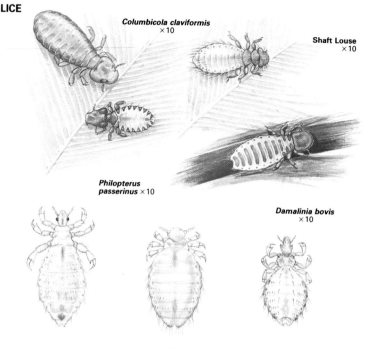

Columbicola claviformis × 10

Shaft Louse × 10

Philopterus passerinus × 10

Damalinia bovis × 10

Human Louse × 10   *Linognathus vituli* × 10   Hog Louse × 6

LICE Wingless parasites of birds and mammals, all strongly flattened and with strong claws to grip feathers and hairs. Sometimes placed in a single order – the Phthiraptera – but mouthparts are of two very different kinds and the insects are here regarded as belonging to two separate orders. Nymphs very like adults, with virtually no metamorphosis.

BITING LICE Order Mallophaga Head quite large, with biting jaws: eyes and antennae very small. Prothorax distinct. Found mainly on birds, feeding on flakes of skin and feather and also on blood from wounds. Longer-bodied species generally among longer plumage: short species generally on head and neck. Examine freshly-dead birds to find lice. There are many species, but most have strong host preferences.

▲ **Columbicola claviformis** Philopteridae. A common parasite of pigeons.

▲ **Philopterus passerinus.** One of several similar species infesting sparrows and other passerine birds.

▲ **Shaft Louse** *Menopon gallinae* Menoponidae. Less flattened than *Philopterus* and with less obvious antennae – more or less concealed in grooves. A very common cosmopolitan pest of poultry and other game birds.

▲ **Damalinia bovis** Trichodectidae. Antennae prominent and clearly 3-segmented. Tarsi 1-clawed. Widely distributed on cattle: closely related spp on other hoofed mammals.

SUCKING LICE Order Anoplura Blood-sucking lice confined to mammalian hosts. Head very narrow: body pear-shaped.

△ **Human Louse** *Pediculus humanus* Pediculidae. Eyes distinctly pigmented. Exists in 2 forms – head and body lice, of which latter is the larger (about 4 mm long). Carries typhus fever, but unlikely to be a problem in hygienic conditions.

▲ **Linognathus vituli** Linognathidae. Eyes absent. Front legs smaller than others. A parasite of cattle. Related species on other hoofed mammals and also on dogs.

▲ **Hog Louse** *Haematopinus suis* Haematopinidae. All 3 pairs of legs equally developed. Eyes virtually absent. On pigs.

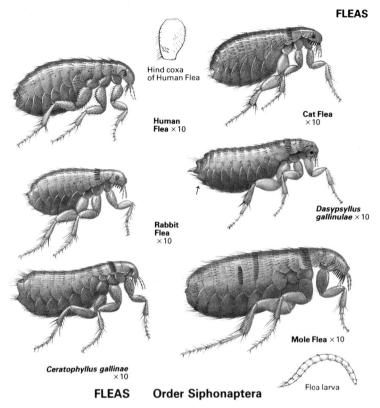

Hind coxa
of Human Flea

**Human
Flea** × 10

Cat Flea
× 10

*Dasypsyllus
gallinulae* × 10

**Rabbit
Flea**
× 10

Mole Flea × 10

Ceratophyllus gallinae
× 10

Flea larva

FLEAS   Order Siphonaptera

Wingless insects, strongly flattened from side to side and with enlarged hind legs for jumping. Generally dark brown or black. Adults all blood-suckers living on birds and mammals. Pearly white eggs are scattered in host nest, including sleeping quarters of domestic cats and dogs, and worm-like larvae feed there on debris, including droppings of adult fleas. Identification of fleas generally requires a microscope, and specimens should first be soaked in 10–20% caustic potash for a day or two: this makes them more transparent and easier to examine. The combs of strong bristles on head and thorax are important features. The illustrations are paler than living fleas to show up the bristles.

▲ **Human Flea** *Pulex irritans* Pulicidae. Small spines on inner side of hind coxa characterise this family. Front of head smoothly rounded. Cosmopolitan in dwellings: also on fox and badger, which may have been original host.

▲ **Cat Flea** *Ctenocephalides felis*. Distinguished from human flea by elongate head and strong genal and pronotal combs. The commonest household flea, often biting man. ▲ Dog flea (*C. canis*) has a more rounded head, with 1st spine of genal comb much shorter than 2nd.

▲ **Rabbit Flea** *Spilopsyllus cuniculi*. Antennal club symmetrical. Genal comb of 4–6 blunt spines. On rabbits, usually attached to ears: carrier of myxomatosis. S & C.

▲ *Dasypsyllus gallinulae* Ceratophyllidae. Distinguished from *Ceratophyllus* spp by many more bristles (3 rows) in front of antennae. Male readily identified by prominent spurs at rear. Abundant on small birds.

▲ *Ceratophyllus gallinae*. Pronotal comb with at least 24 spines: no genal comb. Infests a very wide range of birds, especially those with rather dry nests. Commonest bird flea in B: abundant in tit nest boxes and a real pest in poultry houses.

▲ **Mole Flea** *Hystrichopsylla talpae* Hystrichopsyllidae. One of our largest species – up to 6 mm long. On moles, shrews, and some small rodents.

ANT-LIONS, LACEWINGS, and ALLIES   Order Neuroptera

Soft-bodied holometabolous insects with wingspans ranging from about 3 mm to more than 10 cm. Wings are membranous, usually with dense network of cross-veins which gives the order its name: Neuroptera means nerve-winged. Except in the alder flies (p. 108), the veins usually fork prominently at the wing margins.

Flight is weak in most species and the wings are held roofwise over the body at rest. Antennae usually thread-like: sometimes moniliform (composed of bead-like segments) and occasionally toothed or clubbed. Compound eyes large, sometimes accompanied by 3 ocelli. Tarsi 5-segmented. Largely carnivorous, feeding mainly on other small insects, although some eat pollen and some hardly feed at all. Larvae are carnivorous or parasitic, with several species living in water. More than 6,000 species are known, of which about 300 occur in Europe. The snake flies and alder flies are sometimes placed in a separate order – the Megaloptera.

ANT-LIONS Myrmeleonidae Dragonfly-like insects with long narrow body and narrow wings, spanning up to about 10 cm in European species. Antennae short and stout, and always clubbed in European species. Flight slow and fluttery: mostly nocturnal or crepuscular, often coming to artificial light. Nocturnal species often take flight when disturbed by day. Difficult to see when resting among vegetation with wings pulled tightly back along the body. Mostly carnivorous, plucking small insects from plants, but some nibble pollen. All like warm, dry areas. Males have prominent claspers at the rear.

Larvae prey on a wide range of spiders and small insects, which are captured with large jaws. Some larvae roam in soil and leaf litter: others construct pitfall traps in sandy soil. The pit is conical and the larva buries itself at bottom with just jaws protruding. Insects blundering into pit slither to bottom, often helped by sand grains hurled by ant-lion, and are grabbed by the jaws. Ants are among the commonest victims – hence the ant-lion's name. There are 41 European species, mainly in Mediterranean area. None occurs in B.

Dendroleon pantherinus. Characteristic eye-spot on hind edge of forewing may be rather indistinct. Dry, open oakwoods with many old trees. 7–8. Larva lives in old leaf litter and builds no pit. S & C.

Myrmeleon formicarius. Top of head black or brown. Wings clear. Dry, open places. 5–8. Larva makes pit in soil, rarely in leaf litter. One of the commonest European ant-lions, from southern Scandinavia southwards. *M. inconspicuus* has top of head yellow with brown spots. Wings clear, spanning 50–70 mm. Veins dark with just a few pale spots (several similar species have pale veins with a few dark spots). Abdomen chequered. Open habitats, especially near the sea. 5–8. Larva makes pit in fine sand, especially on dunes and in stream banks, S & C.

Palpares libelluloides. Day-flying, often in dense colonies, and quite unmistakable. Rough grassland, dunes and rocky maquis (not too dense): avoids the driest places. 5–9. Larva lives in soil and debris around vegetation but makes no pit: head protrudes from soil and larva rushes out to grasp passing prey in huge jaws (p. 294). Mediterranean.

Euroleon nostras. Both wings spotted, but hind wing has just a few small spots in front half. Several cross-veins between radius and media in basal part of hind wing (see below). Open woodland, but avoids driest places: sometimes flies with *M. formicarius*. 6–9. Baltic islands southwards, but very local. Larva makes small pit in bare ground.

The hind wing venation helps to identify the smaller ant-lions. *Myrmeleon* and *Euroleon* (left) have several cross-veins between radius and media in basal region: *Creoleon, Distoleon,* and *Macronemurus* (right) have just one such cross-vein.

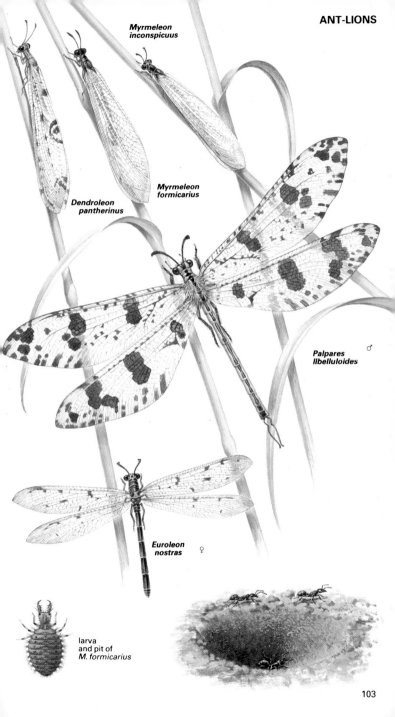

ANT-LIONS

Myrmeleon inconspicuus

Dendroleon pantherinus

Myrmeleon formicarius

Palpares libelluloides ♂

Euroleon nostras ♀

larva and pit of *M. formicarius*

103

Creoleon lugdunensis ♂

Distoleon tetragrammicus

Creoleon lugdunensis. Yellowish thorax with dark brown central stripe. Female abdomen does not extend beyond wings. Two branches of cubital vein in forewing run ± parallel to hind margin. Hind wing with just one cross-vein between radius and media in basal region (see p. 102). Common in rough grassland and rocky places 5–8. Larva in soil and debris, but makes no pit. SW, as far north as Loire Valley. *C. plumbeus* of SE is very similar.

Distoleon tetragrammicus. Conspicuously spotted, similar to *Euroleon nostras* but with only one cross vein between radius and media in basal part of hind wing (see p. 102). 6–8 in dry oak and pine woods: local but sometimes abundant. Larva lies in dry leaf litter and makes no pit. S & C.

Acanthaclisis baetica. One of our largest ant-lions. Wings virtually unspotted and with two rows of cells along front edge of forewing. 6–9, mostly on coastal dunes. Larva lives in sand but makes no pit. SW, as far north as Normandy.

Macronemurus appendiculatus. Thorax yellow with 3 brown stripes on top. Abdomen yellow and brown, extending beyond wings in male, who has very long claspers. Often swarms over roadsides and waste land and also among cereals and other crops. 5–9. Larva lives in soil but makes no pit. S.

ASCALAPHIDS Ascalaphidae

Fast-flying relatives of ant-lions, generally shorter and stouter but with very long clubbed antennae. Males have prominent claspers. Mostly diurnal, with fast undulating flight commonly 2 to 3 metres above ground. Capture flies and other small insects in mid-air. Often bask on plants with wings open as illustrated, but wings folded roofwise over body when truly at rest. Larvae like those of ant-lions but make no pits. They live on the ground, among debris, and under stones: often camouflage bodies with debris. Ascalaphids prefer warm, dry places and the 15 European species occur mainly in the south. None lives in B.

Libelloides longicornis. Black area at base of hind wing stops well short of anal angle. Yellow veins run through dark area of forewing. General venation pale yellow to golden. 6–8 in sunny meadows. SW (including southern Switzerland). *L. macaronius* of eastern Europe is similar but lacks dark patch at base of forewing. *L. coccajus* has black area at base of hind wing extending almost or quite to anal angle. Veins all dark. Pale patches white or yellow. Dry, open woods and grassy areas (rarely far from trees). 4–7. S & C.

Puer maculatus. Forewing ± clear: hind wing densely spotted and sometimes almost black in distal part. Garrigue and rough grassland in summer. Almost confined to southern France: uncommon.

Deleproctophylla dusmeti. Forewing clear: hind wing with brown patch just behind pterostigma. SW. (Insects found from Corsica eastwards have brown patch on all four wings and have recently been treated as a separate species – *D. australis.*)

Bubopsis agrioides. Wings very narrow: first 2 long veins very dark and forming a prominent streak near front edge of all wings. Active at dusk and most often seen at artificial light. 5–8, mainly in and around open woodland, especially pinewoods, SW.

ANT-LIONS and ASCALAPHIDS

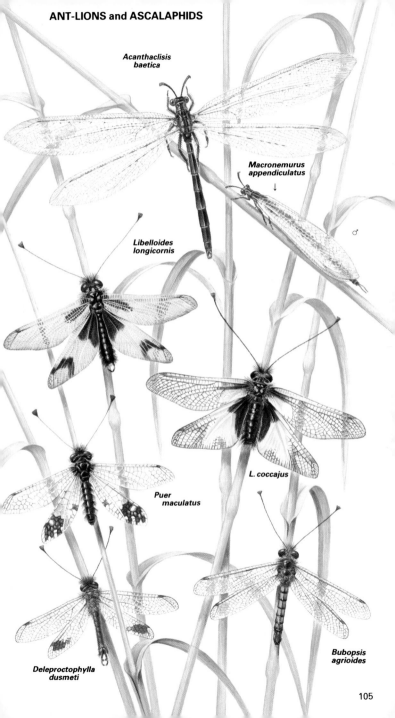

Acanthaclisis baetica

Macronemurus appendiculatus

↓

♂

Libelloides longicornis

L. coccajus

Puer maculatus

Deleproctophylla dusmeti

Bubopsis agrioides

Mantis Fly *Mantispa styriaca* Mantispidae. Resembles mantis, but wings flimsy and insect more timid, feeding mainly on small flies. Active day and night in warm, dry places, especially light woodland with plenty of ground cover. 5–8. Larva enters egg cocoons of spiders, especially wolf spiders, and feeds on eggs. S & C. 4 other similar species in S.

Mantis Fly ×2

Nemoptera bipennis Nemopteridae. Easily recognised by ribbon-like hind wings and lazy up-and-down flight at dusk. Dry, stony and grassy hillsides and coastal pinewoods. 4–8. Larva has long neck and lives on ground. Iberia only. 2 similar species in S.E.

▲ *Conwentzia psociformis* Coniopterygidae. One of many very similar small insects clothed with mealy white powder. Resembles a whitefly (p. 96) but rests with wings steeply roofwise. Often comes to lights at night. Common in many habitats. 4–11. Larva eats aphids on trees.

△ *Osmylus fulvicephalus* Osmylidae. Identified by large size and spotted wings. Streamside vegetation, especially in woods. 4–8. Larva hunts in wet moss and debris. Most of Europe but absent from much of N.

GREEN LACEWINGS Chrysopidae

Long veins reduced, with one – the pseudomedia – almost straight and very prominent in centre of wing. Two zig-zag veins – the gradates – rise stair-like in outer part of wing. Generally green: sometimes brown. Mainly nocturnal. Eggs on slender stalks. Larvae (p. 294) mostly aphid-eating, often camouflaging themselves with empty skins of victims.

△ *Chrysopa perla* is bluish-green, heavily marked with black. Deciduous woodland. 5–8.
△ *C. 7-punctata* is large and bright green with 7 tiny black spots on head. Woods, hedges and gardens. 5–8.

▲ *Chrysoperla carnea* is pale green, becoming pinkish in autumn when it seeks hibernation sites in building. All kinds of well-vegetated habitats.

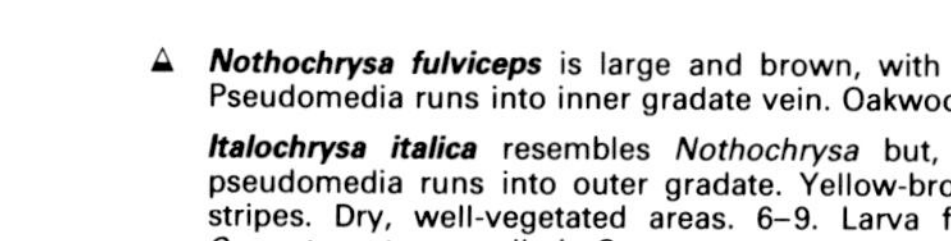

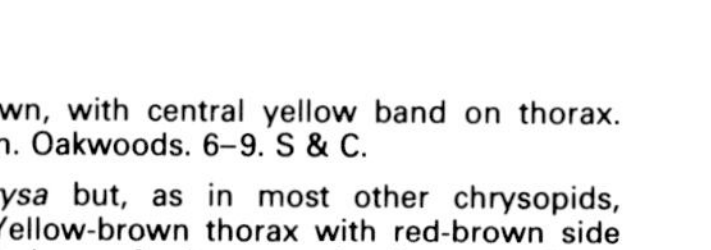

Chrysoperla carnea ×2

Chrysopa perla ×2

△ *Nothochrysa fulviceps* is large and brown, with central yellow band on thorax. Pseudomedia runs into inner gradate vein. Oakwoods. 6–9. S & C.

Italochrysa italica resembles *Nothochrysa* but, as in most other chrysopids, pseudomedia runs into outer gradate. Yellow-brown thorax with red-brown side stripes. Dry, well-vegetated areas. 6–9. Larva feeds on grubs in nest of ant *Crematogaster scutellaris*. S.

▲ *Sisyra fuscata* Sisyridae. Few cross veins and non-forking veins along front of wing distinguish this genus from *Hemerobius*. All-dark antennae separate *S. fuscata* from similar species. Streamside vegetation. 4–10. Larva feeds on sponges.

Dilar meridionalis Dilaridae. Recognised by pectinate antennae of male or long slender ovipositor of female. Flies weakly at dusk. Lush vegetation, especially in woodland clearings. 6–9. Larvae live under bark. SW.

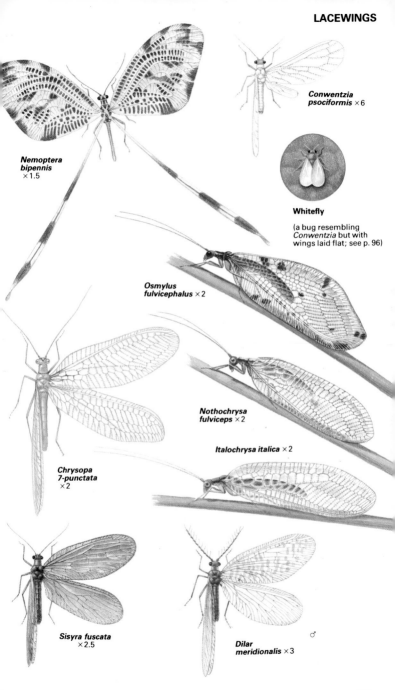

Nemoptera bipennis ×1.5

Conwentzia psociformis ×6

Whitefly

(a bug resembling *Conwentzia* but with wings laid flat; see p. 96)

Osmylus fulvicephalus ×2

Nothochrysa fulviceps ×2

Italochrysa italica ×2

Chrysopa 7-punctata ×2

Sisyra fuscata ×2.5

Dilar meridionalis ×3

♂

BROWN LACEWINGS Hemerobiidae A large family of mainly small greyish or brown insects. Distinguished from Chrysopidae by numerous long veins and from Sisyridae by the forked veins along front margin of wing. Larvae less bristly than chrysopids: mainly aphid-eating.

▲ **Wesmaelius quadrifasciatus** flies in dry, warm habitats, especially among conifers. 5–9. ▲ **Micromus variegatus** prefers low-growing vegetation and is common in gardens and hedgerows. 4–9. △n **Drepanepteryx phalaenoides** is immediately identified by its pointed and strongly hooked wing-tips. Flies in light woodland with well-vegetated clearings. 4–10. N & C. ▲ **Hemerobius humulinus** is one of several very similar species. Front wing pattern varies. Abundant in hedgerows and deciduous woods. 3–11.

Alder Fly *Sialis lutaria* Sialidae. One of 6 very similar species in N & C. Veins not forked at margins. Flies near water, spending much time resting on vegetation. 4–8. Larva (p. 296) aquatic. Eggs laid in batches on reeds etc.

SNAKE FLIES Raphidiidae Named for the long 'neck', on which the head can be raised way above the body. Mainly woodland insects and largely aphid-eating. Female with long ovipositor. Larvae (p. 294) eat various insects under bark and in dead wood. Several very similar species in Europe, differing in detailed wing venation and also in shape of head.

▲ **Raphidia notata** is associated mainly with oaks. 2 cross-veins in pterostigma. 4–8. Larva in stumps of various trees, but mainly oak. N & C. △ **R. confinis** is a smaller species (c. 20 mm wingspan) with only 1 cross-vein in pterostigma. Associated with pines. 5–7. S & C. ▲ **R. maculicollis**, one of the commonest species, is confined to conifers. About the same size as *confinis*, but with narrower head. 1 cross-vein in pterostigma. 5–7. S & C: mainly western.

Inocellia crassicornis resembles *Raphidia* spp but has no ocelli and no cross-veins running through the pterostigma (*Raphidia* has at least one such vein). Associated with conifers. 5–7. N & C.

Raphidia   **Inocellia**

SCORPION FLIES   Order Mecoptera

Named because male abdomen is often up-turned, but main diagnostic feature is downward extension of head to form stout beak. There are some 400 known species. About 30 live Europe, mostly *Panorpa* species (Panorpidae). These fly weakly in shady places, eating mainly dead animal matter and fruit. Fly mainly 5–8, but 2 or more broods in S and may fly all year in Mediterranean area. Larvae (p. 294) are caterpillar-like. The species are often difficult to separate, especially the females.

▲ **Panorpa communis** is a typical species with fairly heavy spotting on wings. △ **P. germanica** is similar but spotting may be lighter and may be absent altogether in N. It is distinguished from *communis* by the parallel appendages on male abdomen (caliper-shaped in *communis*).

△ **P. cognata** is slightly smaller and usually paler: 6th abdominal segment in male is square, and appendages divergent. **P. alpina** of S & C has almost spotless wings but is readily identified by short subcostal vein. **P. rufostigma** of SE can be recognised by red pterostigma. **P. meridionalis** is a heavily spotted species from Iberia and southern France.

P. alpina

Bittacus italicus Bittacidae clings to vegetation with front legs and grabs small insects with long back legs. Male has no up-turned tail. All four wings long and narrow. Shady places in spring and summer S.

▲ **Boreus hyemalis** Boreidae is the Snow Flea. Flightless: wings much reduced. No up-turned tail. Lives among mosses. 10–4. Often seen hopping over snow.

P. rufostigma

P. meridionalis

Boreus hyemalis

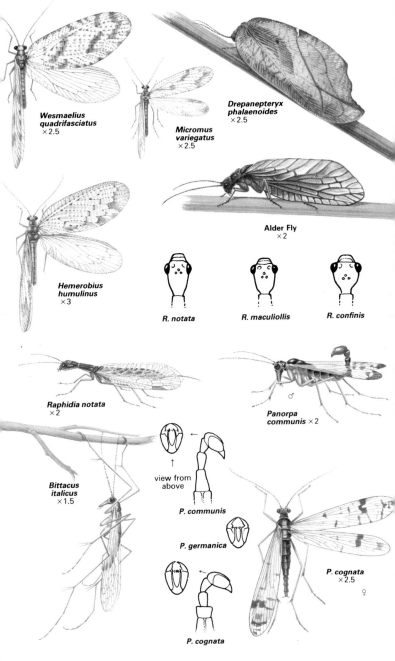

Wesmaelius quadrifasciatus ×2.5

Micromus variegatus ×2.5

Drepanepteryx phalaenoides ×2.5

Hemerobius humulinus ×3

Alder Fly ×2

R. notata

R. maculiollis

R. confinis

Raphidia notata ×2

Panorpa communis ×2 ♂

Bittacus italicus ×1.5

view from above ↑

P. communis

P. germanica

P. cognata

P. cognata ×2.5 ♀

109

BUTTERFLIES and MOTHS   Order Lepidoptera

A very large order, with nearly 150,000 known species. About 5,000 species occur in Europe; about half of them live in Britain. A few moths have wingless females, but the insects generally have two pairs of membranous wings clothed with minute scales. The scales provide the wing colour and pattern, but they are easily detached: if you touch the wings you will find scales on your fingers. Those which have been flying around for several weeks often look dull and worn as a result of losing many of their scales. Lepidopterans show little variation in general structure and are easily recognised as such, but they exhibit a remarkable range of sizes. European species have wingspans ranging from 3 mm to 150 mm, and some tropical species exceed 300 mm.

Adult **mouthparts** are almost always in the form of a slender tube called the proboscis. They use this to drink nectar from flowers, and sometimes to suck up other fluids. When not in use, the proboscis is coiled neatly under the head. Many moths lack a functional proboscis and take no food in the adult state. Some of the more primitive moths, e.g. *Micropterix* species (p. 124), have retained biting jaws and feed on pollen.

The simple division of the order into **"butterflies"** and **"moths"** is an artificial split, based on simple observation and with no real scientific basis. There are about 25,000 known butterfly species and over 120,000 moths. No one feature separates all the butterflies from all the moths, and moth groups differ from each other just as much as they do from butterflies. However, the butterfly/moth distinction is well-established and never likely to be abandoned.

Butterflies are day-flying insects, usually brightly coloured, generally resting with their wings brought together vertically above the body, and have clubbed antennae. Moths are generally nocturnal, rather dull in colour, hold their wings either flat or roof-wise over the body at rest, and seldom have clubbed antennae. However, there are exceptions: in Europe the burnet moths (p. 134) are colourful, diurnal, and have clubbed antennae – while some butterflies are quite drab. Most moth antennae are either hair-like or feathery, with the male's more feathery than the female's, since the greater surface area helps him to pick up the female's scent more easily during courtship.

Many moths, including the burnets, also have a *frenulum* on the underside of the hind wing. This is a bristle springing from the 'shoulder' of the wing and running forward to be held in a small catch on the underside of the forewing, its function being to link the wings together during flight. No butterflies have a frenulum: they and moths without one generally link their wings simply by means of a large overlap.

retaining hook on forewing

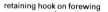
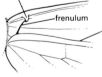

frenulum

front edge of hind wing

Underside of a moth's wings, showing the frenulum which connects front and hind wings

The Lepidoptera are arranged in numerous **families**, based largely on wing-venation. This can sometimes be seen through the covering of scales, and one can usually make out a prominent cell (called the discal cell or simply *the* cell) near the centre of the wing. But with living insects venation is of little use, and one must rely on general appearance to assign them to their families. With a little practice this is not difficult. With the butterflies, colour alone may be enough: predominantly white or yellow species belong to in the **Pieridae** (p. 114), blue to the **Lycaenidae** (p. 122), brown with eye-spots to the **Satyridae** (p. 120). Moths are a little more difficult, but many families have characteristic shapes. The **Noctuidae** (p. 156) are generally rather stout-bodied with drab brown or grey wings laid flat or held roof-wise over the body at rest. The **Notodontidae** (p. 148) are similar but with slightly different forewing venation. The **Geometridae** (p. 170) are rather flimsy and generally rest with their wings flat. Some members of the **Pyralidae** (p. 128) look like them but are distinguished by the hind wing venation. The presence or absence of tympanal 'ears' may also help to distinguish certain families. These membranes, when present, occur either at the rear of the thorax or at the front of the abdomen. At least some moths are known to be able to pick up bats' echo-location signals and to take avoiding action.

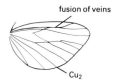

fusion of veins

Cu_2

Venation of hind wing of *(left)* pyralid and *(right)* geometrid moths

Life-histories. Among the butterflies the sexes are usually brought together initially by visual signals emanating during flight, though scent signals come into play during the later stages of courtship. Most moths rely entirely on scent, and this is why it is much easier to breed moths in captivity than butterflies, which need plenty of flying space. **Eggs** are usually laid on the appropriate food-plant, and a lens will reveal that many are exquisitely sculptured. Some species pass the winter in the egg stage, but most eggs hatch within a couple of weeks or so and the larvae or **caterpillars** start to feed. Almost all lepidopteran larvae are vegetarian, feeding on or in almost every kind of terrestrial plant and attacking every part, from the root to the flower and seed, though most species feed on the leaves. Many are serious pests of agriculture. A few feed on animal matter, such as clothes moths on woollen materials. Their natural habitats are the nests of birds and mammals, where they find plenty of fur to eat.

The typical caterpillar has three pairs of true legs at the front and five pairs of stumpy or fleshy prolegs at the back. The last pair are known as claspers. All the prolegs are furnished with numerous minute hooks, with which the caterpillar keeps a firm hold on the food plant. Some have fewer than five pairs of prolegs. The Geometridae have only two pairs, including the claspers. They move by stretching out along a twig and taking a grip with the front legs, then bringing the claspers right up behind them. In doing so, the body is arched up (e.g. p. 176) and these caterpillars are commonly known as loopers.

After three or four moults, the caterpillar is ready to turn into a **chrysalis** or pupa. Many moth larvae spin silken cocoons in which to pupate – usually among the leaves of the food plants. Others burrow into the soil and make silk-lined chambers. Most butterfly larvae pupate naked on their food plants, either hanging from the tail-end, or held upright against the stem by a silken girdle. Many butterfly and moth species pass the **winter** in the chrysalis stage. Others overwinter as larvae, either completely quiescent (hibernating) or remaining active and feeding when conditions allow. A few species hibernate as adults.

A typical moth pupa

Butterfly pupae: *left*, suspended and *right*, upright (succinct)

Apollo

SWALLOWTAIL and APOLLO BUTTERFLIES Papilionidae Mostly large and brightly coloured butterflies, often with tails on the hind wings. Hind margin of hind wing generally concave. Antennal club generally rather slender. When disturbed, larvae stick out a colourful tuft – the osmeterium – just behind head: strong odour from this deters enemies. Pupae usually attached to food plant in upright position and secured by a silken belt.

Apollo *Parnassius apollo* Colours vary slightly from place to place. A mountain butterfly, rarely below 700 m except in north. 6–8. Flies lazily in sunshine: basks on flowers and stones. Larva on stonecrops and houseleeks: pupates in loose cocoon. Most European mountains. **Small Apollo** *P. phoebus* is similar but a little smaller and has a small red spot near the front edge of the forewing. It lives in the Alps, usually between 1500 and 2500 m, where its larvae feed on saxifrages and houseleeks.

Clouded Apollo *P. mnemosyne* is like a Black-veined White (p. 114) but black spots and concave margin of hind wing distinguish it. Wings become almost transparent with age. Dark form only in female. As in all members of the genus, mated females have large horny pouch (sphragis) below abdomen – secreted by male during copulation to prevent further mating by female. 5–7. Damp meadows in N: mountain pastures elsewhere. Larva on *Corydalis*.

△ **Common Swallowtail** *Papilio machaon*. 4–9 in open habitats with plenty of flowers. Single brooded in N: 2 or 3 broods further south. First brood has less yellow dusting on black markings and a completely black abdomen. Larva on wild carrot, fennel, and other umbellifers. All Europe, but only in Norfolk Broads in B. The British race can survive only in moist habitats, for the male genitalia are very sensitive to humidity and become hard and unable to function in drier climates.

Corsican Swallowtail *P. hospiton* is quite similar but the dark band on the underside of the forewing has distinctly wavy margins. Confined to Corsica and Sardinia, it flies 5–7, mainly in upland areas.

Southern Swallowtail *P. alexanor* has no black patch at the base of the forewing but a prominent black stripe runs right across the basal part of both front and hind wings. It has a scattered distribution in southern Europe from Provence eastwards. 5–7.

Scarce Swallowtail *Iphiclides podalirius*. 3–9 in scrubby habitats, including orchards and gardens. 1 or 2 broods: spring insects pale yellow and summer ones almost white. Larva on blackthorn and various cultivated fruit trees. Common in S & C, despite its English name: absent from B other than as a vagrant.

Spanish Festoon *Zerynthia rumina*. Red spots in forewing cell: translucent 'window' near tip. 2–5 on rocky hillsides. Larva on birthworts (*Aristolochia* spp). Iberia and southern France only. **Southern Festoon** *Z. polyxena* has no red spots in cell and no 'window'. 4–5. SE, overlapping with *rumina* in Provence.

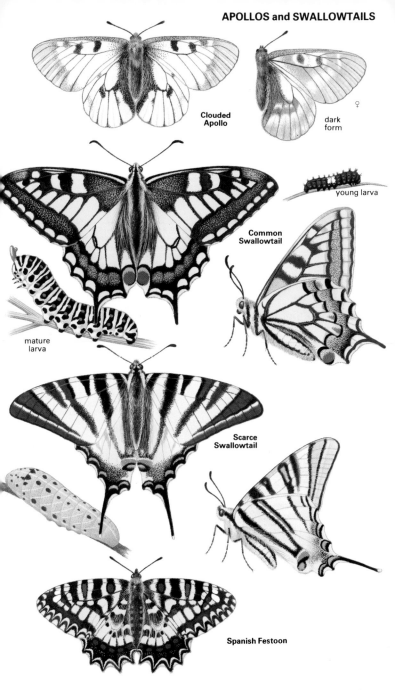

APOLLOS and SWALLOWTAILS

Clouded Apollo

dark form ♀

young larva

Common Swallowtail

mature larva

Scarce Swallowtail

Spanish Festoon

113

WHITE and YELLOW BUTTERFLIES Pieridae A large family whose members are basically white or yellow, often with black markings. Often marked differences between the sexes. Pupae are attached in an upright position on food plant or other vertical surface and supported by a silken belt. The single point on the head distinguishes them from pupae of all other families.

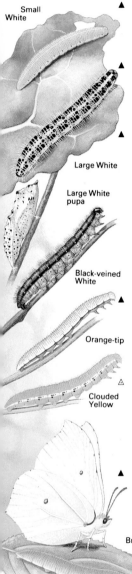

Small White

Large White

Large White pupa

Black-veined White

Orange-tip

△ Clouded Yellow

Brimstone ♀

▲ **Small White** *Artogeia rapae*. Male may lack spot on upper side of forewing: female has 2 spots. 3–10 in 2 or more broods. Dark markings much greyer in 1st brood. Open country and cultivated land everywhere. Larva on wild and cultivated brassicas: a serious pest.

▲ **Green-veined White** *A. napi* is easily identified by greenish black or grey lines along veins of underside of hind wing. Female has 2 spots on upperside of forewing: male has only 1. 3–10 in 2 or 3 broods. Open country and light woodland. Larva resembles that of *rapae*: on various crucifers but rarely on cultivated forms.

▲ **Large White** *Pieris brassicae*. Only female has black spots on upper side of forewing. 4–9 in 2 or 3 broods. Spring insects have greyer wing-tips. Hind wings range from white to deep yellow on underside, often dusted with greenish black scales. Larvae gregarious: serious pests of cultivated brassicas: also on nasturtiums and wild crucifers. Vast numbers of larvae destroyed by *Apanteles glomeratus* (p. 230). Adults strongly migratory, with large numbers arriving in B from the continent each summer.

Black-veined White *Aporia crataegi*. Veins black or dark brown. Wings thinly scaled, especially in female where brown membrane is clearly visible. 5–7 in open habitats, often at altitude. Larva on hawthorn and other rosaceous trees and shrubs: gregarious and hibernating in web when young. S & C.

▲ **Orange-tip** *Anthocharis cardamines*. Only male has orange wing-tips. Female is distinguished from several similar species by rounded wing-tips with solid grey or black patch. 4–6 in flowery meadows, especially where damp: not uncommon in country gardens. Larva on cuckooflower and other crucifers, including garden honesty and sweet rocket.

Clouded Yellow *Colias croceus*. Female generally like male but black borders contain yellow spots. About 10% of females are very pale (form *helice*). 4–10, with up to 3 broods. Flowery fields and hillsides. Larva on clovers and other legumes. Resident in S, spreading northwards each spring and reaching as far as southern Sweden. There are several similar species, most of them a good deal paler.

▲ **Brimstone** *Gonepteryx rhamni*. Male sulphur yellow: female greenish white. Both sexes very leaf-like at rest, showing pale yellow or green underside. 6–9, and again in spring after hibernation: one of the first butterflies to appear in spring in cooler regions. Light woodland, gardens, and open country. Larva on buckthorn. *G. cleopatra* is similar but male has large orange flush on upper side of forewing. S.

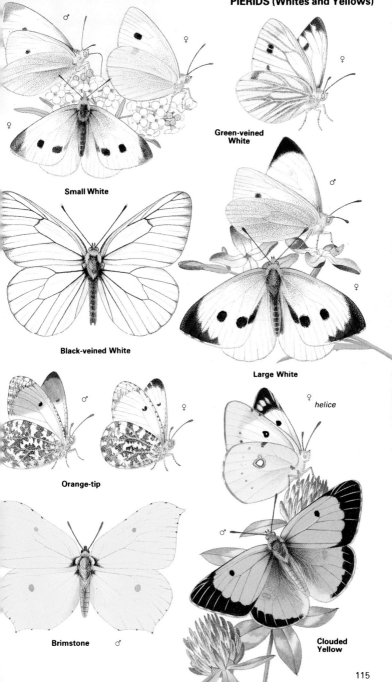

♂

♀

♀

Green-veined White

Small White

Black-veined White

♂

♀

Large White

♂

♀

Orange-tip

♀ *helice*

♂

Brimstone ♂

Clouded Yellow

Nettle Tree Butterfly *Libythea celtis* Libytheidae. The only European member of its family, this butterfly is easily recognised by its wing pattern, with a strongly toothed forewing, and very long palps. Female has all three pairs of legs fully developed. Open and lightly-wooded country: 6–9 and again in early spring after hibernation. Larva is green with white and pink stripes and feeds on nettle tree (*Celtis australis*). S & C (southern and eastern).

Nettle Tree Butterfly

ADMIRALS, TORTOISESHELLS and kin Nymphalidae A family of about 5,000 species, which also includes the fritillaries (p. 118). Upperside generally very colourful: underside commonly drab and cryptically coloured, especially in those species which hibernate as adults. Front legs much reduced and not used for walking. Larvae are generally spiny. Pupae often bear bright metallic spots and are suspended freely from foodplant or other support.

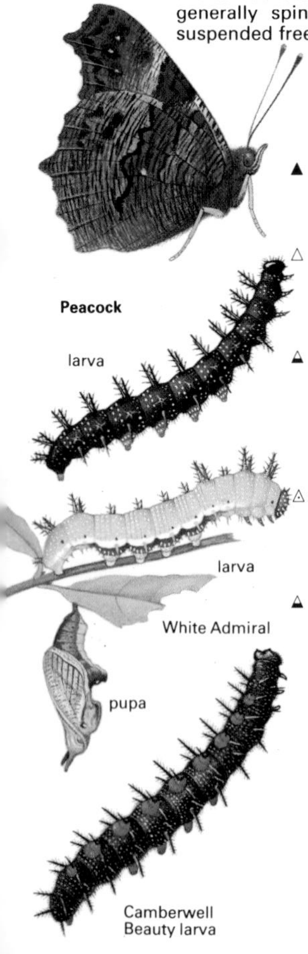

Two-tailed Pasha *Charaxes jasius*. 5–6 and 8–9. Fast-flying: commonly attracted to ripe fruit. Larva is green with yellow stripes, two eye-spots on back, and reddish horns on head. It feeds on strawberry tree (*Arbutus unedo*). S: rarely far from coast, but inland in Spain.

▲ **Peacock** *Inachis io*. 6–9 and again in spring after hibernation. Flowery places, including gardens. Hibernates in hollow trees and buildings. Larva (left) feeds on stinging nettle. Absent far from north.

△ **Camberwell Beauty** *Nymphalis antiopa*. Underside similar to upperside, but duller and with less blue. 6–9 and again in spring after hibernation. Light woodland. Larva (below left) feeds on sallows and other trees. Most of Europe, sometimes migrating as far as North Cape: a rare visitor to B.

Peacock

larva

▲ **White Admiral** *Limenitis camilla*. Velvety black when fresh, becoming browner with age. Two rows of black dots on underside of hind wing. 6–7 in woodland. Larva on honeysuckle. S (northern) and C. **Southern White Admiral** *L. reducta* has only one row of black dots on underside of hind wing, and an extra white spot near middle of forewing. 5–10. S & C.

△ s **Purple Emperor** *Apatura iris*. Female lacks purple sheen and has larger white markings. 7–8 in woodland, especially around oaks. Larva feeds on sallows. S & C. **Lesser Purple Emperor** *A. ilia* is smaller, with orange-ringed dark spot near outer edge of forewing. 5–9. S & C.

larva

White Admiral

pupa

▲ **Comma** *Polygonia c-album*. Named for comma-like mark on underside of hind wing. Summer generation, flying 6–7, is paler than autumn generation shown here. Autumn generation flies 8–9 and again in spring after hibernation. Larva is black and white and resembles bird dropping. It feeds on nettle, elm, and hop. **Southern Comma** *P. egea* is less heavily marked, with 'comma' replaced by indistinct 'v' SE.

Camberwell
Beauty larva

Two-tailed Pasha

Peacock

White
Admiral

Camberwell Beauty

Purple
Emperor
♂

Comma

Purple Emperor larva

117

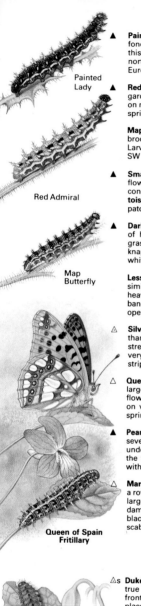

▲ **Painted Lady** *Cynthia cardui*. 3–10 in open flowery places: very fond of thistles and various garden flowers. Larva mainly on thistles and burdock. Resident only in extreme S, but migrates northward each spring and produces summer brood all over Europe. Some insects move south again in autumn.

Painted Lady

▲ **Red Admiral** *Vanessa atalanta*. 3–10 in flowery places, especially gardens and woodland margins. Very fond of over-ripe fruit. Larva on nettles. Resident in S, hibernating as adult and moving north in spring like Painted Lady.

Map Butterfly *Araschnia levana*. 4–9 in open woodland, 2 or 3 broods, with spring and summer insects markedly different. Larvae, black with brownish spines, feed gregariously on nettles. SW and C.

Red Admiral

▲ **Small Tortoiseshell** *Aglais urticae*. 3–10 in gardens and other flowery places. Hibernates as adult: underside very dark for concealment. Larva on nettles: gregarious at first. △ **Large Tortoiseshell** *Nymphalis polychloros* is larger and lacks deep black patch on hind wing.

Map Butterfly

▲ **Dark Green Fritillary** *Mesoacidalia aglaja*. All spots on underside of hind wing are silver. 6–8 in rough flowery places – open grassland, woodland clearings, and moorland. Very fond of knapweed and scabious flowers. Larva is black and spiny with white stripe on back and red spots on sides. It feeds on violets.

Lesser Marbled Fritillary *Brenthis ino*. One of several rather similar species, but distinguished from most by the continuous heavy brown margins on upperside together with purplish brown band across underside of hind wing. 6–8 in damp meadows and open woodland. Larva on meadowsweet.

△ **Silver-washed Fritillary** *Argynnis paphia*. Male much brighter than female, with smaller black markings on upperside and black streaks (scent scales) on some forewing veins. 6–8 in woodland: very fond of bramble flowers. Larva, black and brown with yellow stripe and long brown spines, feeds on violets.

△ **Queen of Spain Fritillary** *A. lathonia* is instantly identified by the large and very shiny silver spots on the underside. 2–9 in rough flowery places, with up to 3 broods: adults hibernate in S. Larva on violets. Most of Europe, with much northward migration in spring: rare visitor to B.

▲ **Pearl-bordered Fritillary** *Boloria euphrosyne*. Distinguished from several superficially similar species by silver marginal spots on underside of hind wing together with large silver spot in middle of the yellow band. 4–8 in open woodland. Larva, black and grey with yellow spines, feeds on violets.

△ **Marsh Fritillary** *Eurodryas aurinia*. Very variable, but always with a row of black dots in outer part of underside of hind wing. Female larger than male. 5–7 in rough grassy places – not necessarily damp – with plenty of flowers: often on moorland. Larvae are black and spiny and feed in a communal web on plantains and scabious.

Queen of Spain Fritillary

───────────────

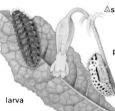

△s **Duke of Burgundy Fritillary** *Hameartis lucina*. Riodinidae. Not a true fritillary and the only European member of its family. Male front legs greatly reduced. 5–8 in light woodland and scrubby places. Larva on primrose and cowslip. S & C.

pupa

Duke of Burgundy Fritillary

larva

Painted Lady

spring

Map Butterfly

summer

Red Admiral

Dark Green Fritillary

Lesser Marbled Fritillary

Small Tortoiseshell

♂

♀

Silver-washed Fritillary

Pearl-bordered Fritillary

♀

Duke of Burgundy Fritillary

Marsh Fritillary

119

BROWN BUTTERFLIES Satyridae A large family of predominantly brown butterflies characterised by prominent eye-spots (ocelli) near wing margins. The spots lure bird attacks away from the head to the less vulnerable wing-tips. Several veins are distinctly swollen near base. Sexes similar, but females often larger and somewhat paler: males often have dark patch of scent scales – the scent is important in courtship – in middle of forewing. Front legs much reduced and brush-like in both sexes. Larvae all feed on grasses and are generally green or brown: 2 prongs at hind end. Pupae either hang upside down like Nymphalidae or lie in flimsy cocoon in the turf.

Marbled White *Melanargia galathea*. Pattern variable, often much darker in mountains. 6–8 in rough grassy places: very fond of knapweed flowers. Larva has brown and green forms. S & C. **Western Marbled White** *M. occitanica* has a black line across cell in forewing and veins on underside of hind wing are brown. 5–7. SW. Several similar species in S.

Grayling *Hipparchia semele*. Rather variable pattern: female has more extensive pale patches on upperside. 5–8 on heaths and dry grassland, usually resting on ground and tilting over to reduce shadow. Not in far north.

Ringlet *Aphantopus hyperantus*. Upperside very dark in both sexes. Ocelli of upperside indistinct or absent in male but always present in female. 6–8 in woodland margins and clearings, hedgerows, and scrubby places: very fond of bramble flowers. Larva like that of Grayling but hairier.

Gatekeeper or Hedge Brown *Pyronia tithonus*. 6–8 in hedgerows and open woodland, especially on bramble blossom. Larva like that of Grayling but yellower and more hairy. S & C.

Small Heath *Coenonympha pamphilus*. Upperside almost plain orange. 4–10 in grassy places and heathland everywhere. Normally rests on grass or ground: rarely on flowers. Larva like green form of Marbled White, but smaller.

Dryad *Minois dryas*. Eye-spots with blue pupils. Female paler, with larger eye-spots. Hind wings distinctly scalloped. 7–9 in open woods and scrub. Larva dirty yellow with darker lines and brown head. S (northern) & C.

Speckled Wood *Pararge aegeria*. 3–10 in woodland clearings. Orange-spotted form (*P. a. aegeria*) occurs in SW and Italy: cream-spotted form (*P. a. tircis*) elsewhere. Not in far north.

Meadow Brown *Maniola jurtina*. Upperside of male with little, if any, orange, but with black patch of scent scales in middle of forewing. 6–9 in grassy places everywhere

Scotch Argus *Erebia aethiops*. Size rather variable. Male darker and often with fewer eye-spots. Underside resembles upperside but hind wing with a greyish band containing 3 tiny white dots. 6–9 in damp grassland, mainly in uplands: often associated with conifers. C.

Wall Brown *Lasiommata megera*. Female often paler and less heavily marked: without broad brown band (scent scales) in middle of forewing. 3–9 in rough grassy places, including roadsides. Sunbathes on rocks and walls. Larva is pale green with white spots and lines. Not in far north.

Great Banded Grayling *Brintesia circe*. Upperside very dark brown with cream band crossing both wings and reaching hind edge of hind wing. Forewing with just one eye-spot (always blind on upperside). No eye-spots on upperside of hind wing. 6–8 in open woodland and on scrubby hillsides. Larva is brown with paler stripes on sides. S & C.

Marbled White

Grayling
↓

Speckled Wood

Meadow Brown

Scotch Argus

Wall Brown

SATYRID BUTTERFLIES

Marbled White

Grayling

Ringlet

♂

♀

Gatekeeper

Small Heath

Dryad

tircis

aegeria

Speckled Wood

♂

♀

Meadow Brown

Scotch Argus

Wall Brown

Great Banded Grayling

HAIRSTREAKS, COPPERS and BLUES Lycaenidae Relatively small butterflies, often brilliantly coloured in male: sexes often markedly different. Hairstreaks, named for the fine streaks on underside, have small 'tails' on hind wings. Larvae are short and squat, with legs concealed from above to give a slug-like or woodlouse-like appearance. Pupae attached upright to the food plant or fixed to debris on the ground by a few strands of silk. There are about 100 species in Europe.

△ **Purple Hairstreak** *Quercusia quercus*. Male has purple sheen all over upper surface. 7–8 in oakwoods, often high in trees and feeding on honeydew on leaves. Larva on oak. Absent from far north.

△s **White-letter Hairstreak** *Strymonidia w-album*. One of several similar species, but distinguished by plain upper surface *and* conspicuous W-shaped line on underside of hind wing. Female is paler, with no sex brand near front of forewing. 7–8 in and around woods: very fond of bramble blossom. Larva is yellowish green with a dark head and diagonal green stripes on the sides: mainly on elm.

▲ **Green Hairstreak** *Callophrys rubi*. 3–7 in scrubby habitats, including woodland clearings, hedgerows, and damp heathland. Larva is bright green with oblique yellow stripes and feeds on gorse, broom, heathers, and other shrubs.

Scarce Copper *Heodes virgaureae*. Distinguished from several similar species by yellowish green underside. Males sometimes bear small black spots in mountain areas. 7–8 in flowery places. Larva on docks.

▲ **Small Copper** *Lycaena phlaeas*. 3–11 in grassy and flowery places, including gardens. Larva on docks and sorrel. All Europe below 2000 m.

▲ **Common Blue** *Polyommatus icarus*. Male distinguished from several rather similar species by distinctly violet tinge. Amount of blue on female very variable: often absent. 4–9 in flowery grasslands, including roadsides. Larva on legumes.

△s **Chalkhill Blue** *Lysandra coridon*. Silvery blue upperside distinguishes male from most other blues. Female is brown, with or without some blue scales near base. 7–8 on flowery hillsides on chalk and limestone. Larva, green with yellow stripes and a black head, feeds on legumes – mainly horseshoe vetch. S & C. *L. hispana* of southern Europe is similar but flies 4–5 and again 9.

▲ **Holly Blue** *Celastrina argiolus*. 4–5 and 7–9: females of summer brood with much more black than spring insect shown here. Open woods, gardens, and hedgerows. Larva is yellowish green to brownish green with yellow and red markings. Summer larvae on holly or ivy, autumn larvae on ivy: mainly in flower heads.

Large Blue larvae are pink at first and feed on wild thyme flowers. They are then taken into ant nests, where they receive ant grubs to eat in return for a sugary secretion eagerly lapped up by the adult ants.

?△ **Large Blue** *Maculinea arion*. Greyish underside with blue flush at base distinguishes this from several similar species. Spots vary in size: generally larger in female. 6–7 on rough hillsides. Most of Europe but not far north: believed extinct in B.

SKIPPERS   Hesperiidae Small butterflies with rapid, darting flight. Antennae widely separated at base: club gradually thickens and often ends in hooked point. Larvae feed and pupate in silken shelters at base of food plant. Only the Dingy Skipper occurs in Ireland.

▲ **Small Skipper** *Thymelicus flavus*. Male has dark stripe (sex brand) in centre of forewing. Wings held vertically above body at night but, like most skippers, when feeding or resting by day front and hind wings held as illustrated. 6–9 in grassy places. Larva, yellowish green with a darker head, feeds on grasses. S & C. △s **Essex Skipper** *T. lineola* is similar but has black under tip of antenna instead of orange.

▲ **Dingy Skipper** *Erynnis tages*. 5–9 in rough flowery places. Rests moth-like, with wings roofwise over body. Larva on various legumes. Absent from far north.

▲ **Large Skipper** *Ochlodes venatus*. Underside mottled orange. 6–9 in rough grassy places, including roadsides and woodland clearings. Rests like small skipper. Larva on various grasses. Not in far north. △s **Silver-spotted Skipper** *Hesperia comma* has silvery spots on underside.

▲ **Grizzled Skipper** *Pyrgus malvae*. Distinguished from several similar species by clear row of white spots in outer part of hind wing: underside never very green. 4–9 in flowery places: basks with wings almost flat. Larva, purplish brown above and green below, feeds on many low-growing herbs.

Purple Hairstreak

White-letter Hairstreak

Green Hairstreak

Scarce Copper

Small Copper

Common Blue

Chalkhill Blue

Holly Blue

Large Blue

Small Skipper

Dingy Skipper

Large Skipper

Grizzled Skipper

△ **Micropterix mansuetella** Micropterigidae. One of several similar pollen-feeding moths with functional jaws. Hind wings purplish brown. Diurnal in damp places on flowers of sedges and marsh marigolds. 5–6. Larvae live in leaf litter. N & C. ▲ **M. calthella**, common on marsh marigolds, has golden head and unbanded wings.

▲ **Eriocrania semipurpurella** Eriocraniidae. One of several very similar day-flying moths with scattered bright blue scales on forewings. Swarms on birches 3–4. Larvae make blotch mines in young birch leaves. Pupate in soil. N & C.

▲ **Stigmella aurella** Nepticulidae. One of many very similar tiny moths with leaf-mining larvae. 1st antennal segment expanded to form pale orange cap over eye. 5–9, in 2 broods. Larvae make serpentine mines in bramble leaves, but escape before pupation. Most of Europe, but not in coldest regions because larvae over-winter in mines.

▲ **Tischeria marginea** Tischeriidae. Distinguished from several similar species by dark edged forewings. All rest with front end raised and wing-tips pressed against surface. 4–8. Larvae make blotch mines in bramble leaves. Absent from far north.

△ **Nemophora degeerella** Incurvariidae. Male has longest antennae of all British moths; female antennae much shorter. Hind wings purplish brown. 4–6, fluttering slowly up and down at dusk. Usually in woodland. Larva feeds in leaf litter like Adela.

▲ **Adela reaumurella**. Female antennae much shorter. Hind wings purplish brown. 4–6. Males swarm round trees and shrubs in sunshine, drifting slowly with antennae held up in front. Larvae live in leaf litter in cases made from small fragments.

▲ **Incurvaria masculella**. Female antennae not toothed. 4–6; diurnal. Young larva mines leaves of hawthorn and other trees and shrubs, then makes itself a small leafy case and falls to ground to continue feeding on dead leaves. S & C. ▲ **I. pectinea** is similar, but paler and with greyish head.

▲ **Lampronia rubiella**. Spots pale yellow or cream in varying patterns. 5–6. Larvae feed in central stalk of raspberry fruit in summer, overwinter in soil, and then complete growth in buds in spring. ▲ **L. praeletella** flies 4–6. Larva mines near leaf tip of strawberry in summer, and then makes a small case for itself and continues to feed externally on the leaf. N & C.

▲ **Tapestry Moth** Trichophaga tapetzella Tineidae. Largest of the 'clothes moths', whose larvae feed on wool and other animal fibres, although this species does not do much damage to normal fabrics indoors. Its larva prefers coarser materials, such as horse hair, and is more often found in stables and other buildings with high humidity. Common in owl pellets, which may be the moth's natural food. Adult 6–7.

▲ **Case-bearing Clothes Moth** Tinea pellionella. Hind wings quite dark. Larva lives and pupates in portable case made of silk and collected fibres. It eats a wide range of animal fibres and damages clothes, carpets, etc. Adult all year indoors; 6–10 out of doors, where it commonly breeds in birds' nests. It needs a relatively high humidity and is less common in houses with central heating.

▲ **Common Clothes Moth** Tineola bisselliella. Hind wings rather pale. All year in houses: rarely out of doors. Reluctant to fly, preferring to scuttle into crevices. Larva is white with a pale brown head: makes no portable case although it builds a shelter of fibres. Attacks a wide range of woollen fabrics and furs. The commonest and most destructive clothes moth.

▲ **Yponomeuta padella** Yponomeutidae. One of several similar species known as small ermines. Hind wings grey. 6–8. Larvae feed communally in silken tents on hawthorn and blackthorn: pupate in tents.

▲ **Diamond-back Moth** Plutella xylostella. Named for row of pale diamonds along back when wings folded. 5–9. Larva, green with brown or black head, feeds on various crucifers: often a serious pest of cultivated brassicas.

▲ **Ypsolopha dentella**. Woods and hedgerows 7–8. Rests in characteristic pose resembling bud or twig. Larva feeds on honeysuckle.

Diamond-back Moth ×2

Yponomeuta padella ×2 with larval tent

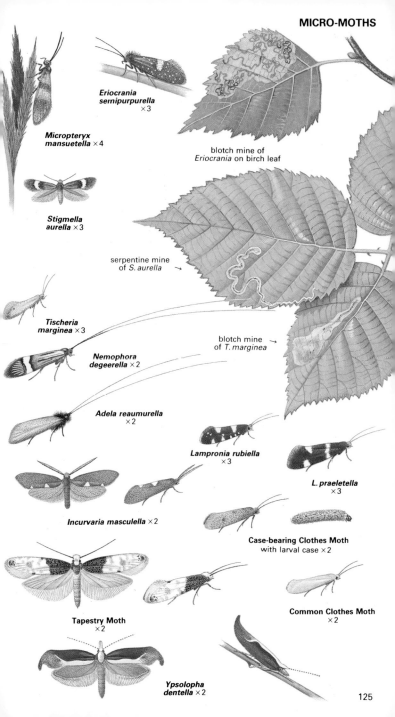

MICRO-MOTHS

**Eriocrania
semipurpurella**
×3

**Micropteryx
mansuetella** ×4

blotch mine of
Eriocrania on birch leaf

**Stigmella
aurella** ×3

serpentine mine
of *S. aurella* →

**Tischeria
marginea** ×3

blotch mine
of *T. marginea* →

**Nemophora
degeerella** ×2

Adela reaumurella
×2

Lampronia rubiella
×3

L. praeletella
×3

Incurvaria masculella ×2

Case-bearing Clothes Moth
with larval case ×2

Tapestry Moth
×2

Common Clothes Moth
×2

**Ypsolopha
dentella** ×2

125

▲ **Coleophora caespitiella** Coleophoridae. Larval cases are abundant on seed heads on rushes. Each larva spins a silken case and remains in it until maturity. There are many similar species on other plants. Adults all small and brown or cream, with pointed wings.

larval cases

▲ **Depressaria pastinacella** Oecophoridae. One of many rather similar flattened moths. As in most members of family, antennae have a tiny comb of hairs near base. 9–4, hibernating as adult. Larvae, grey with black spots, feed communally in silken webs on umbellifers.

▲ **Dasycera sulphurella**. Day-flying in open woodland 5–7. Rests with antennae held forward. Pale grey larva feeds in dead wood. S & C.

▲ **Brown House Moth** Hofmannophila pseudospretella. 5–9 in and around buildings: one of the commonest household pests. Larva, white with a brown head, feeds on a wide range of stored foods, fabrics, and debris: also breeds in old birds' nests.

Coleophora caespitiella
×2

▲ **White-shouldered House Moth** Endrosis sarcitrella. All year in buildings. Larva resembles that of previous species: also eats dried animal droppings in nests.

▲ **Carcina quercina**. Hind wings pale yellow with rosy apex. 7–8 in woods and hedges. Pale green larva feeds in silken envelope under leaves in spring. S & C.

△ **Alabonia geoffrella**. Palps very long. Hind wings dingy brown. Day-flying, 5–6 in wooded areas. Larva, white with black dots, feeds in rotting wood. S & C.

Family Tortricidae A large family of rather small moths with more or less rectangular forewings. Most hold wings roofwise over body at rest, many resembling bird droppings and leaf fragments. Hind wings usually greyish brown. Larvae generally live in folded or rolled leaves, but some tunnel in plants.

▲ **Pine Shoot Moth** Rhyacionia buoliana. Silvery markings often reduced. 6–9 in pine woods. Reddish brown larva feeds on buds and shoots, causing much damage in plantations. ▲ **R. pinicolana** is similar but less orange.

▲ **Codlin Moth** Cydia pomonella. 5–10, wherever apples grow. Larva, cream at first and then pink, tunnels in apples and some other fruits, eating flesh and seeds.

▲ **Pammene regiana**. 5–7 in wooded areas, including town parks. Usually high up in trees. Larva, greyish white with a brown head, feeds on maple and sycamore. N & C.

▲ **Epiblema cynosbatella**. One of several very similar 'bird-dropping' species, distinguished by its yellow palps. 5–6 in gardens and hedgerows. Reddish brown larva lives in rose buds and shoots.

▲ **Acleris emargana**. Colours vary, but deep notch in forewing readily identifies this species. Falls to ground like a piece of leaf if disturbed. 6–9 in wooded areas. Green larva feeds in folded leaves of sallow and other trees. ▲ **A. literana** is easily identified by colour, although pattern varies. Woodland, 8–10 and again in spring after hibernation. Greyish green larva feeds on oak. ▲ **A. variegana** is very variable: black spots often absent from white patch. 7–9 in hedges and other rough places. Greenish larva feeds on roses and related shrubs.

▲ **Ancylis badiana**. 4–8 in rough grassy places. Greyish larva feeds on clovers and vetches, first as a leaf miner and then in a pouch of folded leaves.

▲ **Hedya nubiferana**. Often much browner. 5–7 in hedgerows and other scrubby places. Larva, greenish with a black head, feeds on flowers and shoots of trees and shrubs.

△n **Philedonides lunana**. Male has slightly feathery antennae and greyer wings, with less obvious brown areas. 3–6 on heaths and moors. Greenish larva feeds on flowers and leaves of various plants. N & C.

△ **Cacoecimorpha pronubana**. Day-flying 5–9 in gardens, hedges, and other scrubby habitats. Larva, greyish green to brown, is polyphagous.

▲ **Archips podana**. One of several similar species with prolonged wing-tips. Rests with wings fairly flat, like a dead leaf. 6–8, especially in gardens and orchards. Larva is greenish and feeds on leaves, buds, and fruits of apple.

▲ **Pandemis corylana**. Like Archips but without prolonged wing-tips. Hind wings never orange. 6–9 in woodland. Green larva feeds on many trees and shrubs. N & C.

▲ **Exapate congelatella**. Female with vestigial wings. 10–12 in woods and other scrubby places and moorlands. Light green larva feeds on shrubs. N & C.

▲ **Green Oak Tortrix** Tortrix viridana. 5–8 on oaks. Larva feeds in buds and rolled oak leaves, often defoliating small trees in summer.

▲ **Croesia bergmanniana**. Amount of brown banding and spotting varies. 6–7 in hedgerows and gardens. Larva, greenish grey or yellowish, feeds on roses. N & C.

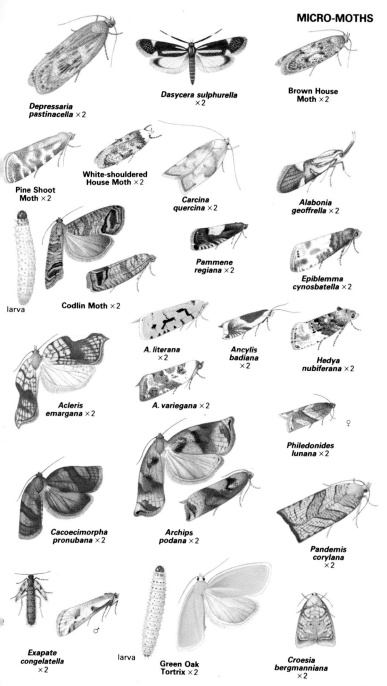

Depressaria pastinacella ×2

Dasycera sulphurella ×2

Brown House Moth ×2

Pine Shoot Moth ×2

White-shouldered House Moth ×2

Carcina quercina ×2

Alabonia geoffrella ×2

larva

Codlin Moth ×2

Pammene regiana ×2

Epiblemma cynosbatella ×2

A. literana ×2

Ancylis badiana ×2

Hedya nubiferana ×2

A. variegana ×2

Acleris emargana ×2

Philedonides lunana ×2

♀

Cacoecimorpha pronubana ×2

Archips podana ×2

Pandemis corylana ×2

Exapate congelatella ×2

♂

larva

Green Oak Tortrix ×2

Croesia bergmanniana ×2

127

Family Cochlidae A family closely related to the Tortricidae (p. 126) but differing in details of wing venation.

▲ **Agapeta hamana.** Ground colour pale to deep yellow: markings pale to dark brown. 5–9 in rough grassy places in lowlands. Larva is greyish and feeds in roots of thistles.
▲ **A. zoegana** occasionally has orange ground colour. 4–9 in rough grassy places. Larva is pale yellow and feeds in roots of scabious and knapweed.

▲ **Aethes cnicana.** One of several very similar species. Ground colour pale yellow to light brick. 5–8 in rough vegetation, especially where damp. Larva is pale yellow and feeds in stems and seed heads of thistles.

▲ **Cochylis roseana.** 5–9 on rough ground and waste land. Larva is pale green with a brown head and feeds in seed heads of teasel. N & C.

Family Pyralidae A very large family whose members generally have rather narrow forewings. The two front veins in hind wing are fused for a short distance (see below). Tympanal organs are present on abdomen. Legs are relatively long and spiky. Many of the larvae live in silken tubes or webs. Several are serious pests of crops and stored food.

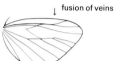

↓ fusion of veins

Venation of *Pyralid* hind wing

▲ **Crambus pratella.** Forewings generally paler in female. 5–9 in grassy places. One of many rather similar slender moths known as grass moths, which rest vertically on grasses, usually head down, with wings wrapped tightly around body. Larvae of all species live in silk tubes at base of grasses, chewing the stems at or below ground level.

▲ **Catoptria pinella.** 6–9 in damp habitats, especially in or near woods. Larva feeds on cotton grass (a sedge) as well as on various true grasses.

▲ **Chrysoteuchia culmella.** Wings relatively short. 5–9: abundant in grass everywhere.

▲ **Agriphila tristella.** Ground colour ranges from straw to deep brown. Central stripe white to pale orange. 6–9 in grassy places everywhere.

Ancylolomia tentaculella. Female larger and brighter, with nearly white hind wings. 7–9 in grassy places. Larva lives in silken tunnel at base of grasses. S & C.

▲ **Garden Pebble** *Evergestis forficalis.* 5–9 in hedges and cultivated land. Larva is greyish green with black and white spots and feeds on wild and cultivated brassicas, often drawing leaves together with silk to form a retreat.

▲ **Parapoynx stagnata.** One of a group of moths known as china-marks, because their wing patterns are thought to resemble the markings under plates and other china articles. The markings vary in intensity and are sometimes absent. 6–8, usually near water. Larva, yellow or pale brown, feeds underwater on bur-reed and other aquatic plants, usually inside the stems at first.

▲ **Brown China-mark Moth** *Nymphula nymphaeata.* 5–8, usually near still or slow-moving water. Larva is brown and hairy and lives underwater. It cuts pieces from floating leaves of pondweeds and other plants and sticks them together with silk to form a little case, in which it lives attached to undersides of leaves.

△ **Pyrausta aurata.** 5–8 in rough grassy places. Larva, dull green with black spots, feeds on catmint. ▲ **P. purpuralis** is similar but forewings are paler and hind wing markings off-white.

▲ **Scoparia arundinata.** One of many similar moths with a tuft of scales in middle of forewing. Markings vary from black to brown: occasionally much reduced. 5–7 in dry grassland, including dunes. Larva feeds on various roots at ground level.

△ **European Corn Borer** *Ostrinia nubilalis.* Male is pink to dark brown: female cream to brick-coloured, often bright yellow. 5–9 on cultivated land. Whitish larva tunnels in stems of many plants and causes much damage to stems and cobs of maize. Much of Europe, but a sporadic visitor to B.

▲ **Small Magpie** *Eurrhypara hortulata.* 6–8 in hedges and waste land. Larva, greenish white at first and then pinkish yellow, feeds in rolled leaf of stinging nettle and labiates. ▲ **E. coronata** flies 5–7 in hedgerows and woodland margins. Larva is pale green and feeds in silken web on foliage of elder. S & C.

▲ **Mother of Pearl** *Pleuroptya ruralis.* 6–8 in hedges and waste land. Slow, ghost-like flight. Pale green larva feeds in rolled leaf of stinging nettle.

▲ **Rush Veneer** *Nomophila noctuella.* Pale to dark grey. 5–9 in grassy places. A strong migrant. Larva is dirty green and feeds on grasses, clovers, and other herbs.

MICRO-MOTHS: GRASS MOTHS and other PYRALIDS

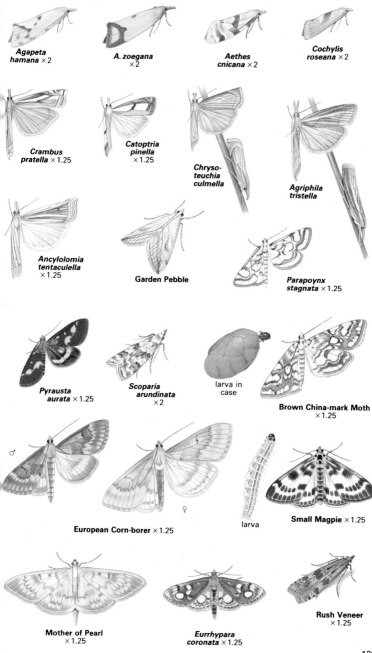

Agapeta hamana × 2

A. zoegana × 2

Aethes cnicana × 2

Cochylis roseana × 2

Crambus pratella × 1.25

Catoptria pinella × 1.25

Chryso-teuchia culmella

Agriphila tristella

Ancylolomia tentaculella × 1.25

Garden Pebble

Parapoynx stagnata × 1.25

Pyrausta aurata × 1.25

Scoparia arundinata × 2

larva in case

Brown China-mark Moth × 1.25

♂

♀

European Corn-borer × 1.25

larva

Small Magpie × 1.25

Mother of Pearl × 1.25

Eurrhypara coronata × 1.25

Rush Veneer × 1.25

129

▲ **Gold Fringe** *Hypsopygia costalis*. 7–10 in and around hedges and grassy places. Rests with wings outstretched and pressed flat against surface, usually with abdomen pointing upwards. Larva is dirty white with a brown head and feeds on dead grasses, including stored hay and even roof thatch. S & C.

▲ *Orthopygia glaucinalis*. Often with a coppery sheen when fresh. 6–9. Larva lives in a silken web among dead grass and other plant material: often in old birds' nests. S & C.

▲ *Dioryctria abietella*. 6–8 in pine woods, where it is very well camouflaged at rest on the trunks. Greyish larva feeds in pine cones or shoots.

▲ **Wax Moth** *Galleria mellonella*. Marked sexual differences. 6–10, around apiaries and wild honey bee colonies. Larvae are pale grey and feed on honeycomb, rapidly chewing through the wax and destroying it. Once a serious pest in beehives, but now much less common.

▲ **Meal Moth** *Pyralis farinalis*. Forewings often tinged with purple. 5–9, usually in and around buildings. Rests with wings flat and abdomen often raised, rarely moving far when disturbed, even if touched. Larva lives in a silken tube and feeds on cereal products in store.

▲ *Myelois cribrella*. Easily confused with *Yponomeuta* spp (especially at rest) but distinguished by clear white fringe on hind wing. 6–8 in rough habitats where thistles grow. Easily overlooked at rest on shiny leaves. Larva is pale grey and feeds in seed heads and stems of thistles.

▲ *Oncocera semirubella*. White streak often missing from front margin of forewing. 6–8 in grassy places. Larva is greenish black and feeds on white clovers and other legumes. S & C. Mainly on chalk in B.

▲ *O. palumbella* flies 6–8 on heathland. Larva is greenish grey and feeds on *Erica* spp.

PLUME MOTHS Pterophoridae

A small family, closely related to Pyralidae, in which the forewings are generally split into 2 feathery plumes and hind wings into 3 similar plumes. Wings are generally rolled around each other at rest and held at right angles to the body, forming a slender T. Legs are long and spiky and flight is rather weak.

▲ *Agdistis bennetii*. Wings not divided, although other features are just like those of typical plume moths. 5–9 in coastal areas, especially on saltmarshes. Larva is green with a yellow line on each side and feeds on sea lavender. S & C.

▲ *Capperia britanniodactyla*. 6–8 on heathland, open woods, and scrubby grassland. Larva, yellowish green with brown dots, feeds on wood sage. S & C.

▲ **White Plume Moth** *Pterophorus pentadactyla*. The most familiar and unmistakable plume moth, flying 5–8 in hedgerows and on waste land. Attracted to light at night and often found on window panes. Larva is green and yellow, with tufts of hair, and feeds in a rolled leaf of hedge bindweed.

▲ *Platyptilia gonodactyla*. Ground colour and intensity of markings rather variable. 5–9 in rough habitats, including roadsides and railways. Larva, dirty white with black dots, feeds in leaves, flowers, and seed heads of coltsfoot.

▲ **Many-plumed Moth** *Alucita hexadactyla* Alucitidae. Each wing divided into 6 slender plumes. 7–10 and again 5–6 after hibernation as adult (occasionally seen on mild days in winter). Hedgerows and woodland margins. Larva is pink and feeds in buds and flowers of honeysuckle.

Thyris fenestrella Thyrididae. Clear membranous areas of wings (characteristic of this small genus) are larger in north of range. Abruptly narrowed abdomen is another characteristic of the genus. 5–8 in hedgerows and other scrubby habitats: swift, darting flight in sunshine. Slightly hairy green larva feeds on *Clematis* spp. S & C.

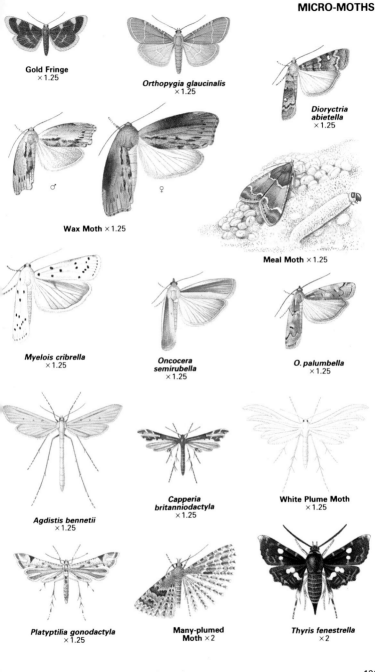

Gold Fringe
× 1.25

Orthopygia glaucinalis
× 1.25

Dioryctria abietella
× 1.25

Wax Moth × 1.25

♂

♀

Meal Moth × 1.25

Myelois cribrella
× 1.25

Oncocera semirubella
× 1.25

O. palumbella
× 1.25

Agdistis bennetii
× 1.25

Capperia britanniodactyla
× 1.25

White Plume Moth
× 1.25

Platyptilia gonodactyla
× 1.25

Many-plumed Moth × 2

Thyris fenestrella
× 2

SWIFT MOTHS Hepialidae Moths with no proboscis and with very short antennae. Front and hind wings of similar shape, with no frenulum. At rest, wings are held tightly along sides of body. Flight is usually fast and darting, with rapid beating of wings. Females generally larger than males and less heavily marked. Eggs are scattered in flight and larvae feed underground on the roots of a wide variety of plants.

▲ **Ghost Swift** *Hepialus humuli*. Named for the ghost-like, hovering flight of male, which rises and falls slowly over the vegetation at dusk. The flashing of its pure white wings attracts the yellowish female. Both sexes are dull brown beneath. 6–8 in grassland and arable land, especially where damp. Larvae (below) may damage crop roots: also harmful in forest nurseries. N & C.

▲ **Orange Swift** *H. sylvina*. Male forewing sometimes tinged with red: hind wing reddish brown. Female much larger and duller: hind wing greyish. 6–8 in open country. Absent from Ireland and SW.

▲ **Map-winged Swift** *H. fusconebulosa*. Forewing pattern very variable, but distinguished from other swift moths by chequered fringes on all wings. The form *gallicus*, found mainly in north, has no more than a white spot near middle. 5–8, mainly on heathland and woodland margins. Larva feeds mainly on bracken roots and rhizomes.

▲ **Common Swift** *H. lupulinus*. Variable forewings: markings often absent in female. Hind wings greyish brown. 5–8. Abundant in open habitats, including gardens and other cultivated land, where larva is often a pest. Adult commonly comes to lighted windows. Absent from SW.

▲ **Gold Swift** *H. hecta*. Light spots often reduced. Hind wings dingy brown. Male with hovering flight. 6–8 on heathland and other bracken-covered habitats. Larva feeds on bracken roots and rhizomes. N & C.

▲ **Goat Moth** *Cossus cossus* Cossidae. A stoutly built moth with a conspicuously ringed abdomen. Hind wings same colour as forewings. 6–8. Larva is purplish red and lives inside trunks of various broad-leaved trees. It takes two or more years to mature and then pupates in soil, leaving a strong smell of goats on the tree.

▲ **Leopard Moth** *Zeuzera pyrina*. Wings thinly scaled in outer part and almost transparent: pulled tightly to sides of body at rest. Female much larger. Male antennae feathery in basal half. 6–8. Not uncommon at light. Larva tunnels in various broad-leaved trees and shrubs and can weaken trunks and branches of young trees. Common in orchards and town parks. S & C.

Dyspessa ulula. Pattern variable: grey areas often very pale. 5–7, in well-drained places, usually on sandy soils. Larva in bulbs of wild and cultivated onions. S & C.

CLEARWING MOTHS Sesiidae Day-flying, sun-loving moths whose wings lose most of their scales during first flight. Many mimic bees and wasps, often buzzing in flight. Usually rest with wings partly open. Larvae live inside roots and stems, usually for two years: pupa works its way partly out of stem before adult emerges.

▲ **Lunar Hornet Clearwing** *Sphecia bembeciformis*. Wasp-like, with black head and clear yellow collar. 6–7, usually in wooded areas, where larva feeds in willows and poplars. C.

△ **Hornet Clearwing** *Sesia apiformis*. Yellow head and two yellow patches on thorax, but no complete collar. Hornet-like in flight. 5–6. Larvae in roots and lower trunks of poplars, usually just under the bark.

△ **Welsh Clearwing** *Conopia scoliaeformis*. Brick red tuft at tip of abdomen distinguishes this from most other clearwings. Named because first British specimen was found in Wales. 6–8. Larvae in birch trunks. N & C. ▲ **Red-belted Clearwing** *C. myopaeformis*. Belt sometimes orange or yellow. 5–8, mainly in gardens and orchards. Larvae in apple and pear trees, especially old and weak ones. S & C.

▲ **Currant Clearwing** *Synanthedon tipuliformis*. Tips of forewing tinged orange. Male usually has 4 yellow belts on abdomen. Sunbathes on leaves of currant bushes 5–8. Larvae in stems of red and black currant, causing them to wilt and die.

△s **Fiery Clearwing** *Bembecia chrysidiformis*. Extensive red colour on forewing identifies this species. Usually 2 yellow belts: sometimes 3 in male. 5–7. Larvae in roots of docks. S & C.

larva of Ghost Swift

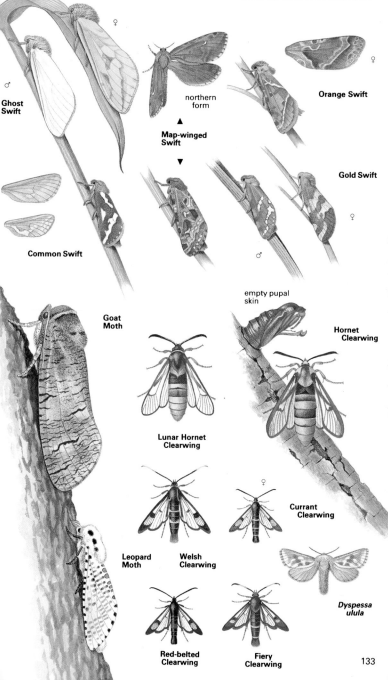

Ghost Swift

♀

♂

northern form

▲

Map-winged Swift

▼

Orange Swift

♀

Gold Swift

♀

Common Swift

♂

Goat Moth

empty pupal skin

Hornet Clearwing

Lunar Hornet Clearwing

Leopard Moth

Welsh Clearwing

Currant Clearwing

♀

Red-belted Clearwing

Fiery Clearwing

Dyspessa ulula

Syntomis phegea Ctenuchidae. Day-flying with weak, drifting flight. 6–7 in flowery habitats, including town gardens: often abundant in sunny valleys in southern Alps. Larva (left) feeds on grasses. S & C. Although burnet-like, this family is not related to the burnets and is closer to tiger moths (p. 152–4).

Syntomis larva

Dysauxes punctata. Spot pattern varies. Day-flying in scrubby places, especially south-facing slopes with scattered trees. Larva feeds on tree-trunk lichens. S & C.

BURNETS and FORESTERS Zygaenidae

Zygaena larva

Day-flying, brightly coloured moths with slow, drifting flight, although wings beat quite rapidly. Generally lethargic and easily picked from flowers. Antennae slightly clubbed in burnets (although frenulum easily distinguishes them from butterflies) and toothed in foresters, especially the males. Larvae are rather plump and usually pale with black spots (left), the species not easy to separate. They generally pupate in a papery cocoon, commonly attached to grass stems. Pupa partly emerges from cocoon before adult escapes.

▲ **6-spot Burnet** *Zygaena filipendulae*. 6 red spots on each forewing, but outer 2 may fuse. Red occasionally replaced by yellow. Abundant in flowery and grassy places 5–8: strongly attracted to knapweed and scabious flowers. Larva feeds on trefoils and other legumes.

▲ **5-spot Burnet** *Z. trifolii* has only a single spot near wing-tip: central spots often touching. Hind wing with thicker border than *filipendulae*. Pupates near ground. S & C.

▲ **Transparent Burnet** *Z. purpuralis* exists in several forms, all with thinly-scaled wings and red stripes reaching nearly to apex of forewing. 6–8 in grassy areas. Larvae feed on various plants.

Z. osterodensis is similar but more thickly scaled and with a broader margin to hind wing. 6–7 in upland meadows. Less sluggish than most other burnets. Larva is golden yellow, feeding on various low-growing plants.

Z. fausta often lacks the red belt. Abundant in rough grassy areas 5–9. Larva feeds on various low-growing plants. S & C.

Z. ephialtes is extremely variable: red is replaced by yellow in *Z. e. coronillae* from Austria and northern Italy. All spots and hind wings may also be red or yellow. 6–9 on scrubby hillsides, mainly in upland regions. Larva feeds on crown vetch and other legumes. S & C.

Z. lavanduli is easily recognised by bluish black hind wings and white collar. 4–6, usually resting head down. Less fond of flowers than most burnets. Larva has red underside and feeds on *Dorycnium*. S.

Z. carniolica is like *fausta* but red spots are more distinct: red usually much deeper than in *fausta*. May have a red belt. 6–8 in scrubby habitats in upland areas. Larva is bluish green with black and yellow dots and feeds on various legumes. S & C.

Rhagodes pruni. Forewings range from green to blue. 6–8 in scrubby places. Larva feeds on heathers and *Prunus* spp. C.

Aglaope infausta. Rather transparent. 6–8 in scrubby places but, unlike its relatives, it has no tongue and rarely visits flowers. Larva feeds on hawthorn, blackthorn, and other rosaceous shrubs. S & C.

▲ **Common Forester** *Adscita statices*. One of several similar species. 5–7 in relatively damp grassland: usually on flowers. Larva is pale green or yellow with a brown stripe on each side and hairy spots on back. It feeds on sorrel.

BAGWORMS Psychidae

A small family named for the larval habit of constructing cases of vegetable fragments held together with silk. The larva carries the case about as it feeds, and then fixes it to a leaf or other object before pupating inside it. Males often fly by day, but females are wingless and remain in their larval cases, where they mate and lay eggs. Neither sex feeds in adult stage.

△ **Sterrhopterix fusca**. Male flies 6–8 in wooded areas, using feathery antennae to detect female in her case. Nocturnal. Larva feeds on various trees. C.

▲ **Psyche casta**. 6–8 in rough grassy places. Males fly soon after daybreak, drifting lazily about in search of females, whose cases are usually fairly well exposed on grass stems. Larvae feed on grasses and lichens.

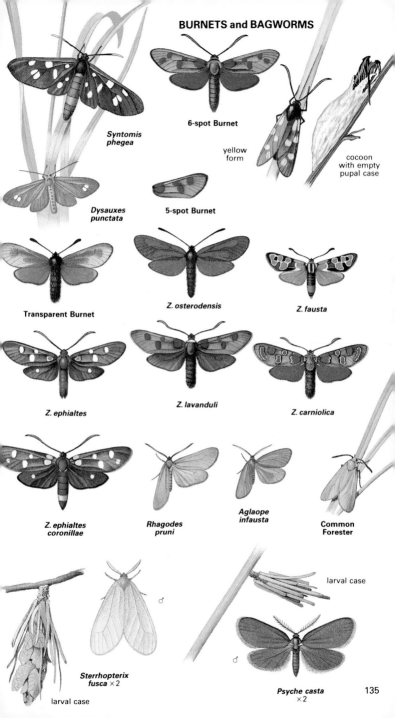

BURNETS and BAGWORMS

Syntomis phegea

6-spot Burnet

yellow form

cocoon with empty pupal case

Dysauxes punctata

5-spot Burnet

Transparent Burnet

Z. osterodensis

Z. fausta

Z. ephialtes

Z. lavanduli

Z. carniolica

Z. ephialtes coronillae

Rhagodes pruni

Aglaope infausta

Common Forester

larval case

Sterrhopterix fusca ×2 ♂

larval case

larval case

Psyche casta ×2 ♂

135

EGGAR MOTHS Lasiocampidae Mostly heavy-bodied moths with sombre colours – usually brown. Females considerably larger than males. No proboscis and no frenulum, the wings being linked merely by a large overlap. The larvae are stout and hairy and usually spin strong silken cocoons on the vegetation. The hairs commonly have irritating properties and the larvae should be handled with care. Several of the species pass the winter as hibernating larvae; most of the others do so in the egg stage.

▲ **Oak Eggar** *Lasiocampa quercus*. Front and hind wings similarly patterned. Male flies rapidly in daytime, but female flies and lays eggs at night. 4–9, mainly on heathland and other open country: sometimes in light woodland. The velvety larva feeds mainly on heather, bramble, and hawthorn.

△s **Grass Eggar** *L. trifolii* generally has uniformly brown hind wings: cross bands may also be missing from forewings. Female usually paler, with less prominent white spot, 5–9 on heathland and coastal dunes: largely nocturnal. Larva like that of *quercus*, but blacker. It feeds on grasses and many other low-growing herbs and shrubs. Coastal in B.

△ **Lappet** *Gastropacha quercifolia*. Varies from deep purple in north to pale brown in south. Female often twice size of male. Rests with wings in unusual position, resembling a bunch of leaves. 5–8 in hedgerows and wooded areas, including orchards. The dark brownish-grey larva has 2 bluish bands near front and feeds on blackthorn, plum, apple, and various other trees: well camouflaged at rest on twigs, especially when hibernating. They are very small at this stage and blend perfectly with the bare, dark twigs.

▲ **Drinker** *Philudoria potatoria*. 6–8 in grassy places, including roadsides, usually where damp. Named for larval habit of drinking from water droplets on leaves. Larva feeds on various tall grasses and pupates in a tough, yellowish sausage-shaped cocoon.

▲ **Fox Moth** *Macrothylacia rubi*. Female much paler and usually greyer. 5–7. Males on the wing day and night: females only at night. Heaths, moors, open woodland, and hedgerows. Larva is velvety black or deep brown, with orange inter-segmental bands. Feeds on bramble, heather, and other low-growing shrubs. Hibernates when fully grown and pupates in spring.

Pine Lappet *Dendrolimus pini*. Very variable: forewing of female may be almost uniformly grey with just the central white spot. Coniferous forests and plantations. 5–8. Larva is greyish brown with 2 blue patches behind head. Feeds on pine and spruce.

▲ **Lackey** *Malacosoma neustria*. Ranges from pale buff to brick red. 6–8 in woods and hedgerows: often common in gardens and orchards. Larva has 2 black spots on face and is remarkably large compared with adult. It lives communally for most of its life in silken tent on hawthorn, blackthorn, and many other trees. It is less hairy than most of its relatives and relies on its warning colours for protection. The species spends the winter as neat batches of eggs on twigs of the foodplant.

▲ **December Moth** *Poecilocampa populi*. Thinly-scaled wings. Flies 9–12, usually at dusk, in woods and hedgerows. In northern regions it may be on the wing as early as August. Larva is pale brown, heavily speckled with black. It feeds on a wide variety of deciduous trees. N & C.

▲ **Small Eggar** *Eriogaster lanestris*. Wings thinly scaled. Female, with much longer wings, has prominent tuft of grey hair at tip of abdomen. 2–4 in lightly wooded areas and hedgerows. Larvae feed communally on hawthorn and blackthorn, forming dense silken tents. The species often spends 2 or 3 years in the pupal state and has been known to take 7 years to emerge. N & C.

E. catax. Female much larger and mostly brown, with narrow yellow band across forewing and a large grey anal tuft. White spot prominent in forewing of both sexes. 9–11 in wooded and scrubby places. Larva is hairy, yellowish brown with velvety black and blue spots. It feeds communally in a silken web on hawthorn and many other trees and shrubs.

Lemonia dumi. Female lighter. 9–10 in open woodland, especially northern and montane coniferous forest. Males fly fast and erratically, like most of the family, and are largely diurnal: females fly at night. Larva, dark brown with yellowish brown hairs, feeds on dandelions and other low-growing herbs. N & C.

▲ **Pale Eggar** *Trichiura crataegi*. Female is often more uniformly grey, but about same size. 7–9 in wooded areas. Larva is dark grey or black, decorated with red and white. It feeds mainly on hawthorn and blackthorn. In southern and central Europe it always overwinters in the egg stage, but in northern areas, including parts of Scotland, it may have a 2-year life-cycle, spending the first winter in the egg stage and the second as a larva.

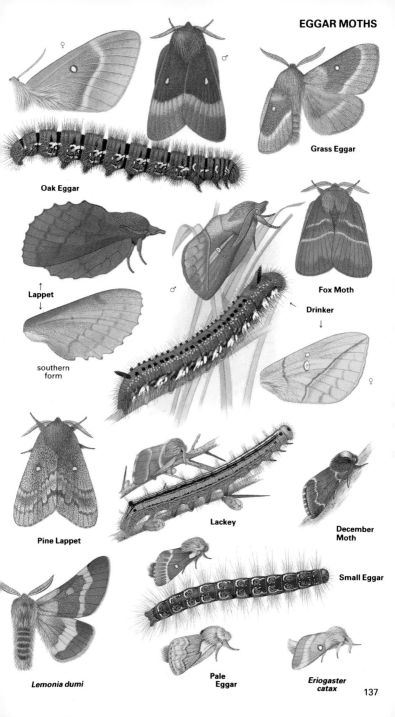

EGGAR MOTHS

Grass Eggar

Oak Eggar

Lappet

southern
form

Fox Moth

Drinker ♀

Pine Lappet

Lackey

December
Moth

Small Eggar

Lemonia dumi

Pale
Eggar

*Eriogaster
catax*

137

Emperor Moth

young larva

older larva

Giant Peacock Moth *Saturnia pyri* Saturniidae. Europe's largest moth, with a wingspan up to 15 cm. 4–6, both sexes flying by night and often mistaken for bats. Lacks proboscis, as do all members of the family. Larva starts off black with red or orange rings, becoming yellowish green with long clubbed spines and rings of blue warts. Feeds on ash, blackthorn, and various other trees. Spins a very fibrous cocoon. S: rarely moving into southern parts of C.

▲ **Emperor Moth** *Saturnia pavonia*. Male flies rapidly by day and can detect female up to 2 km away. She flies and lays her eggs at night, but flight is weak. 4–6, on heathland and other open country. Larva, black and orange to start with, feeds on heather, blackthorn, bramble, and various other plants 5–7.

Tau Emperor *Aglia tau*. Ranges from yellow to very dark brown. Female larger. Eye spots vary in size: underside with eye-spots only on front wings. 3–6, male flying by day and female at night. Rests with wings held vertically like a butterfly. Mainly in woodlands. Larva is pale green, with fine red spines in early stages, and feeds on various trees, especially birch and oak.

Kentish Glory

△n **Kentish Glory** *Endromis versicolora* Endromidae. Flies 3–5, associated with birches of moorland and open woodland. Does not feed. Larva is bright green with pale stripes and a prominent hump at hind end. It feeds on various trees, but especially birch and alder. Widespread, but in B now confined to northern Scotland.

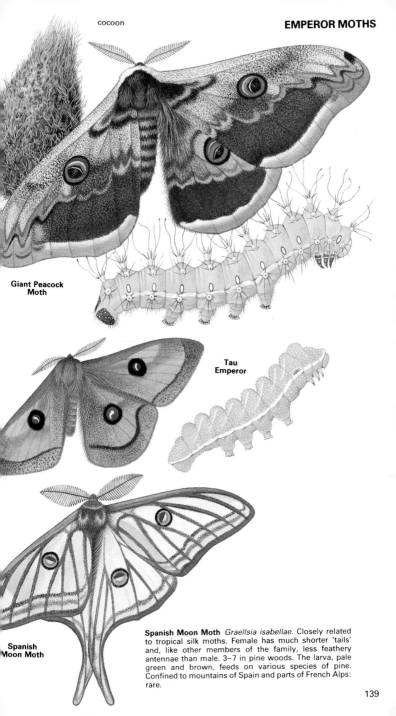

cocoon

Giant Peacock Moth

Tau Emperor

Spanish Moon Moth

Spanish Moon Moth *Graellsia isabellae*. Closely related to tropical silk moths. Female has much shorter 'tails' and, like other members of the family, less feathery antennae than male. 3–7 in pine woods. The larva, pale green and brown, feeds on various species of pine. Confined to mountains of Spain and parts of French Alps: rare.

139

HAWKMOTHS Sphingidae

Stout-bodied and generally fast-flying moths, mostly with narrow, pointed forewings. A few have broader, scalloped wings and fly more slowly. Most have a very long proboscis and feed while hovering at flowers, but some have no proboscis and do not feed. The wings are commonly held flat and swept back like arrow-heads at rest. Many species are strong migrants. The larvae often sport oblique stripes, which camouflage them remarkably well, but species feeding on low-growing plants are often protected by warning colours. There is often a marked colour change before pupation (p. 110). Most species have a curved horn at the hind end.

Lime Hawkmoth *Mimas tiliae*. Ground colour of forewings ranges from greenish, through orange-brown, to buff. Pattern is also variable. One of the slower fliers, it does not feed. The wings are spread rather widely at rest. 5–7. Larva feeds mainly on lime but also on other trees.

Poplar Hawkmoth *Laothoe populi*. Wings range from ash-grey to pinkish brown. The moth flies relatively slowly and does not feed. There is no frenulum, and hind wing projects in front of forewing at rest. Orange spot on hind wing is concealed at rest, but exposed when disturbed as in the Eyed Hawkmoth. 5–9, in 2 broods. Larva, sometimes blue-green, feeds on poplar and sallow.

Pine Hawkmoth *Hyloicus pinastri*. Hind wings dark grey. Especially fond of honeysuckle. Rests on tree trunks by day and is very well camouflaged. 6–8. Larva feeds on pine and spruce. It is green with white stripes at first, when it rests on the needles. Later on it rests on the twigs. Pine and spruce forests throughout Europe.

Eyed Hawkmoth *Smerinthus ocellata*. Flies faster than Poplar Hawkmoth, but rests in the same way with hind wings projecting forwards. The eye-spot on hind wing is exposed when the moth is disturbed, the body heaving up and down at the same time and scaring away inquisitive birds. Does not feed. 5–9, in 2 broods. Larva feeds on sallow and apple, almost always in upside-down position.

Privet Hawkmoth *Sphinx ligustri*. Similar to Convolvulus Hawkmoth (p. 142) but pink banding on hind wings easily distinguishes it: thorax blacker and forewings much browner than in convolvulus. At rest, wings are pulled back and held roofwise over body. 6–7. Larva feeds on privet, lilac, and ash, usually in an upside-down position.

HAWKMOTHS

Lime Hawkmoth

Poplar Hawkmoth

Pine Hawkmoth

Eyed Hawkmoth

Privet Hawkmoth

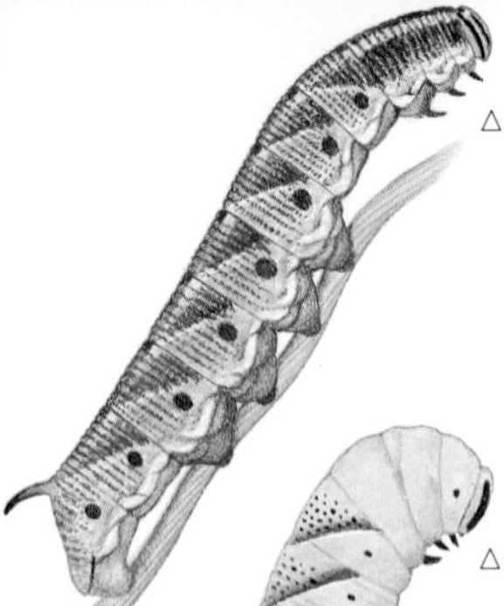

△ **Convolvulus Hawkmoth** *Agrius convolvuli*. Grey thorax and speckled grey wings, with no pink on hind wings, distinguish this from the Privet Hawkmoth (p. 140). It feeds on the wing, with a proboscis much longer than the body (in the pupal stage the proboscis has a special sheath, sticking out from the body like a jug handle). 6–11. Larva feeds on convolvulus leaves. Its ground colour may be apple green or purplish brown. A summer visitor to Europe from Africa, spreading to all parts but rare in N.

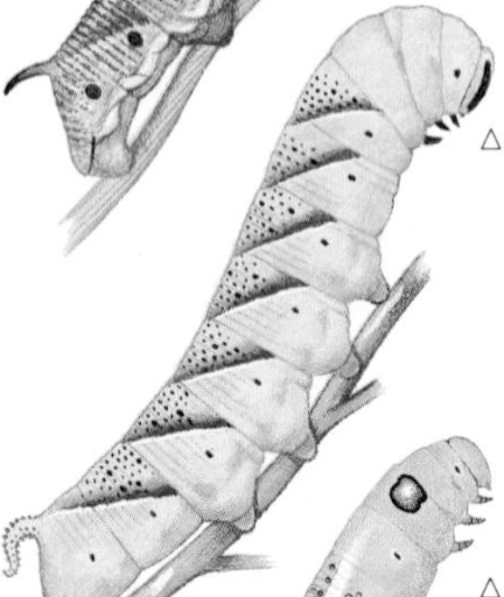

△ **Death's Head Hawkmoth** *Acherontia atropos*. The largest European hawkmoth, named for the skull-like pattern on thorax. The proboscis is short and the moth, which is less streamlined than most other hawkmoths, settles to feed. It will enter beehives to get at the honey. In the normal resting position the wings are pulled back and held roofwise over the body. It squeaks when handled. 5–11. Larva feeds on potato and nightshades. It may be brown, green, or yellow. A summer visitor to Europe from Africa: sporadic in N, but more common in S, where it may survive the winter in the pupal state.

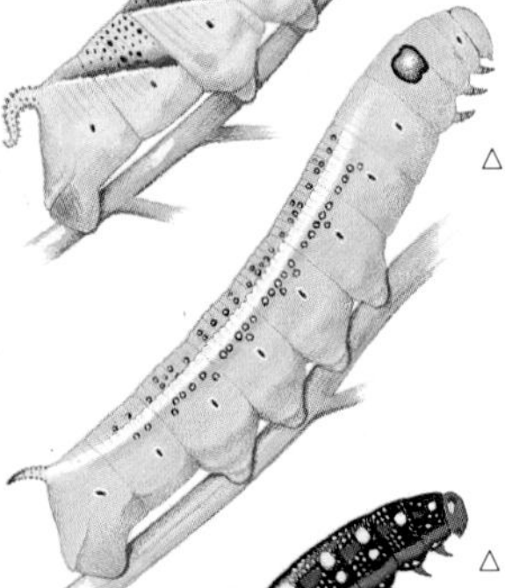

△ **Oleander Hawkmoth** *Daphnis nerii*. This unmistakable moth flies 6–10. Larva feeds on oleander and periwinkle, but rarely found north of the Alps. Essentially a tropical and sub-tropical species, visiting Europe each year from Africa but not surviving the winter. Not uncommon in S. but only an occasional vagrant elsewhere.

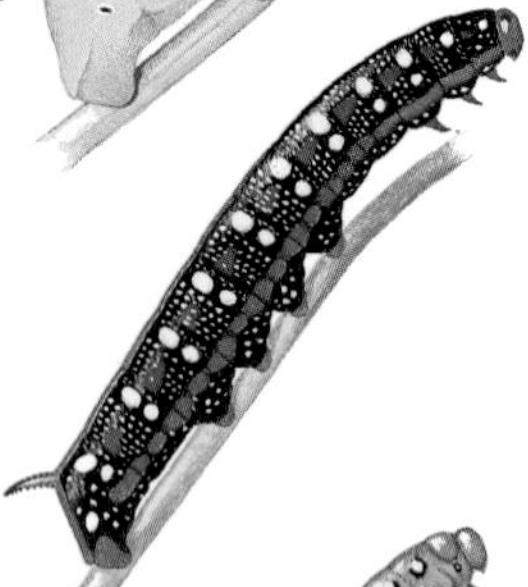

△ **Spurge Hawkmoth** *Hyles euphorbiae*. Forewings are essentially greenish brown and buff, often with a clear pink tinge when freshly emerged. It is similar to the Bedstraw Hawkmoth, but hind wings are usually much pinker and there is no continuous brown band along front margin of forewing. 5–9, in 2 broods. The striking larva feeds on various spurges, especially the larger species. Common in S & C (southern): a rare summer visitor to N and B.

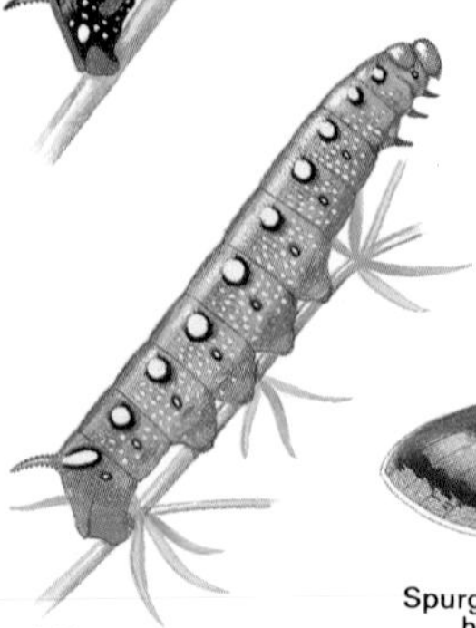

△ **Bedstraw Hawkmoth** *Hyles gallii*. Resembles the Spurge Hawkmoth in looks and habits, but can be distinguished by the continuous brown band along front margin of forewing. The hind wing also has a less extensive pink flush. 5–9, in 2 broods. Larva is greenish, brown, or black and feeds on bedstraws and willowherbs. Resident in most of S & C: summer visitor to N and B.

Spurge Hawkmoth
hind wing

Bedstraw Hawkmoth
hind wing

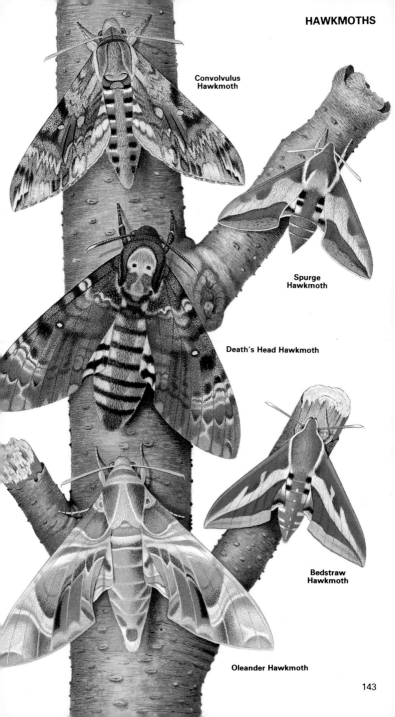

HAWKMOTHS

Convolvulus Hawkmoth

Spurge Hawkmoth

Death's Head Hawkmoth

Bedstraw Hawkmoth

Oleander Hawkmoth

143

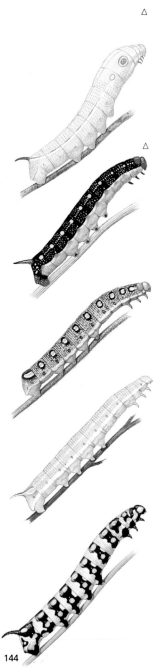

△ **Silver-striped Hawkmoth** *Hippotion celerio*. A very slim hawkmoth with prominent black veins on hind wing. The wings are swept strongly backwards at rest. 4–10, in 2 broods. Larva feeds on vines and bedstraws. When alarmed, the head and thorax can be pulled back into the front of the abdomen, which swells up as in the Elephant Hawkmoth (p. 146), so that the eye-spots present a threatening appearance to any would-be predator. The larva becomes much darker just before pupation. A great migrant, it is a summer visitor to Europe from Africa. It occurs regularly, often in considerable numbers, in S, but is sporadic further north – usually only in autumn.

△ **Striped Hawkmoth** *Hyles lineata livornica*. This is the European race of an almost cosmopolitan species which occurs nearly everywhere outside the tropical and polar regions. It resembles the Spurge Hawkmoth (p. 142) but is clearly distinguished by the white veins on the forewings. Often flies by day as well as by night. 4–9, in 2 broods. Larva varies from green to black, with yellow spots and lines. It feeds on a wide variety of plants, but especially bedstraws and vines. Resident in Mediterranean region, this is a great migrant, reaching far into the north each summer, often in great numbers: an irregular visitor to B.

Hyles vespertilio. Flies mainly in hilly regions. Mainly 6–7, but may be earlier in warm valleys and there may then be a second brood 8–9. Larva is green at first but becomes greyish brown as it grows. Spots may be red or yellowish. There is no horn. It feeds on willowherbs, especially the slender-leaved *Epilobium rosmarinifolium*. Local in S & C, from France eastwards.

Hyles hippophaes. Resembles Bedstraw Hawkmoth (p. 142) but forewing is much greyer. In addition, hind wing has a much deeper and more extensive red patch. 6–7. Larva feeds on sea buckthorn, often sunbathing on upper twigs. Local, from Spain and southern France through the Alps to Switzerland and southern Germany.

Hyles nicacea. Resembles Spurge Hawkmoth (p. 142) but it is larger and has no white on the hind wing. 6–7. The unmistakable larva feeds mainly on spurges. Confined to Mediterranean area, and, unlike many other *Hyles* species, it does not make extensive migrations.

Silver-striped Hawkmoth

Hyles vespertilio

Striped Hawkmoth

Hyles hippophaes

Hyles nicacea

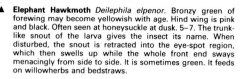

▲ **Elephant Hawkmoth** *Deilephila elpenor*. Bronzy green of forewing may become yellowish with age. Hind wing is pink and black. Often seen at honeysuckle at dusk. 5–7. The trunk-like snout of the larva gives the insect its name. When disturbed, the snout is retracted into the eye-spot region, which then swells up while the whole front end sways menacingly from side to side. It is sometimes green. It feeds on willowherbs and bedstraws.

▲ **Small Elephant Hawkmoth** *Deilephila porcellus*. Smaller and much yellower than its larger relative: hind wing yellow with a pink margin. It feeds at dusk, especially at honeysuckle and rhododendrons. 5–7. Larva is green or brown, with no horn. It feeds mainly on bedstraws and behaves like the previous species.

△s **Broad-bordered Bee Hawkmoth** *Hemaris fuciformis*. Day-flying. Resembles bumble bee at rest, but flight much faster and more darting than bumble bee. Wings are lightly covered with scales at first, but these fall on first flight, leaving just the brown margins. Feeds in flight, especially at bugle flowers. 5–6. Larva feeds on bedstraws and honeysuckle. Woodland clearings and margins.

△ **Narrow-bordered Bee Hawkmoth** *Hemaris tityus*. Resembles previous species but has narrower brown margins. Day-flying. 5–6. Larva feeds on devil's-bit scabious and field scabious. Woodland clearings and margins, moors, and damp heaths and meadows.

Oak Hawkmoth *Marumba quercus*. Less streamlined than most other hawkmoths and relatively slow-flying. Hind wings largely orange-brown. 5–7. Larva feeds on various oaks, especially cork oak. Confined largely to the cork oak forests of the Mediterranean region.

Proserpinus proserpina. Ground colour of forewings usually green, but may be brown or grey, always with a darker central band. Hind wings yellow with a brown margin. Size also varies, and often much smaller than illustrated. 6–8, often flying by day. Larva feeds on willowherbs and purple loose-strife. It is dull green at first and has a small horn at this stage. S & C (southern).

▲ **Hummingbird Hawkmoth** *Macroglossum stellatarum*. Day-flying and most often seen hovering in front of flowers to feed. Also 'sunbathes' by hovering in front of sunny walls. It makes an audible hum while hovering. Common in gardens. All year, especially in S, in two or more broods. Larva is green or brown and feeds on bedstraws. Resident in S, it is a strong migrant and reaches all parts of Europe in spring and summer. Hibernates as an adult, but rarely survives the winter north of the Alps.

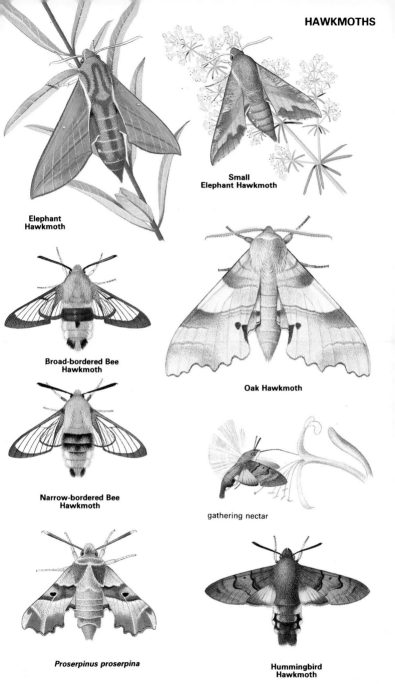

**Small
Elephant Hawkmoth**

**Elephant
Hawkmoth**

**Broad-bordered Bee
Hawkmoth**

Oak Hawkmoth

**Narrow-bordered Bee
Hawkmoth**

gathering nectar

Proserpinus proserpina

**Hummingbird
Hawkmoth**

147

Family Notodontidae Rather stout and often hairy moths with sombre colour-ing. Resemble noctuids (p. 156–68) in many ways, but vein M_2 is not close to M_3 at base. Many are called prominents because hind edge of forewing has a tuft of hair which sticks up in the mid-line at rest. Larvae often rest with front and hind ends raised: usually with little or no hair, but often with fleshy growths on the back.

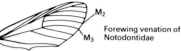

Forewing venation of Notodontidae

▲ **Puss Moth** *Cerura vinula*. Female slightly darker and more strongly marked. 4–7 in lightly wooded areas. Larva, green with a brownish saddle, is well camouflaged on the leaves. It rears head if disturbed and waves highly modified, whip-like hind legs. Feeds on willows and poplars.

△ **Poplar Kitten** *Furcula bifida*. Inner margin of dark band straight and edged with black: outer margin well defined and smoothly curved. 5–7, in lightly wooded areas, including town parks and gardens. Larva like small puss moth larva: on poplar.

▲ **Sallow Kitten** *F. furcula* has yellow edge to forewing band, with outer margin distinctly toothed. Hind wing pale grey in both species. 5–8. Larva like that of *bifida*, but saddle is paler: on sallow.

△ **Alder Kitten** *F. bicuspis* has darker central band than previous 2 species, with both edges concave. 5–7. Larva like that of *furcula*: on alder and birch. N & C.

△ **Lobster Moth** *Stauropus fagi*. Wings sometimes much darker. 4–7 in woodland, especially beechwoods. Pinkish brown larva gives the species its name: it has very long front legs and an upturned tail ending with long, slender claspers. Feeds mainly on beech.

▲ **Buff-tip** *Phalera bucephala*. Named for the buff wing-tips which, with buff thoracic hairs, give it a twig-like appearance at rest. 5–8 in a wide variety of places with trees and shrubs. Larva feeds on many deciduous trees: gregarious when young.

△ **Chocolate-tip** *Clostera curtula*. Clear chocolate on wing-tip does not cross outer white line. 4–10, in 2 or 3 broods. Wooded areas. Larva is hairy: greyish blue, with a broad yellow stripe on the back and orange spots on the sides. Feeds on poplar.

▲ **Small Chocolate-tip** *C. pigra* is smaller, with indistinct chocolate tips. 4–10, with 2 broods in south. Fens and damp woodland. Larva is hairy: largely grey and yellow, speckled with black. Feeds on sallow. N & C.

▲ **Iron Prominent** *Notodonta dromedarius*. Named for rust-coloured patches on fore-wing. 4–9 in lightly wooded areas with birch and alder. Larva is green to brown with 5 slender humps on back. Feeds mainly on birch and alder. N & C.

▲ **Lesser Swallow Prominent** *Pheosia gnoma*. A distinct white wedge near hind margin of forewing. 5–9 in wooded areas. Larva is smooth and slender, purplish brown on top with yellow sides: a hump at hind end. Feeds on birch.

▲ **Swallow Prominent** *P. tremula* is larger and lacks white wedge on forewing. Larva is green with a yellow stripe on each side. Feeds on poplar.

△s **Maple Prominent** *Ptilodontella cucullina*. 5–7, especially in hedgerows and wood-land margins. Larva is glossy green with a pale line on each side and a purple hump at hind end. Feeds on field maple. C: mainly on chalk in B.

▲ **Great Prominent** *Peridea anceps*. Forewing brown to black. Hind wing almost white. 4–7 in open woodland. Larva, pale green with pink and yellow diagonal stripes, feeds on oak.

▲ **Pebble Prominent** *Eligmodonta ziczac*. Named for the pebble-like blotch on wing-tip. 5–10, in 2 or 3 broods. Hedgerows and other wooded areas. Larva is greyish with a brown hind end: sometimes tinged pink or yellow. 2 humps near middle and a third at hind end. Feeds on willows and poplars.

▲ **Coxcomb Prominent** *Ptilodon capucina*. Thorax normally has distinct pale crown of hairs. Wings range from pale to very dark brown. 5–9 in 2 broods. Hedgerows and other wooded areas. Larva usually green with a yellow stripe on each side and a pair of red-tipped humps at hind end. Feeds on a wide variety of deciduous trees.

▲ **Pale Prominent** *Pterostoma palpina*. Long palps project in front of head: very twig-like at rest. 5–8 in wooded areas. Larva is bluish green above, darker green below, with a yellow stripe on each side. Feeds on poplar and sallow.

▲ **Figure of Eight** *Diloba caeruleocephala*. Forewing bears clear figure 8. Hedgerows, woodland edges, and gardens, 9–10. Larva is bluish grey with black spots and yellow lines. Feeds on blackthorn, hawthorn, and other rosaceous trees.

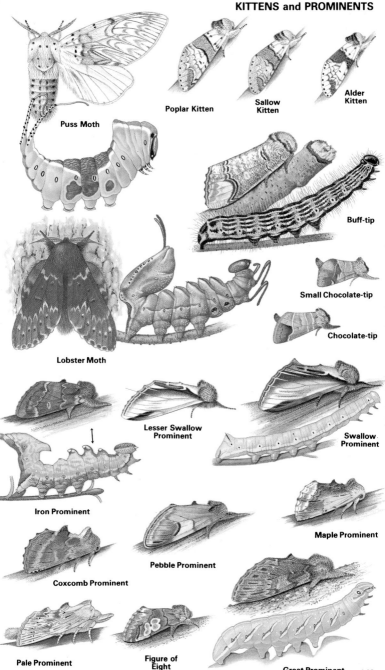

Poplar Kitten

Sallow Kitten

Alder Kitten

Puss Moth

Buff-tip

Small Chocolate-tip

Chocolate-tip

Lobster Moth

Lesser Swallow Prominent

Swallow Prominent

Iron Prominent

Maple Prominent

Pebble Prominent

Coxcomb Prominent

Pale Prominent

Figure of Eight

Great Prominent

149

pine woods infested
by Pine Processionary

Pine Processionary *Thaumetopoea pityocampa* Thaumetopoeidae. Hind wings white. In pine woods 5–7. Larvae are dark with tufts of brown hair and live communally in large silken tents among pine twigs from autumn to spring. They march out to feed on the needles in single file – hence the common name. Feeding expeditions usually take place at night, but when the caterpillars are fully fed in late spring they march out by day to find suitable pupation sites. They may cluster on the ground for a while, as if deciding whether the conditions are right, and then they disperse to pupate singly in silken cocoons on or just under the soil. The larval hairs have extremely irritating properties and the caterpillars should not be handled. S & C (southern), where it is sometimes so common that each tree bears several tents (above). The insect is a serious forest pest.

Oak Processionary *T. processionea* has rather 'dirty' hind wings. 8–9 in oak woods. Larvae in silken tents on oak trunks in spring and early summer. They march in a broader procession when going out to feed on the leaves at night. They pupate communally inside the larval tent.

⌂ **Pale Tussock** *Calliteara pudibunda* Lymantriidae. A very hairy moth flying 4–7 in wooded areas. Adults do not feed – a feature shared by the whole family. Larva feeds on many deciduous trees. N & C.

▲ **Dark Tussock** *Dicallomera fascelina* is slightly smaller, with orange or yellow in forewing lines.

▲ **Vapourer** *Orgyia antiqua*. Male flies by day. Female wingless, mating and laying eggs on her cocoon. 6–10, wherever there are trees and shrubs: often common in towns. Larva, easily identified by horn-like tufts of hair, feeds on a wide range of deciduous trees and shrubs.

⌂ **Brown-tail** *Euproctis chrysorrhoea*. Wings usually pure white in both sexes. Abdomen largely brown above in male: greyish brown in female. Both sexes with tuft of brown hair at tip of abdomen: much larger in female, who uses hairs to cover eggs. It has been shown that, as well as simply concealing the eggs, the hairy covering gives them active protection. The larvae in this family are clothed with irritating hairs and these are incorporated in the silken cocoons when the insects pupate. On emerging from the cocoon the new adult female collects some of these hairs with her abdominal brush and then uses them to protect her eggs. 7–8 in woods and hedgerows. Larvae live communally on blackthorn, hawthorn, and various other trees: sometimes an orchard pest. S & C.

▲ **Yellow-tail** *E. similis* has tuft of yellow or golden hair on abdomen. Male usually smaller and often with small black spot on hind edge of forewing. Wooded areas, especially hedgerows, 6–8. Larva feeds on hawthorn and many other deciduous trees and shrubs.

Gypsy Moth *Lymantria dispar*. Sexes differ greatly. Female flightless, covering eggs with yellow hairs from tuft at tip of abdomen. Male flies by day. 7–9. Larva feeds on many deciduous trees: a serious forest and orchard pest. Most of Europe, but extinct in B, where it was reasonably common in the East Anglian fens until the middle of the nineteenth century. Occasional males occur in the southern counties, having flown across the Channel.

⌂ **Black Arches** *L. monacha*. Female larger and rather sedentary. 7–9 in deciduous and coniferous woods. Larva is grey and hairy with black spots and lines on the back. Feeds mainly on oak, but also on birch and various conifers.

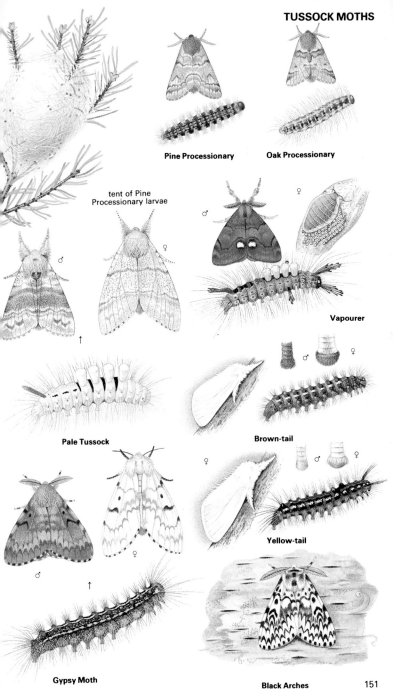

Pine Processionary

Oak Processionary

tent of Pine
Processionary larvae

♂   ♀

Vapourer

↑

Pale Tussock

♂   ♀

Brown-tail

♀

Gypsy Moth

♀

♂   ♀

Yellow-tail

♂

↑

Black Arches

151

TIGER and ERMINE MOTHS Arctiidae Stoutly built, brightly coloured moths, usually hairy and often poisonous. The bold colours, especially on hind wings, warn birds of the unpalatability of these moths, although forewings often have cryptic patterns. The larvae are very hairy – many are known as woolly bears – and usually feed on docks, dandelions, and other low-growing plants. The family also contains the slender-bodied footmen (p. 154).

▲ **Garden Tiger** *Arctia caja*. Pattern very variable on all wings: forewing occasionally all brown and hind wing sometimes yellow instead of orange. 6–8 in almost any habitat.

▲ **Cream-spot Tiger** *A. villica* has cream or white spots on forewing, sometimes running together and occasionally much reduced. 5–7 in scrubby and grassy places. Larva like that of *caja* but has chestnut head and shorter hair. S & C.

△s **Jersey Tiger** *Euplagia quadripunctaria*. 6–9 in open woodland and scrubby places – usually fairly dry. Flies in sunshine and also at night. Roosts in vegetation in dull weather, sometimes in vast numbers, as in the 'Valley of the Butterflies' on the island of Rhodes. Larva is black with a broad yellow stripe on the back and pale spots on the sides. S & C: confined to Devon in B, but common in Channel Isles.

△s **Scarlet Tiger** *Callimorpha dominula*. Markings variable: occasionally yellow replaces the red. Flies in sunshine 6–8. Fens, river banks, and damp woodland. Larva is dark grey with broken yellow lines and grey and black hair. Feeds on bramble, sallow, and other shrubs as well as on herbaceous plants.

▲ **Wood Tiger** *Parasemia plantaginis*. Pattern and colour variable: hind wing sometimes with red spots but may be completely brown, especially in mountains. Pale marks on forewing may also be reduced. Sides of abdomen yellow in male. Heaths, moors, and grassy places, including woodland clearings. 6–8, flying by day and night. Larva is black, clothed with short tufts of black and chestnut hair. N & C.

Pericallia matronula. Spots vary in size: those of hind wing may be separate or joined into a band. 5–6 in many habitats, often flying by day. Larva is dark brown or black with long brown hairs: polyphagous, taking 2 years to mature. Widely distributed in eastern Europe, reaching eastern France.

Ammobiota festiva. Pattern very variable: dark areas in male usually broken into narrower bands and hind wings paler pink. In northern parts of range the colours are much less vivid, often virtually pink and grey. 5–6, often flying by day in dry grassy and scrubby habitats. Larva, very like that of Garden Tiger, is polyphagous on low-growing plants. S & C.

▲ **Ruby Tiger** *Phragmatobia fuliginosa*. Forewings reddish brown to dark brown, rather thinly scaled in centre. Hind wings largely grey in north: elsewhere largely pink. 5–9, with 2 broods in many areas. All kinds of habitats, but most abundant in damp grassland. Larva is dark brown and densely hairy.

P. maculosa has a variable spot pattern: most strongly marked specimens, as illustrated, are found in southern Germany. Hind wing darker red in female. 6–8 in rough and grassy places. Larva, velvety black with short brown hair, feeds on bedstraws. S & C.

Fall Web-worm *Hyphantria cunea*. Sometimes pure white, sometimes black-spotted. 7–8. Larva is yellowish green with black and orange warts and white hairs. It lives communally in a large silken tent on various deciduous trees in autumn: often a pest of fruit trees. An American species now established in Germany and some other parts of Europe.

Cymbalophora pudica. Forewing ground colour ranges from white to deep pink. 8–10 in scrubby and grassy places. Larva is greyish brown with short hairs and feeds on various grasses. S: often abundant on Mediterranean coast.

▲ **White Ermine** *Spilosoma lubricipeda*. Black spots vary in size: occasionally absent. Abdomen yellow. 5–8 in a wide variety of habitats, including gardens. Larva is dark brown and very hairy, with dark red line along the back. Feeds on a wide range of low-growing plants.

▲ **Buff Ermine** *S. lutea* has variable pattern. Habits like those of White Ermine but larva is paler brown.

▲ **Muslin** *Diaphora mendica*. Sexes markedly different: female thinly scaled, with variable amount of black spotting and a white abdomen. 5–6 in hedgerows and open woodland. Male nocturnal but female largely diurnal. Larva like that of Buff Ermine, feeding on low-growing vegetation. N & C.

TIGERS and ERMINES

← Garden Tiger →

Cream-spot Tiger

Jersey Tiger

Scarlet Tiger

Wood Tiger ♂ ♀

Pericallia matronula

Ammobiota festiva ♀

Ruby Tiger

Phragmatobia maculosa

Fall Web-worm

Buff Ermine

Cymbalophora pudica

White Ermine

Muslin ♂ ♀

153

Rhyparia purpurata. Spots vary in number and size and may run together, especially on hind wing. 6–7 in sandy areas, sometimes flying by day. Larva is dark grey with velvety black rings and grey and rust-coloured hairs. It feeds on a wide range of herbs and shrubs, especially *Genista* spp. Much of Europe but not far west.

▲ **Clouded Buff** *Diacrisia sannio*. Sexes markedly different: amount of grey on male hind wing very variable. 6–8 on heaths, moors, and grassland. Male flies by day: female largely nocturnal. Larva is brown with a pale stripe along the back and clothed with brown hair. It feeds on a wide range of herbs and low-growing shrubs.

▲ **Cinnabar** *Tyria jacobaeae*. 5–8 in open habitats, especially on sandy soils. Largely nocturnal, but often seen fluttering weakly by day. Larva feeds on ragwort. Widespread, but mainly coastal in north.

△ **Crimson Speckled** *Utetheisa pulchella*. Day-flying, 4–10, with 2 or 3 broods in south. Open and scrubby habitats. Hairy larva is greyish with white lines and black warts, and an orange band on each segment. It feeds mainly on forget-me-nots and borage. Resident in S, migrating to C each spring: sporadic visitor to B.

Feathered Footman *Spiris striata*. Female lacks thick black veins on forewing and does not have feathered antennae. Day-flying, 5–7 on heaths and grassland. Rests with wings wrapped round body. Larva is black with an orange stripe along the back and yellowish spots. It feeds on various low-growing plants. Widespread but most common in S.

Setina aurita. Lines on forewing often replaced by rows of dots, especially at lower altitudes. Abdomen all black, all yellow, or a mixture. 6–9. Larva is dark brown with yellow spots and feeds on lichens. Alps and neighbouring mountains.

▲ **Common Footman** *Eilema lurideola*. Pale streak at front of forewing tapers strongly and does not reach apex. 6–8 in hedgerows, woods, and orchards. Rests with wings almost flat – very slightly rolled round body. Larva is hairy, grey with black lines on the back and an orange line on each side. Like most true footmen larvae, it eats lichens on trees and shrubs.

▲ **Scarce Footman** *E. complana* has pale streak of constant width from shoulder to wing-tip. Front edge of wing almost straight. 6–8 on heaths and moors and in damp woods. Rests with wings rolled tightly round body. Larva is greyish with a black line on the back and white spots on the sides.

▲ **Dingy Footman** *E. griseola* has uniform pale streak but front edge of wing strongly curved. Abdomen and hind wings dirty yellow. 6–8 in fens and damp woods. Rests with wings virtually flat. Larva is velvety black with a purplish stripe along the back and variable orange spots on each side. C.

△s **4-spotted Footman** *Lithosia quadra*. Sexes markedly different: female often much larger. 7–9, flying by day and by night. Mainly in old woodlands. Larva is black with red and grey spots and a broad yellow stripe along the back. It eats lichens.

▲ **4-dotted Footman** *Cybosia mesomella*. Forewing sometimes much yellower. 6–7 on heaths and moors and in open woods. Larva is velvety black with tufts of black or dark brown hair. It feeds on lichens.

△s **Red-necked Footman** *Atolmis rubricollis*. 5–8, mainly in woodland. Larva is hairy: greyish with paler markings and red spots. It eats lichens. N & C.

▲ **Rosy Footman** *Miltochrista miniata*. Female is smaller. 6–8 in damp wooded areas, including hedgerows. Larva is dark grey and very furry. It eats lichens. N & C.

△ **Dew Moth** *Setina irrorella*. Wings thinly scaled. Female smaller and darker. 6–8, male often active by day. Mainly in coastal and montane habitats: also chalk and limestone hills with bare rock. The hairy larva is dark brown with yellow and white lines. It eats lichens on rocks.

▲ **Short-cloaked Moth** *Nola cucullata* Nolidae. Dark patch at base of forewings resembles a short cloak at rest. 6–7 in wooded and scrubby habitats. Larva is reddish brown with grey hair and white spots. It feeds on blackthorn, hawthorn, and other rosaceous trees and shrubs. Absent from far north.

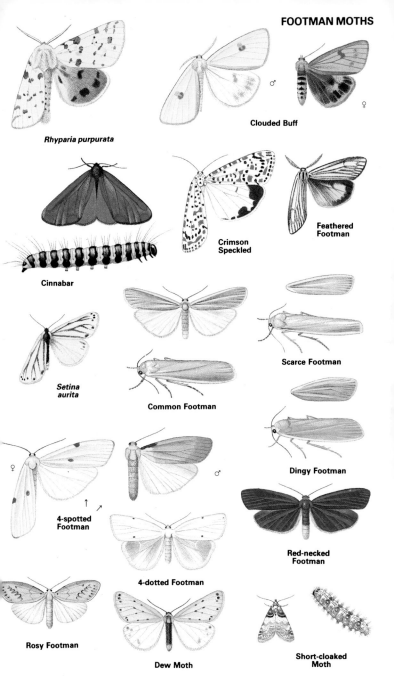

FOOTMAN MOTHS

Rhyparia purpurata

Clouded Buff ♂ ♀

Cinnabar

Crimson Speckled

Feathered Footman

Setina aurita

Common Footman

Scarce Footman

Dingy Footman

♀ 4-spotted Footman ♂

4-dotted Footman

Red-necked Footman

Rosy Footman

Dew Moth

Short-cloaked Moth

Family Noctuidae A very large family with over 25,000 known species of stoutly-built moths. Forewings generally sombre and cryptically coloured, although hind wings may be brightly coloured. Sexes usually alike, but males often have tufts of hair at tip of abdomen. Vein M_2 of forewing is close to M_3 at base, thus distinguishing the family from the Notodontidae (p. 148). Forewing usually with 3 prominent spots or stigmata – the orbicular near the middle, the kidney-shaped reniform outside it, and the elongate claviform below it. At rest, wings may be held roof-wise or flat and overlapping. Larvae are usually plump, with little hair.

Forewing venation
of Noctuidae

▲ **Garden Dart** *Euxoa nigricans*. Forewing pale to very dark brown: claviform stigma usually indistinct. 6–8 on cultivated land and grassland: mainly lowlands. Larva is pale brown or green with a double white stripe low on each side. It feeds on a wide variety of low-growing plants.

△ **Archer's Dart** *Agrotis vestigialis*. Ground colour grey to rich brown. Well-marked claviform stigma (dart) and dark wedges near outer edge of forewing. 6–9, mainly on sandy coasts and heaths. Larva is grey and eats a variety of low-growing plants.

▲ **Turnip Moth** *A. segetum* is distinguished from most other noctuids by pearly hind wings – white in male, grey in female. Forewings pale grey to black. 5–10 in cultivated areas and waste land. Glossy larva, grey and tinged with purple, feeds mainly underground and damages crop roots.

▲ **Shuttle-shaped Dart** *A. puta* has dart-shaped orbicular stigma. Female darker, with pale border to orbicular stigma. Hind wing white in male, grey in female. 5–10 in most habitats. Mottled brown larva eats many kinds of herbaceous plants. S & C.

▲ **Heart and Dart** *A. exclamationis* is named for prominent reniform and solid black claviform stigmata. Forewings pale to dark brown. Open habitats, especially cultivated land. 5–9. Larva is brown above and grey below and feeds on numerous herbaceous plants.

▲ **Flame Shoulder** *Ochropleura plecta*. Readily identified by the pale streak on front edge of forewing. Hind wings shiny white. 5–9, almost everywhere. Larva, yellowish grey with a yellow stripe on each side, feeds on a wide range of herbaceous plants.

▲ **Flame** *Axylia putris*. Pale areas of forewing sometimes tinged with red. Wraps wings round body at rest and resembles broken twig. 5–7 in hedgerows, woodland margins, and cultivated land. Larva is mottled greyish brown with black markings and a hump at hind end. It eats numerous herbaceous plants.

▲ **True Lover's Knot** *Lycophotia porphyrea*. Ground colour of forewing brick-coloured to purplish brown. Hind wings grey. 6–8, mainly on heaths and moors. Larva, reddish brown with paler lines, feeds on heathers.

▲ **Large Yellow Underwing** *Noctua pronuba*. Forewings pale grey to rich chestnut, the palest specimens being females and the darkest ones males. Always a jet black spot near wing-tip. Flight is fast and erratic as in all yellow underwings, flashing the yellow hind wings and then dropping rapidly to ground to confuse predators (see p. 44). Rests with wings folded flat over body. 6–10, almost everywhere. Larva is brown or green with rows of tapering black dashes on back. It feeds on almost any herbaceous plant. △ **Lunar Yellow Underwing** *N. orbona* is like a small *pronuba*, but with a black spot in hind wing. 6–9, mainly in open country. Larva feeds mainly on grasses.

▲ **Broad-bordered Yellow Underwing** *N. fimbriata*. Forewings greyish brown to chestnut: females lighter than males and often tinged with green. 6–9 in wooded areas. Larva, brown with black round spiracles, feeds on various deciduous trees.

▲ **Lesser Broad-bordered Yellow Underwing** *N. janthina* has no black spot in hind wing. 7–9 in hedgerows and other wooded areas. Larva brownish with dark V-shaped marks, feeds on various herbs and shrubs. Absent from far north. ▲ **Least Yellow Underwing** *N. interjecta* has greyish brown to chestnut forewings with little marking. Hind wing with black spot underneath. 6–8 in open and scrubby country. Larva feeds mainly on grasses. ▲ **Lesser Yellow Underwing** *N. comes* has black spot in hind wing. Forewings range from grey to chestnut and very dark brown. 7–9 nearly everywhere. Larva, like that of *pronuba*, feeds on various trees and shrubs.

▲ **Beautiful Yellow Underwing** *Anarta myrtilli*. Forewings greyish brown to purplish. Day-flying, 4–8, mainly on heaths and moors. Larva is green, marked with yellow and white, and is very difficult to see on heathers where it feeds. △n **Small Dark Yellow Underwing** *A. cordigera* is similar but forewings are blacker, never with reddish tinge: abdomen without pale bands. 5–6, mainly on moorland. Larva is reddish brown with white lines. Feeds on bearberry. N & C and southern mountains.

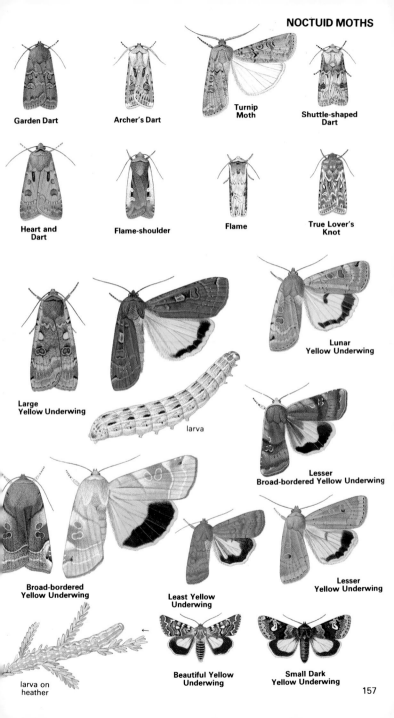

Garden Dart

Archer's Dart

Turnip Moth

Shuttle-shaped Dart

Heart and Dart

Flame-shoulder

Flame

True Lover's Knot

Large Yellow Underwing

larva

Lunar Yellow Underwing

Lesser Broad-bordered Yellow Underwing

Broad-bordered Yellow Underwing

Least Yellow Underwing

Lesser Yellow Underwing

larva on heather

Beautiful Yellow Underwing

Small Dark Yellow Underwing

▲ **Setaceous Hebrew Character** *Xestia c-nigrum*. Ground colour pale grey to purplish chestnut, with characteristic light and dark marking near front of forewing. Wings flat at rest. 5–10, but mainly autumnal: mainly lowland. Polyphagous larva is pale brown or green, heavily speckled with black.

▲ **Double Square-spot** *X. triangulum* has dark mark round orbicular stigma forming 2 almost square spots. Wings flat at rest. 5–7 in wooded areas. Larva is brown with black marks: polyphagous.

▲ **Ingrailed Clay** *Diarsia mendica*. Forewings vary from straw-coloured, through chestnut to dark brown: usually dark in north. Wings flat at rest. 5–7 in woods and moors. Polyphagous larva is brown with black triangles on sides.

▲ **Green Arches** *Anaplectoides prasina*. Black markings variable: green fades after death. Hind wings dark grey or brown with white fringe. 5–7 in deciduous woods. Larva, brown with darker markings, feeds on various herbs and shrubs.

△n **Great Brocade** *Eurois occulta*. Ground colour pale grey to black: white-edged orbicular and reniform stigmata always prominent. 6–8: moors and open woodland. Larva, purplish brown and yellow with white lines, feeds on bog myrtle. N & C.

▲ **Gothic** *Naenia typica*. Hind wings entirely grey. 5–8 in most lowland habitats. Larva is greyish brown with a dark line on each side and a few black dashes at the rear. Polyphagous. △s **Bordered Gothic** *Heliophobus reticulata* is similar but hind wings are white with darker edges.

▲ **Cabbage Moth** *Mamestra brassicae*. Forewing sometimes tinged reddish brown. Hind wings silvery grey with darker margins. All year, but mainly 5–8: very common on cultivated land. Polyphagous larva is green or dull brown with darker spots.

▲ **Broom Moth** *Ceramica pisi*. Ground colour greyish brown to purplish. 5–7. Polyphagous larva is green to dark brown with bold yellow stripes.

▲ **Broad-barred White** *Hecatera bicolorata*. Ground colour white to bluish grey. 5–9. Larva is green or brown with dark diamonds on back. It feeds on flowers and buds of hawkweeds and other yellow-flowered composites.

Dot Moth *Melanchra persicariae*. 5–9, usually in cultivated areas. Larva is green, brown, or purplish, with a distinct hump at rear. Polyphagous.

▲ **Bright-line Brown-eye** *Lacanobia oleracea*. 5–9, especially common in gardens and other cultivated areas. Larva, green or brown with a black and yellow stripe on each side, is polyphagous, but prefers goosefoots and similar weeds.

△ **Tawny Shears** *Hadena perplexa*. Ground colour off-white to dark brown. Claviform stigma broad: usually edged with black. 5–9. Larva is glossy pale brown, feeding on white campion.

△ **Varied Coronet** *H. compta* flies 5–9 in gardens and open country. Larva is dull yellowish brown and feeds in seed heads of pinks and campions. A recent arrival in B (mostly south-east).

▲ **Hedge Rustic** *Tholera cespitis*. Hind wing white (with grey margin in female). 7–9 in grassy places. Larva, green at first and then greyish brown, feeds on various tough grasses.

▲ **Feathered Gothic** *T. decimalis* has feathery antennae only in male. Wings more slender than Gothic: forewings strongly veined in white. Hind wings white with grey border in male: grey in female. 7–9 in grassy places.

▲ **Antler Moth** *Cerapteryx graminis*. Ground colour greyish brown to deep chestnut, pattern varies. Male much smaller than female and normally darker. 6–9 in open country, especially in uplands: often flies by day. Larva is glossy greyish brown and feeds on grasses: often common enough to damage pastures.

▲ **Pine Beauty** *Panolis flammea*. Forewing sometimes greyish brown. 2–5 in pine forests. Larva feeds on pine needles and is a serious forest pest.

▲ **Clouded Drab** *Orthosia incerta*. Pale grey, through reddish brown to purplish black: reniform and orbicular stigmata usually with pale outline. 2–4 (sometimes earlier), mainly in wooded areas: common in gardens. Larva, bluish green with white dots and lines, feeds on shrubs.

▲ **Hebrew Character** *O. gothica* is easily identified by the heavy black mark round orbicular stigma. 1–5. Larva is polyphagous, mainly on shrubs.

▲ **Common Quaker** *O. stabilis* is greyish brown to brick red. 2–4 (sometimes earlier), mainly in wooded areas. Larva, bright green with yellow dots and lines, feeds on most deciduous trees.

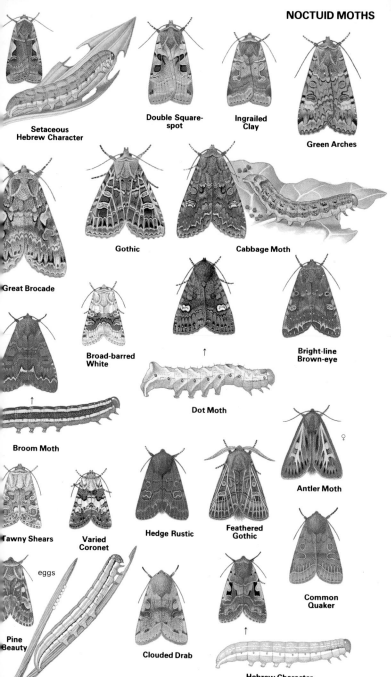

NOCTUID MOTHS

Setaceous Hebrew Character

Double Square-spot

Ingrailed Clay

Green Arches

Great Brocade

Gothic

Cabbage Moth

Broad-barred White

Bright-line Brown-eye

Dot Moth

Broom Moth

Tawny Shears

Varied Coronet

Hedge Rustic

Feathered Gothic

♀

Antler Moth

Pine Beauty

eggs

Clouded Drab

Common Quaker

Hebrew Character

159

▲ **Brown-line Bright-eye** *Mythimna conigera*. Pale yellowish brown to golden orange. 6–9 in hedges and woodland margins. Larva is pale brown with slender yellow lines and feeds on grasses, especially cocksfoot.

▲ **Clay** *M. ferrago*. Pale straw-coloured to brick red. Male has triangular patch of black hair on underside. 5–8. Larva resembles previous species, feeding mainly on grasses.

▲ **Common Wainscot** *M. pallens* has straw-coloured to brick-red forewings: hind wings almost white (sometimes greyish in female). 6–10: especially common in damp grassland. Larva is pale brown with white lines on back and a darker stripe on each side. It feeds on grasses.

▲ **Smoky Wainscot** *M. impura* has 2 or more conspicuous black dots on outer part of forewing: dark streak often less marked than shown here. Hind wing brownish grey. 5–8, mainly in grassy places. Larva like previous species.

▲ **Bulrush Wainscot** *Nonagria typhae*. Pale straw-coloured to brick red. 7–9 in marshy areas, including ditches and river banks. Larva is pale brown and feeds and pupates inside reedmace or bulrush stems (*Typha* spp).

▲ **Mullein** *Cucullia verbasci*. Ground colour pale straw to mid-brown. 4–6 in scrubby places and gardens: remarkably twig-like at rest. Larva is creamy with black and yellow spots: feeds openly on leaves and flowers spikes of mullein. Absent from far north.

▲ **Shark** *C. umbratica* has very narrow forewings, pale grey to rich brownish grey. Hind wings silvery in male, heavily clouded with grey in female. 5–7 in scrubby places, gardens, and waste land. Larva, greyish brown with black spots, feeds on sowthistle and lettuce.

Cucullia argentea flies 6–8 in sandy areas. Larva, dull green with yellow lines along the back and a pink or red streak on each segment, feeds on the flowers and seeds of mugwort and related plants. Germany and Scandinavia eastwards.

▲ **Early Grey** *Xylocampa areola*. Sometimes darker and occasionally with a rosy tinge. 3–5 in hedges, gardens, and woods. Larva, yellowish brown with a dark line on each side and dark brown patches on the back, feeds on honeysuckle. Absent from far north.

▲ **Grey Chi** *Antitype chi*. Distinct black cross near middle of forewing: black marks may be heavier: ground colour often greenish, but this tends to fade after death. 8–10, mainly in open country: common in gardens. Larva is bluish green with green-edged white lines. It feeds on dandelions and other low-growing plants.

▲ **Beaded Chestnut** *Agrochola lychnidis*. Pale brown to brick red, plain or mottled but always with 3 conspicuous spots on front edge of forewing. 9–11, often abundant at ivy blossom. Larva is yellowish green with white lines and spots. It feeds on a wide variety of herbaceous plants and shrubs, especially sallow. Not in far north.

▲ **Merveille-du-Jour** *Dichonia aprilina*. 8–10 around oak trees. Hard to spot at rest on lichen-covered bark. Larva is greenish grey with zig-zag black lines on back. Feeds on oak buds and leaves, hiding on trunks by day. Absent from far north.

△ **Sprawler** *Brachionycha sphinx*. 10–12 in deciduous woodland: very well camouflaged at rest on trunks. Larva is pale green with yellow and white lines: rests with head and thorax raised. It feeds on oak and other deciduous trees. C.

▲ **Swordgrass** *Xylena exsoleta*. Variable amounts of black on forewings. 9–10 and again in spring after hibernation: all kinds of open habitats. Rests with wings wrapped round body. Larva is green with black spots and yellow and red stripes. It feeds on many low-growing plants and also on several trees and shrubs. Absent from far north.

▲ **Orange Sallow** *Xanthia citrago*. Forewings yellow to brick red. 8–10. Larva is greenish grey with white lines and dots: feeds on lime. Not in far north.

△ **Barred Sallow** *X. aurago* has pale yellow to orange ground colour. 8–10, mainly in and around beech woods. Larva, reddish brown with pale dots and lines, feeds on beech and field maple.

▲ **Sallow** *X. icteritia* may have virtually no dark markings. 8–10 in hedgerows and scrubby places. Larva, reddish brown with darker spots and pale lines, feeds on sallow catkins in early spring and then various low-growing plants.

▲ **Green-brindled Crescent** *Allophyes oxyacanthae*. Forewings may lack green brindling, but always with prominent white fleck near hind edge. 9–10 in hedgerows and woodland: often on ivy blossoms. Larva is purplish brown with twin pointed humps at rear. It feeds on hawthorn and related trees. Absent from far north.

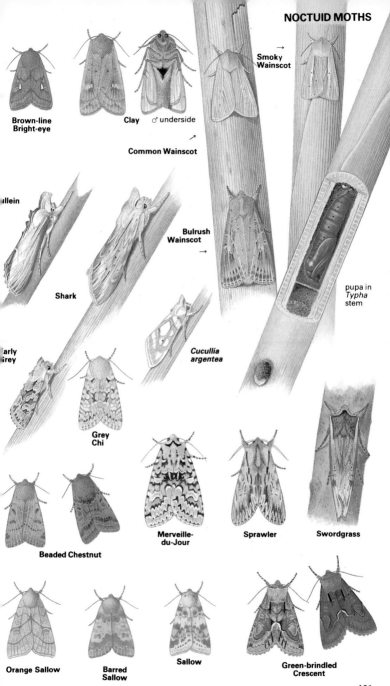

Brown-line
Bright-eye

Clay ♂ underside

Smoky
Wainscot

Common Wainscot

ullein

Shark

Bulrush
Wainscot

pupa in *Typha*
stem

arly
rey

*Cucullia
argentea*

Grey
Chi

Merveille-
du-Jour

Sprawler

Swordgrass

Beaded Chestnut

Orange Sallow

Barred
Sallow

Sallow

Green-brindled
Crescent

161

▲ **Poplar Grey** *Acronicta megacephala*. Hind wings largely white. 5–8 in wooded areas, parks, and gardens. Larva is greyish with black and red markings and a square white patch near rear: hairy. Feeds on poplars and willows.

▲ **Knot Grass** *A. rumicis* resembles previous species but has clear white sub-marginal line: forewings sometimes almost black. Hind wings grey. 6–9. Larva is hairy, blackish brown with red and white spots. Feeds on knotgrass and many other plants.

▲ **Sycamore Moth** *A. aceris* has very white hind wings. 5–7 in wooded areas, including town parks and tree-lined avenues. Larva feeds on sycamore, maple, and other deciduous trees.

▲ **Grey Dagger** *A. psi* is named for black dagger-like marks on grey background. 6–7, mainly in lowlands. Larva feeds on hawthorn and many other trees.

▲ **Dark Dagger** *A. tridens* cannot be distinguished with certainty from *psi* without dissection, although it is often darker. Its larva, however, is very distinct.

△ **Alder Moth.** *A. alni* flies 5–7 in deciduous woods. Young larva is grey with a white patch on the back and resembles a bird dropping: later becomes black and yellow with long spatulate hairs on each side. It feeds on alder and various other deciduous trees.

△ **Miller Moth** *A. leporina* is very pale, with few black marks. 4–7 in woods and on damp heaths. Larva is pale green and almost completely covered with long silky white hairs (often yellowish in north). It feeds on birch and various other trees. N & C.

Malachite Moth *Calotaenia celsia*. 8–10 in coniferous woods. Larva is yellowish green with black 'warts' and a brown head. It eats grasses in summer. N & C (mainly eastern).

▲ **Marbled Beauty** *Cryphia domestica*. Grey may be replaced by green. 6–8, anywhere that lichens thrive: very hard to see at rest on lichens. Larva feeds on lichens.
▲ **Marbled Green** *C. muralis* is very similar but larger. S & C.

▲ **Nut-tree Tussock** *Colocasia coryli*. 5–9 in hedgerows and open woodland. Larva is orange or brown with tufts of red or grey hair behind the head and a broken black stripe on the back. It feeds on hazel and various other trees. N & C.

△ **Copper Underwing** *Amphipyra pyramidea*. 6–8 in wooded areas. Rests with wings nearly flat. Larva is plump and green with white dots and stripes and a pointed hump at rear. It feeds on deciduous trees and shrubs.

△ **Svensson's Copper Underwing** *A. berbera* is almost identical but underside of abdomen has no chequered fringe. Underside of hind wing also has more extensive reddish colour, not just a marginal band as in *pyramidea*, and a less distinct dark band.

▲ **Mouse Moth** *A. tragopoginis* gets its name from the mouse-like way in which it scuttles away when disturbed. Wings held almost flat at rest. 6–9 in woods, hedgerows, and gardens. Larva is green with narrow white lines and feeds on a wide range of herbs and shrubs.

▲ **Old Lady** *Mormo maura*. Named for its shawl-like pattern, this moth flies 6–8 in hedgerows, gardens (including town gardens), and light woodland. Larva is dull brown with white marks and orange spiracles. It feeds herbs and shrubs. S & C.

Polyphaenis sericata. Forewings sometimes flecked with bluish white: stigmata often obscured but dark mark always present at wing-tips. 6–9 in scrubby places. Larva is yellowish grey and feeds on honeysuckle and other shrubs. S & C.

▲ **Straw Underwing** *Thalpophila matura*. 6–8 in grassy and scrubby places. Larva is pale to reddish brown with darker marks on the back. It eats grasses. S & C.

▲ **Angle Shades** *Phlogophora meticulosa*. Green areas may be replaced by brick red: green usually fades after death to dull brown. Abundant everywhere and can be found at all times of year. Rests with wings wrinkled like a dead leaf. Larva is green or brown with darker chevrons on the back. Polyphagous and sometimes a garden pest.

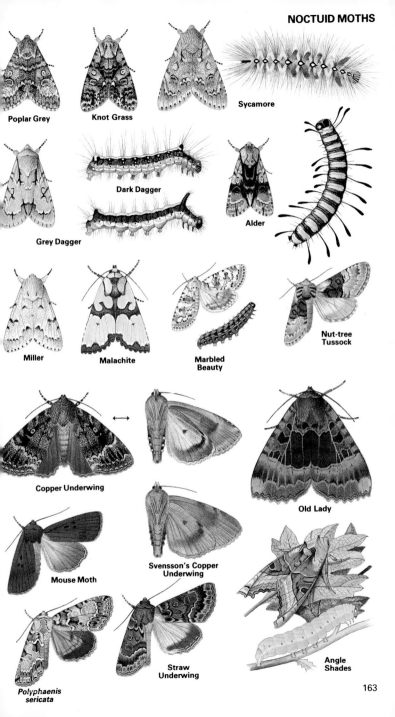

NOCTUID MOTHS

Poplar Grey

Knot Grass

Sycamore

Grey Dagger

Dark Dagger

Alder

Miller

Malachite

Marbled Beauty

Nut-tree Tussock

Copper Underwing

Old Lady

Mouse Moth

Svensson's Copper Underwing

Polyphaenis sericata

Straw Underwing

Angle Shades

163

▲ **Dunbar** *Cosmia trapezina*. Very variable: forewings ranging from greyish buff to deep brick. Cross lines usually distinct and sometimes enclosing rust-coloured or even blackish central band. 6–8 in wooded areas, often on flowers. Larva is green with yellow lines and scattered black and white spots. It feeds on leaves of various deciduous trees and also on other caterpillars, including its own species.

▲ **Olive** *Ipimorpha subtusa*. 6–8, mainly in wooded areas. Larva, green with black dots and white lines, feeds on aspen and other poplars.

▲ **Marbled Minor** *Oligia strigilis*. An extremely variable species, often difficult to separate from its relatives without examining genitalia. Abundant everywhere 6–8. Larva, purplish brown with yellow stripes, feeds on grasses. ▲ **Middle-barred Minor** *O. fasciuncula* often resembles *strigilis* but is usually redder and central band often more distinct. 5–7, mainly in damp habitats. Purplish brown larva feeds on grasses.

▲ **Small Clouded Brindle** *Apamea unanimis*. Reddish tinge may be absent, with more black mottling, especially in female. Reniform stigma usually clearly outlined in white. 6–8 in moist habitats. Larva is pale brown with dark-edged pale lines and feeds on moisture-loving grasses.

▲ **Common Rustic** *A. secalis* is another very variable species, with 3 common forms shown here. 6–8 in a wide variety of habitats. Larva is green with reddish lines on the back and feeds on grasses.

▲ **Dark Arches** *A. monoglypha* has forewings ranging from greyish brown to almost black: pale zig-zag lines always visible near outer margin. 6–10: abundant nearly everywhere and often coming in scores to light traps. Larva is dirty white or flesh-coloured with black spots and a black head. It feeds on grasses, usually chewing through the bases of the stems.

▲ **Light Arches** *A. lithoxylaea* flies 6–8 in most habitats. Larva is like that of *monoglypha* but has a brown head. Absent from far north.

▲ **Bird's Wing** *Dypterygia scabriuscula*. 5–10 in wooded areas: extremely well camouflaged at rest on tree trunks. Larva is reddish brown with black and white lines and yellow dots. It feeds on docks and related plants.

▲ **Rosy Rustic** *Hydraecia micacea*. Pink tinge varies in intensity. 9–10 in open country, especially coastal and cultivated areas. Larva is pinkish grey with black spots and feeds on docks and plantains: also on potatoes and other crops.

▲ **Frosted Orange** *Gortyna flavago*. Outer golden band often indistinct. 8–10 in open country, including both waste and cultivated land, especially in damp situations. Larva is pinkish with black spots and tunnels in stems of thistles and burdock: sometimes a pest of potatoes.

▲ **Ear Moth** *Amphipoea oculea*. Named for shape of reniform stigma. Coastal moths may be paler and larger. 8–9 in damp grassland: often abundant on flowers at night. Larva is pinkish and feeds on grasses.

△ *Calamia tridens*. Reniform stigma often edged with rusty brown. Hind wing yellowish grey in male: whitish green in female. 8–9 in grassy and scrubby places. Larva, greenish brown with black spots, feeds on various low-growing plants. Only British locality is W. Ireland.

Synthymia fixa. Male has ash-grey forewing and pale yellow hind wing. 3–5 on dry hillsides. Larva, dark green with yellow and white lines, feeds on pitch trefoil. S: sporadic visitor to parts of C.

△ **Spotted Sulphur** *Emmelia trabealis*. Black markings vary in number and intensity. 5–8 in rough grassy places, especially on sandy soils. Usually flies late afternoon. Larva, reddish brown with darker lines on back and yellow stripe on each side, feeds on bindweed. Absent from far north: mainly eastern B.

▲ **Four Spotted** *Tyta luctuosa*. Pale spot on forewing white or pink. Day-flying in meadows and rough grassland 5–9. Greyish brown larva feeds on bindweed. S & C.

▲ **Cream-bordered Green Pea** *Earias chlorana*. Pale costal stripe and white hind wings distinguish this from the Green Oak Tortrix (p. 126). 5–8 in damp habitats. Larva, pale green with brown lines, feeds on osier and other willows.

▲ **Green Silver Lines** *Pseudoips fagana*. Female has white hind wings and much narrower red border to forewings. 5–8 in woods and hedgerows. Larva, pale green with thin yellow line on each side, feeds on oak and other deciduous trees.

▲ **Scarce Silver Lines** *Bena prasinana*. 6–7 in oak woods. Larva is green with oblique yellow bars on sides and a yellow-tipped hump near front. It feeds on oak. S & C.

▲ **Marbled Clover** *Heliothis viriplaca*. Pale patch on hind wing may be reduced. Day-flying 5–7 on flowery heaths and grassy places. Larva, green to purplish brown, feeds on a wide range of low-growing plants. Not in far north.

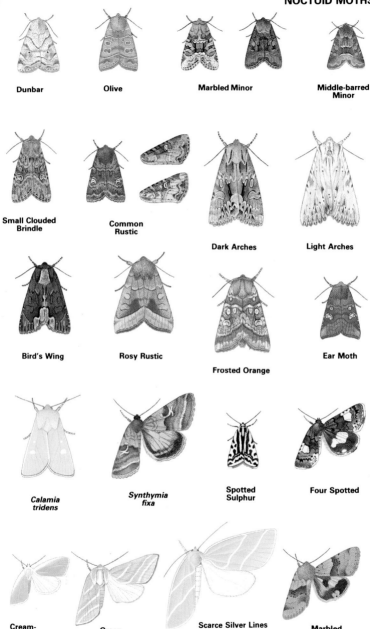

Dunbar

Olive

Marbled Minor

Middle-barred Minor

Small Clouded Brindle

Common Rustic

Dark Arches

Light Arches

Bird's Wing

Rosy Rustic

Frosted Orange

Ear Moth

Calamia tridens

Synthymia fixa

Spotted Sulphur

Four Spotted

Cream-bordered Green Pea

Green Silver Lines

Scarce Silver Lines

Marbled Clover

▲ **Golden Plusia** *Polychrisia moneta*. 6–9 in hedgerows, gardens, and town parks: very fond of garden flowers. Larva white with black dots at first, becoming green with white spots and lines. Like the next 3 species, it has only 3 pairs of prolegs, including the claspers. It feeds on many herbaceous plants – especially garden delphiniums in B.

▲ **Burnished Brass** *Diachrisia chrysitis*. Metallic patches range from green to deep gold: inner and outer bands may join in middle. 6–9 in gardens, hedges, and rough ground. Larva, with just 3 pairs of prolegs, feeds on stinging nettles, deadnettle, and other weeds.

△s **Scarce Burnished Brass** *D. chryson* has one fairly small brassy patch. 7–8 in fens and other damp places. Larva feeds on hemp agrimony. S & C.

Slender Burnished Brass *D. orichalcea* flies 6–9 in rough and grassy places. Larva feeds on various composites. Resident in S. Occasionally wandering to C & N.

▲ **Herald** *Scoliopteryx libatrix*. 8–10 and again in spring after hibernation, often in houses, as adult. Gardens, parks, and rough countryside. Larva feeds on willows and poplars.

△ **Gold Spot** *Plusia festucae*. Ground colour golden brown to chestnut. 6–9 in damp places. Larva feeds on grasses, sedges, and other waterside plants. Like those of the next 4 species, it is green with white spots and lines and has only 3 pairs of prolegs, including the claspers.

△n **Gold Spangle** *Autographa bractea*. Metallic spot sometimes deep yellow. 6–8, mainly in rough, upland country. Larva feeds on many low-growing plants and also on honeysuckle. N & C.

▲ **Beautiful Golden Y** *A. pulchrina*. Y-shaped mark, often broken in middle, sits on a rather confused and indistinct dark patch: reniform stigma clearly outlined in gold. 5–8 in gardens, hedges and other scrubby places. Larva feeds on deadnettle and many other low-growing plants.

▲ **Plain Golden Y** *A. jota* has the Y-shaped mark, often broken, on a distinct and uniform brown rectangle: reniform stigma indistinct. Flies 5–8, usually at dusk, in same habitats as last species and, like all members of the genus, is very fond of flowers. Larva feeds on a wide range of herbaceous plants and also on hawthorn.

▲ **Silver Y** *A. gamma* has grey to velvety black ground colour, occasionally tinged with purple. Upper part of Y sometimes indistinct. Abundant in gardens, town parks, and open country 5–11. Flies day and night and very common at garden flowers – continues to beat wings while feeding and appears as a grey blur. Larva eats a wide range of herbaceous plants and may be a pest of peas and other crops in summer. Resident in S (where it flies all year), migrating to C & N in spring and producing a summer brood, some of which fly south in autumn: cannot survive winter in B.

▲ **Mother Shipton** *Callistege mi*. Named for forewing pattern, thought to resemble witch-like profile of the legendary Mother Shipton. Day-flying in grassy and scrubby places 5–7. Larva is slender, pale brown with a creamy stripe on each side, and has only 3 pairs of prolegs. It feeds on clovers and other legumes.

▲ **Spectacle** *Abrostola triplasia*. Named for the pattern of hairs on front of thorax. 5–8 in gardens, hedgerows, and rough ground. Larva, pale green with white stripes and darker chevrons on back, has two humps near the front and a 3rd at the rear. It feeds on stinging nettle. **Dark Spectacle** *A. trigemina* is darker, with brown 'spectacles'.

Syngrapha ain. Resembles Silver Y, but hind wings yellow instead of brown. 7–8 in montane larch woods. Larva is green with pale lines and 3 pairs of prolegs, including the claspers. It feeds on larch needles and has a long hibernation. C.

△ **Blackneck** *Lygephila pastinum*. Amount of brown dusting on forewing varies, as does amount of black in reniform stigma. 6–7 in rough grassland and scrubby places, especially woodland clearings. Flies weakly. Larva, long and tapering, is greyish brown with 3 reddish brown stripes on the back. It feeds on tufted vetch. S & C.

▲ **Burnet Companion** *Euclidia glyphica*. Day-flying, 5–7 in rough grassy places. Larva has 3 functional pairs of prolegs, including claspers, and a vestigial pair in front of them. It feeds on clovers and other legumes.

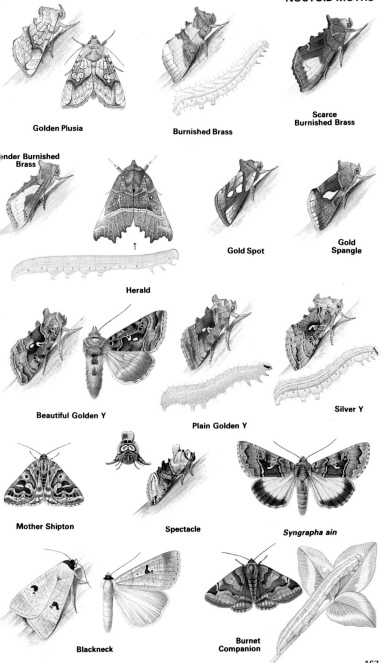

NOCTUID MOTHS

Golden Plusia

Burnished Brass

Scarce Burnished Brass

nder Burnished Brass

Herald

Gold Spot

Gold Spangle

Beautiful Golden Y

Plain Golden Y

Silver Y

Mother Shipton

Spectacle

Syngrapha ain

Blackneck

Burnet Companion

167

△ **Clifden Nonpareil** *Catocala fraxini.* 7–8 in light woodland. Well camouflaged at rest on tree trunks. Larva, like those of the red underwings, is extremely hard to see when stretched out on a twig. It feeds on poplars and ash. N & C (including arctic): sporadic visitor to B.

▲ **Red Underwing** *C. nupta* flies 8–9 in light woodland, hedgerows, gardens, and town parks. Well camouflaged at rest but, like the yellow underwings (p. 156), it flies erratically when disturbed and flashes the red hind wings to mislead predators. Larva has several bud-like 'warts' on the back: fringes along the sides allow it to blend remarkably well with twigs when stretched out along them at rest. It feeds on willow and poplar. Absent from far north.

△ **Rosy Underwing** *C. electa* resembles the last species but hind wings are somewhat paler and front wings lighter grey with thin black lines. 7–9. Larva like that of the last species. S & C: sporadic visitor to B.

△s **Dark Crimson Underwing** *C. sponsa* usually has darker forewings than Red Underwing, with prominent white marks near centre: hind wings also darker red, with strongly angled central black band. 7–8 in oak woods. Larva, somewhat greener than that of Red Underwing, feeds on oak. S & C.

△s **Light Crimson Underwing** *C. promissa* is smaller than the last species: forewings much greyer and hind wings with much straighter central band. 7–8 in oak woods. S & C.

Ephesia fulminea. Forewings range from pale to dark grey, often with a violet tinge. 6–8 in scrubby places, including gardens. Larva is grey or brown with prominent 'warts' and a horn at the rear. It feeds on blackthorn and various other trees. S & C (southern).

Anua tirhaca. 5–6 in dry, scrubby habitats. Some specimens have complete black border to hind wing, much broader in female than male. Larva is reddish or greyish brown, with thin dark lines on the back. It feeds on cistus and mastic shrubs (*Pistachia* spp). S.

▲ **Beautiful Hooktip** *Laspeyria flexula.* Greyish brown to purplish brown, always dotted with black. 6–8 in hedgerows and woodland margins. Larva is bluish green with dark green points and black-tipped 'warts' on the back. Lower edges are fringed. It feeds on arboreal lichens. C. Unrelated to the true hooktips (p. 170).

▲ **Snout** *Hypena proboscidalis.* Much more slender than most noctuids, this moth is named for the long palps which project forward from the head. 6–9 in hedgerows and other rough habitats. Larva, slender and green with scattered black hairs arising from raised spots, feeds on stinging nettle.

▲ **Fanfoot** *Herminia tarsipennalis.* Another slender species, named because male has a large tuft of hair on the front leg. Male also has a swelling half way along the antenna. Sub-marginal line starts before wing-tip. 6–7 in scrubby habitats, including gardens. Larva is greyish brown with black streaks and clothed with short hair. It feeds on bramble and various other shrubs. Most of Europe but not far north or south.

▲ **Small Fanfoot** *H. nemoralis* has sub-marginal line starting at wing-tip. Male has no tuft on front leg and no antennal swelling. 6–7 in woods and hedgerows. Larva, similar to that of last species, feeds on oak. Absent from far north.

The noctuid moths form the largest of the moth families and their larvae include some important crop pests. Many live in the upper layers of the soil and are known as cutworms for their habit of coming out at night to chew right through the bases of young plants and leave the stems and leaves lying on the surface. Even if they are not cut right through, the plants generally wilt and die. Freshly planted brassicas and lettuces are common targets for the cutworms, but most species will attack and eat any plant of the right size. Many feed right through the winter, although they burrow deeply in very cold weather.

They pupate in the soil when fully grown and most of the shiny brown, bullet-shaped pupae which you dig up in the garden belong to this group. The worst offenders include the Large Yellow Underwing, the Turnip Moth and the heart and Dart, all described on p. 156.

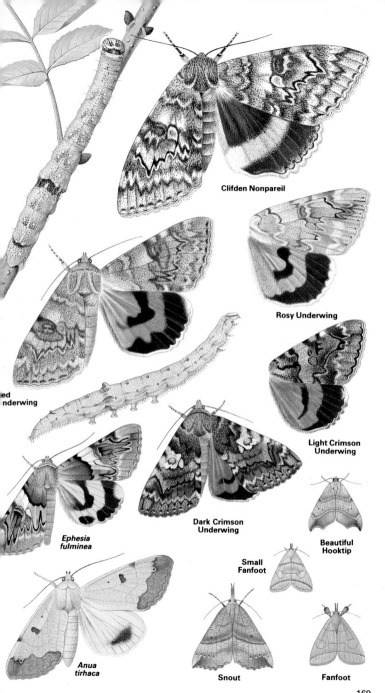

Clifden Nonpareil

Rosy Underwing

ed
nderwing

**Light Crimson
Underwing**

*Ephesia
fulminea*

**Dark Crimson
Underwing**

**Beautiful
Hooktip**

**Small
Fanfoot**

*Anua
tirhaca*

Snout

Fanfoot

▲ **Pebble Hooktip** *Drepana falcataria* Drepanidae. Ground colour may be paler. 5–9 in woods and heathland. Wings held flat at rest. Larva, like all members of the family, tapers to a point at the rear and rests with both ends raised. It eats birch and alder.

▲ **Oak Hooktip** *D.binaria* flies 5–9 in woodlands. Larva, pale brown with yellowish marks on the back and a double-pointed hump behind the head, feeds on oak and birch, S & C.

▲ **Scalloped Hooktip** *Falcaria lacertinaria*. 5–9 in wooded areas and heathland. Rests with wings roofwise. Larva is light and dark brown with 2 humps behind the head and a 3rd at the rear. It feeds on birch and alder. Absent from far south.

▲ **Chinese Character** *Cilix glaucata*. 5–9 in gardens, hedgerows, and woods. Just like a bird dropping at rest. Larva has typical hooktip shape and is reddish brown, often purplish below, with 3 humps behind head. Mainly on hawthorn and blackthorn. S & C.

▲ **Peach Blossom** *Thyatira batis* Thyatiridae. 6–9, mainly in woodland. Larva is dark brown with oblique white lines and several humps along the back. It feeds on bramble and rests with both ends raised. N & C.

▲ **Buff Arches** *Habrosyne pyritoides*. 6–9 in woods and hedgerows. Larva is brick-coloured with a dark line on the back and a large white spot near the front on each side. It feeds mainly on bramble.

▲ **Figure of Eighty** *Tethea ocularis*. 80-mark usually distinct. 5–6 in wooded areas. Larva, dirty white with a grey line on the back, feeds on poplars.

▲ **Frosted Green** *Polyploca ridens*. 3–5 in wooded areas. Larva is yellowish green with black and white dots. It feeds on oak. S & C.

Family Geometridae A very large family, containing about 12,000 species of mainly flimsy moths with slender bodies and relatively large wings. The latter are generally spread horizontally at rest, often swept back into a triangular shape, although a few species hold their wings up like butterflies. Flight is generally weak. The larvae are hairless or only slightly hairy and have only 2 pairs of prolegs, including the claspers. They are known as loopers, from the way they arch their bodies into loops as they move along. Many are amazingly stick-like at rest.

△s **Purple-bordered Gold** *Idaea muricata*. Costal margin always purple, but wings otherwise completely yellow to completely purple. 6–7 in fens and other damp places, often flying at sunrise. Larva, pale brown with darker lines, feeds on marsh cinquefoil and other herbaceous plants. ▲ **Riband Wave** *I. aversata* may be greyish white or yellowish: bands may be indistinct. 6–9. Larva is brown and wrinkled and tapers strongly towards the front. Polyphagous.

Rhodostrophia calabra. Rosy areas may be darker red, especially in far south. 4–7. Larva, yellowish brown or grey with black bristles, feeds on broom and other legumes. S & C. **R. vibicaria** is normally paler than *calabra* and has sharply angled hind wings. Pink bands strong or faint, but always with distinct edges. S & C.

▲ **Lace Border** *Scopula ornata*. 5–9 in rough, grassy places, especially on chalk and limestone. Larva is pale brown above and greyish below, with several dark V-shaped marks on the back. It feeds on wild thyme and marjoram. S & C. ▲ **Cream Wave** *S. floslactata* commonly has only 2 prominent cross lines and is sometimes almost unmarked. Ground colour sometimes yellowish white: may be smoky grey all over. 4–7 in wooded areas. Larva, greyish brown with darker markings and a notched head, feeds mainly on bedstraws. There are several similar species. △ **Small Bloodvein** *S. imitaria* has very angular wings. Ground colour is often less orange: stripe varies in thickness. 6–9 in hedgerows and other rough places. Larva is pale brown with 3 darker lines on the back. Polyphagous. S & C.

▲ **Bloodvein** *Timandra griseata*. Ground colour ranges from cream to pale grey. 'Vein' is pink or purple and varies in thickness. 5–9 in hedgerows and other rough places, especially where damp. Larva is greyish brown with 4 dark spots on the back. It feeds on docks and other low-growing plants.

△ **Clay Triple-lines** *Cyclophora linearia*. Ground colour ranges from yellow to pale brick: inner and outer cross lines often missing. 4–9 in and around beech woods. Larva, pale brown with yellow markings, feeds on beech leaves. S & C.

△ **Mocha** *C. annulata*. Ground colour off-white to pale yellow: rings may be absent, especially on forewing. 5–9 in hedgerows and other wooded areas. Larva, dark green with yellow markings and a brown head, feeds on maple. S & C.

170

Scalloped Hooktip

Pebble Hooktip

Chinese Character

Oak Hooktip

Peach Blossom

Buff Arches

Figure of Eighty

Frosted Green

Purple-bordered Gold

Mocha

Rhodostrophia calabra

R. vibicaria

Riband Wave

Lace Border

Cream Wave

Small Bloodvein

Bloodvein

Clay Triple-lines

171

▲ **Orange Underwing** *Archiearis parthenias*. 3–5 on heaths and in open woodland. Male flies around birches in sunshine: female flies little. Larva, green with white stripes and a black line along the back, feeds on catkins and leaves of birch. △ **Light Orange Underwing** *A. notha* is similar, but smaller and with plainer forewings.

▲ **Large Emerald** *Geometra papilionaria*. Bright green at first but, as in all emeralds, it fades after a few days: green may disappear altogether after death. 6–8 in woods, heaths, and hedgerows. Twig-like larva is brown at first and then green. It feeds on birch, hazel, and beech.

▲ **Grass Emerald** *Pseudoterpna pruinata*. Bluish green at first, soon becoming grey. 6–8 on moors, heaths, and damp scrubby grassland. Larva is green with a dark line on the back and a pink line on each side. It feeds on broom and gorse. S & C.

△ **Small Emerald** *Hemistola chrysoprasaria*. 5–8 in hedgerows and woodland margins, mainly on chalk and limestone. Larva is pale green with white dots and a brown head and feeds on traveller's joy.

△ **Blotched Emerald** *Comibaena pustulata*. 6–7 in and around oak woods. Larva is reddish brown but camouflages itself with debris. It feeds on oak. C.

△s **Thalera fimbrialis**. Hind wing distinctly notched in front of angle. 7–8 in scrubby and grassy places. Larva is yellowish green with red at front and rear and a red dorsal stripe. It feeds on spurges and other herbs. C.

Euchrostes indigenata. 5–10 in rough and cultivated areas. Larva, bright green with red at each end, feeds on spurges. S.

△ **Common Emerald** *Hemithea aestivaria*. 6–8 in hedgerows and wooded areas. Larva is green with reddish brown marks and black V-shaped marks on back. It feeds on low-growing plants when young, and then on deciduous trees. S & C.

▲ **Little Emerald** *Jodis lactearia*. Pale green at first, soon fading to shiny white. 5–7 in hedges and woodland. Larva, thin and green with red spots, feeds on various deciduous trees and shrubs. S & C.

▲ **Light Emerald** *Campaea margaritata*. 5–7, mainly in woodland. Larva is dark green to purplish brown and feeds on various deciduous trees 8–5, often chewing buds and young bark in winter. Not closely related to the other emeralds.

▲ **Mallow** *Larentia clavaria*. Forewings pale to deep brown: cross bands often indistinct. Chequered margins give wings a scalloped appearance. 9–11 in rough habitats. Larva is slender and green and feeds on mallows.

▲ **Shaded Broad-bar** *Scotopteryx chenopodiata*. Resembles Mallow but lacks chequered margins. 6–8 in grassy places. Larva, pinkish grey with black spots, eats grasses and assorted legumes. △s **Chalk Carpet** *S. bipunctaria* flies 6–8 on chalk and limestone grassland. Larva, pale pinkish brown, feeds on clovers and trefoils. S & C.

△ **Chimney Sweeper** *Odezia atrata*. Jet black at first, becoming brown with age. Day-flying 5–7 in grassy places. Larva, green with dark lines on back, feeds on flowers of earthnut and other small umbellifers. N & C and southern mountains.

▲ **Treble-bar** *Aplocera plagiata*. 5–9 in rough grassy places: 2nd brood insects smaller and often with faint bars. Larva, dark green to reddish brown with darker and paler lines, feeds on *Hypericum* spp.

▲ **Barred Yellow** *Cidaria fulvata*. 5–7 in gardens, hedges, and other scrubby places. Rests with abdomen raised. Larva, wrinkled green with yellow rings, feeds on roses.

▲ **Dark Spinach** *Pelurga comitata*. Central band varies in intensity. 6–8 in scrubby and grassy places, especially on coasts. Larva is brownish with V-shaped marks on back and feeds on seeds of goosefoot and related plants. N & C.

▲ **Phoenix** *Eulithis prunata*. 7–8 in gardens, hedges, and woodland margins. Larva, green to brown with pale triangular markings, feeds on currants and gooseberries.

▲ **Spinach** *E. mellinata*. Forewing ground colour pale yellow to brick: hind wing cream: chequered fringes on all wings. Rests with forewings at right angles to body and hind wings more or less concealed beneath them. 6–8, mainly in gardens. Larva, green with white lines, feeds on currant bushes. ▲ **Northern Spinach** *E. populata* is much darker and has no chequered fringes: forewing sometimes entirely brown. 6–8 in woods and on moors. Grey or brown larva feeds on bilberry and other shrubs. N & C: mainly northern in B. ▲ **Barred Straw** *E. pyraliata* resembles a pale Spinach but has no chequered fringes. Central cross lines closer together. 6–8 in hedges and woodland margins. Larva feeds on cleavers and bedstraws.

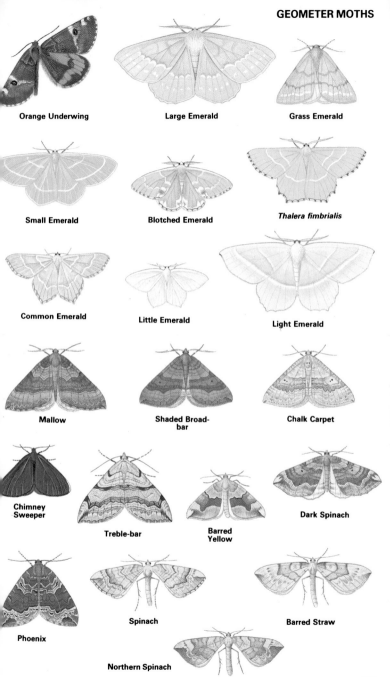

Orange Underwing

Large Emerald

Grass Emerald

Small Emerald

Blotched Emerald

Thalera fimbrialis

Common Emerald

Little Emerald

Light Emerald

Mallow

Shaded Broad-bar

Chalk Carpet

Chimney Sweeper

Treble-bar

Barred Yellow

Dark Spinach

Phoenix

Spinach

Barred Straw

Northern Spinach

▲ **Common Marbled Carpet** *Chloroclysta truncata*. Extremely variable. 5–6 and 8–10 in woods and hedgerows. Green larva is very slender, usually with reddish stripes on the sides, and feeds on many trees and shrubs and also on wild strawberry. N & C.

▲ **Dark Marbled Carpet** *C. citrata* is equally variable and difficult to separate from the last species, but dark basal area of forewing generally has a sharper outline, and hind wing is dirty white instead of mid-grey. 7–8 (more or less in between two broods of *truncata*) in woods and on heaths and moors. N & C.

▲ **Beautiful Carpet** *Mesoleuca albicillata*. 5–8, mainly in open woodland. Larva is green with reddish brown blotches on the back. It feeds mainly on bramble.

△ **Pretty Chalk Carpet** *Melanthia procellata*. 5–8 in old hedges and woodland edges, mainly on chalk and limestone. Larva, pale brown with darker lines, feeds on traveller's joy. S & C.

▲ **Red Twin-spot Carpet** *Xanthorhoe spadicearia*. Ground colour pale to dark grey: central band may be brick coloured: twin spots may be obscure. Hind wings dirty white with grey clouding. 5–9. Larva is brownish grey with pale diamonds and black spots. It feeds on many low-growing plants. ▲ **Dark-barred Twin-spot Carpet** *X. ferrugata* has a darker central band, sometimes purplish, outlined in rich brown. Hind wings dark grey. 5–9. N & C. ▲ **Flame Carpet** *X. designata* flies 5–9 in damp woods and hedges. Larva, yellowish grey with black spots and assorted other markings, feeds on crucifers. N & C. ▲ **Silver-ground Carpet** *X. montanata* may have greyer ground colour and paler cross band. 5–8 in woods and hedges. Larva is purplish brown on the back and greyish on the sides. It feeds on bedstraws and other low-growing plants. N & C. ▲ **Garden Carpet** *X. fluctuata* has ground colour from white to dark grey: black marks also vary in extent. 4–10 almost everywhere. Larva, green to grey with pale diamonds on the back, feeds on brassicas and other crucifers.

▲ **Green Carpet** *Colostygia pectinataria*. Green usually fades to yellowish after a few days. 5–8 in hedges and other scrubby places, including heathland. Larva is greenish brown with red V-shaped marks and feeds mainly on bedstraws.

▲ **Common Carpet** *Epirrhoe alternata*. Dark markings black to greyish brown. Outer white band always contains a thin grey line (absent in the similar ▲ **Wood Carpet** *E. rivata*). 5–9 in woods and hedges. Larva, brown or green with various markings, feed on bedstraws.

△ **Argent and Sable** *Rheumaptera hastata*. Northern specimens smaller and darker. Day-flying 5–7 on heaths and in open woods. Larva is shiny olive green with reddish marks on the sides and feeds on birch and bilberry. N & C.

▲ **Purple Bar** *Cosmorhoe ocellata*. 5–9 in most rough habitats. Larva is pale brown with a darker network and feeds on bedstraws.

▲ **Foxglove Pug** *Eupithecia pulchellata*. Flies 5–7. Larva, normally yellowish green and often marked with purple, feeds in the flowers of foxgloves. ▲ **Currant Pug** *E. assimilata* is one of several similar species but can normally be distinguished by the prominent white mark at hind angle of forewing. 5–9 in gardens and hedges. Larva, yellowish green with darker green lines, feeds on currant and hop. N & C.

▲ **Narrow-winged Pug** *E. nanata*. Pattern varies, but relatively long and pointed forewings distinguish this from most other pugs. 5–9 on heaths and commons. Larva, very pale green with red spots, feeds on heather. N & C. ▲ **Lime-speck Pug** *E. centaureata*. 5–10 in gardens and rough habitats. Like most pugs, it rests with wings outstretched and front edge of forewing more or less at right angles to body. Larva is green or yellow, often with red spots, and feeds on flowers of yarrow, ragwort, and other composites.

▲ **Netted Pug** *E. venosata* may have darker forewings with less distinct network. 5–7 in hedges and other rough places. Larva, greyish brown with a greenish underside and 3 dark lines on the back, feeds in the seed capsules of campions.

▲ **Tawny-speckled Pug** *E. icterata* may lack brick-coloured patch on forewing. 5–8. Larva, reddish brown with a white line on each side, feeds on flowers of yarrow and other composites. △ **Bordered Pug** *E. succenturiata* may have dark clouding over much of forewing. 6–8 in rough grassy places. Larva is reddish brown with black marks on the back and feeds on leaves of mugwort, yarrow, and related composites. N & C.

▲ **Green Pug** *Chloroclystis rectangulata*. Grey to black, often with little green. 5–8. Larva is relatively stout, pale green with a reddish stripe on the back, and feeds in buds and flowers of apple, hawthorn, and related trees. ▲ **V-pug** *C. v-ata* flies 4–9. Larva is green, normally with 3 reddish lines on the back. It feeds on the flowers of many plants, including hemp agrimony, traveller's-joy, and bramble. S & C.

CARPET and PUG MOTHS

Common Marbled Carpet

Beautiful Carpet

Pretty Chalk Carpet

Dark Marbled Carpet

Red Twin-spot Carpet

Dark-barred Twin-spot Carpet

Green Carpet

Flame Carpet

Silver-ground Carpet

↑
Garden Carpet

Common Carpet

Argent and Sable

Purple Bar

Foxglove Pug

Currant Pug

Narrow-winged Pug

Lime-speck Pug

Netted Pug

Green Pug

Tawny-speckled Pug

Bordered Pug

V-Pug

▲ **Magpie Moth** *Abraxas grossulariata*. Pattern rather variable, but usually easily recognised. 6–8 in gardens, hedgerows, and other scrubby places. Larva (left) feeds on blackthorn, gooseberry, currants, and many other shrubs.

△ **Clouded Magpie** *A. sylvata* flies 5–7 in woodland, commonly resting on dog's mercury leaves and resembling bird droppings. Larva, cream with black and yellow lines, feeds mainly on wych elm.

▲ **Clouded Border** *Lomaspilis marginata*. Amount of dark spotting varies, females normally lacking black band across centre of each wing. 5–8, especially in damp woods and hedgerows. Larva is pale green with darker lines and feeds on sallow.

▲ **Scorched Carpet** *Ligdia adustata*. 4–9 in woods and hedgerows. At rest on bark the dark patches break up outline and render it very hard to detect. Larva is bright green with rust-coloured spots and is very like the stalks of spindle leaves on which it feeds.

△ **Large Thorn** *Ennomos autumnaria*. Pale yellow to almost brick-coloured, always with brown wing-tips. 8–10 in woods and hedgerows.. Like most thorn moths, it often rests with wings raised at an angle. A regular visitor to light. Larva (left) feeds on hawthorn and other trees.

▲ **August Thorn** *E. quercinaria* ranges from pale yellow to almost brick-coloured: female usually paler than male. Cross lines almost parallel, but inner line bends sharply inwards near front margin. 8–9 in wooded areas and also tree-lined suburban avenues. Larva is greyish brown and stick-like, with several 'warts' on the back. It feeds on oak and other trees.

▲ **Canary-shouldered Thorn** *E. alniaria* is named for its bright yellow thoracic hair. Wings range from pale to deep yellow, always tinged with brown. 8–10 in wooded areas, especially where damp. Twig-like larva feeds on alder, birch, and other trees.

△ **Dusky Thorn** *E. fuscantaria* is like August Thorn but cross lines converge strongly towards hind edge of forewing. 8–9 in wooded areas. Larva is green and feeds on ash.

▲ **Early Thorn** *Selenia dentaria*. Ground colour yellowish grey to brown. Spring brood (3–5) much larger than summer brood (7–9): females usually paler than males, especially on underside. Summer insects often more boldly marked. Rests with wings partly raised or else closed vertically above body: underside resembles dead leaf. Woodland and hedgerows. Twig-like larva feeds on hawthorn and many other shrubs.

▲ **Purple Thorn** *S. tetralunaria* flies in woodland, with spring brood (4–5) darker and larger than summer insects (7–9). Basal part of wing ranges from chestnut to purplish black. Rests like Early Thorn: underside similar to upper side. Larva feeds on a wide variety of trees and shrubs in summer. △ **Lunar Thorn** *S. lunularia* is distinguished by very jagged wing margins. 5–7 in woods and hedgerows. Brown, twig-like larva feeds on many trees and shrubs.

△ **Lilac Beauty** *Apeira syringaria*. 6–9 in woods, gardens, and hedgerows. Rests with forewings strangely creased to resemble a dead leaf. Larva (below) has 2 hooked outgrowths on the back and is very hard to spot among the twigs. It feeds on lilac, privet, and honeysuckle.

△ **Small Waved Umber** *Horisme vitalbata*. Dark stripe across wings and body breaks up outline and makes the moth very hard to spot at rest on tree trunks and fences. 5–9 in hedgerows and woodland margins. Larva is greyish brown with darker lines and feeds on traveller's joy.

Magpie larva

Large Thorn larva

Early Thorn larva

Lilac Beauty larva

Lilac Beauty

Small Waved Umber

Magpie

Clouded Magpie

Clouded Border

Scorched Carpet

Large Thorn

August Thorn

Canary-shouldered Thorn

Dusky Thorn

♀ spring

♂ summer

spring

Early Thorn

spring

Purple Thorn

Lunar Thorn

summer

▲ **Scalloped Hazel** *Odontopera bidentata*. Ranges from dirty white to black, the latter mainly in north. 4–7 in woods and hedgerows. Brown or green twig-like larva feeds on almost any deciduous tree or shrub.

▲ **Feathered Thorn** *Colotois pennaria*. Pale to dark brick-coloured. Male antennae strongly feathered. 8–11 in woods and hedgerows. Twig-like brown larva feeds on a wide range of deciduous trees and shrubs.

▲ **Scalloped Oak** *Crocallis elinguaria*. Ground colour ranges from pale cream to brick. 6–8 in woods and hedges. Twig-like greyish larva feeds on most deciduous trees.

△ **Orange Moth** *Angerona prunaria*. Sexes differ markedly in colour: sometimes brown with orange (male) or yellow (female) band on each wing. 5–7 in woodland. Twig-like larva feeds on most deciduous trees and shrubs.

▲ **Scorched Wing** *Plagodis dolabraria*. 4–9 in woodlands. Twig-like larva, brown with darker markings and a large 'wart' at the rear, feeds on various trees.

▲ **Brimstone** *Opisthograptis luteolata*. 4–10 in hedgerows and other scrubby places, including gardens. Larva (left), brown or green, feeds on hawthorn and other shrubs.

▲ **Speckled Yellow** *Pseudopanthera macularia*. Brown markings vary. Day-flying 5–6 in scrubby habitats. Bright green larva feeds on wood sage and other labiates.

▲ **Swallowtail Moth** *Ourapteryx sambucaria*. 6–8 in gardens, hedges, and other scrubby places. Larva (left) feeds on ivy, hawthorn, and many other shrubs.

   ▲ **Winter Moth** *Operophtera brumata*. 10–2 in gardens, hedges, and wherever else there are trees. Male often comes to lighted windows: female virtually wingless. Larva, green with pale lines and a darker one on the back, feeds on almost any deciduous tree: a serious pest of apples.

Brimstone

   ▲ **Early Moth** *Theria primaria*.1–3 in hedges and other scrubby places. Female wingless. Larva, generally pale green with darker blotches and pale lines, feeds on hawthorns, blackthorn, and other shrubs.

   ▲ **Spring Usher** *Agriopis leucophaeria*. Often much paler, but forewings may be entirely black. Female wingless. 1–4 in wooded areas. Larva, green with yellowish lines, feeds on oak. ▲ **Scarce Umber** *A. aurantiaria* flies 10–12 in wooded areas. Female is wingless. Larva is brownish yellow with purplish markings on sides and feeds on many trees and shrubs. ▲ **Dotted Border** *A. marginaria* may have forewings darker than shown, but small dots usually visible on outer margins of all wings. Female wingless. 2–4 in hedges and other scrubby places. Larva, greenish brown with dark crosses on back, feeds on many trees and shrubs.

   ▲ **Mottled Umber** *Erannis defoliaria*. Very variable: forewings sometimes uniformly straw-coloured or dark brown. Female wingless. 10–3 in gardens, woods, and hedges. Larva ranges from straw-coloured to deep brown, usually with yellow patches along the sides. It feeds on almost any deciduous tree or shrub: often an orchard pest.

   ▲ **November Moth** *Epirrita dilutata*. 9–12 in wooded areas. Larva is green with deep red spots or lines and feeds on many trees and shrubs.

   ▲ **March Moth** *Alsophila aescularia*. 2–4 in gardens, hedges, and other wooded areas. Wings wrapped partly round body at rest. Female wingless. Larva, pale green with white lines, feeds on most deciduous trees and shrubs.

   ▲ **Small Yellow Wave** *Hydrelia flammeolaria*. 5–7 in woods and hedges: rests with wings widely spread. Larva, green with pale rings, feeds on maple and alder.

   ▲ **Rivulet** *Perizoma affinitatum*. 5–7 in rough grassy places. Larva is pinkish brown and feeds in seed capsules of campions.

Swallowtailed

   ▲ **Yellow Shell** *Camptogramma bilineata*. Ground colour yellow or brown: central band sometimes very dark. 6–8 in gardens and hedges. Larva is brown or green, paler below, and feeds on many low-growing plants. It bends into a question-mark shape when resting.

   ▲ **Shoulder Stripe** *Anticlea badiata*. 3–5 in hedges and other scrubby places. Larva, generally green with paler rings, feeds on roses.

Small Yellow Wave   **Rivulet**   **Yellow Shell**   **Shoulder Stripe**

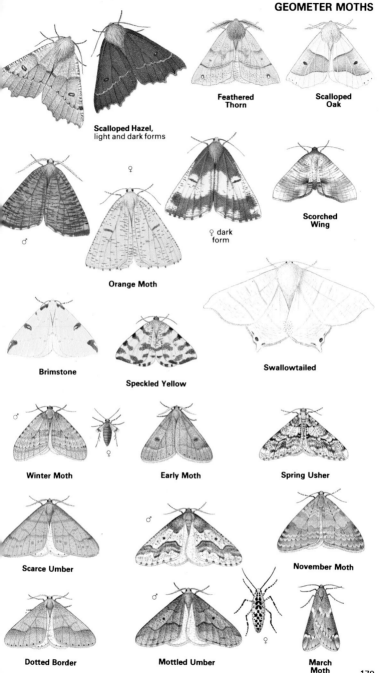

Scalloped Hazel,
light and dark forms

Feathered Thorn

Scalloped Oak

♀

♂

Orange Moth

♀ dark form

Scorched Wing

Brimstone

Speckled Yellow

Swallowtailed

Winter Moth ♀

Early Moth

Spring Usher

Scarce Umber

♂

November Moth

Dotted Border

♂

♀

Mottled Umber

March Moth

Peppered Moth larva

Waved Umber

Oak Beauty larva

Bordered White at rest

▲ **Peppered Moth** *Biston betularia*. Exists in two main forms – the speckled (normal) and the black (melanic). The latter was first noticed in the middle of the 19th century in industrial areas, where it clearly has an advantage on smoke-blackened trees and buildings, but it is now widespread in many other habitats and often much more common than the normal form. This industrial melanism has since been discovered in many other moths. The Peppered Moth flies 5–8 in woods and gardens. The larva (left) is greyish brown or bright green, with a deeply notched head. It feeds on many trees and shrubs. △s **Oak Beauty** *B. strataria* flies 2–5, mainly in woodland. Larva (below left) feeds on oak and many other trees. S & C.

▲ **Pale Brindled Beauty** *Apocheima pilosaria*. 11–4 in hedgerows and woodland. Female is wingless and found mainly on tree trunks. Stick-like larva is greyish brown with darker bud-like 'warts' and feeds on most deciduous trees and shrubs. N & C.

▲ **Brindled Beauty** *Lycia hirtaria*. Ground colour grey or brown, usually heavily speckled with yellow. Female wings somewhat longer and narrower. 2–4 wherever there are trees, including town streets and parks. Larva is reddish brown or grey with yellow and red markings. It feeds on most kinds of deciduous trees and shrubs.

△ **Waved Umber** *Menophra abruptaria*. Ground colour often much darker, especially in male. 3–6 in woods, hedgerows, and gardens. Remarkably well camouflaged at rest on trees and fences, where it always rests with its body horizontal and the wing pattern running vertically to match the furrows – which on tree trunks are almost always vertical. Larva is greyish, often marked with pink, and very twig-like. It feeds on privet, lilac, and other shrubs. Cocoon, spun on twigs and covered with fragments of bark and algae, is almost invisible. S & C.

▲ **Willow Beauty** *Peribatodes rhomboidaria*. Ground colour smoky grey or yellowish. One of several rather similar species, distinguished from most of them by central cross line on forewing having only one bulge (in front of middle). Male antennae strongly feathered. 6–9 in woods and gardens. Larva is reddish brown and feeds on ivy, hawthorn, and many other shrubs. S & C.

▲ **Great Oak Beauty** *Boarmia roboraria*. Black cross lines vary in intensity and sometimes almost absent. 6–7 in oakwoods. The larva feeds on oak and closely resembles the twigs. S & C.

▲ **Engrailed** *Ectropis bistortata*. Markings vary in intensity and ground colour often greyer. Male antennae not feathery. 3–9 in wooded areas. Larva is greyish and feeds on many deciduous trees and shrubs. N & C.

Square Spot *Ectropis consonaria* has a clear square mark near outer margin of forewing. Male antennae not feathered. 4–6 in woodland. Larva feeds on numerous trees and shrubs, including pine. S & C.

▲ **Bordered White** *Bupalus piniaria*. Also called the Pine Looper. Male ground colour is white in northern Europe, including northern B, and yellowish in the south. Female is orange-brown in north and yellowish elsewhere. All forms have brown wing-tips. 5–8 in coniferous woodland. Larva is green with pale stripes and feeds on the needles of many conifers, often causing severe damage in plantations.

▲ **Common Heath** *Ematurga atomaria*. Ground colour yellowish in male and white in female. Dark speckling often so dense as to make wings brown all over, but female usually less heavily speckled than male. Day-flying 5–9 on heathland. Larva is grey to dark green, often with rows of white dashes on back. It feeds on heather, heaths, and various legumes.

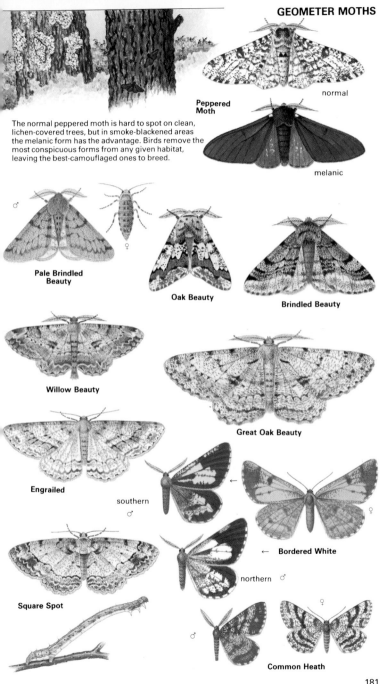

GEOMETER MOTHS

Peppered Moth

normal

melanic

The normal peppered moth is hard to spot on clean, lichen-covered trees, but in smoke-blackened areas the melanic form has the advantage. Birds remove the most conspicuous forms from any given habitat, leaving the best-camouflaged ones to breed.

Pale Brindled Beauty

Oak Beauty

Brindled Beauty

Willow Beauty

Great Oak Beauty

Engrailed

southern
♂

Bordered White

♀

northern ♂

Square Spot

♂

Common Heath

♀

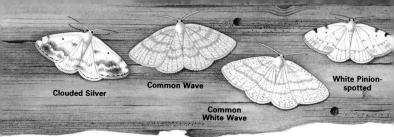

Clouded Silver **Common Wave** **Common White Wave** **White Pinion-spotted**

- ◬ **Clouded Silver** *Lomographa temerata*. Silky white wings with a greater or lesser amount of dark grey shading readily distinguish this species. Clouding may be almost absent in some females, however. 5–6 in woods and hedgerows. Larva, green with reddish spots, feeds on blackthorn and several other trees and shrubs. C.

- ▲ **Common Wave** *Cabera exanthemata*. White, sprinkled with yellowish grey. Outer cross line distinctly curved. 5–9 in wooded areas, especially where moist. Larva is green with yellow rings and black spots and usually has purplish marks on the sides. It feeds on sallow, alder, and various other trees.

- ▲ **Common White Wave** *C. pusaria* resembles the Common Wave but is whiter (sometimes tinged with pink) and outer cross line is virtually straight. 5–9, mainly in wooded country. Larva is normally purplish brown with white spots. It feeds on sallow, birch, and various other trees.

- ◬ **White Pinion-spotted** *Lomographa bimaculata* has silky white wings like the Clouded Silver, but black spots on front edge of forewing readily distinguish it. 4–6 in woods and scrubby places. Larva is dark green with purplish arrowhead marks on the back. It feeds on wild cherry, blackthorn, and other rosaceous trees and shrubs. C.

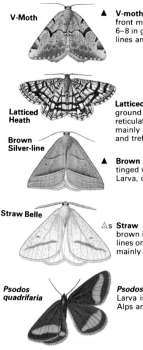

V-Moth

- ▲ **V-moth** *Semiothisa wauaria*. Forewings may be darker: dark V near front margin usually distinct, although posterior arm may be faint. 6–8 in gardens and open woods. Larva is green or brown with white lines and black dots. It feeds on gooseberry and currant.

Latticed Heath

Latticed Heath *S. clathrata* has dirty white to yellowish brown ground colour. Latticed pattern is dark brown or black, always more reticulate than in Common Heath (p. 180). 4–9 in grassy places, mainly day-flying. Larva, green with white lines, feeds on clovers and trefoils.

Brown Silver-line

- ▲ **Brown Silver-line** *Petrophora chlorosata*. Forewings sometimes tinged with pink. 5–7 on heathland and other bracken-rich habitats. Larva, dark green with brown lines, feeds on bracken fronds.

Straw Belle

△s **Straw Belle** *Aspitates gilvaria*. Forewings heavily speckled with brown in female. 6–8 in grassy places. Larva, pinkish grey with dark lines on the back, feeds on many low-growing plants. Local in S & C: mainly on chalk in B.

Psodos quadrifaria

Psodos quadrifaria. Yellow bands may be narrower. Day-flying 6–7. Larva is brown and feeds on a wide range of low-growing plants. Alps and other mountains of S & C.

CADDIS FLIES   Order Trichoptera (pp. 184–9)

An order of nearly 6,000 species of holometabolous insects, almost all of which spend their larval life in water. About 400 species occur in Europe and 189 of them are found in Britain. The adults are mostly brownish, moth-like insects with relatively weak flight. Some fly by day, but most are active at night and often come to lighted windows and light traps, often quite a long way from water. There are normally four rather flimsy wings all covered with fine hairs, although the hind wings are generally less hairy and more transparent than forewings. There are relatively few cross veins, and the wings are held roofwise over the body at rest. The slender antennae, usually as long as the forewings and sometimes much longer, are held out in front of the head at rest. Ocelli may or may not be present. Adult caddis flies rarely feed, although some individuals may occasionally lap nectar from the waterside flowers. There is never a proboscis such as we find in most moths.

The head bears a pair of conspicuous maxillary palps, whose form is important in the classification of the insects: some are very long, while others are short and swollen. Females always have 5-segmented palps, but the males of many species have fewer segments. The spurs on the tibiae are also valuable aids to identification, for their numbers vary from family to family. It is conventional to describe the spur pattern with a series of numbers: 2-2-4, for example, means that there are 2 spurs on the front tibia, 2 on the middle tibia, and 4 on the hind tibia. The spurs are usually very easy to see, but among the families Phryganeidae and Limnephilidae (p. 184) the legs also bear numerous spines, some of which may be at least half as long as the spurs. Take care that you really are looking at the spurs when counting them: and make sure that none has broken off in old and dried specimens.

The venation is another important factor in the identification of caddis fly families, although less easy to use. Classification revolves largely around the forking of the veins near the margin and also on the presence or absence of a discal cell near the centre of the forewing, but most of the caddis flies on the following pages can be recognised without examination of the veins. Separation of closely related species often necessitates examination of the genitalia.

Eggs are commonly laid in gelatinous masses, in or on the water or else on overhanging vegetation. Some are laid under stones on beds of dried-up ponds and streams, and they hatch when water returns in the autumn. The larvae are largely omnivorous, although some species show leanings towards either plant or animal food. The majority make portable homes or cases which camouflage them very well on the bed of the pond or stream. Only the head and legs protrude from the case as the larva crawls along. The case is made of small stones or plant fragments, neatly fitted on to a silken tube surrounding the body.

The silk is produced by the larva's salivary glands. Each species builds to its own pattern, although closely related species have similar cases. The case is open at both ends, and more material is added to the front as the animal grows. A range of cases is shown on the following pages.

The larvae of some caddis flies are completely naked, while others shelter in silken nets. The latter are usually spun among the water plants and they trap small animals and other food particles. Net-spinning species generally live in running water.

The insects pupate in their cases after cementing them to stones or other large objects. Species which make no larval case construct a simple pupation chamber of silk and sand. When the adult is ready to emerge, the pupa bites its way out of the case and swims to the surface or to the bank, where the adult bursts out and immediately flies away. The life cycle generally occupies a year.

▲ ***Phryganea grandis*** Phryganeidae. Spurs 2-4-4. Discal cell long and narrow. Male palps 4-segmented. Male is smaller and lacks black stripe in forewing. 5–8, with peak in early July: the largest British caddis fly. Breeds in still and slow-moving water, including large lowland rivers, with plenty of submerged vegetation. Case of spirally arranged plant fragments. Absent from far south. ▲ ***P. striata*** is very similar but female has more slender black stripe broken in 3 short dashes.

Oligostomis reticulata. Spurs 2-4-4. Mottled pattern combined with size readily distinguishes this species from most others. Hind wing has dark border and a dark stripe across the middle. Male palps 4-segmented. Larval case and habits like *Phryganea*. N & C. △n ***Hagenella clathrata*** is similar but has more dark clouding on hind wing. N & C.

Family Limnephilidae
A large family in which front leg never has more than one spur: formula 1-3-4 in most species. Forewings parchment-like with few hairs: discal cell fairly long and obvious. Hind wings rather broad and very transparent.

▲ ***Glyphotaelius pellucidus***. Spurs 1-3-4. Readily identified by strongly notched outer margin of forewing. Female less strongly marked: forewing often plain yellowish brown. Abdomen generally greenish. 4–10. Ponds and lakes: case of pieces of dead leaf, completely concealing larva from above. Absent from Iberia.

▲ ***Limnephilus lunatus***. Spurs 1-3-4. Forewings, as in all members of this large genus, narrow with an almost straight front edge and sharply truncated at tip. Markings black or brown and variable, but always a pale crescent on outer margin. 5–11. Breeds in all kinds of water: sometimes abundant in watercress beds. Case of overlapping leaf fragments and other debris, sometimes with added shells and sand grains. ▲ ***L. flavicornis*** is similar but lacks pale crescent. Wings rather shiny: British specimens often much less marked, rarely with more than a dark line along hind margin of forewing. 5–11. Breeds mainly in small ponds. Case of various materials arranged in criss-cross fashion: occasionally made entirely of small shells. There are many other *Limnephilus* spp, nearly all with clear patches on forewings, distinguished with certainty only by examining the genitalia.

▲ ***Anabolia nervosa***. Spurs 1-3-4. Size very variable. Forewings often paler. 6–11. Breeds in still and running water but most common in streams. Case of sand grains to which are attached small sticks, the latter preventing trout and other fishes from swallowing the cases.

▲ ***Grammotaulius nigropunctatus***. Spurs 1-3-4. Forewing rather pointed. Hind wing with indented outer margin and a dark streak just in front of indentation: dark streak shows through delicate forewing at rest. 8–10. Breeds in marshy areas, including small ditches. Case of overlapping reed fragments. △ ***G. nitidus*** is larger, with more pointed forewing, especially in male. C.

▲ ***Micropterna sequax***. Spurs 0-3-4 in male: 1-3-4 in female. 5–11: very common at lights. Breeds in small clear streams. Case of sand grains but with a region of small stones, sharply demarcated, at the front. There are several similar species.

▲ ***Halesus radiatus***. Spurs 1-3-3. Apex of forewing smoothly rounded, with a conspicuous pattern of finger-like, pale-edged grey streaks. Grey streaks and patches in cells elsewhere in wing as well. 7–11. Breeds in running water. Case of assorted plant debris neatly fitted together: up to 3 slender twigs run the length of the case and project from both ends. ▲ ***H. digitatus*** is similar but larger: wing-tips slightly less rounded and slightly less obvious pattern. Case of debris and sand grains but usually without sticks.

↑ larval case

Micropterna sequax ×2

Halesus radiatus ×1.5

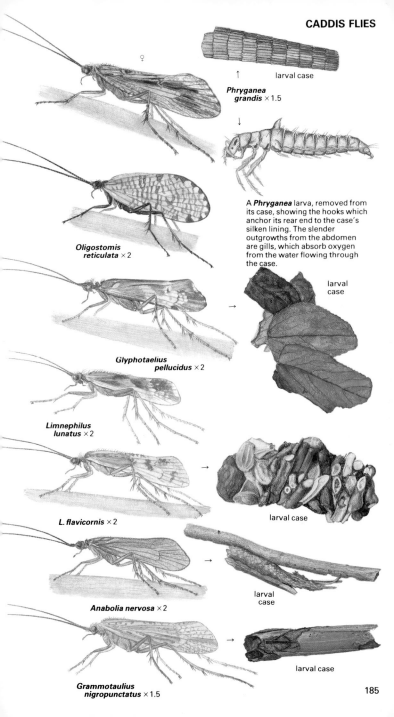

CADDIS FLIES

larval case

Phryganea grandis × 1.5

A *Phryganea* larva, removed from its case, showing the hooks which anchor its rear end to the case's silken lining. The slender outgrowths from the abdomen are gills, which absorb oxygen from the water flowing through the case.

Oligostomis reticulata × 2

Glyphotaelius pellucidus × 2

larval case

Limnephilus lunatus × 2

L. flavicornis × 2

larval case

Anabolia nervosa × 2

larval case

Grammotaulius nigropunctatus × 1.5

larval case

185

▲ **Brachycentrus subnubilus** Brachycentridae. Spurs 2-3-3, distinguishing this from nearly all other caddis flies: no other British species has this formula. Basal antennal segment stout and hairy. Male palps 3-segmented. Female wings longer and more pointed. 3–7: very common around slow-moving rivers. Case of young larva made of plant debris and square in cross-section: older cases of silk only and attached to vegetation. Larva strains food from water with comb-like middle legs.

▲ **Sericostoma personatum** Sericostomatidae. Spurs 2-2-4. Male palps 1-segmented and very broad and hairy: held muff-like in front of face. 6–9. Breeds in streams. Case of sand grains: very smooth and gently curved.

▲ **Goera pilosa** Goeridae. Spurs 2-4-4 and very conspicuous. Basal antennal segment very hairy. Male palps 3-segmented: 3rd segment long and bristly and held close to face. Body and wings yellow or greyish yellow. 5–9, around lakes and rivers. Case of sand grains with small pebbles at the sides.

▲ **Silo nigricornis**. Spurs 2-4-4. Basal antennal segment very stout. Male palps 3-segmented and very hairy: held in front of face. Male black when fresh: female brown. A hairy stripe runs through middle of male hind wing. 5–8, near running water. Case like that of *Goera*. S & C. There are several similar species.

▲ **Lepidostoma hirtum** Lepidostomatidae. Spurs 2-4-4. Basal antennal segment longer than head and bearing long hairs. Male palps 2–3 segmented: short and club-like and very hairy. Female wings longer and narrower and without dark scales. 4–9. Breeds in still and running water. Case of vegetable debris and square in cross-section.

▲ **Hydropsyche pellucidula** Hydropsychidae. Spurs 2-4-4. Basal antennal segment slightly swollen. Last palpal segment much longer than the rest. No ocelli. Discal cell short and broad. Amount of mottling on forewing very variable. 5–9, flying in sunshine: very common. Breeds in still and slow-moving water. Larva spins net among gravel to trap food. There are many similar species, very difficult to distinguish.

△ **Philopotamus montanus** Philopotamidae. Spurs 2-4-4. Last palpal segment longer than all others together. Ocelli present. Hind wings smoky grey. 4–8, mainly around upland streams. Larvae are net spinners in swift-flowing streams. Wing pattern readily distinguishes this species in B, but there are several similar species on the continent.

▲ **Polycentropus flavomaculatus** Polycentropodidae. Spurs 3-4-4 and very large. Last palpal segment about as long as all others together. No ocelli. Antennae brown with *narrow* yellow bands. Wings very hairy. Female up to twice size of male. 5–9: one of the commonest caddis flies. Larva spins pouch-shaped net in slow-moving water. There are several similar species.

▲ **Tinodes waeneri** Psychomyiidae. Spurs 2-4-4. Last palpal segment long and slender. No ocelli. Veins very distinct: discal cell short and broad. Hind wing narrow, with front edge slightly cut away towards tip. 5–8. Breeds in lakes and rivers. Galleries of silk, usually coated with mud: attached to stones. There are several similar but generally smaller species.

▲ **Psychomyia pusilla**. Spurs 2-4-4. Hind wing sharply pointed and with a small spike on front margin. 5–9: day-flying in warm weather, often in great swarms. Breeds like *Tinodes* in streams and rivers.

▲ **Hydroptila sparsa** Hydroptilidae. Wings very narrow, pointed, and extremely hairy. Spurs 0-2-4. 5–9, often scuttling over waterside rocks and plants. Breeds in still or running water. Larva naked until final instar, when it makes a silken, sausage-shaped chamber coated with fine sand grains. There are many very similar species.

Silo:
hind
wing of ♂

Tinodes
hind wing

Psychomyia
hind wing

palp of *Philopotamus*

palp of ♀
Sericostoma

palp of ♀
Lepidostoma

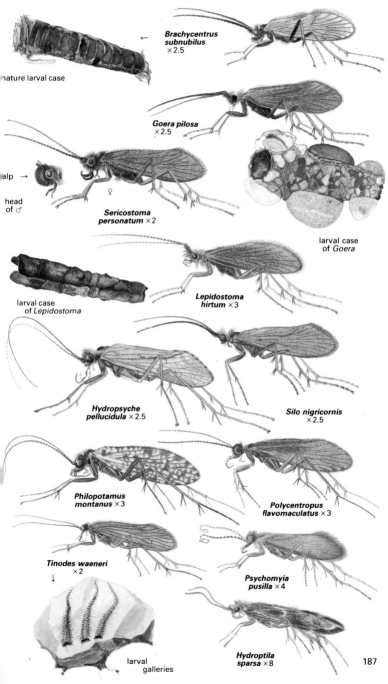

mature larval case

Brachycentrus subnubilus ×2.5

Goera pilosa ×2.5

alp →

head of ♂

Sericostoma personatum ×2 ♀

larval case of *Goera*

larval case of *Lepidostoma*

Lepidostoma hirtum ×3

Hydropsyche pellucidula ×2.5

Silo nigricornis ×2.5

Philopotamus montanus ×3

Polycentropus flavomaculatus ×3

Tinodes waeneri ×2

Psychomyia pusilla ×4

larval galleries

Hydroptila sparsa ×8

187

▲ **Odontocerum albicorne** Odontoceridae. Spurs 2-4-4: large. Best distinguished by antennae, which appear distinctly toothed under a lens: basal antennal segment very thick. Wings silvery grey when fresh, becoming darker or yellowish with age. Hind wing of male with long tuft of hair along inner margin. Female larger than male. 6–10. Breeds in running water with stony bottom. Case of sand grains.

▲ **Molanna angustata** Molannidae. Spurs 2-4-4. No ocelli. Forewings dark grey to brown, with conspicuous venation, especially near tips. Legs rather long. Rests at an angle, with wings folded round body to resemble a piece of dead grass. 5–9. Breeds in still and slow-moving water with a sandy bottom. Case of sand grains: tubular, with a broad flat shield on dorsal side. N & C.

▲ **Beraea pullata** Beraeidae. Spurs 2-2-4. No ocelli. Head projects forward between antennae. Palps long and stout: held upright in front of face when alive. 5–7. Breeds in shallow water at edges of lakes and rivers, as well as in ponds and marshes. Case of sand grains: tubular and tapering and gently curved. There are several similar species.

▲ **Athripsodes cinereus** Leptoceridae. Spurs 2-2-2: all members of this large family have just 2 spurs on hind tibia. Very long antennae, especially in males, are also a feature of the family. Palps very long and hairy. Colour and markings vary. Female smaller. 6–9: very common around lakes and large rivers. Case of sand grains: slender and tapering.

▲ **Ceraclea nigronervosa**. Spurs 2-2-2. Body entirely black. Forewing veins rather conspicuous. Hind wing very broad and triangular. Female smaller. 5–7, around lakes and large rivers. Flight strong. Case of secretion, with irregular bands of sand grains. N & C.

▲ **Mystacides longicornis**. Spurs 0-2-2. Easily recognised as a rule by wing pattern, although this is occasionally obscured. Male eyes very large. Antennae very pale. Palps plumose and spread out to sides, almost like legs, at rest. 5–9: very common around lakes and ponds. Flight strong. Case of small stones or sand grains: almost straight and tapering very gently. Several closely related species have steely blue or black forewings.

▲ **Triaenodes bicolor**. Spurs 1-2-2. Readily identified by chestnut forewings when fresh. Antennae distinctly ringed. Palps very long. 6–9: often abundant around lakes and ponds. Case of very regular, spirally arranged green leaf fragments: long and straight. Larva swims with aid of feathery middle legs: prefers weedy ponds.

△ **Rhyacophila obliterata** Rhyacophilidae. Spurs 3-4-4: large. First 2 palpal segments short and thick, the 2nd being almost spherical. Ocelli present. 6–9, mainly around upland streams. Larva makes no case and lives freely on stream bed. There are several closely related species, but *obliterata* is easily recognised by bright yellow wings when fresh, although colour fades after death.

▲ **Agapetus fuscipes** Glossosomatidae. Spurs 2-4-4. First 2 palpal segments short and thick. Wings narrow: black with golden hairs. Male has long yellow spine under abdomen. 5–12: one of the commonest caddis flies. Breeds in fast-flowing streams with stony bottoms. Case of small stones, domed above and flat below: often clothing submerged rocks in vast numbers.

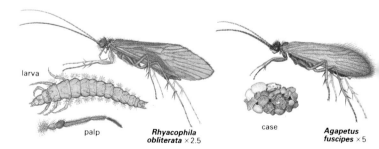

larva

palp

Rhyacophila obliterata × 2.5

case

Agapetus fuscipes × 5

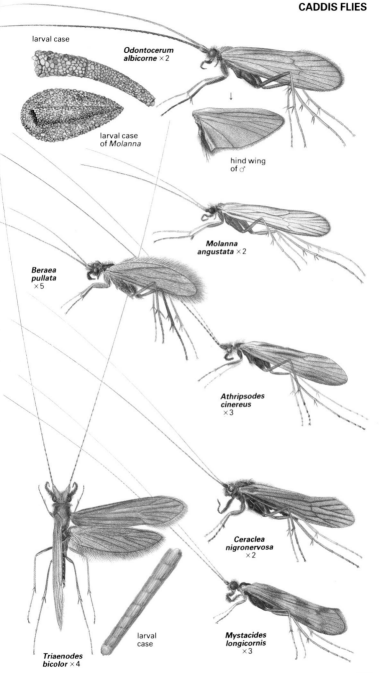

larval case

Odontocerum albicorne × 2

larval case of *Molanna*

↓

hind wing of ♂

Molanna angustata × 2

Beraea pullata ×5

Athripsodes cinereus ×3

Ceraclea nigronervosa ×2

larval case

Mystacides longicornis ×3

Triaenodes bicolor ×4

TRUE FLIES   Order Diptera

An immense order of insects containing nearly 100,000 known species. The hind wings are reduced to minute pin-shaped bodies known as balancers or halteres, which act as gyroscopes and help to maintain stability in flight. The single pair of membranous wings gives the order its name: 'two-winged.' A few species, mainly ectoparasites (p. 213), are entirely wingless.

Feeding. Although a few hover-flies (pp. 204–6) are able to crush pollen-grains, flies feed essentially on liquids: mainly nectar but many other liquids too. Female mosquitoes, horse-flies and several other groups feed mainly on blood, attacking both man and his domestic animals to get it. The blood-sucking in itself is serious only where the insects exist in huge numbers, but many carry dangerous diseases such as malaria. The flies' mouth-parts vary with the diet. Female mosquitoes have needle-like jaws which fit neatly together to form a hypodermic syringe, complete with a protective sheath which is drawn back when the insect is about to pierce a victim. Female horse-flies have more blade-like jaws which cut the victim's skin: a fleshy pad then mops up the blood that flows from the wound. House-flies and blow-flies rely entirely on mopping up surface fluids with a pair of spongy pads at the tip of the mouth-parts, though they can deal with soluble solids like sugar, by pouring digestive fluids on to them first. They spread disease by regurgitating over our food after visiting dung or carrion. Some flies do not feed at all once adult.

Compound **eyes** are always present, and often so large that they meet on the top of the head. This 'holoptic' condition is most often found in males, but the females of some species also have it. The presence or absence of **ocelli**, which generally form a small triangle on the top of the head, often helps identification, as does the form of the **antennae** and the arrangement of bristles on the head and **thorax**. The bulk of the thorax consists of the wing-bearing mesothorax, but the roughly triangular scutellum on its rear margin may be prominent. In some flies, notably the parasitic tachinids (p. 212), there is also a post-scutellum bulging from underneath the scutellum itself. Each **foot** normally has two small pads, but some groups of flies have three on each foot.

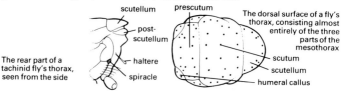

The rear part of a tachinid fly's thorax, seen from the side

scutellum · post-scutellum · haltere · spiracle

The dorsal surface of a fly's thorax, consisting almost entirely of the three parts of the mesothorax

prescutum · scutum · scutellum · humeral callus

Wing-venation is extremely variable. Several schemes are in use for naming and numbering the veins; here we have used a simple system for the major veins. Very close to the base of the front margin there is a small and often inconspicuous cross vein known as the humeral vein. The sub-costa runs close to the front margin, often joining it about half way along though it reaches almost to the wing tip in some species. The other main veins, sometimes termed long veins, can be numbered from the front. The first is commonly known as the radius, while the last two (6 and 7) are the anal veins. Venation is much reduced in many flies, especially towards the rear of the wing and is often complicated by the branching of some or all of the veins. Some main veins may also fuse together, and it is not always possible to determine which vein is which simply by counting. There are useful clues, however: the anterior cross-vein always links veins 3 and 4, while the posterior cross-vein – usually near the centre of the wing – links 4 and 5. Many species have a discal cell near the centre of the wing: its shape varies a great deal, but the anterior cross-vein generally joins its anterior margin. Between the discal cell and the base of the wing are generally two basal cells, whose relative shapes and lengths are important. The anal cell, when present, lies just behind the basal cells.

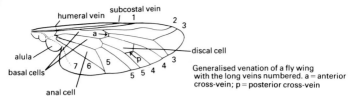

Generalised venation of a fly wing with the long veins numbered. a = anterior cross-vein; p = posterior cross-vein

The front or costal margin of the wing sometimes has one or two minute breaks in it, usually quite near the base; mainly in the smaller flies. The hind margin of the wing may have one or more distinct lobes near the base. The outer lobe, known as the alula, is generally the biggest and quite obvious. The inner lobe, known as the calypter or thoracic squama, is generally minute, but in some it forms a prominent flap covering the haltere. This is particularly noticeable in the house-flies, blow-flies etc., known as the calypterate flies.

Classification. The flies are grouped into three sub-orders: Nematocera, Brachycera and Cyclorrhapha. Members of the **Nematocera**, (pp. 192–7) have slender, many-segmented antennae which are usually longer than the head and thorax together. Most of the antennal segments are alike, and there is no bristle or arista at the tip. There is usually no discal cell, and the anal cell, when present, is open and gets wider towards the wing margin.

Antenna of a, *Nematocera*; b, *Cyclorrhapha*; c, *Brachycera*

The **Brachycera** (= short horns, pp. 198–205) are mostly much stouter flies and their antennae are always shorter than the thorax, although very variable in form. The antennae are basically 3-segmented, but the third segment is strongly annulated and the antennae may then appear to be many-segmented. They are stouter than the nematoceran antennae, however, and often horn-like: many have a terminal arista. The discal cell is nearly always present, and the anal cell is closed or strongly tapered towards the wing-margin.

In the **Cyclorrhapha**, (= 'circular seam', pp. 204–16) the antennae are generally much less prominent. The three main segments are generally pendulous, and a slender bristle springs from the dorsal surface of the third segment rather than from the tip. In most species only the bristle is visible from above. But it is in the young stages that the Brachycera and Cyclorrhapha show their main differences.

Larvae and life-histories. The larvae of flies are incredibly varied in form and habits, some living on land and some in water, some inside plants and others as parasites inside various other animals: they include many serious agricultural pests. The larvae have no true legs, although many have fleshy outgrowths which help them to wriggle about. The head is quite prominent in many nematocerans, and equipped with biting jaws. Brachyceran larvae have a much-reduced head, which can be retracted into the thorax, although still equipped with biting jaws. Among the cyclorrhaphans there is no real head and the larvae are the familiar tapering maggots. Their jaws, at the narrow end, are represented by minute hooks whose main function is to scrape and tear at the food and release fluids which the maggot can imbibe.

There are normally four larval instars among the Nematocera, five to eight among the Brachycera, and only three among the Cyclorrhapha. The **pupa** is quite mobile in the first two groups, very much so in some families such as mosquitoes. The cyclorrhaphan pupa, on the other hand, is quite immobile inside a hard barrel-shaped puparium, formed from the hardened last larval skin. When ready to emerge, they inflate a sac at the front of the head and the pressure forces up a round lid. The pale sac, known as the ptilinum, can often be seen in freshly emerged flies, which therefore appear rather deformed, but it soon deflates and recedes into the head. Its position is then marked by a faint groove, shaped like an inverted U, around the bases of the antennae.

Tipula abdomen

♀   ♂

CRANE-FLIES Tipulidae Rather leggy flies commonly called **daddy-long-legs**. Legs readily break off when handled. Many are only mosquito-sized, but all can be recognised by the V-shaped suture on thorax together with lack of ocelli. A clear discal cell in outer half of wing. Larger species generally rest with wings extended: smaller species generally fold wings flat over body, and often bob up and down on their legs when at rest – hence an alternative name of bobbing gnats. Many of the smaller species form dense mating swarms (see p. 190). Female abdomen is pointed, for laying eggs in ground or other materials. Some females are wingless and can be seen on house walls in late autumn. Adults may lap nectar and other fluids but do not feed much. Larvae live mainly as scavengers in soil or decaying matter, often under water.

▲ **_Tipula maxima_.** One of the largest crane-flies. Like _Tipula_ spp, it rests with wings at about 90° to each other. 4–8, mainly in wooded areas. ▲ **_T. vittata_** is smaller and has a less extensive pattern. 4–6 in damp woods.

▲ **_T. oleracea_** is one of the commonest species. The wing is brown along the front, with brown stigma, but otherwise plain. Antennae 13-segmented, with at least first 3 segments brick-coloured. Female wings as long as abdomen. 4–10, but most abundant 5–6. ▲ **_T. paludosa_** is very like _oleracea_ but antennae are 14-segmented (terminal one minute) and only first 2 segments brick-coloured. Female wings shorter than abdomen, the latter often with rusty tinge. 4–10, but most abundant in autumn. Larvae of last two species are crop-damaging leatherjackets (p. 294).

▲ **_Nephrotoma crocata_.** Sides of thorax almost entirely black. Wings usually folded at rest. 5–8. Especially common in damp woods.

▲ **Spotted crane-fly** _N. appendiculata_ – illustrated here without its wings – has a very faint stigma: wing otherwise clear and shiny. 5–8, especially in cultivated areas. Larva (similar to that of _Tipula_) is a common garden pest. ▲ **_N. quadrifaria_** is similar but has a dark stigma and dark streak below it. Both species fold wings flat over body at rest.

▲ **_Limonia nubeculosa_.** One of several species with spotted wings. Latter are folded flat at rest. Sub-costal vein runs into front margin, not into radius as in most other large crane-flies. No tibial spurs. Femora with 3 dark rings. All year, mainly in woodland.

▲ **_Ctenophora atrata_.** Antennae range from orange to black: strongly pectinate in male, toothed near tip in female. Male abdomen ranges from black to yellow, with spotted intermediate forms: female abdomen sometimes nearly all red. 4–7 in damp woods.

△ **_C. ornata_** has female antennae toothed throughout. 5–7 in woods. Both species breed in decaying timber; _atrata_, with its tougher ovipositor, preferring harder and less rotted wood.

▲ **_Ptychoptera contaminata_ Ptychopteridae.** Resembles crane-flies but thoracic suture is U-shaped. No discal cell and only one anal vein. Legs with strong tibial spurs – much more prominent than in crane-flies. Abundant in damp places 5–10. Larva (p. 296) is aquatic. There are several similar species, all with spotted wings.

Liponeura cinerascens Blepharoceridae. A weak-flying insect with very long legs and a network of fine creases on wings. Ocelli present. Females predatory. Larvae and pupae aquatic. Wings fully expanded, although folded, in pupa: latter 'explodes' at surface and adult flies away immediately, but wings never lose creases. One of several similar species living around upland streams in summer. S & C.

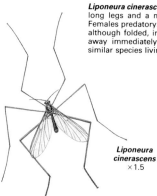

Liponeura cinerascens
× 1.5

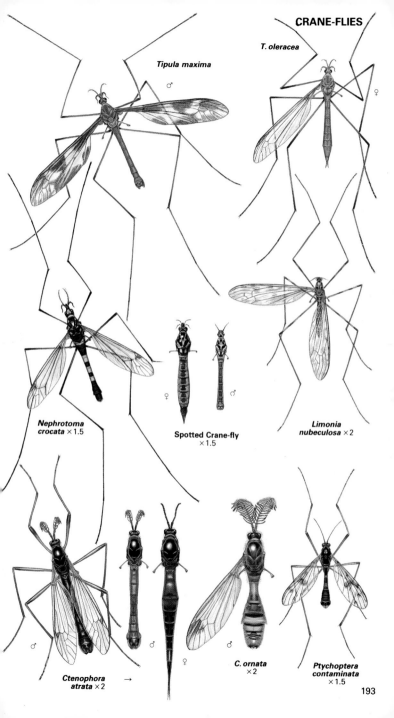

Tipula maxima

T. oleracea

Nephrotoma crocata ×1.5

Spotted Crane-fly ×1.5

Limonia nubeculosa ×2

Ctenophora atrata ×2

C. ornata ×2

Ptychoptera contaminata ×1.5

193

Culicine at rest

Anopheline at rest

▲ *Trichocera relegationis* Trichoceridae. Like a small crane-fly but 2nd anal vein very short and sharply bent. Legs not deciduous. Ocelli present. Abundant everywhere in winter, males forming dense mating swarms. Less common at other times of year. Larvae live in decaying matter. One of several similar species, mostly without a spot in middle of wing, known as winter gnats. ▲ *T. annulata* has a banded abdomen.

MOSQUITOES Culicidae A large family of flies (over 1600 known species) with a long, forward-pointing proboscis which female uses to suck blood. Male, distinguished by bushy antennae, feeds on nectar. Male palps long and hairy: female palps always slender. Wing veins and margins clothed with scales. Mainly nocturnal, although some woodland species are active by day. Larvae (p. 296) are aquatic. Two groups are generally recognised – the culicines and the anophelines. Culicines rest with body slightly arched and abdomen almost parallel to surface: female palps very short. Anophelines, represented in Europe only by *Anopheles* spp, are the malaria-carriers. They rest with body sharply inclined to surface: female palps about as long as proboscis. Both groups fold wings flat over body at rest.

▲ *Culex pipiens*. Abdominal segments dark brown with white bands at front of each. Female abdomen blunt-ended. Male palps up-turned. Abundant everywhere, hibernating as adult in buildings. Rarely bites man in B. There are several similar species, but with less clearly banded abdomen.

▲ *Culiseta annulata*. One of the largest mosquitoes. Wings spotted. Legs and abdomen boldly banded. Common in many habitats, hibernating as adult in buildings. Bites man, often causing blisters.

▲ *Aedes punctor*. Abdomen brown with yellowish bands, each notched in middle. Legs dark. Female abdomen pointed. Male palps swollen at tip. 3–10. Breeds in acidic pools, especially on heathland and in open woods. Regularly bites man. N & C.

▲ *Anopheles plumbeus*. Female palps long: male palps clubbed, with hairy tip. Wings unspotted. Tuft of pure white scales on head (creamy white in *A. claviger* which is generally rather browner). 3–10, mainly in woods. Bites man readily. Breeds mainly in wet tree holes. Many *Anopheles* spp have spotted wings.

▲ *Chaoborus crystallinus* Chaoboridae. One of a group known as phantom midges, closely related to mosquitoes but non-biting. Scales confined to wing margins. Female wings reach tip of abdomen. Male antennae plumose. Abdomen unbanded. Common all year except in coldest weather. Usually near water: larvae (p. 296) aquatic.

▲ *Dixella aestivalis* Dixidae. Closely related to mosquitoes but non-biting. Sub-costal vein only about half length of wing. No scales. Antennae not plumose. Most of year, usually near water. Larvae aquatic, usually bent into U-shape at surface (p. 297). There are several similar species.

▲ *Chironomus plumosus* Chironomidae. No cross vein in middle of wing: hind veins very weak. Wings shorter than abdomen and held roofwise over body at rest. Only male antennae plumose. Non-biting, feeding little if at all as adults. Common everywhere 4–9, males forming dense swarms. Aquatic larva (p. 297) is one of the bloodworms. One of many very similar species known as non-biting midges. Some are green.

▲ *Sylvicola fenestralis* Anisopodidae. Resembles winter gnats (Trichoceridae) but no V-shaped thoracic suture. Discal cell present. 2nd anal vein not sharply bent and not reaching wing margin. Common most of the year, often in houses. Larvae in decaying matter: very common in sewage beds. One of several species known as window midges.

Midge is a general term applied to small flies in several families and with no precise meaning.

Sylvicola fenestralis ×3

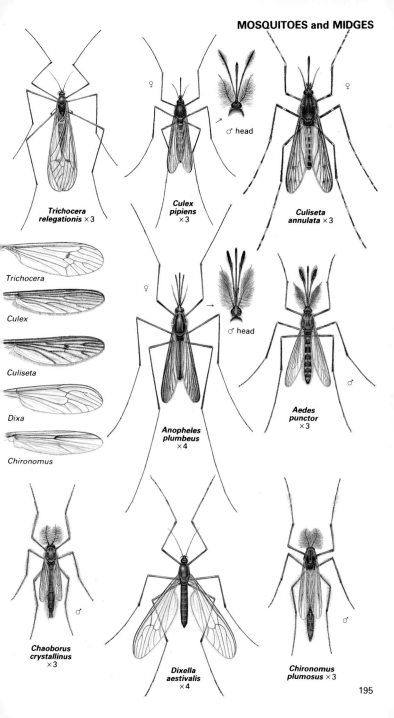

Trichocera relegationis × 3

Culex pipiens × 3

♀
♂ head

Culiseta annulata × 3

♀

Trichocera

Culex

Culiseta

Dixa

Chironomus

♀
♂ head

Anopheles plumbeus × 4

♂

Aedes punctor × 3

♂

Chaoborus crystallinus × 3

Dixella aestivalis × 4

♂

Chironomus plumosus × 3

195

Simulium at rest

gall
of *Jaapiella*

Culicoides

Pericoma

front leg of
St. Mark's-fly

front leg of
Fever-fly

▲ **Simulium equinum** Simuliidae. One of many very similar species known as black-flies – not to be confused with blackfly aphids (p. 94). Broad wings have characteristic venation. Strongly humped thorax, best seen from the side. Female sucks blood and often flies in such dense swarms as to be a serious nuisance to horses and cattle: also attacks people. 3–10, especially common around hill streams. Larvae (p. 297) attached to stones in running water.

▲ **Scatopse notata** Scatopsidae. Venation superficially like *Simulium* but wings narrower and thorax less humped. Ocelli present, unlike *Simulium*. Commonly enters houses and crawls over windows. Breeds in decaying matter. Several similar species.

▲ **Jaapiella veronicae** Cecidomyiidae. Wings hairy, with little venation. Antennae like minute strings of beads, with whorls of hair. Swarms to lighted windows on summer nights. Larva on germander speedwell, causing hairy galls (left) on shoot tips. Many very similar species, collectively known as gall midges, cause galls on a wide range of plants.

▲ **Sciara thomae** Mycetophilidae. Thorax strongly humped. Eyes meet above antennae. Tibiae spiny. Prominent fork in middle of wing. Breeds in all kinds of rotting matter. Common in houses, scuttling rapidly about or drifting slowly through the air. Abundant where mushrooms are grown, commonly damaging the crop. Many similar species. Family as a whole known as fungus gnats. Larvae, like white worms with dark heads, commonly feed in fungi.

△ **Cerotelion lineatus.** First 2 long veins not linked by cross vein. 6–10 in woods and other damp places. Larvae carnivorous on other insects in fungi, especially those on tree trunks.

△ **Platyura marginata.** First 2 long veins linked by cross vein near wing tip. Thorax with yellow hair: abdomen shining black. Femora yellow. 6–9, especially in wooded areas. Larvae inhabit silken web and are carnivorous on other fungus-eaters. C.

▲ **Culicoides obsoletus** Ceratopogonidae. One of the biting midges – very small flies with blood-sucking females. Thorax strongly humped. Forked vein in centre of wing: latter folded flat at rest. Male antennae plumose. Many species attack other insects but *Culicoides* spp take vertebrate blood: *obsoletus* and several similar species swarm in vast numbers in summer and often make life intolerable in northern and upland areas. Breed in waterlogged soil and peat.

▲ **Pericoma fuliginosa** Psychodidae. One of the owl-midges or moth-flies, which are easily recognised by hairy wings with many long veins. Some species rest with wings partly spread: others hold them roof-like over body. Smaller species mostly uniformly grey. Breed in decaying matter of all kinds. Abundant at sewage works. Often come to lighted windows at night.

▲ **St Mark's-fly** *Bibio marci* Bibionidae. Named because it often appears close to St Mark's Day (April 25th). Drifts slowly over low vegetation with legs hanging. Like other members of the family, it has short, stout antennae inserted below eyes. Eyes well separated in female. There is a beak-like spine at tip of front tibia. Breeds in soil and rotting vegetation. Several similar species. ▲ **B. hortulanus** has a brick-coloured upper surface in female. Not uncommon in gardens in spring, often pairing on sunny walls.

▲ **Fever-fly** *Dilophus febrilis*. Distinguished from *Bibio* spp by circlet of small spines around tip of front tibia. Female has smoky wings: male wings clear with a black spot like *Bibio*. On and around flowers, including apples and other fruit trees, 3–10; most common in spring. Flight sluggish.

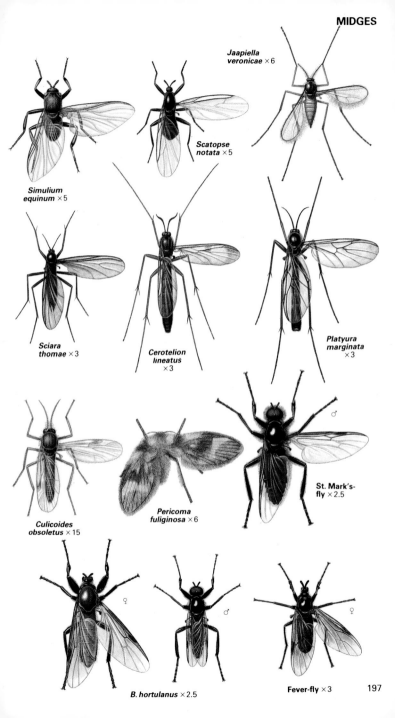

Jaapiella veronicae ×6

Scatopse notata ×5

Simulium equinum ×5

Sciara thomae ×3

Cerotelion lineatus ×3

Platyura marginata ×3

Culicoides obsoletus ×15

Pericoma fuliginosa ×6

♂ St. Mark's-fly ×2.5

♀ *B. hortulanus* ×2.5

♂

Fever-fly ×3 ♀

SOLDIER-FLIES Stratiomyidae Flattened flies named for their usually bright and often metallic colours. Feet with 3 pads. Veins crowded in front part of wing, with small discal cell and relatively faint veins beyond it. Flight often weak, although some males hover and 'dance'. Visit flowers for nectar, but most often seen sunbathing on ground or low-growing vegetation. Wings folded flat at rest (left), often concealing bright colours.

Stratiomys potamida ♀ at rest

△ **Oxycera pulchella.** Scutellum with 2 spines. Legs largely yellow. 6–8 in damp woods and hedgerows. Breeds in moss and leaf litter. There are several similar species.

△ **Stratiomys chameleon.** Antennae long and pointed: distinctly elbowed with 1st segment long. Scutellum with 2 spines. 5–9 in marshy areas; especially fond of umbellifers. Larva aquatic and carnivorous. △ *S. potamida* has smaller yellow spots on 3rd abdominal segment in male and a narrow yellow band in female.

▲ **Chloromyia formosa.** Eyes very hairy. Scutellum not armed. Female abdomen less hairy than male, with blue-green and violet sheen showing through. 5–8 in woods, hedges, and gardens. Breeds in damp soil and leaf litter. *C. speciosa* has darker wings and yellowish hind tarsi. C.

▲ **Microchrysa polita.** Shiny green in both sexes. Antennae and legs black. Scutellum unarmed. 3–9 on shrubs and other lush vegetation: not uncommon in gardens. Breeds in dung and compost heaps.

△ **Beris clavipes.** Venation less crowded than in most soldier-flies. Scutellum with 4–6 black spines. 5–7 in damp areas with lush vegetation. ▲ *B. vallata* has no dark bands on abdomen. Wings are clearer, especially in female, and stigma more conspicuous.

▲ **Sargus bipunctatus.** Scutellum without spines. Veins more distinct in this genus than in most soldier-flies. Sexes differ markedly in abdomen. 8–10. Breeds in dung.

▲ **S. iridatus** has sexes alike, although female is broader at hind end. Wings uniformly smoky. 5–8. Breeds in cow dung.

△s **Odontomyia ornata.** Resembles *Stratiomys* but smaller and with shorter, non-elbowed antennae. Scutellum with 2 small spines. Abdominal spots yellow or orange. 5–8, usually on flowers and leaves near water. Breeds in muddy water.

▲ **O. viridula** abdomen varies from white to orange or green, always with a central black stripe. Green becomes yellowish after death. 6–8 among reeds and other waterside vegetation. Breeds in water.

△s **Xylomyia maculata** Xylomyiidae. Related to soldier-flies but venation is very different, with closed cell behind discal cell. Mid and hind tibiae spurred. Feet with 3 pads. 5–6 in ancient woodland, usually around decaying stumps and logs in which the larvae feed.

△ **Xylophagus ater** Xylophagidae. Superficially like *Ctenophora* (p. 192) but venation and antennae quite different. Feet with 3 pads. Female slightly larger, with just 2 shiny stripes on thorax. 4–8, mainly in woodland. Breeds in dead deciduous trees. N & C. △n *X. cinctus*, in which female abdomen is reddish in middle, breeds in pine stumps. N & C.

▲ **Snipe-fly** *Rhagio scolopacea* Rhagionidae. Feet with 3 pads. 2nd long vein curves forward to costa to enclose stigma. Anal cell open. Hind tibia with 2 spurs. 5–8, mainly in wooded areas. Rests head-down on tree trunks and other vertical surfaces. Larva (p. 294) lives in soil and is carnivorous. There are several related species, mostly with unspotted wings.

▲ **Chrysopilus cristatus.** Clothed with golden hairs and scales, although these easily rub off. Feet with 3 pads. Femora black. Hind tibia with 1 spur. 2nd long vein curves forward to enclose stigma. Anal cell closed and joined to wing margin by a stalk. 5–8 in woods and other damp or shady places. Breeds in rotting wood and leaf mould.

▲ **Atherix ibis.** Feet with 3 pads. Hind tibia with 2 spurs. 2nd long vein curves forward to enclose stigma. Anal cell closed and joined to wing margin by a stalk. Female greyer, with grey stripes on thorax. 5–7, rarely far from water. Larvae are aquatic.

Snipe-fly at rest

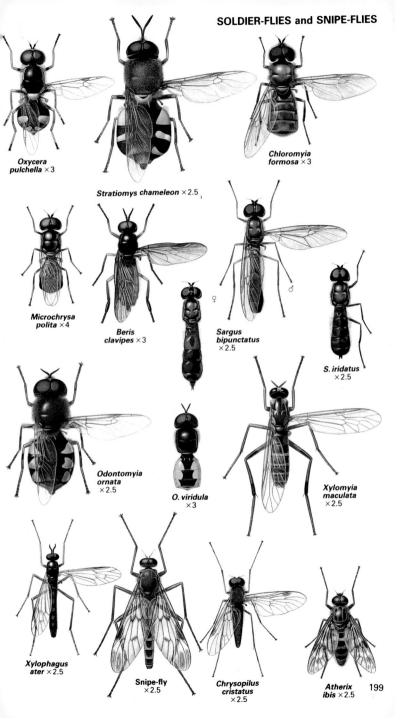

*Oxycera
pulchella* ×3

*Chloromyia
formosa* ×3

Stratiomys chameleon ×2.5

*Microchrysa
polita* ×4

*Beris
clavipes* ×3

♀

*Sargus
bipunctatus*
×2.5

♂

S. iridatus
×2.5

*Odontomyia
ornata*
×2.5

O. viridula
×3

*Xylomyia
maculata*
×2.5

*Xylophagus
ater* ×2.5

Snipe-fly
×2.5

*Chrysopilus
cristatus*
×2.5

*Atherix
ibis* ×2.5

199

HORSE-FLIES Tabanidae Stoutly-built, fast-flying flies with robust antennae. Eyes large and often brilliantly coloured and patterned in life. Veins form a broad fork across wing-tip. Feet have 3 pads. Most females are voracious blood-suckers, attacking large mammals, including man, with their blade-like mouth-parts. Males, often with slightly different patterns from females, are nectar-feeders. Almost always diurnal. Larvae (p. 294) live in damp soil and mud: some are carnivorous, others feed on decaying plant matter. About 160 of the 3,500 species occur in Europe.

▲ **Tabanus bovinus**. Hind margin of head concave when seen from above (as in all *Tabanus* spp). Eyes unbanded. Pale triangles on abdomen indistinct but usually reaching well into front half of each segment. Female palps very pale. 5–8 in pastures, especially near rivers. Breeds in muddy river banks.

▲ **T. bromius** ranges from yellowish grey to almost black. Eyes with one band. 5–9 on pastures: commonest of several similar species.

▲ **T. sudeticus** is very variable and often very like *bovinus* but pale triangles more distinct and generally shorter. Female palps brownish. 6–8 in pastures and open woodland. Mainly upland in B.

△ **Hybomitra micans**. Eyes very hairy, especially in male, with 3 purplish bands. Palps, antennae, and legs all black. Sub-callus (swelling just above antennae) shiny black. 5–9 on moors and damp heaths. C and occasionally on mountains in S.

△s **H. muhfeldi** is distinguished from several similar species by the brownish (not black) swelling just in front of wing base. 5–8. Common in many places, but especially on damp grassland around lakes. (This genus distinguished from most other horse-flies, including all British species, by very hairy eyes.)

Heptatoma pellucens. Distinguished by very long antennae together with clear wings. Eyes with 4 bands. 5–9 in many habitats, wooded or open.

▲ **Cleg-fly** *Haematopota pluvialis*. Eyes fairly hairy. 1st antennal segment deeply notched near tip in female. Mottled wings, held roofwise at rest, characterise this genus. Colour and pattern of abdomen vary. 5–10. Especially common in damp wooded habitats: one of the commonest horse-flies and a real nuisance to man, especially in thundery weather. Approaches silently. Partially replaced in uplands by the very similar ▲ **H. crassicornis**, which has pale V or Y in the discal cell. There are many similar species.

△ **Chrysops relictus**. Middle tibiae brownish yellow. Abdominal pattern varies but always with black lobes on 2nd segment (less divergent in male than female). 5–9 on damp heaths and moors and in light woodland: rarely far from water. Breeds in muddy river banks and other wet places.

▲ **C. caecutiens** has black middle tibiae. Male abdomen largely black: black marks on 2nd abdominal segment of female often much reduced. 5–9 in many habitats near water.

△ **C. viduatus** has brownish middle tibiae. 2nd abdominal segment has a single dark spot, variable in shape and much larger in male. 6–9 in grassland and woodland clearings. The last two species are absent from Ireland. There are several other species, all with brilliant eyes. Wings generally have more extensive dark area in males. All *Chrysops* spp have spurred hind tibiae.

▲ **Bombylius major** Bombyliidae. One of the bee-flies, so called for their furry appearance. Common at flowers in spring, sucking nectar through long proboscis. Quite harmless. Hovers well, especially in sunny spots, with a high-pitched whine. Larvae attack grubs of solitary bees and wasps in their underground nests.

△s **Thyridanthrax fenestratus**. Has same darting and hovering flight as *Bombylius* and the rest of the family. Proboscis short and retracted into head when not in use. 6–8 in sandy habitats. Larvae parasitise caterpillars. N & C. Several similar species in S.

Anthrax anthrax. Dark body, more extensive dark areas of wing, and short proboscis distinguish this from *Bombylius*. 5–9 mainly in dry habitats. Larvae parasitise solitary bees.

△ **Villa modesta**. Like a clear-winged **Bombylius** but proboscis short and head more spherical. Male has no pale abdominal bands. 5–9 in sandy places, mainly coastal. Larvae parasitise caterpillars. There are several species.

Fallenia fasciata Nemestrinidae. Very agile, fast-flying and often hovering. Distinguished from bee-flies by very different venation and a down-pointing proboscis. 5–8 in rather damp places, commonly feeding on thistles. Larvae feed on other insect grubs. S.

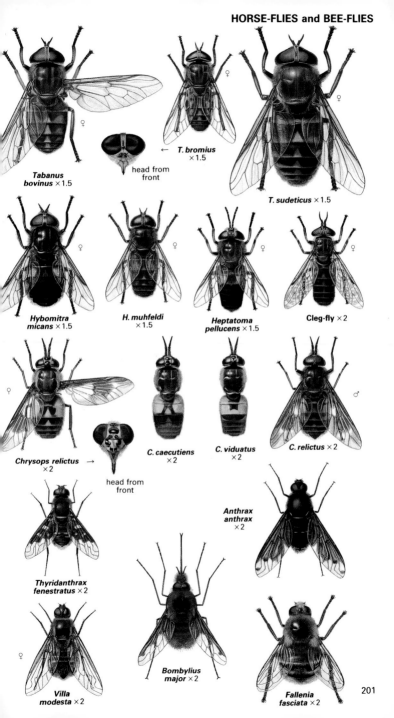

Tabanus bovinus ×1.5

head from front

← *T. bromius* ×1.5

T. sudeticus ×1.5

Hybomitra micans ×1.5

H. muhfeldi ×1.5

Heptatoma pellucens ×1.5

Cleg-fly ×2

Chrysops relictus → ×2

head from front

C. caecutiens ×2

C. viduatus ×2

C. relictus ×2

Anthrax anthrax ×2

Thyridanthrax fenestratus ×2

Villa modesta ×2

Bombylius major ×2

Fallenia fasciata ×2

201

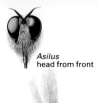

Asilus
head from front

ROBBER-FLIES Asilidae Very bristly predatory flies which generally chase and catch other insects in mid-air. Most species sit in wait and dart out when likely prey appears. The prey is then sucked dry with the stout proboscis, which projects horizontally or obliquely forward. There is a deep groove between the eyes in both sexes, the eyes never touching even in males. A 'beard' on the face protects eyes from struggling prey. Legs are sturdy and feet have 2 pads at most. Wings folded flat over body at rest. Larvae feed mainly on dead vegetable matter.

Asilus
with prey

△s **Asilus crabroniformis**. An unmistakable fly – the largest in B – inhabiting open country 7–10. A very strong flier. Breeds in cow pats and other dung.

Dasypogon diadema. First 2 long veins both reaching wing margin: wing membrane ribbed. Front tibia has curved spine at tip. Male more uniformly black, with dark wings. 6–8 in scrubby places, especially coastal dunes. S.

▲ **Leptogaster cylindrica**. Feet without pads. Hind femur yellow. 3rd antennal segment ends in bristle. Hunts in grassy places, flying slowly amongst grass and plucking aphids from the leaves. Resembles crane-fly in flight. 5–8. △ **L. guttiventris** is similar but has reddish hind femur.

△s **Dioctria atricapilla**. First 2 long veins reach margin. Beard rather sparse and, as in all *Dioctria* spp, antennae spring from a prominence high on the head. Female wings much lighter than male. 5–8 in grassy places.

△n **Laphria flava**. First 2 long veins join before reaching margin. 3rd antennal segment blunt, not with long bristle as in most other genera. Furry in pine woods. Breeds in pine logs and stumps. Confined to Scottish Highlands in B. Several similar species, all furry and bee-like, live on the continent. △s **L. gilva** is much less furry than *flava*, with hairs lying flat. 6–8 in old deciduous woods. Breeds in deciduous stumps. △s **L. marginata** is very similar but has yellow hairs on legs and thorax. 6–8 in oak woods.

△s **Eutolmus rufibarbis**. First 2 long veins join before reaching wing margin. Legs black with yellow hair. 5–9. N & C. Several similar species live on the continent.

△ **Pamponerus germanicus**. First 2 long veins join before reaching margin. Bristles behind eyes bend sharply forward. Femora black: tibiae and tarsi orange or yellow with black tips. Wing base much clearer in female. 5–7, mainly coastal.

───────────

△s **Acrocera globulus** Acroceridae. Minute head appears to consist of nothing but eyes. Antennae on top of head. Thorax strongly rounded. 6–8 in grassy places: often on flowers although adult does not feed. Larva parasitises spiders.

▲ **Thereva nobilitata** Therevidae. Resembles robber-flies but no groove between eyes: male eyes touching. Face very hairy. First long vein much shorter than in robber-flies. Female abdomen largely golden, with last 2 segments shiny black. 5–8. Larvae omnivorous in leaf litter. There are several similar species, difficult to separate. ▲ **T. annulata** male is silvery. Female is greyer and duller, with only last abdominal segment shiny black. 4–8 in sandy places, especially coastal dunes.

▲ **Window-fly** *Scenopinus fenestratus* Scenopinidae. Most often seen in windows, with wings tightly folded to give the fly a dark, bullet-like appearance. No bristles. Larva inhabits birds' nests and buildings, preying on grubs of other insects.

▲ **Empis tessellata** Empididae. Short triangular cell close to wing-tip is typical of this genus. Head almost spherical, with slender down-pointing proboscis. Predatory on other flies, but also taking nectar. Often hunts on hawthorn and umbellifer flowers. 4–8. Larva lives in soil. ▲ **E. stercorea** is easily recognised by its yellow-brown colour with a black stripe along the back. 4–6 in lush grassy places.

▲ **Hilara maura**. Venation like *Empis* but triangular cell near wing tip is longer and narrower. Swollen front tarsi of male produce silk which the fly uses to wrap prey as a courtship gift for female. Swarms over water throughout summer.

Acrocera globulus
×2

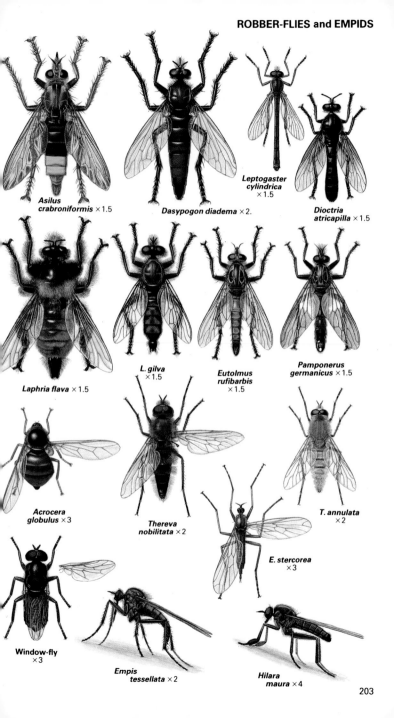

Asilus crabroniformis × 1.5

Dasypogon diadema × 2.

Leptogaster cylindrica × 1.5

Dioctria atricapilla × 1.5

Laphria flava × 1.5

L. gilva × 1.5

Eutolmus rufibarbis × 1.5

Pamponerus germanicus × 1.5

Acrocera globulus × 3

Thereva nobilitata × 2

E. stercorea × 3

T. annulata × 2

Window-fly × 3

Empis tessellata × 2

Hilara maura × 4

203

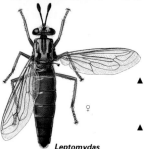

Leptomydas corsicanus × 1.5

Leptomydas corsicanus Mydaidae. Male much smaller and darker. Nectar-feeding, with darting flight. Rough grassy places 5–8. Corsica. 2 similar spp in Spain and 1 in Sardinia, all with clubbed antennae.

▲ **Lonchoptera lutea** Lonchopteridae. Pointed wings with no central cross vein identify this small family. Last 2 veins join before reaching margin only in female. Damp shady places 4–10. Commonest of several similar species.

▲ **Phora atra** Phoridae. One of the scuttle-flies, so called for their active running. Front edge of wing spiny at base: most veins very weak. Abundant on shrubs in summer: males hover in shafts of sunlight. There are many related species.

▲ **Sciapus platypterus** Dolichopodidae. Only one prominent cross vein, as in all the family. 4th vein distinctly forked. Female lacks black and white markings on mid tarsi. Hedgerows and tree trunks in summer. There are several similar species. All members of the family are metallic and prey on other small insects.

▲ **Dolichopus popularis**. Male genitalia very large, as in most members of the family. Female lacks plumes on mid tarsi. Damp places throughout summer, resting with front end raised. There are many similar species.

▲ **Poecilobothrus nobilitatus**. Male easily recognised by wing pattern: female like *Dolichopus*. Both sexes with 3rd and 4th veins wavy and convergent. 5–9 in damp places, resting on mud and floating or waterside plants with front end raised.

HOVER-FLIES Syrphidae A family of about 5,000 species, with hovering and darting flight. Body shape very variable, but all have a false margin formed by veins running more or less parallel to hind margin of wing. There is also a false vein near the centre – simply a thickening of the wing membrane and unconnected to any real vein. Vein pattern important in identification. Antennae generally short and drooping. All are nectar-feeders, especially fond of umbellifers. Many mimic bees and wasps. The larvae live in a wide variety of habitats and include predators, vegetarians, and scavengers.

▲ **Syrphus ribesii**. First 2 long veins both reach margin: central cross vein is before middle of discal cell. Thorax greenish black with brown hair. Face has no black line. 4–11, often in swarms. Larva (p. 294) feeds on aphids.

▲ **Scaeva pyrastri**. Venation like *Syrphus*. Pale lunules on abdomen white or cream and of almost constant width. △ **S. selenitica** has outer lunule arm much thinner than inner one. 6–10. Larva eats aphids.

▲ **Episyrphus balteatus**. Venation like *Syrphus*. Easily identified by additional narrow black bands on 3rd and 4th abdominal segments. 3–11 (may be all year in S). Often forms dense migratory swarms. Abundant in gardens. Larva eats aphids.

△ **Xanthogramma pedissequum**. Venation like *Syrphus*. Distinctive body pattern and dark smudge on wing readily distinguish it from other yellow and black species. Abdomen very flat. 5–9. Larva feeds on aphids.

▲ **Leucozona lucorum**. Resembles *Volucella pellucens* (p. 206) but *Syrphus*-like venation clearly distinguishes it. 5–9. Larva eats aphids.

▲ **Rhingia campestris**. Venation like *Syrphus*, but easily identified by its snout. 4–11, mostly in hedgerows and light woods. Breeds in cow-pats and other dung. △s **R. rostrata** is very similar but has a slaty blue thorax.

▲ **Baccha elongata**. Venation like *Syrphus*. 4–10, hovering in and around damp vegetation but not easily seen because of slim build. Larva eats aphids.

△s **Doros conopseus**. Venation like *Syrphus*. Superficially like *Physocephala* (p. 208) but antennae quite different. Wasp-like in flight. 5–8. Mainly in woodland. Larva believed to be carnivorous in soil and rotting wood.

▲ **Melanostoma scalare**. Venation like *Syrphus*. Male abdomen much slimmer than female: always parallel-sided. 4–11. Very common in gardens: especially fond of hawthorn blossom in spring. Larva eats aphids. There are several similar species.

▲ **Neoascia podagrica**. One of the smallest hover-flies. Venation like *Syrphus*, but outer cross veins almost upright, destroying false margin. Abundant everywhere 3–10. Larva eats aphids. There are several similar species, but cross veins not clouded.

Venation of *Neoascia*

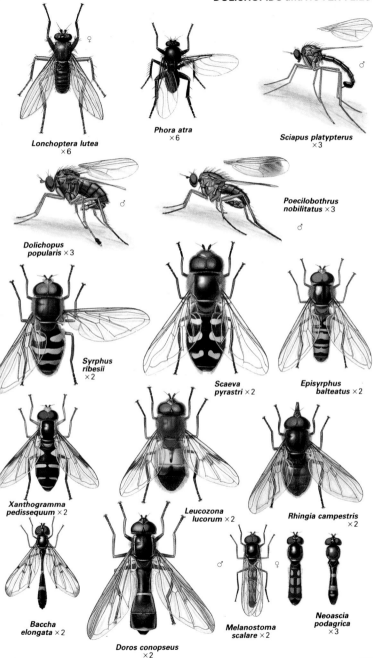

Lonchoptera lutea
×6

Phora atra
×6

Sciapus platypterus
×3

*Dolichopus
popularis* ×3

*Poecilobothrus
nobilitatus* ×3

*Syrphus
ribesii*
×2

*Scaeva
pyrastri* ×2

*Episyrphus
balteatus* ×2

*Xanthogramma
pedissequum* ×2

*Leucozona
lucorum* ×2

Rhingia campestris
×2

*Baccha
elongata* ×2

Doros conopseus
×2

*Melanostoma
scalare* ×2

*Neoascia
podagrica*
×3

▲ **Volucella bombylans**. As in all *Volucella* spp, the first 2 long veins meet before reaching the wing margin and the central cross vein is before the middle of the discal cell. The antennae are distinctly feathery. Distinguished from its relatives by its dense hair, *bombylans* is a very variable species mimicing several kinds of bumble bee. 5–9.

△s **V. zonaria** is easily recognised by its size and colour. 5–9, mainly in wooded areas.

▲ **V. pellucens** resembles *Leucozona* (p. 204) but is distinguished by larger size and venation. 5–9, mainly in wooded areas. Hovers just above head height (mainly the males) and is very fond of bramble blossom.

△ **V. inanis** resembles *zonaria* but is much smaller and has narrower black abdominal bands. 6–9. *Volucella* larvae (p. 294) all live as scavengers in nests of bees and wasps.

Milesia crabroniformis. First 2 long veins meet before reaching wing margin. Central cross vein well beyond middle of discal cell. Anal vein bends sharply back to wing margin. 6–9 on flowers, especially in sunny places. Larva develops in rotting beech wood. S, mainly western.

▲ **Drone-fly** *Eristalis tenax*. Named for its remarkable resemblance to honey bee drone. First 2 long veins meet before reaching wing margin: 3rd long vein with a deep U-shaped bend. Central cross vein at about the middle of the discal cell. Yellow or orange marks on base of abdomen often indistinct. Face has a wide black stripe down the centre. All year, hovering at about head height in sunshine: very common in gardens. Larva (p. 297) is the rat-tailed maggot, living in stagnant water. There are several similar species. ▲ *E. pertinax* is very similar but has a narrow facial stripe and yellow tarsi on front and middle legs. 3–11 almost everywhere.

▲ **E. arbustorum** is smaller and has no facial stripe. Front and mid tarsi are dark. 4–10, mainly in open habitats.

▲ **Helophilus pendulus**. First 2 long veins both reach wing margin: 3rd long vein with a deep U-shaped bend. Central cross vein at about middle of discal cell. Black line down centre of face. 4–10. Most frequent in damp places: fond of sunbathing on waterside vegetation. Males hover just above water surface. Larva is like that of *Eristalis* and lives in muddy water. △ *H. hybridus* is similar but only basal third of hind tarsus is yellow.

▲ **Narcissus-fly** *Merodon equestris*. Venation like *Helophilus*. Hind femur with prominent bulge on underside of apex. Body essentially black with grey, tawny, or black hair. Mimics various worker bumble bees. 3–8. Larva lives in bulbs of narcissi and other plants, often causing severe damage. There are several similar species on the continent, mainly in S.

▲ **Myathropa florea**. Resembles a brightly marked Drone-fly, but readily distinguished by thoracic pattern and *Helophilus*-like venation. Pale markings vary in size, with western specimens tending to be darker. 5–10, mainly in wooded areas. Larvae live in stagnant water in hollow trees and similar places.

△s **Xylotomima lenta**. First 2 long veins reach wing margin. Central cross vein beyond middle of discal cell and strongly oblique. Abdomen very flat. Red patch on abdomen together with black legs distinguish this from several related species. 5–7. Breeds in rotting wood. Widespread, but uncommon.

△ **Chrysotoxum cautum**. Antennae long and forward-pointing, with 3rd segment about as long as other 2 together. First 2 long veins both reach wing margin. 5–8, mainly in woods and hedgerows: not uncommon in gardens and very fond of sunbathing on leaves. Breeds in rotting wood. S & C. There are several similar species, usually less hairy and with a shorter 3rd antennal segment. ▲ *C. festivum* is much blacker than *C. cautum* with 3 pairs of narrow yellow bars on the abdomen. The bars curve distinctly backwards in the outer region and do not reach the sides of the abdomen. The front half of the wing is yellowish-brown, although this colour does not reach the wing-tip. 6–10 in grassy places. ▲ *C. bicinctum*, the commonest member of the genus in Ireland, has just 2 prominent yellow bands on the abdomen – on segments 2 and 4 – and an intensive brown patch on the outer part of the wing. 5–9 in grassy places.

Chrysotoxum
cautum × 2

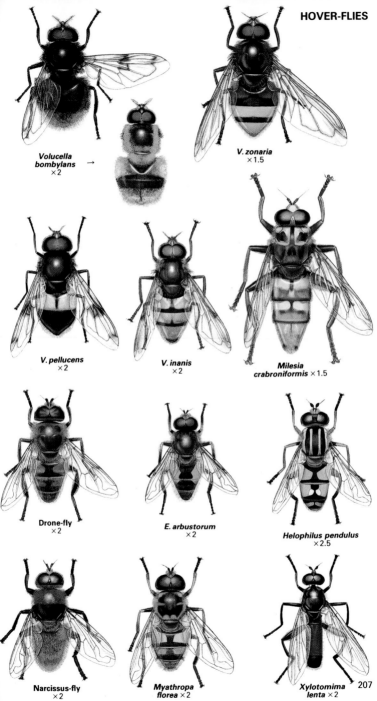

Volucella bombylans ×2

V. zonaria ×1.5

V. pellucens ×2

V. inanis ×2

Milesia crabroniformis ×1.5

Drone-fly ×2

E. arbustorum ×2

Helophilus pendulus ×2.5

Narcissus-fly ×2

Myathropa florea ×2

Xylotomima lenta ×2

207

Pipunculus campestris Pipunculidae. Female abdomen much shinier. Stigma often yellow at first but may darken with age. 4–10 in woods and hedgerows: especially fond of bramble blossom. Larvae are internal parasites of leafhoppers. Large head, nearly all eyes, is typical of all of this large family. Venation, usually with a distinctly beaked sub-apical cell, is also characteristic. All are superb hoverers, often hovering low down in dense vegetation.

Pipunculus campestris × 4

△ **Conops quadrifasciata** Conopidae. Long proboscis and long, pointed anal cell near hind edge of wing characterise this family. Hind femora yellowish brown. Female has small yellow pouch under 5th abdominal segment. 6–9 on umbels and composites, especially ragwort: mainly in dry habitats. Larvae are internal parasites of bumble bees. There are several similar species.

△ **Physocephala nigra.** 5–7 on a wide range of flowers, especially in wooded and scrubby places. ▲ **P. rufipes** has a browner body and black antennae. Larvae of both species parasitise bumble bees.

△ **Myopa buccata.** Ocelli and short antennae distinguish this from the two previous conopids. Tip of 1st long vein very close to sub-costal vein. 4–8 on a variety of flowers: very fond of dandelions and hawthorn blossom. Several similar species.

▲ **Platystoma seminationis** Platystomatidae. Prominent cream patch under end of abdomen. 5–10. Crawls rather slowly over rank vegetation in many habitats, especially in woods, hedgerows, and gardens. Little attracted to flowers but has been seen sucking dead insects. Breeds in decaying matter. There are many similar species on the continent.

⬭ **Melieria omissa** Otitidae. Face has deep grooves to accommodate antennae. Wing with 7 dark spots. Commonly waves wings slowly up and down as it rests on or walks slowly over vegetation. 5–8 on river banks and other damp places. Breeds in decaying matter. S & C. There are several similar species, differing slightly in pattern.

▲ **Seioptera vibrans.** Head red at front: face grooved. Body shiny blue or black. 3rd and 4th long veins converge slightly. Resembles sepsids (p. 210) in frantic wing waving, but distinguished by larger size. 5–9 on trees and shrubs, especially lime. Feeds on aphids and other small insects. Breeds in decaying vegetation.

Family Tephritidae A large family of rather small flies in which the wings are heavily mottled, or pictured, as in the previous two families. Sub-costal vein sharply bent towards costa about halfway along its length. Anal cell usually with a characteristically pointed extension. Female abdomen pointed, with rigid ovipositor. Larvae develop in fruit or elsewhere in plants, often causing galls.

▲ **Urophora cardui.** Anal cell blunt. Dark markings heavier in male. 5–8 in open country. Larvae cause very hard, egg-shaped, plurilocular galls on stems of thistles. Many similar species cause galls in composite flower heads.

▲ **Cerajocera ceratocera.** Male has bristly horn on antenna. 6–8. One of several species causing galls in flower heads of greater knapweed. The carpels become very hard and woody and can be felt by squeezing the dead flower heads. N & C.

▲ **Celery-fly** *Euleia heraclei.* Eyes become reddish after death. Body and wing markings either blackish brown or pale reddish brown. 4–11. Larvae excavate mines in leaves of celery, parsnip, and other umbellifers.

△ **Mediterranean Fruit-fly** *Ceratitis capitata.* Wings with pink and yellow blotches. Thorax strongly humped. Female lacks the two spatulate, horn-like bristles on head. Most of the year: continuously brooded in south. Larvae infest a wide range of fruits, including cherries, peaches, and oranges. S & C: not native in B but often imported in fruit. A serious pest in all the warmer parts of the world.

Rhagoletis cerasi. Head rather square in profile. Scutellum yellow: rest of thorax shiny black. 5–7. Larvae in wild and cultivated cherries. N & C: in B only through introduction in fruit. ▲ **R. alternata** has the whole thorax orange-yellow. Larvae in cherries and rose hips. N & C. Both species with very slow flight.

▲ **Phagocarpus permundus.** Eyes green with 2 transverse red bands in life: becoming red when dead. Wing pattern very characteristic. 8–10. Larvae in hawthorn fruits. N & C.

Conops quadrifasciata × 2

Physocephala nigra × 2

Myopa buccata × 2

Platystoma seminationis × 3

Melieria omissa × 3

Seioptera vibrans × 3 ♀

Urophora cardui × 3 ♀

gall on thisle

→

Cerajocera ceratocera × 3 ♀

Celery-fly × 3 ♀

→ leaf mine in celery

Mediterranean Fruit-fly × 3 ♂

Rhagoletis cerasi × 4

Phagocarpus permundus × 3 ♀

grubs in cherry

209

▲ **Calobata petronella** Micropezidae. One of several long-legged flies known as stilt-legged-flies. 5–7, walking rather hesitatingly on foliage, mainly in damp places, and feeding on other small insects. Breeds in decaying matter. N & C.

▲ **Micropeza corrigiolata.** An even more slender stilt-legged-fly. Head very flat and pointed. Mid and hind coxae brownish. 5–9 on vegetation in damp and shady places. Not uncommon in gardens, where probably breeds in compost heaps. △ **M. lateralis** has coxae all yellow and more yellow on abdomen. 8–10. S & C. **M. brevipennis** is all black, with short wings. C.

Micropeza corrigiolata × 2.5

▲ **Coelopa frigida** Coelopidae. One of the kelp-flies, a small family distinguished from several similar groups by very straight vein closing anal cell but best recognised by seashore habitat. **C. frigida** has a very flat body and swarms over shore throughout the year: on coastal flowers in summer. Breeds in rotting seaweeds on beach. ▲ **C. pilipes** is similar but much hairier in male. The closely related ▲ **Malacomyia sciomyzina** flies with them but is not flattened. N & C.

▲ **Carrot-fly** Psila rosae Psilidae. One of many similar species, all with a pale streak running across basal part of wing, although this is not always obvious. Front margin of wing with a distinct break about ¼ of the way along. Ocellar triangle very clear. 5–9. Larvae infest carrots: leaves of infested plants often become rust coloured.

▲ **Helcomyza ustulata** Dryomyzidae. Wings longer than abdomen and with prominent spines on front margin. 6th long vein reaches margin. Size varies a good deal. On seashore all year, with characteristic darting flight. Larvae live in sand or mud below high tide level. N & C.

▲ **Coremacera tristis** Sciomyzidae. Dappled wings laid very flat over body at rest. Conspicuous, forward-pointing antennae. 6–10 in damp grassy and scrubby places. Larvae prey on small molluscs. A few related species have yellow femora.

▲ **Lonchaea chorea** Lonchaeidae. One of several very similar shiny blue or greenish black flies with large, clear wings. Front margin distinctly broken at tip of sub-costal vein. Female with pointed ovipositor. 2–12 on bushes and other herbage: movements rather sluggish. Breeds in decaying matter and under bark.

▲ **Sepsis fulgens** Sepsidae. One of several very similar species which wave their wings as they scuttle over the vegetation. Common on umbellifer flowers. Often forms dense swarms in autumn, with hundreds of thousands of flies scurrying about on a small patch of plants. Hibernate as adults. Breed in dung.

▲ **Psilopa nitidula** Ephydridae. One of many very small and shiny flies known as shore-flies, recognised by the presence of one very long cell in hind region of wing: anal vein absent. Front margin with 2 small breaks. All year on margins of ponds and streams.

▲ **Suillia variegata** Heleomyzidae. Spines along front edge of wing. Distinguished from Helcomyza by smaller size, spotted wings, and much smaller anal cell. 3–12 in damp places. Breeds in fungi and decaying matter. Never on sea shore.

▲ **Opomyza germinationis** Opomyzidae. One of several similar small flies with spotted wings, but distinguished from most by the extensive darkening on front margin. 1st vein extremely short. 2nd and 3rd long veins converge strongly towards tip. Very common in leaf litter and grasses in moist habitats. Walks slowly: reluctant to fly. 6–10. Breeds in grass stems.

▲ **Frit-fly** Oscinella frit Chloropidae. A very small fly, frequently even smaller and paler after mid-summer. Ocellar triangle plate-like and very distinct, as in all members of this family. Anal cell absent. Abundant in cereal fields, especially oats and barley, 3–11. Larvae tunnel in stems and ears and cause much damage.

▲ **Lipara lucens.** One of the largest chloropids, but with relatively small eyes – well separated and with a very large ocellar plate between them. 2–11, mainly in marshy places. Larva in a cigar-shaped gall (left) on common reed. There are several smaller but otherwise similar species.

▲ **Thaumatomyia notata.** Ocellar triangle very large in relation to the head. This tiny fly is sometimes called the yellow swarming-fly, because of its habit of entering buildings in vast numbers in autumn prior to hibernation. At other times it lives in rough grassy places.

gall of
Lipara

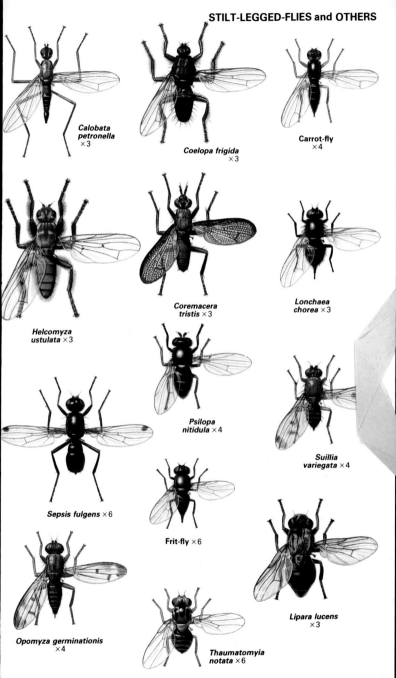

*Calobata
petronella*
×3

Coelopa frigida
×3

Carrot-fly
×4

*Helcomyza
ustulata* ×3

*Coremacera
tristis* ×3

*Lonchaea
chorea* ×3

*Psilopa
nitidula* ×4

Sepsis fulgens ×6

Frit-fly ×6

*Suillia
variegata* ×4

Opomyza germinationis
×4

*Thaumatomyia
notata* ×6

Lipara lucens
×3

211

▲ **Drosophila funebris** Drosophilidae. One of many closely related species known as fruit-flies or vinegar-flies because of their liking for rotting fruit and other fermenting materials. Arista of antenna bears fine bristles and appears forked at tip (strong lens!). 2 clear breaks in front border of wing. Long cell in hind region of wing: short anal cell present behind it, unlike Ephydridae and Chloropidae (p. 210). Most common summer and autumn: all year in food and drink factories. Fond of wine and often settle on opened bottles and glasses. Breed in decaying vegetable matter.

△ **Leucophenga maculata**. Closely related to *Drosophila* but arrangement of head bristles is different. Easily identified by body pattern: thorax silver-haired in male, orange brown in female. Breeds in fungi. S & C.

▲ **Phytomyza ilicis** Agromyzidae. This large genus is distinguished from many similar groups by lack of posterior cross vein, but specific identification of adults is difficult. 4–7 in woods, hedgerows, and gardens. Larva excavates distinctive mine in holly leaf. Mined leaves at all seasons, but grubs or pupae present only in spring and early summer. Easy to breed out adults. All members of family are leaf miners in early stages.

LOUSE-FLIES Hippoboscidae All flattened blood-sucking parasites of birds and mammals. Head partly sunk into thorax. Long, toothed claws grip feathers or fur of host. Many have reduced wings, and even fully-winged species rarely fly. Instead of laying eggs, female periodically gives birth to fully-grown larva which pupates immediately. The related Nycteribiidae is a small family of completely wingless bat parasites. Head folds back into a groove on thorax.

▲ **Sheep Ked** *Melophagus ovinus*. Entirely wingless, never leaving hosts although it can move from one sheep to another when they come into contact. It seems to do the sheep little real harm. *M. rupicaprinus* lives on the chamois.

▲ **Forest-fly** *Hippobosca equina*. Fully winged in both sexes. On horses, cattle, and deer. Scuttles sideways with crab-like gait when disturbed. Mostly in wooded areas. 5–10, most noticeable when new adults are seeking hosts.

▲ **Deer-fly** *Lipoptena cervi*. On deer, especially red deer, mainly in wooded areas. Winged at first, but sheds wings on reaching host. New adults emerge in autumn and fly into trees, from where they drop on to passing animals.

▲ **Ornithomyia avicularia**. Fully winged. On a wide range of woodland birds, including owls, pigeons, and thrushes. 6–10, mainly on young birds, perhaps because older ones preen themselves better.

▲ **Crataerina hirundinis**. Flightless, with much reduced wings. On martins and swallows. 5–10. Pupae overwinter in the nest and new adults emerge when the birds return in spring. ▲ *C. pallida* has broader wings and infests swifts.

Family Tachinidae A large and rather variable family whose larvae are internal parasites of caterpillars and other young insects. Some attack adult bugs and grasshoppers. Usually only one grub per host. Adults are bristly and resemble Calliphoridae (p. 214) but distinguished from them by the prominent post-scutellum bulging beneath the scutellum. 4th long vein sharply bent. Thoracic squamae usually very large. Many species are common on flowers.

▲ **Gymnochaeta viridis** resembles *Lucilia* (p. 214) but more bristly and with hairy eyes. Thorax may have golden stripes. On vegetation 3–7. Eggs laid on plants and young grubs bore into various moth larvae.

△ **Alophora hemiptera**. Size and colour vary a good deal, but male always with very broad wings and rather bug-like at rest. 4–8. Parasitises various heteropteran bugs, eggs being laid directly into the host by the female fly.

△ **Dexia rustica**. Female much blacker. 6–8. Eggs laid on soil and larvae seek out grubs of cockchafer and related beetles.

△ **Gonia divisa**. Resembles *T. fera* but wings lack yellow and head is much more swollen in front. 3–6 in rough grassy places. Eggs are scattered and larvae seek out caterpillars of various noctuid moths.

▲ **Tachina fera**. Jowls with yellow hair. 4–9 in woods and moist habitats: often abundant on waterside plants in late summer. Parasitises many butterfly and moth larvae: breeding behaviour as *Gymnochaeta*.

▲ **T. grossa** resembles a bumble bee in flight. 2–9 in woods and heathland. Attacks large caterpillars.

Gymnochaeta viridis × 2

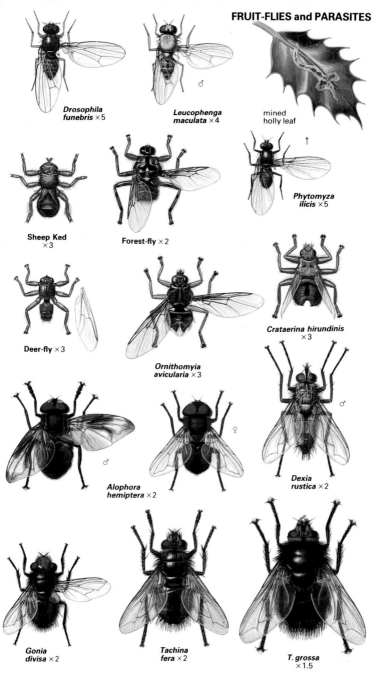

FRUIT-FLIES and PARASITES

Drosophila funebris ×5

Leucophenga maculata ×4

mined holly leaf

Sheep Ked ×3

Forest-fly ×2

Phytomyza ilicis ×5

Deer-fly ×3

Ornithomyia avicularia ×3

Crataerina hirundinis ×3

Alophora hemiptera ×2

Dexia rustica ×2

Gonia divisa ×2

Tachina fera ×2

T. grossa ×1.5

213

BLOW-FLIES Calliphoridae A large family of rather stout flies, resembling Tachinidae (p. 212) in having a fan of bristles close to haltere, but with little or no post-scutellum. 4th long vein usually bends *sharply* forward near tip. Adults soak up surface fluids with mop-like mouthparts. Most common in summer, but many species are drawn out by the sun in mid-winter. Most breed in carrion and other decaying animal matter. A few larvae are parasites.

▲ **Flesh-fly** *Sarcophaga carnaria*. One of several very similar species with large feet and red eyes. Size is very variable. Common around houses but not often inside. Breeds in carrion, female bringing forth young larvae instead of eggs.

▲ **Bluebottle** *Calliphora vomitoria*. One of several similar flies common in and around houses: rests on sunny walls all year. Female attracted to meat and fish indoors for egg-laying. Larva (p. 294) is typical of whole family. ▲ *C. vicina* is almost identical but has reddish jowls (below eyes) instead of black.

▲ **Cluster-fly** *Pollenia rudis*. Golden hairs on thorax and chequered abdomen identify this fly, named for its habit of hibernating in dense clusters in attics and out-houses. Larvae parasitise earthworms.

▲ *Cynomya mortuorum*. Brilliant green or blue-green: very like *Lucilia* but with yellowish jowls. On carrion but less common than *Lucilia*.

▲ **Greenbottle** *Lucilia caesar*. Bluish-green to emerald, often becoming coppery with age. Eyes red. Jowls silvery. 4th long vein sharply bent. Size varies. On carrion, dung, and flowers everywhere: rarely indoors. Larvae sometimes live in wounds on sheep and other animals. Commonest of several very similar species in this genus.

HOUSE-FLIES and kin Muscidae A large and rather variable family: often resemble blow-flies but generally smaller and never with fan of bristles near haltere. 4th long vein rarely bends sharply forward. Most species mop up fluids like blow-flies. Most breed in dung and other decaying matter, larvae being like that of bluebottle. Identification of many smaller species difficult, relying on bristle patterns and genitalia.

▲ *Dasyphora cyanella*. Like *Lucilia* but 4th long vein bends gently forward. Eyes hairy. Green becomes coppery with age. Viviparous. 2–6. Several related species.

△ *Orthellia cornicina*. Like *Lucilia*, with 4th long vein sharply bent, but jowls metallic green. On flowers, dung, and carrion. Larvae live in dung and are blue.

▲ *Mesembrina meridiana*. Enjoys sunbathing on ground or vegetation: especially fond of umbellifer flowers. 3–10, mainly in woods and hedgerows. Breeds in dung.

M. mystacea is much hairier, especially on middle tibiae. Resembles *Volucella bombylans* (p. 206) in flight. 6–9, mainly on umbellifers and other flowers. Most of Europe but only on mountains in S.

▲ *Helina duplicata*. 4th long vein curving gently backwards. Enjoys sunbathing. 4–10 in all kinds of vegetation from pine woods and hedges to marshes. Many similar species.

▲ *Polietes lardaria*. Like a small flesh-fly but with 4th long vein almost straight. 4–10 in open country and light woodland. Larva predatory in dung.

▲ *Phaonia viarum*. 4th long vein almost straight, but differs from *Helina* and *Mydaea* in having a strong bristle on dorsal side of hind tibia (not easily detected). 4–11, basking on tree trunks and flowers. Breeds in leaf litter. Many similar species.

▲ *Hydrotaea irritans*. Males of this genus have oddly-shaped front legs. Female plain grey, although abdomen may be reddish at base. 6–9, often swarming round human heads seeking sweat, especially in woodland. Larva partly predatory.

▲ *Mydaea scutellaris*. Scutellum yellow. A few bristles at base of 3rd long vein. 5–8, basking on flowers, foliage, and ripe fruit: especially fond of elder flowers.

▲ *Graphomya maculata*. 4th long vein bends quite sharply forward, thus distinguishing female from *Polietes*. Male wings have yellowish tinge, but female wings yellow only at base. 5–10, mainly on umbellifers. Larvae predatory in muddy pools and damp leaf litter.

▲ *Ophyra leucostoma*. Hind tibia of male curved and with tuft of soft hair. 4–10 on and around lush vegetation, especially among trees. Common in orchards. Hovers in shafts of sunlight. Breeds in decaying vegetation, and manure. Abundant in poultry houses and on pig farms, where larvae feed on other fly grubs. The very similar ▲ *O. capensis* occurs in the same places.

Ophyra leucostoma × 3

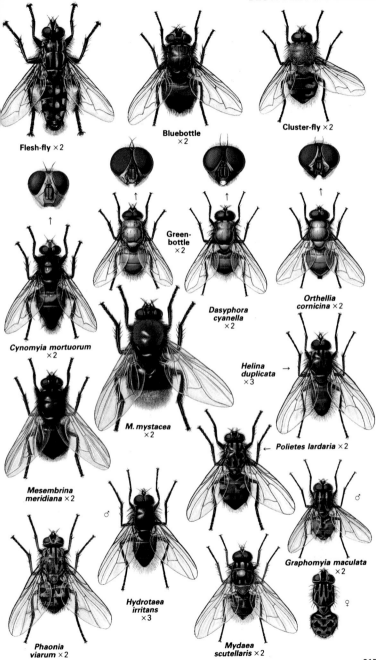

Flesh-fly ×2

Bluebottle ×2

Cluster-fly ×2

Green-bottle ×2

Cynomyia mortuorum ×2

Dasyphora cyanella ×2

Orthellia cornicina ×2

Helina duplicata ×3

M. mystacea ×2

Polietes lardaria ×2

Mesembrina meridiana ×2

Graphomyia maculata ×2

Hydrotaea irritans ×3

Phaonia viarum ×2

Mydaea scutellaris ×2

215

▲ **Stable-fly** *Stomoxys calcitrans*. One of the 'biting house-flies', both sexes being bloodsuckers. Piercing proboscis points forward at all times, readily distinguishing this from the House-fly. 4th long vein gently curved. 4–10, mainly around farms and stables: occasionally bites man. Breeds in dung and stable litter.

▲ **Common House-fly** *Musca domestica*. 4th vein sharply-bent. Most common 6–9. Breeds in and around houses throughout the world. Especially numerous around farms and rubbish dumps where decaying matter abounds. ▲ **Face-fly** *M. autumnalis* is very similar, especially female, but her eyes closer together and body more rounded than in *domestica*. Male has more orange on abdomen. Swarms round cattle: sunbathes on walls and fences. Enters houses for hibernation in autumn – when House-fly population is declining.

▲ **Lesser House-fly** *Fannia canicularis* Fanniidae. Smaller and more slender than *Musca* and with 4th long vein almost straight. Female very dull, without clear patches at base of abdomen. Male flies incessantly round lights and other objects indoors. Larva (p. 294) feeds in various decaying materials. Many similar species.

▲ *Eustalomyia festiva* Anthomyiidae. Closely related to muscids but 6th long vein reaches wing margin. 4th vein almost straight. On flowers 5–8. Breeds in bodies of flies stored by solitary wasps.

▲ *Anthomyia pluvialis*. Abdomen much broader than *Eustalomyia* and very flat. On umbellifers and other flowers, especially in damp places, 4–8. Males 'dance' before rain. Breeds in decaying vegetation.

▲ *Anthomyia pluvalis*. Abdomen much broader than *Eustalomyia* and very flat. On umbellifers and other flowers, especially in damp places, 4–8. Males 'dance' before rain. Breeds in decaying vegetation.

▲ **Cabbage Root-fly** *Delia radicum*. One of many very similar small flies. 3–11 on flowers and leaves. Susceptible to fungal attack and corpses not uncommonly found in masses clinging to vegetation. Larvae damage roots of brassicas.

▲ *Cordilura impudica* Scathophagidae. Outer half of costa hairy (lens!): wing clearly darker towards apex. Legs very spiky. 4–9, mainly in damp places. Frequents cow pats and other dung, preying on other small insects. Breeds in dung. Many similar species.

▲ *Norellisoma spinimanum*. Identified by double row of bristles under front femur (lens!). Tibiae very bristly. Narrow brown (not black) bands on thorax. 6–9, mainly in damp places. Predatory, but larva breeds in stems of docks.

▲ **Yellow Dung-fly** *Scathophaga stercoraria*. Golden-furred males swarm on fresh cow pats and horse dung. Females are less furry and rather greyish: less common than males. Adults prey on other flies on the dung, while larvae develop in the dung. Several similar species.

▲ **Warble-fly** *Hypoderma bovis* Oestridae. Hairy and bee-like, with 4th long vein bent sharply forward in line with posterior cross vein. 6th vein reaches wing margin. 5–6. Adult does not feed. Eggs laid on cattle legs and grub works its way through body to spend final 3 months in a swelling (the warble) just under skin on the back. Falls out when mature to pupate on ground. Hides are ruined by the warbles and exit holes.

▲ *H. lineatum* is similar, although a little slimmer and with blackish veins and orange hair at tip of abdomen. ▲ *H. diana* has a similar life history but attacks red deer.

Oedemagena tarandi. A parasite of reindeer, with a life history like *Hypoderma*. N.

▲ **Sheep Nostril-fly** *Oestrus ovis*. Wrinkled or warty surface characterises this fly. 3rd and 4th long veins join before reaching wing margin: 6th vein does not reach margin. 5–6, resting on rocks and walls in sheep country: does not feed. Viviparous, with female depositing young larvae in sheep nostrils, where they feed for about 9 months. Pupate in soil. Also attacks goats and other mammals.

Pharyngomyia picta. Life cycle like that of *Oestrus* but attacks deer. Widespread, but rare.

▲ **Bot-fly** *Gasterophilus intestinalis* Gasterophilidae. 4th long vein almost straight. 7–9. Adult does not feed. Eggs are laid on legs of horses, donkeys, and mules: larvae enter mouth when legs are licked and then pass into stomach where they complete growth attached to lining. Pupate in soil. There are several similar species, mostly without brown on wings.

Bot-fly ×2

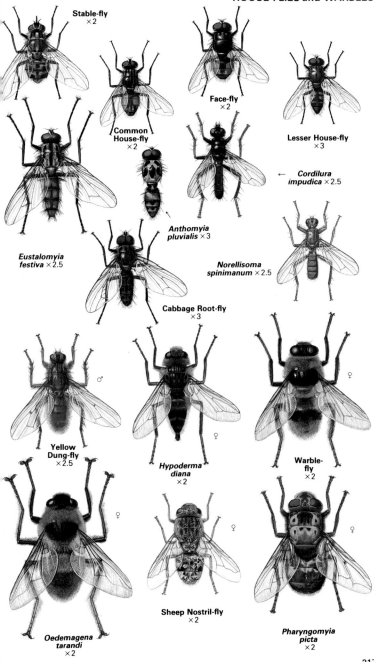

Stable-fly
×2

Common
House-fly
×2

Face-fly
×2

Lesser House-fly
×3

*Eustalomyia
festiva* ×2.5

*Anthomyia
pluvialis* ×3

← *Cordilura
impudica* ×2.5

*Norellisoma
spinimanum* ×2.5

Cabbage Root-fly
×3

Yellow
Dung-fly
×2.5 ♂

*Hypoderma
diana*
×2 ♀

Warble-
fly
×2 ♀

*Oedemagena
tarandi*
×2 ♀

Sheep Nostril-fly
×2 ♀

*Pharyngomyia
picta*
×2 ♀

ANTS, WASPS, BEES, and their relatives
Order Hymenoptera

This immense order contains well over 100,000 species. As well as the bees, wasps, and ants, it contains the sawflies and gall wasps and a bewildering assortment of ichneumons and other parasites. The range of size is enormous, from huge spider-hunting wasps down to the minute fairy flies (family Mymaridae) which pass their larval stages in the eggs of other insects and are strong contenders for the title of the world's smallest insect.

The typical hymenopteran has two pairs of membranous wings, the front and hind wings being coupled by a row of minute hooks on the leading edge of the hind wing. The latter is usually very much smaller than the forewing and not always easy to detect, especially when the insects are at rest. Wing venation is often much reduced, producing a network of large and often rather square cells not seen in any other group of insects. There is frequently a pigmented pterostigma towards the tip of the forewing, with a generally elongated cell, known as the marginal cell, beyond it. Just behind the pterostigma and marginal cell lies a row of two or three sub-marginal cells, which are of great value in identifying the insects, especially the bees and wasps. The pronotum is often no more than a narrow collar at the front of the thorax, but it sometimes extends back along the sides of the thorax to meet the tegulae. The latter are scales or swellings over the bases of the forewings. The form of the pronotum is another useful guide to the identification of bees and wasps.

The head is usually rather hard and extremely mobile, being attached to the thorax by a slender neck. Three ocelli are usually present in addition to the compound eyes. The antennae are extremely variable in form, especially among the sawflies, and are often longer in males than in females. Mouthparts are essentially of the biting type, equipped with toothed jaws for dealing with solid food, but many hymenopterans also lap up liquids and the bees feed almost entirely on nectar. Most bees have developed long, tubular tongues in connection with their nectar-feeding habits, but they retain their biting jaws for nest-building and other chores.

The order is divided into two very distinct sub-orders – the Symphyta, containing the sawflies, and the Apocrita.

SAWFLIES   Sub-order Symphyta

The sawflies are readily distinguished from the other hymenopterans by the absence of any 'waist', the abdomen being joined to the thorax across its full width and showing little, if any narrowing at the front end. The insects get their name for the female's ovipositor, which in most species is in the form of a minute saw. This saw is used to cut slits in plants, and the eggs are then laid in the slits. Each species has a distinct pattern of teeth on the saw, and it is often possible to identify a species just from the ovipositor. The horntails or wood-wasps (p. 222) are sawflies with drill-like ovipositors which are used to bore into timber.

The saw-like ovipositor of a sawfly

Adult sawflies are mostly quite sturdy insects, although the stem sawflies in the family Cephidae (p. 222) are notable exceptions. The wings are folded flat over the body at rest. The antennae are mostly thread-like, but they are clubbed or feathery in some species. Most of the species are active by day and some, notably the pamphilids (p. 222), fly very rapidly in the sunshine. Others are rather sluggish and are more likely to scuttle away through the vegetation than to take to the air if disturbed. Some species are at least partly carnivorous, capturing other insects on the flower heads of umbellifers and other plants, but most sawflies are vegetarians. They lap nectar and nibble pollen as they roam over the flowers.

Larval sawflies are all vegetarians. Most of them feed freely on leaves and resemble the caterpillars of butterflies and moths but they differ from these caterpillars in having at least six pairs of fleshy abdominal prolegs. The lepidopterous larvae have no more than five pairs of these prolegs (p. 111). Some sawfly larvae tunnel inside their food plants and they have no abdominal legs. They look more like beetle larvae (p. 295) than caterpillars. These tunnelling larvae usually pupate inside the food plant, but the other sawfly larvae generally pupate in cocoons in the soil or leaf litter or attached to the food plant.

Sub-order Apocrita

By far the larger of the two sub-orders of the Hymenoptera, this contains a very wide range of insects, including many parasitic and social species. The most obvious difference between this group and the sawflies lies in the possession of the typical 'wasp-waist'. Although appearing to divide the thorax from the abdomen, the waist is, in fact, entirely in the abdomen if we abide strictly by anatomical criteria. The first segment of the abdomen, known as the propodeum, is firmly fused to the rear of the thorax and the waist comes just behind it. The whole of the abdomen behind the propodeum is known as the gaster, but for practical purposes we can consider the propodeum part of the thorax and equate gaster with abdomen. The narrow front part of the abdomen, which forms the waist, is known as the petiole and may consist of one or two segments or just part of one segment. In a few families (p. 228) it is attached to the top of the propodeum, but it is generally attached near the bottom. In the ants this region is called the pedicel.

Entomologists split the Apocrita into two sections – the **Parasitica** and the **Aculeata**.

The **Parasitica** are almost all parasites, the females using their ovipositors to pierce the host tissues and to lay their eggs there. A wide range of other insects are used as hosts, and it is almost always the young stages that are attacked. Some of the parasites have extremely long ovipositors (p. 231) which can reach hosts tunnelling deep inside plants or even inside other animals. In this last instance the parasite is known as a hyperparasite – parasitising an insect which is itself already living parasitically inside its host. Clearly, these parasites have extraordinary powers of detection – based on scent and vibration – to enable them to seek out their hidden hosts. Although most of the Parasitica attack other insects, some lay their eggs in the egg cocoons of spiders.

The young parasites grow up inside, or firmly attached to the outside of the host. Depending on the relative sizes of the parasite and its host, there may be anything from one to several hundred parasitic larvae in each host, which is gradually eaten alive. But the parasites are careful not to damage any vital organs until they themselves are almost mature. It would obviously not be in the parasite's interest to kill its host too early. The host usually dies at about the time that the parasites pupate – either inside or outside its shrivelled skin. Insects with this type of life history, resulting in the eventual death of the host, are often known as parasitoids. They are also known as protelean parasites, indicating that they are parasitic only in the larval state.

Best known of the parasitic hymenopterans are the ichneumons (p. 230), an immense and very varied group which can usually be recognised by having a prominent stigma in the forewing and more than 16 antennal segments. The front edge of the forewing is somewhat thickened, owing to the virtual fusion of the first long vein with the front margin and the consequent obliteration of the long narrow cell found in most other hymenopterans. Many ichneumons are quite large, but the rest of the Parasitica are mostly very small insects. They include the chalcids (p. 228), which often have beautiful metallic sheens, and the plant-feeding gall wasps (p. 226).

The bees, wasps, and ants belong to the **Aculeata**, in which the female's ovipositor is generally modified as a sting and used for paralysing prey or for defence. Wasps are essentially predatory insects: the adults often feed on nectar and fruit juices, but the larvae are almost always fed on animal matter. Bees are entirely vegetarian, feeding mainly on nectar and pollen, while the ants include predatory, vegetarian, and omnivorous species. Many social insects belong to this section, including all the ants and many bees and wasps. They live in colonies consisting of one or more fertile females (queens), a sprinkling of males (often only at certain times of the year), and numerous sterile females called workers. There are often marked differences between these castes – especially among the ants, where the workers are wingless. Ant and honey bee colonies are perennial, but the bumble bees and wasps produce annual colonies, with over-wintered queens starting new nests in the spring.

There is no hard and fast dividing line between the Parasitica and the Aculeata and there are several transitional families, such as the ruby-tailed wasps and velvet ants (p. 232). These families contain species with parasitic larvae, although the adults are anatomically closer to the Aculeata than to the Parasitica.

The larvae of the sub-order Apocrita – both Parasitica and Aculeata – are always surrounded by food and are poorly developed in comparison with the sawfly larvae. They are always legless and even the head is commonly reduced, especially in the parasitic species.

The following simplified pictorial key will enable you to identify the major groups of the Apocrita and to turn to the appropriate page, although only a very small proportion of species can be illustrated in this book.

Insects with abdomen attached near the top of the propodeum
Superfamily Evanioidea

Insects with abdomen attached near the bottom of the propodeum

Antennae with more than 16 segments (lens!). Forewing with a distinct stigma: costal cell almost or quite obliterated.

Ichneumons p. 230

Antennae with less than 16 segments. With or without a stigma in forewing: costal cell may or may not be distinct.

Hind wing smoothly rounded, without any lobes or notches close to body on hind margin. Mostly very small insects.

Petiole of one or two segments, either scale-like or bearing distinct dorsal swellings. Antennae strongly elbowed. Often wingless

Ants p. 234

Abdomen laterally compressed. Antennae not elbowed.

Gall Wasp p. 226

Abdomen fatter. Antennae elbowed.

Chalcids p. 228

Hind wing usually with one or two distinct lobes close to body on hind margin (sometimes only a small notch is discernible). Mostly medium-sized or large insects.

lobes

Hind wing with no closed cells.

Ruby-tailed wasps and relatives p. 232

Hind wing with at least one closed cell.

Pronotum reaches back to tegulae at bases of forewings.

pronotum

Forewings folded longitudinally at rest.
Eyes strongly emarginate.

tegula

Potter, Mason, and Social Wasps pp. 240–2

Forewings held flat at rest. Hind legs very long – much longer than abdomen. Body rarely very hairy.

Spider-hunting Wasps p. 240

Forewings held flat at rest. Hind legs never much longer than abdomen. Body often very hairy. Often wingless.

Velvet Ants and **Scoliids** p. 232

Pronotum does not reach back to tegulae, but forms a lobe on each side of thorax.

tegula

Hind tarsi broad and often very hairy.

Bees p. 244

Hind tarsi not broad and never very hairy.

Digger Wasps p. 236

SAWFLIES   Sub-order Symphyta

Sawflies get their English name from the saw-like ovipositors of most females (p. 218), although the horntails and a few others have drill-like ovipositors. The adults feed mainly on pollen, although some are partly carnivorous. Mostly fly weakly, usually by day. The larvae are vegetarians, feeding openly on leaves or else tunnelling inside the plants. The free-living forms generally resemble the larvae of butterflies and moths, although they usually have more prolegs (p. 218), but the tunnellers and some other larvae have greatly reduced legs. Some larvae induce gall-formation.

Megalodontes klugii Megalodontidae. Flat-bodied and fast-flying, mainly in sunshine. Antennae with flaps on underside (below). 5–8, usually on umbellifer heads. Larva has no prolegs and lives in communal webs on umbellifers. S & C.

▲ **Pamphilus sylvaticus** Pamphilidae. One of several similar fast-flying, flattened insects. On flowers 5–7: usually active only in sunshine. Larva has no prolegs and lives in rolled leaves of hawthorn and other rosaceous trees.

△n **Acantholyda erythrocephala.** Male head black behind antennae. Flies rapidly in pine woods 4–6. Larvae live communally in webs among pine needles. N & C.

▲ **Xyela julii** Xyelidae. Varied shades of brown, with filamentous antennae. Female has long, slender ovipositor. Weak-flying 3–6, often visiting birch catkins. Larva has many legs and lives in male pine cones. Common on heathland. N & C.

△s **Xiphydria prolongata** Xiphydriidae. Long neck distinguishes this family. 6–8 in wooded habitats. Larvae are almost legless and tunnel in sallows and poplars.
△ **X. camelus** is similar but lacks red on abdomen. It breeds in birch and alder.

▲ **Horntail** *Urocerus gigas* Siricidae. Named for prominent ovipositor: also called Wood Wasp, although harmless. 5–10, mainly in pine woods but not uncommon on new housing estates, where adults emerge from building timbers. Fly in sunshine, with males usually around tree tops. Eggs are drilled into tree trunks and almost legless larvae take 2 or 3 years to mature in the timber. The northern race (subspecies *taiganus*) has a black ovipositor sheath and male has more black on front of abdomen. There are several similar species in Europe.

▲ **Sirex juvencus.** Male resembles *Urocerus*, but has no pale patch behind eye. Antennae usually reddish at base, but may be all black in north. 5th tarsal segment always yellow. 5–10 in coniferous forests. Larvae tunnel in pine trunks.
▲ **S. noctilio** is similar but antennae always black and 5th tarsal segment brown.

Orussus abietinus Orussidae. Antennae inserted below eyes, not between them as in most sawflies: more slender in male. 5–8 in coniferous forests, but rare. Larva parasitises grubs of wood-boring beetles (no other sawfly has parasitic larvae). S & C.

ssp *taiganus*

△ **Cephus pygmaeus** Cephidae. One of several similar species, all with the slender bodies characteristic of this family. Yellow bands variable. Slow-flying 5–8. Common on flowers, especially yellow composites, in grassy places. Larvae are almost legless and tunnel in grass stems: serious pests of cereals.

▲ **Arge ustulata** Argidae. Metallic blue or green: wings yellowish with yellow stigma. Antennae with only 3 segments, as in all this family, the 3rd being very long: less clubbed in male. 5–7. Slow-flying in scrubby places, mainly where damp. Larva is fully legged and feeds on sallow, birch, and hawthorn. ▲ **A. cyanocrocea** has yellow costa in forewing, with dark smudge extending right across wing below stigma. Hind legs yellow with black tips: sometimes all black in south. 5–7, usually on umbellifers. Larva feeds on bramble.

Orussus head

Antenna of *Megalodontes* with much enlarged section to show the flaps.

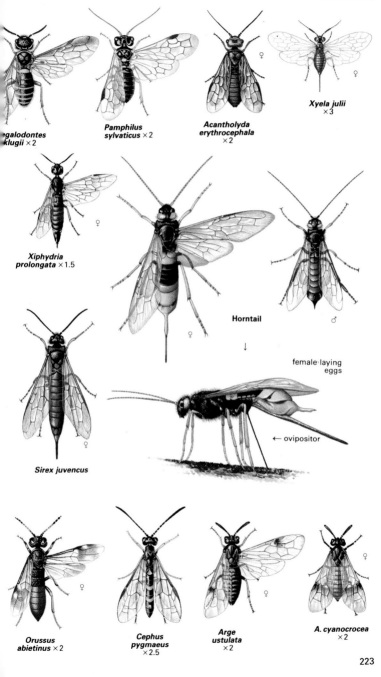

galodontes
klugii ×2

**Pamphilus
sylvaticus** ×2

**Acantholyda
erythrocephala**
×2

♀

Xyela julii
×3

♀

**Xiphydria
prolongata** ×1.5

Horntail

♂

↓

female laying
eggs

♀

Sirex juvencus

← ovipositor

**Orussus
abietinus** ×2

♀

**Cephus
pygmaeus**
×2.5

**Arge
ustulata**
×2

♀

A. cyanocrocea
×2

♀

Hawthorn Sawfly
emerging from
cocoon

Blasticotoma filiceti Blasticotomidae. A rare insect (the only European member of its family), recognised by distinctly pear-shaped cell in middle of forewing and short antennae with only 3 obvious segments (4th forms a minute hook at tip). 5–7. Larva tunnels in fern stems. N & C.

▲ **Abia sericea** Cimbicidae. Male's thorax metallic green like abdomen. Fast-flying in grassy places 5–8: attracted to various flowers. Larva feeds openly on scabious leaves.

▲ **Birch Sawfly** *Cimbex femoratus*. Dark band around apices of all wings. Fast-flying with buzzing sound in wooded areas 5–8. Larva is plump, greyish or bluish green, and feeds on birch. Spins a tough, sausage-shaped cocoon on twigs like next species.

△ **Hawthorn Sawfly** *Trichiosoma tibiale*. Hair may be very pale. 5–6 in hedgerows and scrubby places. Larva (p. 297) feeds on hawthorn and spins a tough cocoon, from which adult cuts its way out. N & C. There are several very similar species, not easy to separate.

▲ **Pine Sawfly** *Diprion pini* Diprionidae. Abdomen dull, sometimes with pale bands in female. Antennae with more than 9 segments: strongly feathered in male. 5–8 in pine woods, female rather sluggish and flying little. Larvae feed freely on pine needles, often in large groups: a serious forest pest. There are several similar species.

Family Tenthredinidae

The largest sawfly family, with nearly 1000 European species, many of them difficult to separate. Antennae usually 9-segmented. Larvae usually free-living, with 6–8 pairs of prolegs: often gregarious. Many raise hind ends and wave them about when alarmed. Some are slug-like with reduced legs (see **Pear Slug** *Caliroa cerasi* on p. 295). Many are garden pests.

△ **Turnip Sawfly** *Athalia rosae*. One of several very similar species. Antennae with 10–12 segments. Costa black. Thorax yellow beneath. 5–10. Larva, greyish brown or black, feeds on various brassicas, especially turnips.

▲ **Allantus cinctus.** One of several similar carnivorous species with large, asymmetrical jaws. 5–8, often on umbellifers where it catches other small insects. Larvae feed on wild and cultivated roses and related plants.

▲ **Tenthredopsis litterata.** Colour ranges from orange to black: female commonly with thorax and base of abdomen black and rest of abdomen red. 5–7. Larvae feed on grasses, especially cocksfoot grass.

▲ **Rhogogaster viridis.** Amount of black varies, and green fades soon after death. Stigma uniform green or straw-coloured. 5–7 in woods and scrubby places, usually on flowers where it catches other small insects. Larva is polyphagous on woody and herbaceous plants. There are several similar species.

▲ **Tenthredo atra.** Antennae and stigma completely black. Female lacks red band on abdomen. 5–8. Larva feeds on a wide range of herbaceous plants, including potato and brassicas. One of several very similar species (65 *Tenthredo* spp in N & C).

▲ **T. arcuata** is one of a number of very similar species with slightly clubbed antennae. Underside of male entirely yellow. Flagellum of antennae entirely black. 4–8 in grassy places. Larva feeds on red clover.

▲ **Cladius pectinicornis.** Male antennae feathery, but much less so than Pine Sawfly. 5–9 almost everywhere: one of the commonest sawflies. Larva is flat and green and rather hairy and feeds on undersides of rose leaves: also on strawberries and other related plants. ▲ **C. difformis** is very similar.

▲ **Gooseberry Sawfly** *Nematus ribesii*. The amount of black on male abdomen varies a great deal. 4–9. Larva (p. 293) feeds on gooseberry and currant leaves, often stripping whole bushes. There are many similar species (about 40 in B).

▲ **Pontania proxima.** 5–8, wherever white or crack willows grow. Larva causes red bean galls on the leaves (paler on white willow than on crack willow). Pupates in the soil. N & C. There are many similar species, whose larvae all live on willow, either in galls or in rolled-up leaves.

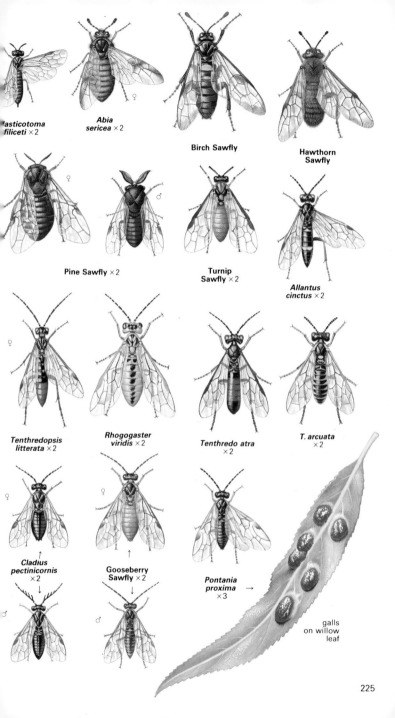

lasticotoma filiceti ×2

Abia sericea ×2 ♀

Birch Sawfly

Hawthorn Sawfly

Pine Sawfly ×2 ♀ ♂

Turnip Sawfly ×2

Allantus cinctus ×2

Tenthredopsis litterata ×2 ♀

Rhogogaster viridis ×2

Tenthredo atra ×2

T. arcuata ×2

Cladius pectinicornis ×2 ♀ ♂

Gooseberry Sawfly ×2 ♀ ♂

Pontania proxima → ×3

galls on willow leaf

WASPS, ANTS AND BEES   Sub-order Apocrita

GALL WASPS Cynipidae Small, ant-like insects with laterally compressed abdomen and distinctive venation. Sometimes wingless. Nearly all species induce gall formation in plants, especially in oaks. Female lays eggs in the plants, and when eggs hatch the tissues swell up around the grubs to form the galls. The larvae thrive on the nutritious tissues. Unilocular galls contain just one chamber and usually a single larva, while plurilocular galls contain several chambers, each with its own larva. The insects always pupate in the galls, and most spend the winter in the pupal stage. Many species have complex life cycles, involving the alternation of bisexual and parthenogenetic generations. Each generation causes its own kind of gall. The parthenogenetic females differ slightly from females of the sexual generation. A few gall wasps do not cause gall formation, but lay eggs in the galls of other species: their grubs may deprive the rightful occupants of food and cause them to die. Many parasites, including chalcids and ichneumons, also attack the gall wasp grubs. The insects emerging from a gall are thus not necessarily the gall causers.

△ **Phanacis hypochoeridis** causes plurilocular galls in cat's-ear stems. The galls start to swell before the eggs hatch. Gall mature 8–9. Adult 5–7. Life cycle normal.

△ **Liposthenus latreillei** causes unilocular galls on ground ivy leaves. Gall pea-sized, but several may coalesce. Gall mature 8–9. Adult 3–4. Life cycle normal.

△ **Diastrophus rubi** attacks young bramble stems, causing cigar-shaped plurilocular galls up to 15cm long. Gall mature 10–11. Adult 4–6. Life cycle normal.

▲ **Diplolepis rosae** causes the bedeguar gall or robin's pincushion on wild roses: a plurilocular gall with a hard woody centre. Gall mature late autumn. Adult 4–6. Males very rare: females lay eggs without mating. No alternation of generations.

△ **D. eleganteriae** and ▲ **D. nervosus** resemble *rosae* but cause pea-like unilocular galls on the underside of rose leaves. Those of *nervosus* are usually spiky. Usually pink when mature in late summer, the galls fall to the ground in autumn. Adult insects emerge in spring.

▲ **Neuroterus quercusbaccarum** causes common spangle galls on oak leaves in autumn. Galls fall to ground, and parthenogenetic females emerge early in spring to lay eggs in oak buds. The new generation of grubs induces the formation of currant galls on young leaves and catkins 5–6. Male and female gall wasps emerge from these galls and, after mating, eggs are laid on oak leaves, leading to more spangle galls. Silk button and smooth spangle galls also appear on oak leaves in autumn, caused by ▲ **N. numismalis** and ▲ **N. albipes** respectively. These insects resemble *quercusbaccarum* but galls of the sexual generation are rather inconspicuous swellings on young leaves.

▲ **Andricus kollari** induces unilocular marble galls on oak – green at first, but brown and woody when mature 8–9. Parthenogenetic females emerge 9–10 and overwinter in a sheltered spot before laying eggs in oak buds in spring. If eggs are laid on common oak, new marble galls develop, but if laid on turkey oak a bisexual generation is produced in little galls in the buds. Artichoke galls are caused by ▲ **A. fecundator**, similar to *kollari* but about half its size. The grub lives in a hard, egg-shaped inner gall, which falls out when mature in autumn. Parthenogenetic females emerge in spring and lay eggs in buds. Bisexual generation develops in tiny furry galls on male catkins 5–6.

artichoke galls

marble galls with
A. kollari

226

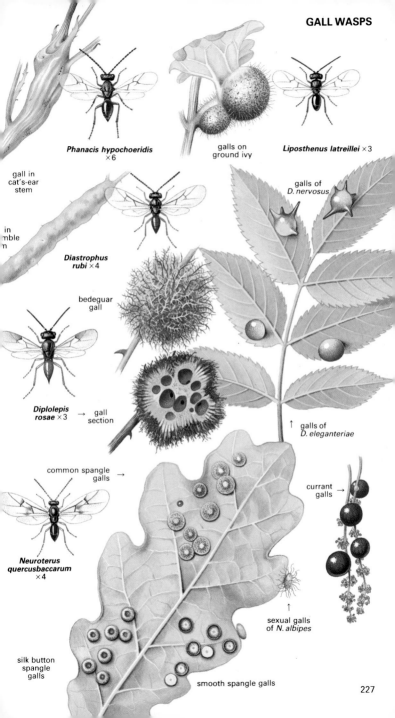

GALL WASPS

Phanacis hypochoeridis ×6

galls on ground ivy

Liposthenus latreillei ×3

gall in cat's-ear stem

in mble n

Diastrophus rubi ×4

galls of *D. nervosus*

bedeguar gall

Diplolepis rosae ×3 → gall section

galls of *D. eleganteriae*

common spangle galls →

Neuroterus quercusbaccarum ×4

currant galls →

sexual galls of *N. albipes*

silk button spangle galls

smooth spangle galls

asexual
(knopper) gall
of *A. quercus-*
calicis on acorn

sexual
gall of
A. quercus-
ramuli

asexual
gall of
Cynips coronatu

△ **Andricus quercusramuli**. Reddish brown with yellow legs. Males and females emerge 5–7 from cotton wool-like galls which develop on male oak catkins. Parthenogenetic generation (rarely seen) develops in bud galls in early spring. △ **A. quercuscalicis** causes the knopper gall, a hard and irregular umbrella-like object on acorns. Larva is in a hard inner gall as in *A. fecundator*. Parthenogenetic adults emerge 2–4. Bisexual generation induces galls on turkey oak catkins.

Cynips coronatus. Parthenogenetic generation induces spiky brown galls on downy oak in autumn. S & C. ▲ **C. quercusfolii** causes the pale green to red cherry galls on undersides of oak leaves in autumn. Parthenogenetic adults emerge 12–2 and lay eggs in buds, where bisexual generation induce purple or black galls in spring. ▲ **C. divisa** has a similar life history, but autumn galls are small yellow or red spheres with very hard walls.

▲ **Biorhiza pallida**. Males and females emerge from oak apple galls 6–7. The spongy, plurilocular galls contain many insects, but each gall contains only one sex. Females lay eggs on fine roots, where parthenogenetic generation develops in small brown galls. Parthenogenetic adults are wingless and emerge 2–4 of second year.

PARASITIC HYMENOPTERA

Hymenoptera, belonging to many different families, which spend their early lives inside or firmly attached to the young stages of other insects. The hosts remain alive until the parasites have grown up, but are eventually completely destroyed (see p. 218). Only a few of the families can be mentioned here.

△s **Evania appendigaster** Evaniidae. Gaster very small and attached to top of propodeum by very slender petiole: often waved flag-like, hence American name of ensign wasps. On flowers throughout summer. Larvae in oothecae of cockroaches.

△s **Gasteruption jaculator** Gasteruptiidae. Long, slender gaster attached to top of propodeum. Wings folded longitudinally at rest. On umbellifers in summer. Larvae feed on grubs of solitary bees and also on the stored food. N & C.

△s **Aulacus striatus**. Pear-shaped gaster attached to top of propodeum by short petiole. Ovipositor long. Around logs and tree trunks and on umbellifers and other flowers 6–9. Larvae parasitise grubs of wood-boring beetles and sawflies. N & C.

▲ **Torymus nitens** Torymidae. Hind coxae very large, as in whole family. Female uses long ovipositor to pierce young oak apples and other oak galls in summer. The grubs parasitise those of the gall wasps. There are hundreds of similar metallic species in this and related families (collectively known as chalcids), all sharing the same simple wing venation and elbowed antennae. They are abundant in vegetation in summer.

▲ **Pteromalus puparum** Pteromalidae. Hind coxae not much larger than others. Larvae parasitise pupae of white butterflies, the female inserting her eggs before pupal case hardens. Adults emerge in large numbers from each infested chrysalis, with 2 or 3 generations per year.

Leucospis gigas Leucospidae. One of the largest of the chalcids. Hind coxae very large; hind femora much swollen and strongly toothed. Wings folded longitudinally at rest, like a wasp. Flies in summer. Larvae feed on grubs of solitary bees, especially *Chalicodoma parietina* (p. 246). S & C.

Pteromalus
emerging from
host pupa

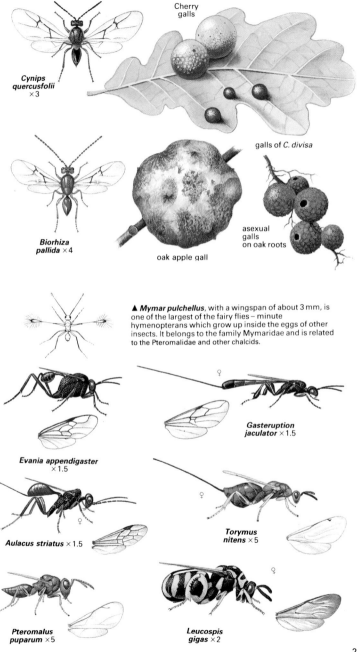

GALL WASPS, CHALCIDS and other parasites

Cherry galls

Cynips quercusfolii ×3

galls of *C. divisa*

Biorhiza pallida ×4

oak apple gall

asexual galls on oak roots

▲ *Mymar pulchellus*, with a wingspan of about 3 mm, is one of the largest of the fairy flies – minute hymenopterans which grow up inside the eggs of other insects. It belongs to the family Mymaridae and is related to the Pteromalidae and other chalcids.

Evania appendigaster ×1.5

Gasteruption jaculator ×1.5 ♀

Aulacus striatus ×1.5 ♀

Torymus nitens ×5 ♀

Pteromalus puparum ×5

Leucospis gigas ×2 ♀

ICHNEUMON FLIES Ichneumonidae An immense group of parasitic insects whose larvae live in or on the young stages of other insects. Adults are rather slender, with long antennae of at least 16 segments. The front edge of the forewing appears rather thick due to obliteration of the costal cell, and there is a prominent stigma. A few species are wingless. Ichneumons are abundant in hedgerows and other dense vegetation, scuttling around and vibrating their antennae as they search for the scents of their hosts. Butterfly and moth caterpillars are the main hosts, and generally just one egg is laid on or in each one. Endoparasitic species generally emerge after pupation of the host, much to the dismay of many people who collect caterpillars to breed into adult butterflies or moths. Many other insects are used as hosts, and some ichneumons even use spiders. Female ichneumons often have a very long ovipositor to reach hosts deep inside plants or other animals. The family Braconidae is very similar in habits, but readily distinguished by its venation: there is a long open cell towards the rear of the wing (see below). Braconids tend to be smaller than ichneumons and often lay many eggs in each host.

△ **Agriotypus armatus**. Thorax has long, curved spine. Wings distinctly clouded. An ectoparasite of various case-bearing caddis flies. Female crawls into water and lays an egg in a case containing a fully grown larva or a pupa. The grub consumes the pupa and then pupates in the case: adult remains in case for the winter and emerges in spring or early summer. Cases containing pupae or resting adult *Agriotypus* can be recognised by a silken ribbon attached to one end and used for respiration.

▲ **Rhyssa persuasoria**. One of the largest ichneumons. Ectoparasitic on horntail larvae (p. 222): slender ovipositor drills deep into pine trunks to reach the host. Not uncommon in pine woods in summer. The brown and yellow **Megarhyssa superba** is even larger.

▲ **Pimpla instigator**. A very common ectoparasite of various moth larvae, notably those of the Snout moth (p. 168). All summer. There are several similar species, mostly a little smaller: one is an endoparasite of Large White butterfly pupae.

▲ **Lissonota setosa**. Resembles *Pimpla*, but larger and female has a very long ovipositor. Endoparasitic in goat moth larvae, the ovipositor being used to drill into tree trunks. The smaller, but otherwise similar ▲ *L. fundator* attacks clearwing larvae in stems. There are many similar species.

▲ **Diplazon laetatorius**. An abundant endoparasite of various hover-fly larvae. The egg may be laid in the host egg, and adult emerges from host pupa. There are several similar species.

▲ **Netelia testaceus**. A very common ectoparasite of moth larvae. Abdomen flattened from side to side and arched upwards. Short ovipositor capable of piercing human skin if molested. Flies all summer: markedly nocturnal and abundant in light traps. There are several similar species, but only *testaceus* has dark tip to abdomen.

▲ **Ophion luteus**. Very like *Netelia*, but venation differs. Scutellum distinctly triangular. Late summer and autumn: very common. Endoparasitic in various caterpillars. One of many similar species, with or without dark hind ends.

▲ **Protichneumon pisorius**. An endoparasite of hawkmoth larvae. Adult 5–9: not uncommon on umbels and other flowers.

▲ **Amblyteles armatorius**. Scutellum cream or yellow. Hind trochanter yellow. Very common on umbels in summer: hibernates as adult, often in caves. An endoparasite of many caterpillars, especially noctuids. One of several very similar species.

▲ **Ichneumon suspiciosus**. One of many very similar species, difficult to separate with certainty. Very common on umbels in summer: hibernates as adult. An endoparasite of swift moth larvae and various noctuid caterpillars.

▲ **Apanteles glomeratus** Braconidae. Endoparasitic in larvae of large white and related butterflies. Up to 150 grubs in each caterpillar, emerging before it reaches pupal stage to leave just a shrivelled, empty skin. The grubs themselves pupate around it in silken yellow cocoons. Adult in spring and summer.

Apanteles glomeratus ×5

cocoons surrounding
dead host larva

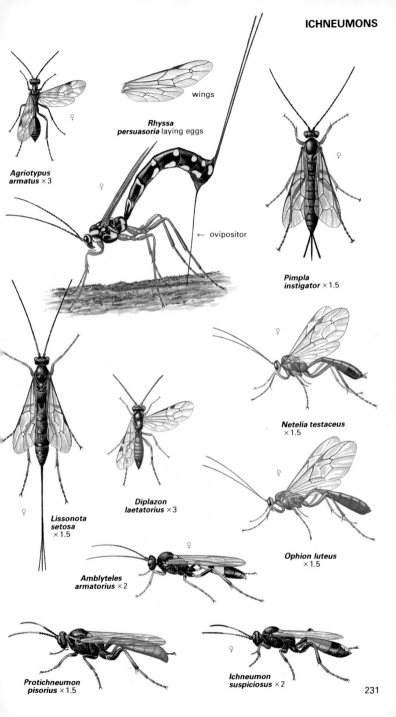

wings

Agriotypus armatus ×3 ♀

Rhyssa persuasoria laying eggs

♀

← ovipositor

Pimpla instigator ×1.5 ♀

Netelia testaceus ×1.5 ♀

Lissonota setosa ×1.5 ♀

Diplazon laetatorius ×3 ♀

Ophion luteus ×1.5 ♀

Amblyteles armatorius ×2 ♀

Protichneumon pisorius ×1.5

Ichneumon suspiciosus ×2 ♀

231

RUBY-TAILED WASPS Chrysididae Metallic-coloured insects, commonly called cuckoo wasps because they lay their eggs in the nests of other insects – mainly solitary wasps and bees. The ruby-tail grubs then eat the wasp or bee larvae. A very hard cuticle protects adults from the stings of the host species, and most ruby-tails can also roll themselves up for extra protection – thanks to the flat or concave underside of the abdomen. Only three abdominal segments are usually visible from above. Female has ovipositor in a retractable tube. A sting is present, but not usually functional: there is no venom in most species.

Stilbum cyanurum. Tip of abdomen distinctly tapered, with 4 pointed teeth. Generally clear green with golden reflections, but head and thorax may be dull green or blue and abdomen reddish with a blue tip. Parasitises mason wasps and bees. 6–9. S & C (southern).

▲ *Chrysis ignita*. Commonest of several very similar species. Head and thorax green or blue, sometimes with golden sheen. 4 teeth at tip of abdomen sharply pointed and almost equidistant. Parasitises mason bees mainly, and often seen running over walls and tree trunks in search of their nests. 4–9.

△s *C. fulgida* is readily distinguished from *ignita* by blue area at front of gaster. Parasitises digger and mason wasps. 5–9 in woods.

Parnopes grandior. Male has 4 abdominal segments visible from above: female has only 3, of which 3rd is much larger than the others. A thin, leaf-like projection from hind end of thorax. Abdomen not toothed at tip, but with several very tiny points. Tongue very long. Parasitises *Bembix* digger wasps. 6–8. S & C (southern).

▲ *Cleptes nitidulus*. Pronotum strongly narrowed at front and leading to a distinct neck. Thorax green or blue in male: black, red, and blue in female, usually tinged with green. Male has 5 abdominal segments visible from above: female only 4. Functional sting present. A parasite of sawfly larvae. 5–8. S & C. Sometimes placed in a separate family – the Cleptidae.

△s *Methocha ichneumonides* Tiphiidae. Male with 2 sub-marginals and a long, pointed marginal cell. Female wingless. Very shiny in both sexes. Males very rare: reproduction largely parthenogenetic? 5–9 on heathland. Larvae parasitise those of tiger beetles in their burrows. S & C.

△s *Tiphia femorata*. 2 sub-marginals: marginal cell open in female but closed in male. Middle and hind legs red in female: black in male. Pronotum rather square in front. 7–8. Parasitises larvae of various chafers and dung beetles. S & C.

△ **Velvet Ant** *Mutilla europaea* Mutillidae. Male fully winged: female wingless and without any divisions on thorax. Both sexes with patches of silvery hair. 7–9 and again in spring after hibernation. A parasite of various bumble bee species, feeding on larvae in the nest. Most of Europe, but local. There are several species on the continent.

Myrmilla capitata. Wingless in both sexes. Head relatively large and square. Thorax parallel-sided. A parasite of various solitary bees. 4–8. S. There are several similar species, some with winged males.

Dasylabris maura. Male fully winged, with dark wing-tips, and with 2 grey bands across abdomen. Female thorax strongly pear-shaped. A parasite of *Ammophila* and other sand wasps. S & C (southern).

Scolia flavifrons Scoliidae. One of Europe's largest hymenopterans, with female up to 40 mm long. Her head is larger than that of male and orange-brown in colour. Each yellow band may be split into 2 spots. Thorax and tip of abdomen may have reddish hairs in some areas. 6–8 in hot, sunny places: commonly seen on flowers. Harmless to man despite size. A parasite of the beetle *Oryctes nasicornis* (p. 264). S.

S. hirta is distinguished from several similar species by the 2 yellow bands and the strong violet tinge on wings. 7–10. A parasite of chafer grubs. S & C (southern).

△s *Sapyga quinquepunctatum* Sapygidae. 3 sub-marginals. Antennae distinctly thickened towards tip. Pronotum square in front. Male lacks red on abdomen but has yellow spots on 3rd and 4th segments. 5–8. A parasite of *Osmia* and other mason bees.

♀

Sapyga quinquepunctatum ×2

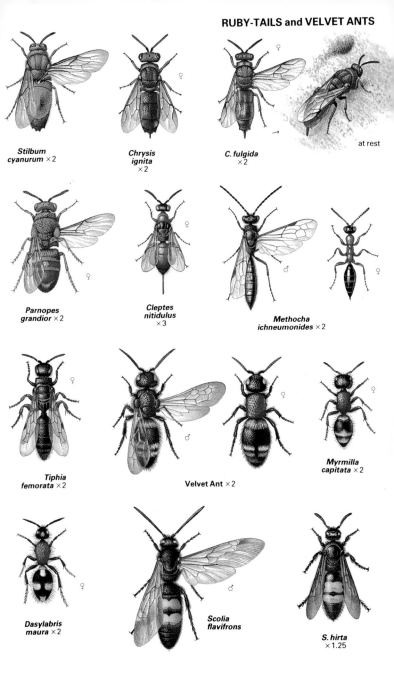

Stilbum cyanurum ×2

Chrysis ignita ×2

♀

C. fulgida ×2

at rest

Parnopes grandior ×2 ♀

Cleptes nitidulus ×3 ♀

Methocha ichneumonides ×2 ♂ ♀

Tiphia femorata ×2 ♀

Velvet Ant ×2 ♂ ♀

Myrmilla capitata ×2 ♀

Dasylabris maura ×2 ♀

Scolia flavifrons ♂

S. hirta ×1.25

ANTS Formicidae A family of some 15,000 known species, all social. Workers are always wingless: sexual forms winged, but queens break off wings soon after mating. Antennae usually clearly elbowed. The narrow 'waist', known as the pedicel, has one or two segments. Sting not present in all species (usually absent in species with 1-segmented pedicel). There are carnivorous, herbivorous, and omnivorous species, with aphid honeydew prominent in many diets. European ants nest mainly in the ground. Some species have more than one queen in each colony. The dense swarms of flying ants that appear in summer and autumn are mating swarms. Unless otherwise stated, all ants illustrated here are workers.

Ants of the sub-family Myrmicinae have a 2-segmented pedicel. Other European ants have just one segment, generally scale-like.

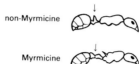

non-Myrmicine

Myrmicine

▲ *Myrmica rubra*. Pedicel of 2 segments. Male blackish brown: queen and worker chestnut. Propodeum with 2 spines. Worker with sting. Omnivorous. Abundant in garden soils. Mating flights 7–10. One of several very similar species. **M. ruginodis** is almost identical but the pedicel differs slightly in shape.

Pheidole megacephala. A very small ant with 2-segmented pedicel. Two types of worker, one with a very large head and jaws for cracking seeds which are a major component of omnivorous diet. Nests under stones and in soil, often close to houses. S & C (southern): sometimes in buildings further north.

△ **Argentine Ant** *Iridomyrmex humilis*. A small and very slender ant with a 1-segmented pedicel and well-developed scale on it. Omnivorous. A native of S. America, now well established in and hard to eradicate from European buildings. Colonies increase and spread by fragmentation, without mating flights. Widespread in S & C: sporadic in B (heated buildings only).

▲ **Pharaoh's Ant** *Monomorium pharaonis*. A very small ant with 2-segmented pedicel. Antennae 12-segmented, the last 3 broader than others and forming a faint club. Omnivorous. A native of Africa and now a troublesome pest in heated buildings. Nests in tiny crevices. No mating swarms.

Camponotus vagus. One of the largest European ants, although sizes vary. Pedicel 1-segmented and much of body dotted with long pale hairs. Several similar species live on the continent but none in B. Omnivorous, with especial liking for honeydew. Nests in dead tree trunks, often causing losses to forestry by excavating galleries in felled trunks before they are taken to sawmills. S. *C. lateralis* nests under stones and logs. Queen has brown head only: male is all black. Omnivorous. Workers forage on ground and tree trunks, often forming long columns and frequently associating with the superficially similar *Crematogaster scutellaris*, although latter is distinguished by 2-segmented pedicel and habit of carrying abdomen almost vertically when alarmed. S.

▲ **Black Garden Ant** *Lasius niger*. Pedicel 1-segmented. Dark brown to black. Omnivorous but regularly 'milking' aphids for honeydew. Abundant everywhere, often under pavements and garden paths and sometimes nesting in or under house walls. ▲ **Yellow Meadow Ant** *L. flavus* is yellowish brown but otherwise very like *niger*. Inhabits rough grassland, making the familiar ant-hills. Both species produce huge mating swarms, usually 7–8.

Messor barbara. Petiole with 2 relatively long segments. Head red or black according to race: rest of body brown to shiny black. Two types of worker, one with much larger head than the other. Males have very small heads. Nests underground and feeds almost entirely on seeds, which are cracked open by the large-headed workers. Workers can be seen dragging seeds back to the nest from considerable distances. S.

△s **Wood Ant** *Formica rufa*. Pedicel of one flattened, leaf-like segment. No sting, although the ant can fire formic acid from rear end when disturbed. Mainly in woods, making large mound nests with leaves and other debris. Several or many queens in each nest. Omnivorous, with bias towards animal food. Protected by law in some European countries because of its great value in destroying forest pests. Most of Europe but mainly upland in S. Mating flight 5–6. There are several similar species.

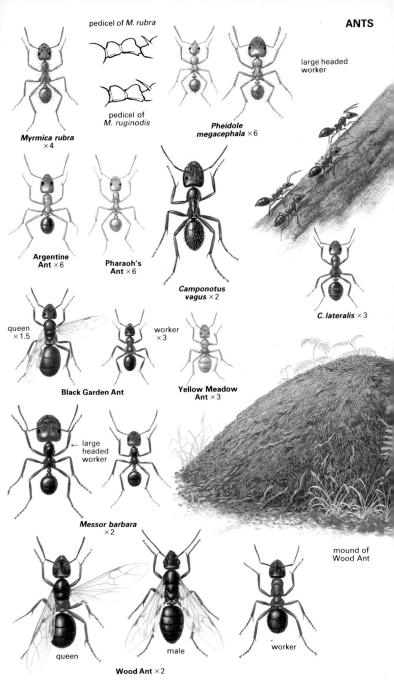

ANTS

pedicel of *M. rubra*

pedicel of *M. ruginodis*

Myrmica rubra ×4

Pheidole megacephala ×6

large headed worker

Argentine Ant ×6

Pharaoh's Ant ×6

Camponotus vagus ×2

C. lateralis ×3

queen ×1.5

worker ×3

Black Garden Ant

worker ×3

Yellow Meadow Ant ×3

large headed worker →

Messor barbara ×2

mound of Wood Ant

queen

male

worker

Wood Ant ×2

235

DIGGER WASPS Sphecidae Solitary wasps with a relatively broad head. Pronotum forms only a small collar, not reaching back to tegulae. Wings held flat over body at rest. Most species nest in ground: females often have a spiny comb on front legs for digging. Some species nest in decaying wood or hollow stems, and a few are masons which build with mud. The nests are stocked with various insects, paralysed by the female's sting. Several insects are usually put into each burrow, often in several separate chambers. Eggs are laid and the wasp grubs rely on the stored food until they pupate. There are some 9,000 known digger wasp species.

▲ **Trypoxylon figulus.** One of several similar species with slender, tapering abdomen. 1 sub-marginal. Inner margin of eye deeply notched. Nests in woodworm holes, hollow stems, and similar cavities: builds mud cells therein and stocks them with small spiders. 5–9.

▲ **Crabro cribrarius.** 1 sub-marginal. Only male front tibia broad and plate-like. Male antennae appear deformed. Central yellow bands of abdomen divided. Continental specimens often with yellow on thorax. 5–9. Nests mainly in sandy soil: stocked with flies. There are many similar species.

▲ **Ectemnius cephalotes.** One of several similar species, distinguished from *Crabro* by normal front tibiae in male and by grooved prolongation of abdomen in female. 6–9. Nests in rotten wood: stocked with flies.

△ **Crossocerus palmipes.** 1 sub-marginal. Face largely yellow. Front tibia and 1st tarsal segment of male expanded. 5–9 in sandy places, stocking nest with flies. One of several similar species.

Lestica clypeata. 1 sub-marginal. Body coarsely punctured. Male instantly recognisable by shape of head and front legs: female more normal, with yellow on thorax and a narrow grooved spike at tip of abdomen. 5–9. Nests in dead wood: stocked with small moths.

▲ **Oxybelus uniglumis.** Venation much reduced. Rear of thorax with 2 transparent flaps: propodeum with a small spine. Female with comb. 5–9. Nests in sand: stocked with flies which are carried back impaled on sting. Several similar species.

Larra anathema. 3 sub-marginals. Abdomen sometimes entirely black: always shining. 6–9. Makes no nest. Follows mole crickets along their burrows and temporarily paralyses them with the sting. An egg is laid in each cricket, which soon wakes up and continues activity with the wasp larva inside it. S.

▲ **Pemphredon lugubris.** 2 sub-marginals, the first much larger than second. Abdomen distinctly stalked. Head and thorax hairy. 5–9. Nests in rotten wood: stocked with aphids. One of many similar species, most of which nest in bramble stems.

▲ **Mellinus arvensis.** 3 sub-marginals. Scutellum with large yellow spot. Abdomen with short petiole. 5–9. Nests in sand: stocked with large flies, especially hover-flies. △s **M. crabroneus** has paler markings and reddish antennae.

Palarus variegatus. 3 sub-marginals. Abdomen with distinct grooves between segments as in *Cerceris*, but more triangular and much yellower. 5–7. Nests in ground: stocked with assorted hymenopterans, including other digger wasps. S.

△ **Astata boops.** 3 sub-marginals. Male eyes meet on top of head. Female antennae much shorter. Female with comb. 5–8. Nests in sandy soil: stocked with shield bug nymphs.

△ **Mimesa lutarius.** 3 sub-marginals. Petiole shorter than 1st abdominal segment: keeled on top and straight when seen from the side. Female has more red on abdomen. 5–8. Nests in sand: stocked with leafhoppers. There are several similar species.

▲ **Argogorytes mystaceus.** 3 sub-marginals. Male antennae extra long. Female with short comb. 1st abdominal tergite almost semi-circular. Yellow spot may be missing from 4th gastral segment. Nests in soil: stocked with froghopper nymphs. 5–9.

▲ **Nysson spinosus.** 3 sub-marginals, the second being stalked in front. Hind edges of propodeum spiny. Front of abdomen often reddish. Cuticle very hard. 5–8. A cuckoo species, laying eggs in nests of *Argogorytes*. There are many similar species.

△ **Cerceris arenaria.** 3 sub-marginals, the second being stalked at front. Female with comb. 1st abdominal segment rounded, with 2 large yellow spots. Abdominal segments separated by distinct grooves. 5–9. Nests deep in sand: stocked with weevils. S & C. One of several similar species.

△s **Bee-killer** *Philanthus triangulum.* 3 sub-marginals. Head more rounded in front than in most digger wasps. Female with strong comb. Abdomen largely yellow, with or without black triangles. 7–9. Nests in sand: stocked with honey bees which are carried slung upside-down under body. S & C.

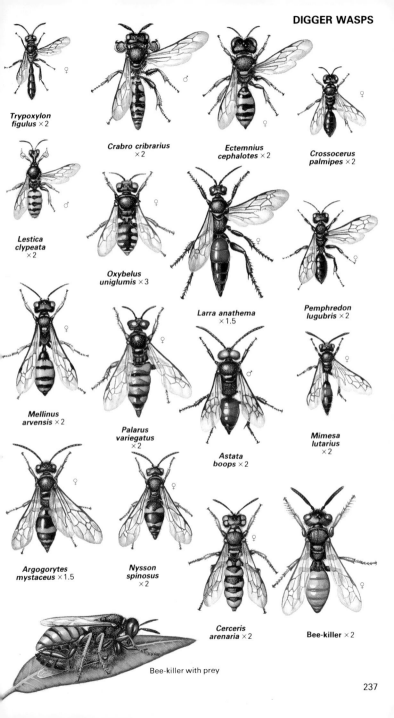

DIGGER WASPS

Trypoxylon figulus × 2 ♀

Crabro cribrarius × 2 ♂

Ectemnius cephalotes × 2 ♀

Crossocerus palmipes × 2 ♀

Lestica clypeata × 2 ♂

Oxybelus uniglumis × 3 ♀

Larra anathema × 1.5 ♀

Pemphredon lugubris × 2 ♀

Mellinus arvensis × 2 ♀

Palarus variegatus × 2 ♀

Astata boops × 2 ♂

Mimesa lutarius × 2 ♀

Argogorytes mystaceus × 1.5 ♀

Nysson spinosus × 2 ♀

Cerceris arenaria × 2 ♀

Bee-killer × 2 ♀

Bee-killer with prey

A female *Sphex* dragging a bush cricket to her burrow. She grips the victim by an antenna, and straddling its body with her long legs, makes for home. She can negotiate surprisingly rough ground, although the journey might take several hours.

Sphex rufocinctus. 3 sub-marginals. Wing tinted yellow in female. Face clothed with silvery hair. Female with comb. 6–9. Size very variable. Nests in sandy soil: stocked with crickets and grasshoppers. S & C (southern): most common around Mediterranean. Commonest of several similar species.

Sceliphron destillatorium. 3 sub-marginals. Wings yellowish at base. Petiole yellow and almost as long as rest of abdomen. 5–8. Makes a nest of mud, attached to walls, rocks, tree trunks, etc: sometimes in buildings. Nests stocked with spiders. S & C (southern). **S. spirifex** is very similar but has no yellow on thorax: tegulae are black.

Liris praetermissa. 3 sub-marginals. Propodeum sub-rectangular and strongly grooved. 4–8. Nests in ground, often in pre-existing holes: stocked with crickets. S.

Dolichurus corniculus. 3 sub-marginals. Long pronotum with distinct neck. Almost square propodeum, strongly sculptured and keeled on top. Abdomen very shiny. Nests in hollow stems of bramble and other shrubs: stocked with cockroaches of genus *Ectobius*. 6–9. S & C (southern).

▲ **Ammophila sabulosa**. 3 sub-marginals. Petiole 2-segmented, very long and slender and not sharply separated from rest of abdomen. Female with strong comb. 5–9. Nests in sandy places: stocked with non-hairy caterpillars. One of several similar species known as sand wasps, but distinguished from most others by entirely black legs.

▲ **Podalonia hirsuta**. 3 sub-marginals. Thorax with bristly hairs: whitish in male, black in female. Petiole shorter than in *Ammophila* and more sharply separated from gaster. 3–8. Nests in sandy places: stocked with hairless or sparsely hairy caterpillars. Unlike most digger wasps, it catches prey before excavating the nest.

Bembix rostrata. 3 sub-marginals. Resembles social wasps, but wings are held flat at rest. Mouthparts with a beak-like extension. Comb on front leg in both sexes, but very large in female. Yellow abdominal bands sinuous and often broken in middle. 5–8. Nests in sandy places, often densely clustered: stocked with flies. Female brings more flies later on to top up the larder, adjusting size of her captures to the increasing size of her larvae. There are several similar species.

Stizus fasciatus. 3 sub-marginals. Stigma very small. Female has abdomen markedly oval and antennae entirely red. 5–8. Nests in sandy soil: stocked with crickets and grasshoppers. S. There are several similar species.

Ammophila tapping down the sand to close her burrow with a small stone held in her jaws. Some species use their heads to tap down the sand.

238

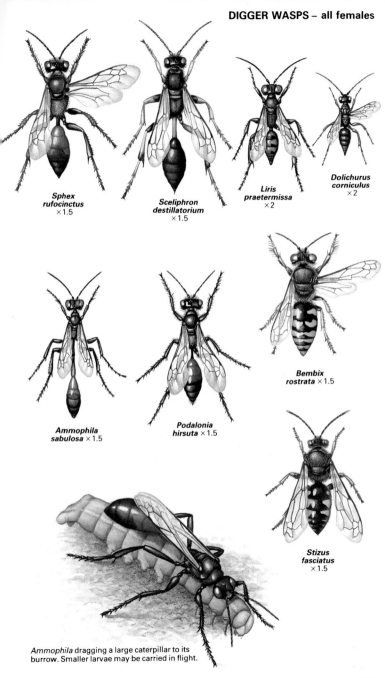

Sphex rufocinctus ×1.5

Sceliphron destillatorium ×1.5

Liris praetermissa ×2

Dolichurus corniculus ×2

Ammophila sabulosa ×1.5

Podalonia hirsuta ×1.5

Bembix rostrata ×1.5

Stizus fasciatus ×1.5

Ammophila dragging a large caterpillar to its burrow. Smaller larvae may be carried in flight.

SPIDER-HUNTING WASPS Pompilidae Solitary wasps using spiders as food for their young. Distinguished from digger wasps (p. 236) by pronotum extending back to tegulae at base of wings. Latter laid flat at rest: almost all with 3 sub-marginals. Males often much smaller than females: female antennae generally coil up after death. Legs long and slender: hind femur especially long. Generally nest in sandy ground, many females having strong combs on front legs for sweeping away the sand. Female makes several burrows, each one usually with a single spider and a single egg. Burrow is closed by tapping down sand with end of abdomen. Unlike most digger wasps, these insects catch prey before digging the burrow. A few species make mud nests.

Cryptocheilus comparatus. One of the largest European pompilids. Collects wolf spiders, including the infamous tarantula, by following them into their burrows or chasing them on the surface. Male often paler. 6–7. S.

△s **Caliadurgus fasciatellus**. Pronotum rather square in front. Male lacks red on abdomen and has no brown patch on wings. 6–9. Nest is short vertical burrow in hard clay. Collects orb-web spiders and instals them vertically in burrows.

△s **Ceropales maculata**. Female with visible sting sheath: male genitalia exposed. Female antennae do not coil after death. Legs not spiny. A cuckoo species, watching other pompilids excavating their burrows and then nipping in to lay an egg on the paralysed spider as it is being dragged into the nest. The *Ceropales* egg hatches quickly and its grub devours the rightful pompilid larva as well as the spider. Adults often on umbellifer flowers. 5–9.

Eoferreola rhombica. Thorax (with propodeum) distinctly rectangular. Wings almost clear in male, which also has only 2nd abdominal tergite orange. Follows eresid spider into its silken tunnel, paralysing it temporarily and laying egg on it. Spider recovers and wasp grub feeds on it externally. 6–7. S & C (southern).

▲ **Anoplius viaticus**. Outer sub-marginal almost triangular. Tip of abdomen clothed with numerous stiff black hairs in female: broad and flat in male. 4–10, especially common on umbellifer flowers in spring. Chases wolf spiders. One of the commonest pompilids. S & C. Several similar species, but abdominal patterns differ.

▲ **Episyron rufipes**. Claws on all feet distinctly bifid. Female with strong comb. Thorax and propodeum with silvery scales (may be missing in worn specimens). White abdominal markings variable. Plucks orb-web spiders from webs. 6–9. *E. tripunctatus* of S & C is similar but has entirely black legs.

▲ **Pompilus cinereus**. Hairy bands on abdomen are blue-grey. Tip of female abdomen with scattered fine hairs. Female with strong comb. 5–9. Collects wolf spiders mainly, burying them temporarily while digging the permanent burrow. There are many similar species, often with orange bands on abdomen.

Celonites abbreviatus Masaridae. 2 sub-marginals. Wings folded longitudinally at rest. Pronotum reaches back to tegulae. Abdomen very square in front. A solitary wasp making a small nest of clay cells on a stone. Unlike most wasps, it stocks the nest with pollen and nectar. 5–8. S & C (southern), esp. near Mediterranean.

Ceramius lusitanicus. 2 sub-marginals. Antennae spirally twisted at tip in male: normal in female. Abdomen rounded in front. Digs nest burrow in clay, forming several cells and stocking them with pollen and nectar. 5–7. SW.

POTTER and MASON WASPS Eumenidae Solitary wasps, but closely related to social Vespidae (p. 242) and resembling them in folding wings longitudinally at rest. 3 sub-marginals. Pronotum reaches back to tegulae. Middle tibia with 1 spur. Almost all species black and yellow. Small nests built of clay or mud.

Delta unguiculata. 1st abdominal segment bell-shaped and clearly separated from the rest. Nest is an irregular cluster of several cells, fixed to rocks or walls like a lump of hardened mortar: stocked with caterpillars. 6–8. S & C (southern).

△s **Eumenes coarctatus** is the common potter wasp of heathland. One of several similar species making vase-shaped nests on rocks or plants. Each vase is stocked with small hairless caterpillars and contains a single wasp grub. 6–9.

▲ **Odynerus spinipes**. Male antennae spirally rolled at tip, the rolled section entirely black. Male with 3 teeth on underside of mid femur. Male with paler hairs. 5–9. One of many similar species nesting in sandy ground, especially on slopes: burrow entrance often with a curved chimney. Nest stocked with weevil larvae.

△ **Ancistrocerus antilope**. Male antennae not coiled: last segment bent back like a hook. Tegulae pointed at rear. 5–9. Nests in a wide range of cavities, divided by mud partitions and stocked with small caterpillars. Largest of several similar and very common species, not easily distinguished from each other.

SPIDER-HUNTERS, POTTERS and MASON WASPS

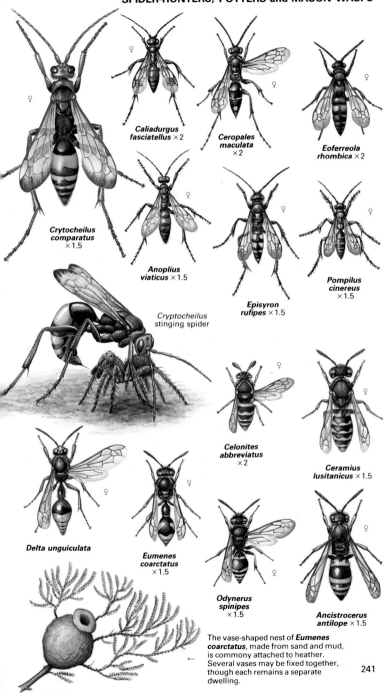

Crytocheilus comparatus ×1.5

♀ **Caliadurgus fasciatellus** ×2

♀ **Ceropales maculata** ×2

♀ **Eoferreola rhombica** ×2

♀ **Anoplius viaticus** ×1.5

♀ **Episyron rufipes** ×1.5

♀ **Pompilus cinereus** ×1.5

Cryptocheilus stinging spider

♀ **Celonites abbreviatus** ×2

♀ **Ceramius lusitanicus** ×1.5

♀ **Delta unguiculata**

♀ **Eumenes coarctatus** ×1.5

♀ **Odynerus spinipes** ×1.5

♀ **Ancistrocerus antilope** ×1.5

The vase-shaped nest of **Eumenes coarctatus**, made from sand and mud, is commonly attached to heather. Several vases may be fixed together, though each remains a separate dwelling.

241

SOCIAL WASPS Vespidae Eyes deeply notched or crescent-shaped. Wings folded longitudinally at rest, with most of abdomen exposed from above. Pronotum reaches back to tegulae. Insects live in annual colonies, each founded by a mated female (queen) in spring. Nests are built of paper, which wasps make from wood. A few hundred to several thousand female workers are reared in summer: always smaller than queens. Males appear in late summer: most often seen on flowers. They have longer antennae than females (13 segments compared with 12): base of antenna usually yellow beneath in males but yellow or black in females. Adults feed mainly on nectar and other sweet materials. Young reared mainly on other insects collected by the workers. The colony disintegrates in autumn and only mated females survive the winter. Some species, known as cuckoo wasps, have no workers: they lay their eggs in the nests of other wasps. The following notes refer only to females: male patterns are more variable.

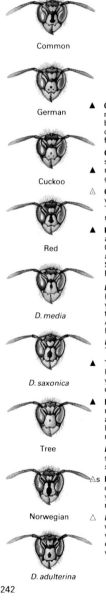

Common

German

Cuckoo

Red

D. media

D. saxonica

Tree

Norwegian

D. adulterina

▲ **Common Wasp** *Vespula vulgaris*. Face usually with anchor mark: malar space (between bottom of eye and jaw) very short. Antennae black at base. Thoracic stripes parallel-sided. 4 yellow spots at rear of thorax. Nests in holes in ground or buildings: paper yellowish and formed into shell-like plates on outside.

▲ **German Wasp** *V. germanica*. Face with 3 dots: malar space very short. Antennae black at base. Thoracic stripes usually bulge in middle. 4 yellow spots at rear of thorax. Nest like that of *vulgaris* but greyish.

△ **Cuckoo Wasp** *V. austriaca*. Face with 2 or 3 black spots: malar space very short. Antennae yellow at base. Only 2 yellow spots on thorax. Tibiae and 1st abdominal segment with long black hairs. Never any red on abdomen. A cuckoo species in the nest of *V. rufa*. N & C.

▲ **Red Wasp** *V. rufa*. Face with thick vertical line, sometimes forming anchor-like mark: malar space very short. Antennae black at base. Only 2 yellow spots on thorax. Tibiae without long hairs. 1st abdominal segment with long black hairs and often distinctly red. Subterranean nest covered with more or less smooth sheets. All Europe but rare in S.

Dolichovespula media. Face with slim black bar: malar space long (nearly as long as distance between antennal bases). Antennae yellow at base. Eye notch completely filled with yellow. Thorax often tinged red, especially in female, and with 4 yellow spots at rear. Abdomen often tinged red with very variable amount of black. Nest hung in bushes and clothed with smooth sheets.

D. saxonica. Like Norwegian Wasp but face bar often irregular. Thorax with pale hairs at sides. Abdomen never red.

▲ **Tree Wasp** *D. sylvestris*. Face clear yellow or with 1 dot: malar space long. Antennae yellow at base. Thorax with pale hairs at sides and 2 yellow spots at rear. Nest a rather small ball, hung in bushes and covered with thin but tough sheets. Absent from far south.

▲ **Norwegian Wasp** *D. norvegica*. Face divided by vertical black bar: malar space long. Antennae yellow at base. Thorax with black hairs at side and 2 yellow spots at rear. Abdomen often red in front. Nest like that of Tree Wasp but with looser covering. Widespread but most common in N.

D. adulterina. Black bar sometimes completely divides face. Malar space long. Antennae yellow at base. A cuckoo species in nest of *saxonica*, but not common.

△s **Hornet** *Vespa crabro*. The largest wasp. Nests in hollow trees, chimneys and wall cavities, sometimes using same site year after year (although a completely new colony). Populations fluctuate markedly from year to year in B.

△ *Polistes gallicus*. One of several very similar species known as paper wasps. Abdomen tapering in front and not hairy: pattern very variable. Nest is a small 'umbrella' without protective envelopes: often on buildings. S & C: most common in S: only occasional vagrants reach B.

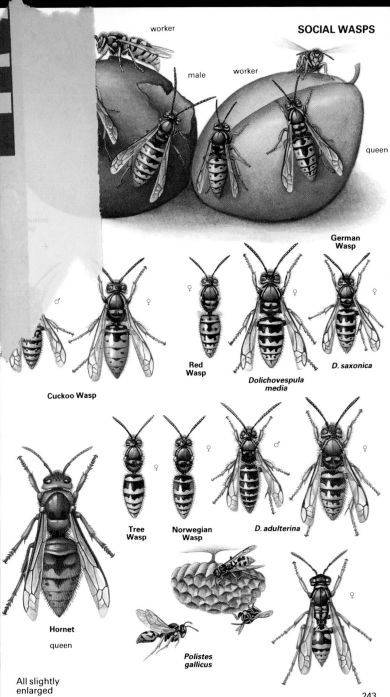

SOCIAL WASPS

worker

male

worker

queen

German Wasp

♂

♀

♀

♀

♀

Red Wasp

Dolichovespula media

D. saxonica

Cuckoo Wasp

♀

♀

♂

♀

Tree Wasp

Norwegian Wasp

D. adulterina

Hornet

queen

Polistes gallicus

♀

All slightly enlarged

BEES A large group of Hymenoptera, belonging to several families and all feeding on pollen and nectar. The pronotum does not extend back to the tegulae (p. 218) and the body is generally rather hairy – an adaptation to pollen gathering. Pollen is often carried back to the nest attached to the broad and hairy hind legs: among the honey bees and bumble bees the hind tibiae are fringed with stiff hairs which form distinct 'baskets'. Some bees carry their pollen on the underside of the body. Only females are equipped for carrying pollen. Important features for identifying bees include the sub-marginal cells (p. 218) and the form of the tongue. The latter is short and broad in the Colletidae, but otherwise pointed and often quite long.

Unless otherwise stated, all bees described here are solitary.

▲ **Colletes succinctus**. Colletidae 3 sub-marginals. Tongue short and broad. 7–9: ground-nesting in sandy areas. One of several similar species with bands of pale hairs on abdomen. Thoracic hairs paler in male.

△s **Hylaeus signatus**. 2 sub-marginals. Tongue short and broad. Face almost entirely white in male: white-spotted in female. Almost hairless: pollen carried in crop. Abdomen very parallel-sided, especially in male. 6–8 on bramble and umbellifers: nest mainly in sandy banks. S & C: one of several similar species.

Andrena Andrenidae. A large genus with many species superficially like honey bees. Abdomen often rather flat. 3 sub-marginals. Tongue short and pointed. Often known as mining bees, *Andrena* spp generally nest in ground and appear mainly in spring. △ **A. hattorfiana** is largest British species, largely dark brown with yellow near tip of abdomen. 6–9. △s **A. labiata** forages 5–6, almost entirely at speedwell flowers. Male has white hairs on legs, female pale golden. S & C. △ **A. cineraria** male has less obvious black band on thorax and has white hairs on all femora: female has white hairs only on front femora. ▲ **A. haemorrhoa** is one of the earliest spring species – on blackthorn, dandelions, and sallow. Female has white face: male has pale brown face and yellower tip to abdomen. N & C. △s **A. pilipes** has paler hairs on thorax. Female has white pollen brush on hind legs. 3–5 and sometimes again 7–8: mainly on dandelions. △s **A. florea** male has paler head and thorax and very short antennae. Width of reddish abdominal bands varies, but first 2 segments usually largely red. Feeds mainly on white bryony. S & C. **Tawny Mining Bee** *A. fulva* feeds at currant and gooseberry flowers in spring, especially brightly coloured female. Commonly nests in lawns, with small mound around opening. C. △s **A. marginata** has yellowish or reddish brown abdomen in female: shiny black in male. 6–8 on scabious. S & C.

⍄ **Panurgus banksianus**. 2 sub-marginals. Tongue short and pointed. Abdomen with black hair in male, brown in female. Latter with very prominent golden pollen brush on hind legs. Other legs with tawny hairs. 7–8 in sandy places.

Halictus Halictidae. Another large genus of ground-nesting bees. Abdomen more cylindrical than in *Andrena*: female with prominent bare patch at tip. Tongue short and pointed. 3 sub-marginals: basal vein (near centre of forewing) strongly curved, not ± straight as in *Andrena*. Mated females survive winter and fly again in spring: new generation of both sexes flies mid to late summer. ▲ **H. rubicundus** has clear yellow hind tibiae. Abdominal bands of male entire. ▲ **H. tumulorum** is one of several greenish species. Female has paler legs. **H. scabiosae** is recognised by the very broad bands of pale hairs on abdomen. S & C. (southern). Many species show sub-social habits, with a few sterile females appearing late spring and doing a little food-gathering for the younger larvae in the nest.

▲ **Lasioglossum calceatum**. 3 sub-marginals. Tongue short and pointed. Male narrower, with more red on abdomen. Both sexes often with tufts of white hair. Usually nests in steep banks. △s **L. malachurus** resembles *calceatum* but has paler hair. S & C. ⍄s **L. smeathmanellum** is metallic bronze or bluish green: male has less bright abdomen. This genus is ground-nesting, with flight times as in *Halictus*. Some species are sub-social, like some *Halictus* species.

△s **Sphecodes spinulosus**. 3 sub-marginals. Tongue short and pointed. A cuckoo bee, laying eggs in nests of *Lasioglossum xanthopum*. Body ± hairless, for it collects no pollen. One of several similar species, some with dark wings and almost all with entirely black antennae. Flies late summer: mated females again in spring with host. S & C.

Sphecodes spinulosus × 1.5

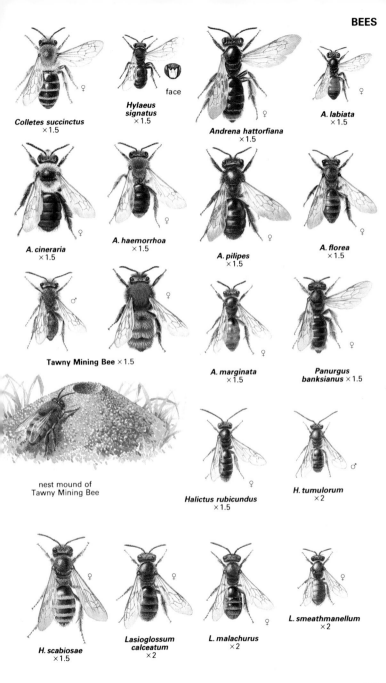

Colletes succinctus
×1.5

Hylaeus signatus
×1.5

face

Andrena hattorfiana
×1.5
♀

A. labiata
×1.5
♀

A. cineraria
×1.5
♀

A. haemorrhoa
×1.5
♀

A. pilipes
×1.5
♀

A. florea
×1.5
♀

Tawny Mining Bee ×1.5
♂

A. marginata
×1.5
♀

Panurgus banksianus ×1.5
♀

nest mound of
Tawny Mining Bee

Halictus rubicundus
×1.5
♀

H. tumulorum
×2
♂

H. scabiosae
×1.5
♀

Lasioglossum calceatum
×2
♀

L. malachurus
×2
♀

L. smeathmanellum
×2
♀

Anthidium florentinum Megachilidae. 2 sub-marginals. Tongue long and slender. Distinguished from most of its relatives by yellow or brick-red borders to thorax. Flies all summer and nests in holes in ground, trees, or walls. Nest lined with hairs plucked from plants. As in all members of this genus, males are notably larger than females. S & C (southern).

▲ **A. manicatum** has thorax almost entirely black. 6–8. Nests in existing holes in timber or masonry: lined with plant hairs carried back in a ball under body.

A. variegatum has thorax bordered with yellow and legs entirely yellow. Nests like manicatum. S & C (southern). There are about 30 similar species in Europe, some using plant hairs to line nest and some using resin from conifers. Only manicatum occurs in B.

△s **Stelis punctulatissima**. 2 sub-marginals. Tongue long and slender. Pale hind margins of abdominal segments distinguish it from the very similar △s **S. phaeoptera**. A cuckoo species, with very little hair. Invades nests of Osmia and Anthidium spp.

▲ **Chelostoma campanularum**. 2 sub-marginals. Tongue long and slender. A very slender, fly-like bee specialising in Campanula flowers. Female has dense orange pollen brush on underside of body. Nests in holes of furniture beetles (woodworm) and other minute holes. Cannot turn round in burrows: backs in to off-load pollen, but enters head-first to disgorge nectar. 6–8.

▲ **C. florisomne** is larger and female has creamy pollen brush. Male face with long pale hairs. Feeds mainly at buttercups. 6–9. Often nests in hollow stems, including straw of thatch. Males of both species often curl up in flowers at night.

▲ **Osmia rufa**. 2 sub-marginals. Tongue long and slender. Male much smaller than female but with much longer antennae. Male face clothed with pale hairs: female face has black hairs and a pair of short horns below antennae. Abdominal hairs denser in female. 4–7, nesting in holes in a variety of situations, often in walls. Cells made with mud. There are many similar species.

▲ **Hoplitis spinulosa**. Resembles Osmia spp. Female has brick-red pollen brush under abdomen. Nests in empty snail shells, using dung for cell partitions. 4–7. S & C.

Chalicodoma parietina. 2 sub-marginals. Tongue long and slender. Male lacks dark wing colour and has browner body. 4–6, building small clay nests attached to stones, sometimes in large groups. S & C. There are several similar species, some building clay chambers in hollow stems.

△s **Macropis europaea** 2 sub-marginals. Tongue short and pointed. Thorax bordered by longer hairs in male, which also has swollen and curved hind legs: female hind tibia with pale yellow pollen brush. 7–8, feeding mainly on yellow loosestrife. Nests in ground and lines burrow with sticky sap of foodplant.

▲ **Megachile maritima** 2 sub-marginals. Tongue long and slender. Head relatively broad. Front of abdomen scooped out on dorsal surface: each segment with an entire pale terminal band. Female less brightly coloured and without dilated front legs: she has a dense pollen brush under abdomen – white at front, orange to black below. One of several species known as leaf-cutter bees because females cut semi-circular pieces from leaves and use them to form sausage-shaped nest cells in plant stems and other crevices. 6–8. Mainly coastal.

▲ **M. centuncularis** female has a bright orange pollen brush under abdomen. Commonest of the leaf-cutters, it often attacks garden roses. Usually nests in wood. 5–8.

△s **Dasypoda altercator** Melittidae. 2 sub-marginals. Tongue pointed. Hind legs with conspicuous golden tufts in female: male legs all clothed with dense yellow hairs. Male also has dense yellow hair on face. Abdominal hair yellower than in female. 6–9, nesting in sandy soil. Mainly coastal in B.

△ **Melitta haemorrhoidalis** 3 sub-marginals. Tongue pointed. Male with longer and paler hairs on both thorax and abdomen. Resembles Andrena (p. 244) but tongue somewhat longer. 6–8, mainly on calcareous grassland. Often feeding at harebell. There are several similar species.

▲ **Coelioxys inermis** 2 sub-marginals. Tongue long and slender. One of several similar species with tip of abdomen pointed in female and spiny in male: no pale band on hind margin of 5th abdominal segment in this species. A cuckoo species laying eggs in nests of Megachile spp. Coelioxys egg hatches first and grub destroys rightful egg. 6–8.

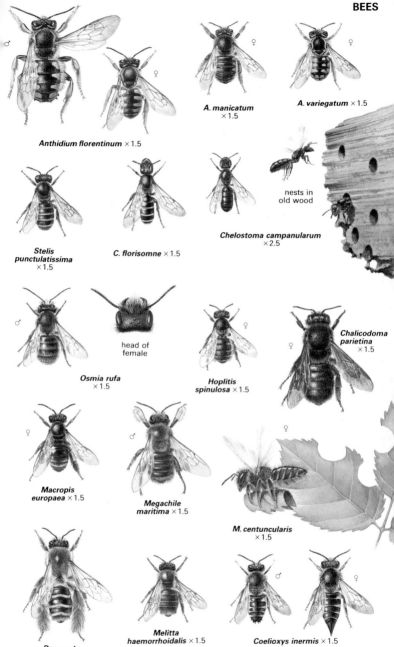

♂ ♀

Anthidium florentinum ×1.5

A. manicatum ×1.5

A. variegatum ×1.5

Stelis punctulatissima ×1.5

C. florisomne ×1.5

Chelostoma campanularum ×2.5

nests in old wood

Osmia rufa ×1.5

head of female

Hoplitis spinulosa ×1.5

Chalicodoma parietina ×1.5

Macropis europaea ×1.5

Megachile maritima ×1.5

M. centuncularis ×1.5

Dasypoda altercator ×1.5

Melitta haemorrhoidalis ×1.5

Coelioxys inermis ×1.5

247

△s **Nomada fulvicornis** Anthophoridae. 3 sub-marginals. Tongue ovate. A wasp-like bee, almost hairless and with variable amount of yellow on abdomen: 2nd & 3rd yellow bands always broken. 1st band often reduced to 2 small spots in female. 4–6, breeding as cuckoo in nests of *Andrena* spp. There are many closely related species, some black and yellow and others red and black or brown and black.

▲ **Epeolus cruciger**. 3 sub-marginals. Tongue long and slender. Female legs entirely red. Almost hairless. 7–8, mostly in sandy areas. A cuckoo in nests of *Colletes* spp. N & C.

△ **Eucera longicornis**. 2 sub-marginals. Tongue long and slender. Male has extremely long antennae and a bright yellow face. He lacks the pale bands at tip of abdomen. His legs are also less hairy, 4–7, nesting in ground. There are several similar species.

▲ **Anthophora plumipes**. 3 sub-marginals. Tongue very long and slender. Extreme sexual dimorphism: female is jet black except for orange pollen brushes on hind legs, while male is brownish. Male has prominent fans of hairs on middle legs. Resembles bumble bees (p. 250), but eye reaches down to meet the jaw (left) with no cheek area such as occurs in bumble bees. Much quicker in flight than bumble bees, with much higher-pitched flight noise. Hovers well. 3–6. Very common in gardens, where fond of lungwort and other tubular flowers. Nests in ground and in soft mortar of walls. There are several similar species. △ **A. retusa** has only basal part of abdomen clothed with brown hair in male: no fans of hairs on middle leg. **A. hispanica** flies 1–3 in SW, nesting in sandy ground.

head of
Anthophora

△ **Melecta luctuosa**. 3 sub-marginals. Tongue long and slender. 4–6, breeding as cuckoo in nest of *Anthophora retusa*. Absent from far north. △s **M. albifrons** is very similar but has much smaller pale spots of abdomen and browner hairs on thorax. It is a cuckoo in the nests of *Anthophora* spp.

head of
bumble bee (p. 250)

Tetralonia salicariae. 3 sub-marginals. Tongue long and slender. Male antennae very long, as in *Eucera*. 7–8, feeding mainly at flowers of purple loosestrife: occasionally at viper's bugloss and wild thyme. Local in S & C.

Xylocopa violacea Xylocopidae. Readily identified by its colour, this handsome bee flies in summer and autumn and again in spring after hibernation. It nests in dead wood, hence its common name of carpenter bee. Despite its fast flight and fearsome appearance, it is not aggressive and rarely stings. S & C: vagrant to B and other more northerly areas. There are 3 other very similar species in western Europe.

△s **Ceratina cyanea**. 3 sub-marginals. Tongue long and slender. Metallic blue with white face in male, black face in female. Very little hair, even on legs of female. 4–6, nesting in hollow stems of bramble and other shrubs. Several similar species on continent.

▲ **Honey Bee** *Apis mellifera* Apidae. 3 sub-marginals. Apical cell slender and very long, reaching almost to wing-tip. Tongue long and slender. A social bee living in permanent colonies of perhaps 50,000 individuals. A native of southern Asia, but well established in Europe – in the wild as well as in domestic hives. The queen, who rules the colony, is rarely found outside the nest except when on her mating flight or when swarming, and in the latter instance she is completely surrounded by a mass of workers. The latter make up bulk of the colony and forage from early spring to autumn. Drones (males) are plumper and appear mainly in summer. There are several distinct strains or races of honey bee, some almost black and some with an extensive orange patch at the base of the abdomen. The Italian race, now common all over Europe, has a very marked orange patch. The strains hybridise very easily, however, and wild bees combine the features of many different strains.

Wild colonies usually build in hollow trees and similarly protected situations, but will occasionally build in the open. The nest consists of several wax combs, suspended vertically – not horizontally like the wasps' combs – and without a protective envelope. Each comb consists of hundreds of 6-sided cells which are used for rearing the brood and for storing honey and pollen. New queens are reared when the colony becomes overcrowded and also when the old queen gets too old for the job. The workers enlarge selected cells on the combs and, by special feeding of the young grubs already in those cells, they produce the new queens, one of which will eventually take control of the colony.

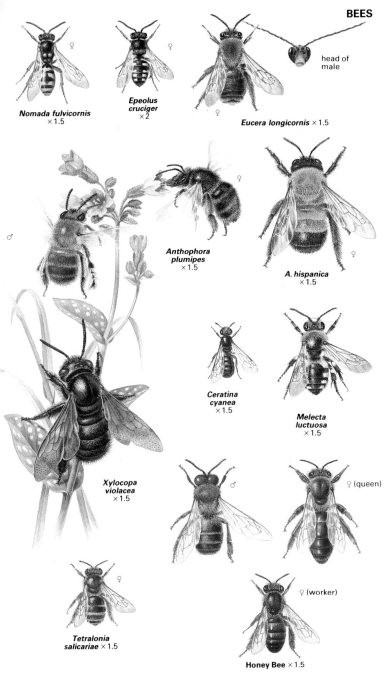

Nomada fulvicornis ×1.5

Epeolus cruciger ×2

Eucera longicornis ×1.5

head of male

Anthophora plumipes ×1.5

A. hispanica ×1.5

Ceratina cyanea ×1.5

Melecta luctuosa ×1.5

Xylocopa violacea ×1.5

♀ (queen)

Tetralonia salicariae ×1.5

♀ (worker)

Honey Bee ×1.5

BUMBLE BEES Relatively large and very hairy social bees of the genus *Bombus*, readily distinguished from *Anthophora* (p. 248) because eyes do not reach down to the jaws. The bees form annual colonies, with only mated queens surviving the winter to start new colonies in the spring. The nest may be under the ground – often in old mouse holes – or amongst the bases of tall grasses, especially on sunny banks. The nest is essentially a ball of grass and moss with wax cells inside it. The young are reared on pollen and nectar, the pollen being carried home in large pollen baskets on the back legs. Some early spring workers are very small and it is hard to believe that they belong to the same species as the queens, but later workers are much larger as a result of more copious food supplies. Males, recognisable by their longer antennae, appear in summer. The bees illustrated here are all queens: workers and males are basically similar unless otherwise stated, but the identification of all castes is complicated by marked regional colour variations. Some northern species produce very few workers – even none at all in the Arctic – because the short summer season in the far north simply does not allow time to build up a colony.

Bombus lapponicus. A very variable species with several sub-species. May have greyish yellow collar and scutellum. Abdomen almost entirely reddish, but yellow hairs often mingle with the red ones towards the rear. Nests on or just under the ground: few workers. Confined to northern Scandinavia, where often the dominant species, and high mountains.

△ **B. soroeensis**. Typical subspecies (*B. s. soroeensis*) has collar and 2nd abdominal segment yellowish and tail white. Male has 1st abdominal segment yellowish as well. Nests underground. The subspecies *B. s. proteus*, not found in B, is all black with an orange tail. Both subspecies are widely distributed on the continent, where they overlap and interbreed to produce numerous colour varieties.

▲ **B. jonellus**. Generally has yellow hairs on top of head. Collar, scutellum, and 1st abdominal segment yellow: tail white. Pollen basket reddish. Like a small *hortorum* but face is shorter and rounder. Mainly on coasts and heathland.

▲ **B. hortorum**. A relatively large bee with collar, scutellum, and 1st abdominal segment yellow. Tail white. A rather 'scruffy' species with long hair. Pollen basket of black hair. Abundant everywhere: especially common in gardens. Usually nests on or just under the ground.

△s **B. ruderatus**. Often similar to *hortorum*, but yellow bands often narrower and darker and sometimes absent altogether. 1st abdominal band often broken. Hair generally shorter than in *hortorum*. Wings sometimes very dark. Much rarer than *hortorum* and absent from far north. Nests below ground.

B. hypnorum. Identified by entirely brown thorax and white tail: front of abdomen may be black. Nests in hollow trees and other cavities above ground. In wooded areas in most parts of Europe.

△s **B. subterraneus**. A large, short-haired bee with a dull yellow collar and very narrow yellow band on scutellum: both bands may be much reduced. Tail off-white. Hind edges of abdominal segments often with brown fringes. Males largely greenish brown or brownish yellow with black bands. Nests below ground.

▲ **B. lucorum**. Collar and 2nd abdominal segment lemon yellow. Tail white. Male may have yellow scutellum as well, and other yellow bands may be extensive. A very early bee, abundant nearly everywhere. Nests below ground.

▲ **B. terrestris**. Collar and 2nd abdominal segment orange or golden yellow (often reduced). Tail buff or tawny in B: white on continent. Worker and male always with whitish tail, sometimes tinged with ginger. Nests below ground. Very common, but not in far north.

▲ **B. pratorum**. A relatively small bee with collar and 2nd abdominal segment yellow (sometimes interrupted). Tail deep orange-red. Coat rather shaggy. Worker may lack yellow on abdomen. Male has wide collar and more yellow on abdomen. An early bee, often finished by end of July, but may have 2nd brood. May nest well above ground – in birds' nests and nest boxes, for example.

B. alpinus. Easily identified by black thorax and largely golden abdomen. Hind legs and pollen baskets very black: not brownish as in *lapponicus*. Nest above or below ground. Heaths and montane pastures in Alps and Scandinavia.

△ **B. monticola**. Collar and scutellum usually pale yellow, but scutellum may be black: whole thorax occasionally black. Abdomen largely red, becoming more orange towards the rear. Mountain and moorland: mainly northern.

B. confusus. Short-haired with swollen or humped thorax. Tail red and rather pointed. Male has very large eyes and greyish hairs on prothorax. S & C.

B. pomorum. Red tail has a pinkish tinge. Male has yellowish grey collar and scutellum, with abdomen mainly red. Sandy areas.

Bombus lapponicus

B. soroeensis soroeensis

B. s. proteus

B. jonellus

B. hortorum

B. ruderatus

B. hypnorum

B. subterraneus

B. lucorum

B. terrestris

B. pratorum

B. alpinus

B. monticola

B. confusus

B. pomorum

△? **Bombus cullumanus**. The insect illustrated is from Spain. The males show this general colour pattern everywhere, but in most parts of Europe the queens are black with a red tail and just a faint trace of yellow on collar and scutellum. They are thus superficially like *lapidarius*, but 1st segment of hind tarsus is shiny black, not downy yellow as in *lapidarius*. Widespread, but rare: probably extinct in B.

B. mendax. A variable species: pale bands may be missing from thorax and front of abdomen in Alps, but always present in Pyrenees. Tip of abdomen may be red, especially in male. Only in mountains.

B. mesomelas. The pale brown or fawn hair and prominent black band between wings easily identify this species. Front of abdomen sometimes golden: tip of tail black. Males greyish white and quite shaggy, with blacker band on thorax. Hind end more yellowish grey. Alps and Pyrenees.

△n **B. distinguendus**. A long-haired bee, predominantly brown with a black band between the wings. Much brighter than *mesomelas*. Nests below ground. Not common. N & C (northern).

▲ **B. pascuorum**. Largely tawny, with variable amounts of black: very dark in N, but often foxy red in S. Coat thin and rather 'scruffy'. Nests on or above ground – often in birds' nests. One of the last bumble bees to disappear in autumn.

B. hyperboreus   **B. wurfleini pyrenaicus**   **B. lapidarius**

B. gerstaeckeri. Thorax golden or orange-yellow. Abdomen with scattered white hairs: sometimes entirely black. Face long and narrow. Alps and Pyrenees, usually feeding at *Aconitum* spp.

△ **B. sylvarum**. Thorax pale brown with black central area. Abdominal segments with pale fringes at rear. Tail orange to pinkish red. A relatively late species. Absent from far north.

B. hyperboreus. A large brightly coloured, long-haired bee. Orange bands may be replaced by yellow. Black inter-alar band not wider than collar. Basal part of wing distinctly darker than outer edge. N.

B. wurfleini pyrenaicus. A colourful bee from the Pyrenees. Resembles Spanish form of *cullumanus*, but much larger and with less yellow hair on abdomen. Nests below ground. Further north, *B. w. mastrucatus* is just black with an orange tail.

▲ **B. lapidarius**. Abdomen relatively long. Hair longer and thorax less humped than in *confusus* (p. 250). Male has broad yellow collar. Often nests under stones. Especially common in open country: often coastal in N. ▲ **B. ruderarius** is similar but has red pollen baskets instead of black.

CUCKOO BEES Social parasites in the genus *Psithyrus*. No workers: females lay in nests of *Bombus* spp, often killing the *Bombus* queen, and bumble bee workers rear young cuckoos. Generally resemble the bees they parasitise, but coats less dense and abdominal plates shine through. Females without pollen baskets. Wing membrane often darker than in *Bombus*. Females hibernate, but wake later than *Bombus* – waiting for the bumble bee nests to be started.

▲ **Psithyrus barbutellus**. Collar and scutellum yellow: front of abdomen may also be yellowish. Tail always white. Parasitises *B. hortorum*.

▲ **P. vestalis**. Mainly black, but with prominent golden collar and yellow and white patches near rear of abdomen. Parasitises *B. terrestris*. Rare in N.

▲ **P. campestris**. Amount of yellow hair on scutellum varies. Abdomen sometimes all black, but usually with variable amounts of yellow hair, especially towards rear. Male very variable: generally mainly yellow but may be all black. Parasitises *B. pascuorum* and is unusual in not resembling its host.

△ **P. rupestris**. Female very like *B. lapidarius*, which it parasitises. Male usually has some yellowish grey hairs on collar, scutellum, and front of abdomen. Widespread, but not common.

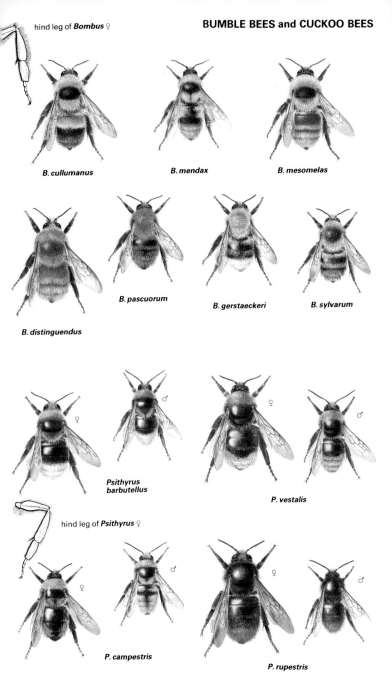

hind leg of *Bombus* ♀

B. cullumanus

B. mendax

B. mesomelas

B. distinguendus

B. pascuorum

B. gerstaeckeri

B. sylvarum

Psithyrus barbutellus

P. vestalis

hind leg of *Psithyrus* ♀

P. campestris

P. rupestris

BEETLES   Order Coleoptera

This is the largest order of insects, with well over 300,000 known species in the world and some 20,000 in Europe. About 4,000 live in Britain. The order contains the bulkiest of all insects – the fist-sized Goliath beetle, weighing 100 g – and some of the smallest, many less than 0.5 mm long.

Beetles are easy to recognise as such, for the front wings, known as *elytra*, are tough and horny; and with the notable exception of the rove beetle (p. 260), they usually cover the whole abdomen. They normally meet neatly in the mid-line without overlap, giving the insects their characteristic armoured look. The hind wings are membranous, and folded beneath the elytra when not in use. They are sometimes absent, in which case the elytra may be fused together for extra protection. Rarely, as in the female glow-worm, the elytra are absent too. The only possible confusion is with some of the heteropteran bugs (p. 72), but these all have overlapping forewings whose tips are usually distinctly membranous. Also, the bugs have needle-like suctorial mouths, whereas all beetles have biting mouths.

Compound eyes are usually well developed in the beetles, as are antennae, whose shape is important in classification. Some antennae are distinctly 'elbowed', with the first segment (the scape) very long and the other segments forming an angle with it – e.g. as in the weevils (p. 284–6). Weevils generally carry their antennae on a prominent snout, and the scapes can be retracted into grooves, called scrobes, on each side of it.

The prothorax is always large, and covered by a tough and often highly ornamented shield called the pronotum. In some beetles this shield almost covers the head as well. The rest of the thorax is generally covered by the elytra, except for a small triangle called the scutellum, which sits in the mid-line between the bases of the elytra. The **legs** vary a great deal with the beetles' habits. Dung beetles, for example, have broad front legs with strong teeth for excavating their burrows, while most water beetles have paddle-like hind legs for swimming. The number of tarsal segments on each leg (usually 4 or 5) and the shape of the coxa – the first segment of the leg – are also important, but these features are not readily appreciated in the field.

Most beetles can fly, but most spend relatively little time in the air. They are essentially insects of the ground and vegetation. Many live among stones and leaf litter, where the tough elytra provide valuable protection: the armoured and often tank-like look is no masquerade and it is surprisingly difficult to crush even a small specimen. With their biting jaws, both adults and larvae exist mainly on solid foods, though some species can lap nectar from flowers and some larvae have hollow mandibles through which they suck the juices of their prey. Different beetles exploit almost every kind of solid food: even the dried bones of animals, pepper, grain, or the dried wood of a chair-leg. These dry foods present them with no great problems as the elytra and general thickness of the adult cuticle effectively prevent loss of body moisture. Nevertheless, the majority feed on living plant material, including roots and woody stems as well as leaves and fruits. The ability to exploit such a wide range of food – made possible by the retention of biting jaws – has been one of the main factors in the success of beetles throughout the world.

Life histories. All beetles undergo a complete metamorphosis, rarely with any form of parental care. The larvae (pp. 295–7), are much more varied than the adults, though most have the same kind of food as their parents. Most have three pairs of legs, but weevil larvae, mostly inside their food plants and surrounded by provisions, are generally legless. Most European beetles have just one generation each year, normally passing the winter as larvae or adults – either active or in hibernation. Very few species pass the winter in the egg stage.

Water beetles. Beetles of several families, notably the Dytiscidae and Hydrophilidae, have opted for life in the water, though most of them retain the power of flight to enable them to move from pond to pond. The adults have generally evolved smooth outlines (pp. 290–2), and many have broad, paddle-like hind legs. They remain essentially air-breathing insects and carry air-supplies with them under water. Among the dytiscids, the air is carried in the space between the elytra and the body, and the abdominal spiracles draw air directly from this reservoir. When the oxygen content has been exhausted, the beetle rises tail-first, breaks through with the tip of the abdomen, and draws fresh air into the reservoir. The hydrophilids carry only part of their air supply under the elytra, the rest in a bubble 'strapped' to the underside in a coat of fine, water-repellent hairs. This bubble gives the beetles a bright, silvery appearance in the water. The hydrophilids come up head-first, breaking the surface with one of their club-shaped antennae. These are clothed with water-repellent hairs which form channels through which air is drawn down into both reservoirs.

A few small water beetles have managed to dispense with surface visits altogether, by developing a physical gill. A film of air is held around the body by a dense coat of extremely fine hairs. This film acts as a gill: it is in direct contact with the spiracles, and as oxygen is drawn from it more oxygen flows in from the surrounding water to redress the balance. This system is sometimes known as plastron breathing. The larvae of some water beetles have evolved true gills, which absorb oxygen directly from the water, but most are air-breathers like the adults and come to the surface tail-first to draw air into their posterior spiracles. Although both larval and adult stages are spent in the water, nearly all water beetles pupate in the soil.

The Stylopids. Although there are vast numbers of predatory species, very few beetles have become parasitic, living in or on other creatures. One strange group, however, are entirely parasitic – the stylopids. They are not uncommon, but rarely seen because only the short-lived adult males emerge. The larvae live inside the bodies of various bees, wasps and bugs, where the females remain throughout their lives, with just part of the body exposed when mature. Males, only 2–3 mm long, have relatively huge hind wings but the forewings are club-like and act rather like the halteres of flies (p. 190). They escape through the intersegmental membranes of the host's abdomen. Adult females also protrude from these membranes but do not become free. The males spend their few hours of freedom flying rapidly about in search of females, which they smell out with their large antennae. Mated females give birth to small larvae which then search out new hosts. Unlike ichneumons and tachinid flies, stylopids do not normally kill their hosts, although they commonly render them sterile. About 400 species are known, with about 30 in Europe.

A stylopid male, showing large hind wings and club-shaped halteres derived from the forewings

TIGER BEETLES and GROUND BEETLES
Carabidae Long-legged, fast-running, predatory beetles with powerful jaws and very fine sensory bristles scattered over the body. The antennae are filamentous and usually 11-segmented. Tarsi are 5-segmented. Many species exhibit beautiful metallic or iridescent colours.

Cicindela
germanica
× 1.5

Tiger Beetles (*Cicindela* spp) are sun-loving insects with huge eyes and jaws. The antennae are attached above the jaws and their bodies are somewhat flattened. Most fly well, with a loud buzzing sound. They hunt ants and other prey on the ground and usually live in open habitats. They are among the fastest runners in the insect world. The larvae (p. 295) construct burrows from which to ambush prey. About a dozen species live in Europe.

▲ **Green Tiger Beetle** *Cicindela campestris.* Legs and sides of thorax are coppery or purplish bronze and very shiny. Underside of abdomen is metallic green. Elytral pattern varies and ground colour may be very dark. 5–7. Mainly on heathland, sand dunes, and other sandy places.

△ *Cicindela hybrida.* Elytra may have a greenish tinge, but margins always reddish, as are the edges of the thorax. Each elytron has 3 or 4 yellow marks. Underside of body is metallic green. 8–9 and again 4–6 after hibernation. Heathland and dunes. Absent from far north.

△s **Wood Tiger Beetle** *Cicindela sylvatica.* Similar to *hybrida*, but darker and with a distinct purplish tinge: yellow markings less heavy. Metallic blue below. Heathland and pine woods. 5–9. N & C.

△s *Cicindela germanica.* Smaller and more cylindrical than the other tiger beetles. Thorax distinctly bronze, and elytra usually very dark green, often almost black. Elytral pattern usually confined to three small spots on outer margin on each side. Rarely flies. 5–9. Dry grassy places in lowlands. S & C: south coast only in B.

Ground Beetles are generally less flattened and largely nocturnal, although some of the more metallic species are active by day. The antennae are attached between the eyes and the jaws. Many are flightless, with vestigial hind wings and often with the elytra fused together. Front tarsi are strongly dilated in males. They eat a wide variety of invertebrates and also take carrion: many eat plant matter as well. The larvae (p. 295) are active hunters like the adults. Most species are long-lived and adult throughout the year, although many hibernate in the coldest months. Several hundred species live in Europe.

△s *Calosoma sycophanta.* Elytra are golden green to brassy red and strongly striated. Flies well. Diurnal. Mainly in woodlands. Adults and larvae live in trees, where they feed on moth larvae. They are important predators of gypsy and processionary moth caterpillars. Most of Europe, but only a sporadic visitor to B.

C. auropunctatum. Recognised by the three rows of golden green dots on each elytron. Adults and larvae prey on moth larvae on the ground, although adult flies well. Diurnal. Most frequent in moist fields and on roadsides. C.

▲ *Carabus auratus.* Elytra and thorax green with a golden or brassy iridescence. Three broad ridges on each elytron. Flightless, with vestigial hind wings like most *Carabus* spp. Common in gardens and on other cultivated land, mainly in spring. Eats slugs and snails and cockchafer grubs. S & C.

▲ **Violet Ground Beetle** *C. violaceus.* Elytra almost smooth, with a bright violet sheen around their edges and around the edges of the thorax. Common in many habitats, including gardens and hedgerows, hiding under stones and litter by day and emerging to hunt slugs and other prey at night. ▲ *C. nemoralis* Elytra very convex, especially in male, and marked with fine ridges and rows of conspicuous pits. Bronzy to bright brassy green, becoming violet on the sides. The thorax is also purplish or bronze on the sides. Females are less shiny. Found in many habitats: especially common in gardens on the continent. Its habits are much like those of *C. violaceus* and most other *Carabus* spp.

C. coriaceus. Resembles a large violet ground beetle in shape, but thorax and elytra are dull black. Elytra patterned with coarse dots and wrinkles. Mainly in damp deciduous woodland.

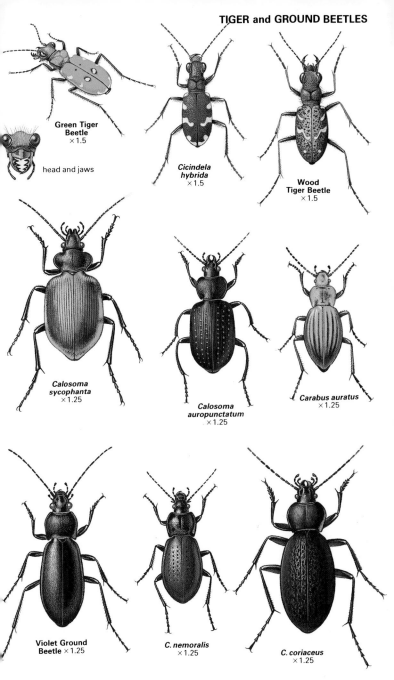

Green Tiger Beetle ×1.5

head and jaws

Cicindela hybrida ×1.5

Wood Tiger Beetle ×1.5

Calosoma sycophanta ×1.25

Calosoma auropunctatum ×1.25

Carabus auratus ×1.25

Violet Ground Beetle ×1.25

C. nemoralis ×1.25

C. coriaceus ×1.25

△ **Cychrus caraboides**. The narrow front end of this very convex beetle is associated with its diet of snails, the head being plunged deeply into the shells when feeding. Flightless, with elytra fused together. It squirts a jet of yellow liquid from the hind end when alarmed. Mainly in damp woodland.

▲ **Notiophilus biguttatus**. A sun-loving beetle with a bronze sheen which obliterates the elytral pattern from some angles. Flattened and very fast-running, feeding on mites and springtails and other small arthropods on the ground. Flightless. Abundant in gardens, grasslands, and many other habitats. Several similar species.

▲ **Elaphrus riparius**. Elytra sometimes metallic blue or bronze. Tarsi green. Sun-loving and fast-running. Fully winged. On bare sand and silt by ponds and streams.

antenna-cleaning notch on front tibia of many ground beetles

△ **Omophron limbatum**. The shape and colour immediately identify this ground beetle. Fast-running, on bare ground around ponds and streams. Burrows in the sand.

△ **Broscus cephalotes**. Huge jaws and appetite to match. A prominent antenna-cleaning notch. Elytra dull black. Fully winged, but rarely flies. Lies in wait for prey in a burrow. Sandy places: mainly coastal.

△s **Callistus lunatus**. Dark areas of elytra with blue or green reflections. Antenna-cleaning notch. Fully winged. Diurnal, running rapidly over dry grassland, usually on chalk or sand: often coastal. S & C.

△ **Badister unipustulatus**. Several similar species with asymmetrical jaws. Antenna-cleaning notch. Fully winged. Among leaf litter and moss, usually near water.

▲ **Dyschirius globosus**. Smallest of many very similar species. Flightless. Usually lives near water, using spiny front legs to dig burrows in soft sandy ground.

▲ **Dromius 4-maculatus**. Yellow spots may join on each elytron. Fully winged. Antenna-cleaning notch. Flattened body. Lives in trees and hibernates under bark.

▲ **Harpalus affinis**. Green to black, often strongly metallic: female less shiny. Antenna-cleaning notch. Fully winged. Open country, often on cultivated land. Largely vegetarian. A distinctive member of this very large family.

▲ **Pterostichus madidus**. Body and elytra black, like most members of this large genus, but legs usually chestnut, especially the femora. Antenna-cleaning notch present. Flightless. Common in gardens and other cultivated land, where it is fond of fruit and often known as the Strawberry Beetle. ▲ **P. nigrita** is similar but legs are black and hind angles of pronotum sharp. Sides of pronotum are strongly rounded. Fully winged. ▲ **P. cupreus** elytra range from brassy green to black: legs may be chestnut. Fully winged. Usually found near water.

△ **Agonum 6-punctatum**. Each elytron with a row of six small punctures. Fully winged. Antenna-cleaning notch. Usually found near water, often on bare soil and peat.

△ **Panagaeus bipustulatus**. Has antenna-cleaning notch. Lives in short, dry grassland. △ **P. cruxmajor** is slightly larger and lives in damp places.

△ **Lebia cruxminor**. Black elytral marks may link up with black scutellum to form a larger cross. Antenna-cleaning notch present. Climbs on grassland vegetation, feeding on other beetle larvae.

▲ **Amara aenea**. Elytra black with very fine striations and brassy green lustre. Fully winged. Antenna-cleaning notch. In short, dry vegetation in summer.

△ **Odacantha melanura**. Thorax and elytral tips reflect blue or green. Fully winged. Antenna-cleaning notch. On reeds and other tall waterside plants.

▲ **Leistus ferrugineus**. Body and elytra yellow or brown. Jaws very broad and flat. Amongst grass tufts and debris, usually in open country.

△ **Bombardier Beetle** *Brachinus crepitans*. When disturbed, it fires a burning, volatile liquid from its hind end like a puff of smoke, accompanied by a soft popping sound. Elytra reflect blue or green. Fully winged. Antenna-cleaning notch. Under stones in dry, open country, especially on chalk.

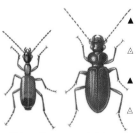

Odacantha melanura × 2.5   **Leistus ferrugineus** × 2.5

Bombardier Beetle × 2.5

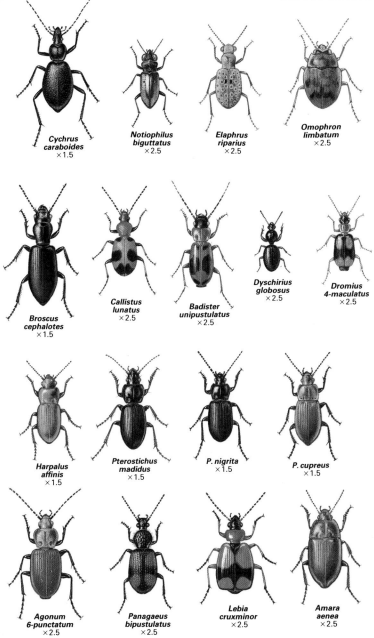

Cychrus caraboides
×1.5

Notiophilus biguttatus
×2.5

Elaphrus riparius
×2.5

Omophron limbatum
×2.5

Broscus cephalotes
×1.5

Callistus lunatus
×2.5

Badister unipustulatus
×2.5

Dyschirius globosus
×2.5

Dromius 4-maculatus
×2.5

Harpalus affinis
×1.5

Pterostichus madidus
×1.5

P. nigrita
×1.5

P. cupreus
×1.5

Agonum 6-punctatum
×2.5

Panagaeus bipustulatus
×2.5

Lebia cruxminor
×2.5

Amara aenea
×2.5

259

▲ **Sphaeridium scarabaeoides** Hydrophilidae. A terrestrial member of a largely aquatic family (p. 292), with slender palps almost as long as antennae. Usually found tunnelling in fresh cow dung.

▲ **Hister 4-maculatus** Histeridae. Red spots may join up on each elytron. Feeds on fly maggots and other scavenging insects in horse and cow dung. There are several similar species, all somewhat flattened with shiny, truncated elytra, elbowed antennae, and strongly toothed front tibiae (tooth pattern may help to separate species). Some live in carcases instead of in dung.

BURYING BEETLES Silphidae
Scavenging and carnivorous beetles with clubbed antennae and a very good sense of smell. The elytra are often strongly truncated, but most species fly well.

Nicrophorus spp are the true burying beetles, burying small carcases (mice, birds, etc) by digging a shaft underneath them and hauling them down. They usually work in pairs and the female lays eggs close to the buried corpse. Adults and larvae feed on the carrion and also on the other scavenging insects. They are also known as sexton beetles. Adults are seen mainly in spring and summer and are often attracted to lights at night. The antennae are very abruptly clubbed in this genus.

▲ **Nicrophorus humator** is one of few species with all-black elytra, but it can be recognised by the orange clubs to its antennae.

▲ **N. vespillo** is one of several species with orange bands on the elytra. Both bands are virtually complete in this species and the hind tibiae are strongly curved.

▲ **N. investigator** has the posterior orange band narrowly broken in the mid-line, where the elytra join.

△ **N. interruptus** has both orange bands broadly interrupted.

▲ **N. vespilloides** has a broadly interrupted posterior orange band – often reduced to a small spot on each elytron – and entirely black antennae. ▲ **N. vestigator** is similar but has orange antennal clubs.

▲ **Necrodes littoralis**. Resembles *Nicrophorus humator* but the antennae are gradually thickened towards the tip and not abruptly clubbed. Each elytron has three strong ridges and a large 'pimple' towards the back. Size is very variable. Usually on large carrion, which is not buried. Sometimes among stranded seaweeds on the shore. Summer.

▲ **Oiceoptoma thoracicum**. Elytra silky, each with three longitudinal ridges. A non-burying species found mainly in woodland – under dung and carcases and also in rotting fungi. Feeds on other insect larvae. Summer.

▲ **Dendroxena 4-maculata**. Lives mainly in oakwoods, feeding on moth larvae in the trees and on the ground. Most numerous in autumn and spring.

▲ **Silpha atrata**. A predator of snails, reaching deep into the shells to devour them. In woods and other damp, shady places. Very glossy.

ROVE BEETLES Staphylinidae
A very large group, with well over 1,000 species in Europe, in which the elytra are very short and leave most of the abdomen exposed. Very variable in size, with many very tiny species. Despite the short elytra, the hind wings are usually well developed and most species fly well. Many of the smaller ones fly by day, but the larger ones are mainly nocturnal. They are predators and omnivorous scavengers.

▲ **Creophilus maxillosus**. Elytral and abdominal pattern formed by grey and black hairs. Head and pronotum hairless. 5–10. Preys on other insects on dung and carrion and in rotting vegetation.

△s **Emus hirtus**. Very large and very hairy. 4–8. Feeds on other insects around fresh horse and cow dung. S & C.

▲ **Staphylinus caesareus**. Patches of golden hair on abdomen. 4–9. Usually on dung and carrion, where it feeds on other insects.

▲ **Devil's Coach-horse** *S. olens* is clothed with fine black hairs. Hides under stones and debris by day and hunts slugs and other invertebrates at night. Also called the cocktail because, when disturbed, it raises its hind end and opens the jaws wide in a threatening attitude. Common in woods, gardens, and hedgerows.

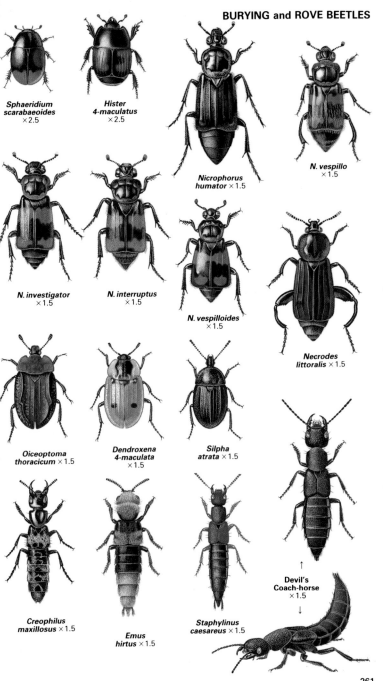

Sphaeridium scarabaeoides ×2.5

Hister 4-maculatus ×2.5

Nicrophorus humator ×1.5

N. vespillo ×1.5

N. investigator ×1.5

N. interruptus ×1.5

N. vespilloides ×1.5

Necrodes littoralis ×1.5

Oiceoptoma thoracicum ×1.5

Dendroxena 4-maculata ×1.5

Silpha atrata ×1.5

Creophilus maxillosus ×1.5

Emus hirtus ×1.5

Staphylinus caesareus ×1.5

↑
Devil's Coach-horse ×1.5
↓

▲ **Oxyporus rufus.** Smooth and shiny and distinctly arched in the middle. Adults and larvae live in various woodland toadstools. Most common in summer and autumn.

▲ **Paederus littoralis.** A flightless predatory species with metallic blue elytra. Lives among debris on marshes, river banks, and other damp places. S & C.

▲ **Stenus bimaculatus.** Hairy, with black and yellow legs. Large bulging eyes are used for stalking springtails and other small prey. Lives around ponds and streams and in other damp places. Can skim over the water surface by exuding an oily secretion from the hind end. Diurnal and sun-loving. One of many similar species.

⌂ **Bledius furcatus.** Prominent horns on head and thorax of male: smaller in female. Gregarious, like other members of this large genus. Burrows in damp soil and feeds on algae. May emerge to fly in groups in the evening. S & C.

▲ **Philonthus marginatus.** Orange sides of thorax distinguish this species from other members of this large genus. It lives in dung and other decaying matter.

▲ **Tachyporus hypnorum.** One of several strongly tapering species. Lives among mosses and vegetable debris, including compost heaps. Most common in winter and spring.

⌂s **Stag Beetle** *Lucanus cervus* Lucanidae. Named for the huge jaws (antlers) of the male, which are used to fight rival males in the breeding season. Female sometimes almost black. Antennae, as in all members of the family, are elbowed and have small flaps at the end, but the flaps cannot be brought together to form a club. Middle tibia

Stag beetles battling with their antlers. The stronger one wins but neither is usually hurt.

has three small teeth. Size is very variable. 5–8. Flies well, usually in the evening. Feeds on sap oozing from trees. Larva (p. 295) lives in decaying trees and posts, especially oak. S & C: becoming rare.

⌂ **Lesser Stag Beetle** *Dorcus parallelipipedus.* Resembles female stag beetle but middle tibia has only one tooth. Male never has antlers. 4–10, mainly in deciduous woods. Feeds on sap. Breeds in rotting stumps. S & C.

Platycerus caraboides. Rather flat, with a bluish iridescence in male and green in female. 4–9, flying mainly by day. Chews leaves and buds. Breeds in rotting wood. Widely distributed in deciduous woodland.

▲ **Sinodendron cylindricum.** Distinctly cylindrical. Male has a rhinoceros-like horn on head: female just a small knob. 5–8, feeding on oozing sap. Breeds in rotting stumps, especially beech.

▲ **Trox scaber** Trogidae. Roughly sculptured elytra and pronotum, with bristly scales on the elytral ridges. Antennal flaps can be brought together to form a small club. Feeds mainly on small carcases, especially when dry, and often scavenges in owls' nests. Rarely flies. 4–8. Widely distributed but rare in N.

⌂s **Odontaeus armiger** Geotrupidae. Strongly domed and very shiny. Male has slender movable horn on head and smaller horn on thorax: female is hornless. As in the whole family, the antennal club is composed of movable flaps. 6–9, flying in the evening and also by day. Larva feeds on rabbit dung.

▲ **Dor Beetle** *Geotrupes stercorarius.* Superficially like some of the scarabs (p. 264) but easily distinguished because the jaws are clearly visible from above. Seven ridges on each elytron. Metallic blue or green below. Mainly on cow dung, digging shafts below it and burying the dung for breeding. Often flies in the evening. Also called the Lousy Watchman because it is commonly heavily infested with mites. 4–10. One of several similar species.

⌂ **Minotaur Beetle** *Typhaeus typhoeus.* Very shiny, strongly ribbed elytra. Male has three thoracic horns. Found mainly in sandy places, where it buries rabbit droppings on which adults and larvae feed. Also on sheep dung. Flies in the evening.

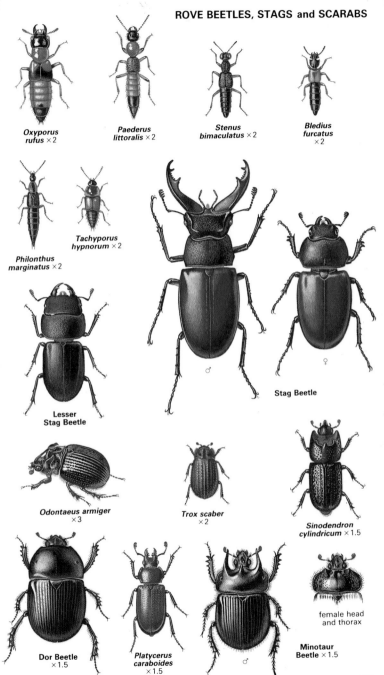

ROVE BEETLES, STAGS and SCARABS

Oxyporus rufus ×2

Paederus littoralis ×2

Stenus bimaculatus ×2

Bledius furcatus ×2

Philonthus marginatus ×2

Tachyporus hypnorum ×2

Lesser Stag Beetle

Stag Beetle

Odontaeus armiger ×3

Trox scaber ×2

Sinodendron cylindricum ×1.5

Dor Beetle ×1.5

Platycerus caraboides ×1.5

female head and thorax

Minotaur Beetle ×1.5

263

Scarabaeus pushing a
ball of dung along
with its hind legs

antenna of a chafer,
showing characteristic
fan-like flaps

SCARABS and CHAFERS Scarabaeidae A very large family, with some 20,000 species in the world. The antennae are distinctly clubbed, the club consisting of several flaps which can be opened out to form a fan – especially noticeable in the chafers. The jaws are not visible from above. The elytra are normally truncated, markedly so in the chafers, leaving the tip of the abdomen exposed. Most species fly well. Many stridulate by rubbing the tips of the elytra against the abdomen. The scarabs are dung-feeders, while the chafers are vegetarians and often serious pests.

Scarabaeus semipunctatus. Numerous pits on pronotum. Elytra almost smooth. Rolls balls of dung about with its hind legs, eventually burying them and eating them. Neighbouring beetles often wrestle fiercely over ownership of a ball. The rake-like front tibiae and the spiky pronotum are used for raking up the dung and also for digging. Sandy shores around the Mediterranean. **S. laticollis** is similar but has ribbed elytra. S. **S. sacer** has smooth elytra but no pronotal pits: usually larger. S.

△ **Copris lunaris.** Female has shorter horn on the head. Usually associated with cow dung, digging shafts under it and burying large quantities in which to lay their eggs. Seen mainly in spring and autumn.

▲ **Aphodius fimetarius** and **A. rufipes** are two very common members of a large genus of dung beetles, all rather cylindrical. They are often attracted to light at night. They feed on all kinds of herbivorous dung, but do not burrow beneath it or bury it. A. rufipes is one of the largest European members of the genus.

Pine Chafer Polyphylla fullo. Female is slightly larger, but without the enormous scent-detecting flaps of the male antennae. Stridulates loudly. 6–8, in and around pine woods, especially on sandy soil. Adults chew pine needles. Larvae feed on roots of sedges and grasses. S & C.

▲ **Cockchafer** Melolontha melolontha. Also called May-bug. Inhabits gardens, woods, and hedgerows 5–6. Swarms around trees in evening and often crashes into lighted windows. Chews leaves of various deciduous trees. Larva (p. 295) feeds on roots of a wide range of plants, often causing severe damage to crops.

▲ **Summer Chafer** Amphimallon solstitialis. Like a cockchafer but pronotum is brown and much hairier. Only three segments to antennal club (4–7 in cockchafer). Swarms round deciduous trees, mainly in dry places, 6–7. Larvae feed on roots.

▲ **Garden Chafer** Phyllopertha horticola. Thorax sometimes almost black. Elytra often with green or blue iridescence. Dry habitats, often swarming in sunshine. 6–7. Adults feed on various trees and shrubs, often damaging fruit crops. Larvae feed on roots of cereals and other grasses.

Rhizotrogus aestivus. Resembles Summer Chafer but less hairy, with long hairs only on thoracic margins. Usually a dark line in centre of pronotum. Grassy places. 4–6. Larvae feed on grass roots. S & C.

Oryctes nasicornis. Up to 40 mm long. Male has long, curved horn on the head: female has just a small point. Flies on summer evenings. Breeds in rotting wood and leaves, and also in piles of sawdust at sawmills.

Hoplia caerulea. Clothed with scales, which are brilliant blue in male and greyish brown in female. 6–8 in damp grassy places, especially near rivers. Larvae feed on roots. S & C (southern). **H. argentea** is greenish yellow, while several other species are reddish brown – like small Summer Chafers, but easily distinguished by their coatings of scales and also by the single large claw on the hind leg.

Anisoplia cyathigera. Found mainly in low-lying grassy places, often causing damage to cereals. 5–6. Larvae feed on roots and on decaying vegetation. S & C (southern)

Anisoplia cyathigera × 1.5

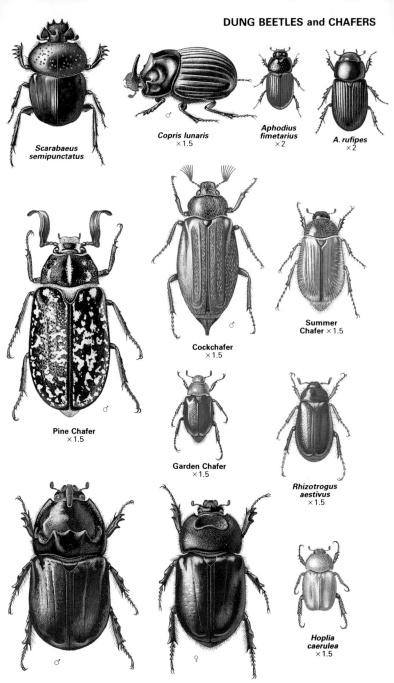

Scarabaeus semipunctatus

Copris lunaris
×1.5

Aphodius fimetarius
×2

A. rufipes
×2

Pine Chafer
×1.5

Cockchafer
×1.5

Summer Chafer ×1.5

Garden Chafer
×1.5

Rhizotrogus aestivus
×1.5

Hoplia caerulea
×1.5

Oryctes nasicornis

△ ***Gnorimus nobilis***. Superficially like the Rose Chafer, but elytra distinctly wrinkled and clearly separated from pronotum. 6–8, especially common on umbellifer flowers and flying strongly in sunshine. Breeds in rotting wood. Absent from far north.

△ **Bee Beetle** *Trichius fasciatus*. Very hairy. Elytra range from pale yellow to deep orange: black bars very variable. 5–7, usually seen on flowers, especially thyme and roses. Breeds in rotting timber. ***T. zonatus*** and ***T. abdominalis*** are similar.

Oxythyrea funesta. Usually a coppery iridescence: white spots very irregular. Abundant in flowers of many kinds, often destroying flower buds of vines and fruit trees. 4–7. Larvae eat roots. S & C. (southern).

▲ **Rose Chafer** *Cetonia aurata*. Elytra clearly flattened, usually green but may be bronze or even bluish black: always with some white marks. Coppery red beneath. 5–10, mainly in sunny places: nibbles many kinds of flowers, including roses. Larvae live in rotting timber, especially old willows.

▲ ***C. cuprea*** is green with a gold or bronze sheen, distinguished from the Rose Chafer by the narrowing of the elytra towards the rear. White spotting is variable. Coppery violet beneath. 5–9, visiting various flowers, especially in woods, and also nibbling ripe fruit. Enjoys sunshine. Larvae live in ant nests.

C. aeruginosa is larger, with very smooth and shiny elytra and no white spots. 5–8, on flowers and also feeding at sap oozing from trees. Larvae feed in old oak trunks and stumps. S & C.

▲ ***Serica brunnea***. Elytra dull yellowish brown and strongly ribbed. Like a Summer Chafer (p. 264) but smaller and less hairy and with a dark head. 6–8, mainly in sandy places. Often attracted to lights in evening. Larvae feed on roots.

△s ***Omaloplia ruricola***. Similar to the Garden Chafer (p. 264) but smaller and more rotund. 5–8, usually in warm and dry places. Flies day and night. Larvae feed on roots. C: on chalk soils in B.

BUPRESTID BEETLES Buprestidae A family of some 15,000 rather metallic beetles living mainly in the tropics. Often bullet-shaped, with sharply pointed rear ends. They fly in the sunshine and are often seen on flowers. The larvae are flattened and tadpole-shaped, with a broad thorax, and live mainly under bark. They are long-lived and often carried far from home in timber. Only 12 species occur naturally in Britain.

Chalcophora mariana. Brown with a bright bronze sheen. Pronotum and elytra with broad ridges and furrows. 5–10, in pine woods.

Buprestis 8-guttata. Iridescent blue or green: pronotum with narrow yellow sides. Coniferous forests in summer. Larvae in young pines. Much of Europe, but rare.

B. rustica Metallic green or blue, with a coppery or violet sheen. Summer, usually in pine woods. The larvae live in rotting stumps and trunks.

Capnodis tenebrionis. Non-metallic, with grey pronotum and dull black elytra speckled with white. Summer, usually in sunny habitats and associated with blackthorn and other *Prunus* species. The larvae live in the older stems. S & C.

Lampra rutilans. Green, with a golden or bluish sheen. Elytra reddish on outer edges. 5–9, usually near old lime trees in which larvae feed.

△ ***Anthaxia nitidula***. Male is green all over. Female head and pronotum purple or reddish: elytra blue or green. 4–7 on a variety of flowers. Larvae live in stems of rose, hawthorn, and related shrubs. S & C.

A. candens is easily identified by its striking colouration. 4–7, often on cherry blossom. Larvae feed in cherry trunks and branches. S & C.

A. hungarica. Male generally entirely green above, often with purplish sheen: female elytra green or blue. Both sexes are bright metallic purple beneath. 4–7 on various flowers, especially in and around oak woods. Larvae live in decaying oak timber. S.

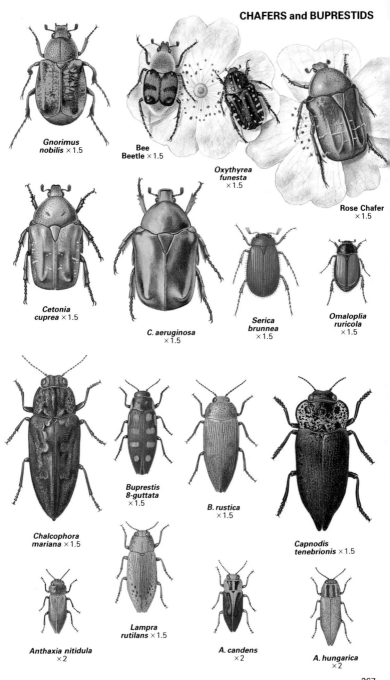

Gnorimus nobilis ×1.5

Bee Beetle ×1.5

Oxythyrea funesta ×1.5

Rose Chafer ×1.5

Cetonia cuprea ×1.5

C. aeruginosa ×1.5

Serica brunnea ×1.5

Omaloplia ruricola ×1.5

Chalcophora mariana ×1.5

Buprestis 8-guttata ×1.5

B. rustica ×1.5

Capnodis tenebrionis ×1.5

Anthaxia nitidula ×2

Lampra rutilans ×1.5

A. candens ×2

A. hungarica ×2

Phaenops cyanea. Entirely blue but often tinged with green. Pine forests in warm regions. 6–8. Larvae develop in pine trunks.

Ptosima 11-maculata. Black with blue iridescence. Pale marks orange or yellow and very variable. 5–6. Larvae feed in *Prunus* spp and are pests of cherry. S & C.

▲ ***Agrilus pannonicus***. Ground colour dark green or blue. 5–7. Breeds in old oaks.

△ ***A. viridis*** is unmarked: often entirely green, sometimes entirely copper-coloured. 6–7, on sallows and other deciduous trees.

Isorhipis melasoides Eucnemidae. Like click beetles, but with some anatomical differences. 5–7. Adults and larvae (legless) in rotting beech and oak. S & C.

▲ ***Melasis buprestoides***. Matt black, sometimes tinged with red. Thorax widest at the front. Female antennae only lightly toothed. 5–7. Breeds in various deciduous trees. Larvae legless. S & C.

CLICK BEETLES Elateridae
A large family (over 7,000 species) of elongate beetles named for the ability to leap into the air and right themselves when laid on their backs. This action is accompanied by a loud click. The larvae are slender and short-legged, vegetarian or carnivorous, and live in rotting wood or the soil.

△n ***Ctenicera pectinicornis***. Green or coppery and very shiny. Female antennae only lightly toothed. 6–7 in grassy places. Larvae live in the soil. N & C. △n ***C. cuprea*** is sometimes entirely violet or copper-coloured. Female antennae only lightly toothed. Grassland. 5–7. N & C.

△ ***Ampedus cinnabarinus***. Lightly clothed with rust-coloured hairs. Woodland, mainly in spring. Breeds in decaying deciduous trees, where larvae eat other insect grubs.

△ ***A. sanguineus*** is similar but has black pubescence. 5–8, mainly on woodland flowers. Breeds in rotting timber, especially conifers. △ ***A. balteatus*** frequents umbellifers and other flowers. 5–6. Breeds in dead evergreen and deciduous trees.

▲ ***Agriotes lineatus***. Brown or yellowish, with striped elytra. Much of the year, but seen mainly 5–7. Abundant on grassland and cultivated land. The larva (p. 295) is one of the infamous wireworms, causing much damage to crop roots.

▲ ***Athous haemorrhoidalis***. Clothed with grey or brown hair. Elytra strongly grooved. Abundant 5–8, especially in hedgerows and grassland. Larvae eat roots.

Selatosomus cruciatus. Black markings roughly in the form of a cross. 4–7, mainly in woodland and scrub. Larva is soil-living.

Cardiophorus gramineus. Deciduous woodland, especially on hawthorn flowers. 4–5. Larva very long and thin, feeding on other insects under bark. S & C.

▲ ***Oedostethus 4-pustulatus***. Rear yellow spots may be absent. River banks and other damp grassy places, often under stones. 5–7. N & C.

Cebrio gigas Cebrionidae. Female, with short elytra and no hind wings, remains in her larval gallery all her life. Male flies in evening. 8–11. Larva eats roots. S.

△ ***Drilus flavescens*** Drilidae. Male is winged but rarely flies. 6–7 amongst low-growing vegetation: female rarely seen. Larvae feed on snails.

▲ ***Dascillus cervinus*** Dascillidae. Covered with hair – greyish in male, yellowish brown in female. 5–7. Rough grassland, usually on flowers. Larvae eat roots.

▲ ***Byrrhus pilula*** Byrrhidae. Very convex, brown or reddish. Amongst moss and short turf, especially in sandy areas. All year, but hibernates: most common in spring.

▲ ***Microcara testacea*** Helodidae. Thin-skinned and rather soft. Abundant in damp grassland and hedgerows in summer. Larvae are aquatic.

Dascillus cervinus
× 1.5

When disturbed, *Byrrhus* pulls in its legs and antennae and is easily mistaken for a seed.

Byrrhus pilula
×2

Microcara testacea × 4

Phaenops cyanea ×1.5

Ptosima 11-maculata ×1.5

Agrilus pannonicus ×1.5

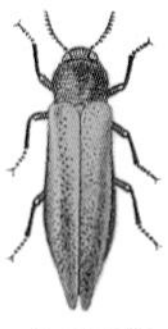

A. viridis ×1.5

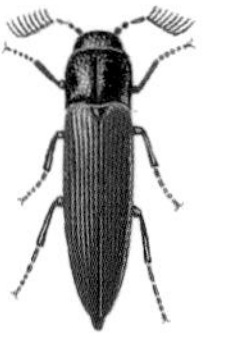

Isorhipis melasoides ×1.5

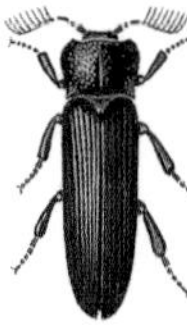

Melasis buprestoides ×1.5

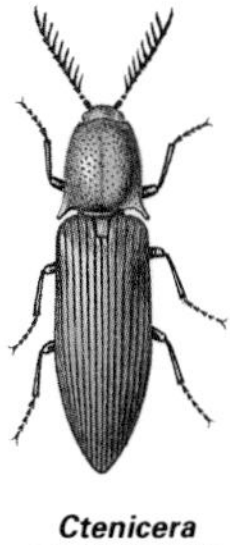

Ctenicera pectinicornis ×1.5

C. cuprea ×1.5

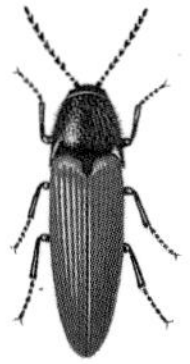

Ampedus cinnabarinus ×1.5

A. sangineus ×1.5

A. balteatus ×1.5

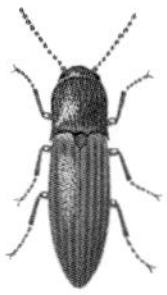

Agriotes lineatus ×1.5

Athous haemorrhoidalis ×1.5

Selatosomus cruciatus ×1.5

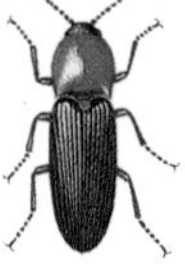

Cardiophorus gramineus ×1.5

Oedostethus 4-pustulatus ×4

♂

Drilus flavescens ×2

♀

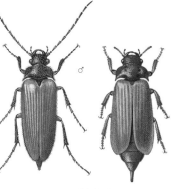

♂

♀

Cebrio gigas

269

SOLDIER and SAILOR BEETLES Cantharidae So called for the bright colours of some species, reminiscent of military uniforms. Elytra are soft. Beetles are predatory, often hunting on flowers of grassland, hedgerow, and woodland margin: fly well in sunshine. The larvae resemble those of ground beetles (p. 295) and hunt mainly on the ground.

▲ *Cantharis rustica*. Femora largely red. Abundant everywhere 5–8. ▲ *C. fusca* is similar but with black femora and the black spot near front edge of pronotum. ▲ *C. livida* has legs partly black and sometimes has black spot on pronotum. 4–8.

▲ *Rhagonycha fulva*. A very common species, often called the bloodsucker because of its colour, although it is harmless. 5–8.

▲ *Malthinus flaveolus*. Elytra short, leaving tip of abdomen exposed. Abundant on shrubs and among grasses, mainly near woodland margins. All summer.

△s **Glow-worm** *Lampyris noctiluca* Lampyridae. Males fly at night in search of wingless, larva-like females which sit in grass and emit greenish light from underside of hind end of abdomen. Males have larger eyes. 6–7 on grassland, including roadside verges. Larvae (p. 295) feed on snails. Absent from far north. *Phausis splendidula*, common on Continent, is a little smaller: female tawny brown, with 3 spots of light.

Firefly *Luciola lusitanica*. Male flies after dusk, emitting bright flashes about once every second from underside of hind end of abdomen. Female has smaller head and eyes and a pointed abdomen. Although winged, she does not fly: she sits in vegetation and responds with flashes when she sees a male overhead. 5–7. Larva feeds on snails. S: not west of Rhône.

△s *Phosphaenus hemipterus*. Wingless female is rarely seen: she sits among turf or stones and attracts wandering male with greenish light after dusk. 5–7. Larva is like that of glow-worm and feeds on snails.

Family Cleridae A family of brightly coloured and rather hairy beetles. Most are predatory as adults and larvae. The latter are often brightly coloured and feed on other grubs under bark and in timber. Most of the 3000 or so species are tropical.

Denops albofasciata. Woodlands and woodland margins, 5–6. Larva feeds on grubs of various bark beetles. S & C.

⚐ *Tillus elongatus*. Female has red thorax: male entirely black. On trunks of various deciduous trees, 6–7.

Opilo domesticus. In coniferous woodland and often in houses, 6–8. Breeds in dry softwoods, feeding on woodworm and other grubs. S & C. ▲ *O. mollis* is very similar.

▲ *Thanasimus formicarius*. Elytral pattern varies, but always with 2 pale cross bars. On tree trunks in spring. Feeds on bark beetle grubs in various trees.

Clerus mutillarius. Spring and summer on old trees and logs, especially oaks. Feeds on other beetle grubs. S & C.

Trichodes alvearius. Front blue band forms a shallow U. Very common on flowers, especially umbellifers, 5–7. Larvae feed on grubs of solitary bees *T. apiarius* is similar but front band straighter. Both species may have blue areas almost black.

▲ *Necrobia ruficollis*. Sometimes seen on flowers, but more often in tanneries and meat stores. Larvae eat skins and bones and dead insects. All year indoors: spring and summer out of doors.

▲ *Pyrochroa coccinea* Pyrochroidae. One of the **Cardinal Beetles**, all rather flat. Found on flowers and old tree trunks and stumps. 5–7. Larva (p. 295) lives under bark and feeds on other insects. N & C. ▲ *P. serraticornis* is similar but head is scarlet.

▲ *Schizotus pectinicornis* resembles *P. coccinea* but has very feathery antennae and a black spot on pronotum. N & C.

Lygistopterus sanguineus Lycidae. Soft elytra. Sun-loving and found on flowers, usually in woodland, 5–9. Larvae eat other grubs in rotting deciduous timber.

△n *Dictyoptera aurora*. Resembles last species but pronotum decorated with sunken pits. Coniferous woods, 5–8. Larvae feed on other grubs under conifer bark. N & C (and mountains further south).

Dictyoptera aurora ×2

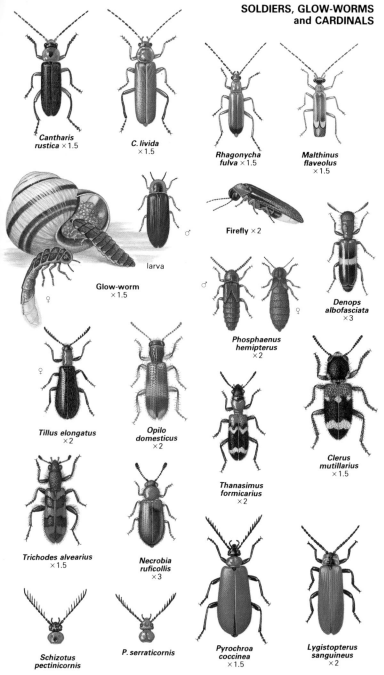

Cantharis rustica ×1.5

C. livida ×1.5

Rhagonycha fulva ×1.5

Malthinus flaveolus ×1.5

Firefly ×2

♂

larva

Glow-worm ×1.5
♀

♂ ♀

Phosphaenus hemipterus ×2

Denops albofasciata ×3

♀

Tillus elongatus ×2

Opilo domesticus ×2

Thanasimus formicarius ×2

Clerus mutillarius ×1.5

Trichodes alvearius ×1.5

Necrobia ruficollis ×3

Schizotus pectinicornis

P. serraticornis

Pyrochroa coccinea ×1.5

Lygistopterus sanguineus ×2

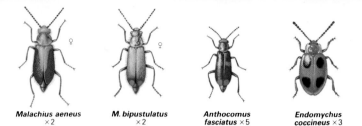

Malachius aeneus ×2   **M. bipustulatus** ×2   **Anthocomus fasciatus** ×5   **Endomychus coccineus** ×3

▲ **Malachius aeneus** Melyridae. A predatory beetle frequenting flowers in spring, esp. in woods. Elytra rather soft. Male has outgrowths near base of antennae, used for holding female. S & C. ▲ **M. bipustulatus** also with antennal swellings in male, hunts other insects among flowers and grasses. 5–8.

▲ **Anthocomus fasciatus** Elytra soft, ground colour black or greenish black. Knees of front legs brownish. Predatory in grass and on various trees. Summer. S & C.

▲ **Endomychus coccineus** Endomychidae. Often mistaken for a ladybird, but much flatter and with longer antennae. A fungus-eater living under bark of dead or dying trees, esp. beech. 4–6.

LADYBIRDS Coccinellidae

Small, domed, usually ± hemispherical, though some are oblong. Head sunk into pronotum. Legs short and retractable: tarsi 4-segmented but 3rd segment very small and concealed in bilobed 2nd. Usually brightly coloured and distasteful but colour-pattern notoriously variable. Mostly carnivorous. Often hibernate in large masses. Larva (p. 295) also carnivorous: pupates openly on plants.

Epilachna chrysomelina. 6 black spots on each elytron, varying and often merging to form heavy black network. Vegetarian on gourd family; sometimes a pest of melons. All year. Mediterranean. ▲ **Subcoccinella 24-punctata** eats all kinds of plants: a carnation pest in France. Very variable. Summer.

▲ **Coccidula scutellata** hunts aphids on various plants in marshy places. 7–8. ▲ **Scymnus frontalis**. Red marks on elytra. Usually on or near pronotum. Front of pronotum often reddish in male, always black in female. Dense vegetation in dry places. 5–7. S & C.

△ **Hippodamia 13-punctata** 4–9 in low marshy areas. More oval than many species.

▲ **7-spot Ladybird** Coccinella 7-punctata. The ladybird, abundant everywhere 3–10. △ **Eyed ladybird** Anatis ocellata. Usually on or near conifers. 6–7. ▲ **Thea 22-punctata** 4–8 in low vegetation of all kinds. Feeds largely on mildews.

▲ **2-spot Ladybird** Adalia bipunctata. Abundant everywhere 3–10. Very variable: black ground colour, especially common in north, helps heat absorption in smoky and cloudy regions. ▲ **10-spot Ladybird** A. 10-punctata is similarly variable but has yellowish legs. 3–10.

▲ **Propylea 14-punctata** Elytra range from almost all yellow to almost all black, with black spots merging together. Common on shrubs 4–9. ▲ **Calvia 14-guttata**. Usually on shrubs and small trees. 4–9.

LARDER BEETLES Dermestidae

Mostly sombre-coloured scavengers, clothed with scales or hairs. Antennae clubbed and can be hidden under body. Many are cosmopolitan pests of stored foods and fabrics. Larvae are bristly and known as 'woolly bears.'

▲ **Larder** or **Bacon Beetle** Dermestes lardarius. Larvae and adults eat carrion in the wild and dried meats in store. All year, but hibernate in the wild. ▲ **Hide Beetle** D. maculatus has similar habits but damages hides and furs as well as stored foods.

▲ **Attagenus pellio**. Visits flowers 3–9: also common in houses. Larvae in birds' nests, furs, carpets, stored grain etc. Sometimes called the fur beetle.

▲ **Varied Carpet Beetle** Anthrenus verbasci. Pattern varies. Adults eat pollen and nectar 3–9. Larvae (p. 295) eat dried materials in birds' nests and buildings; damage woollens and insect collections.

▲ **Khapra Beetle** Trogoderma granarium. Adult does not feed but larva is serious pest of stored grain and cereal products everywhere. All year in heated buildings. **T. angustum**, much narrower than other Trogoderma spp., is native of Chile but established in Germany and Sweden. A pest in insect collections.

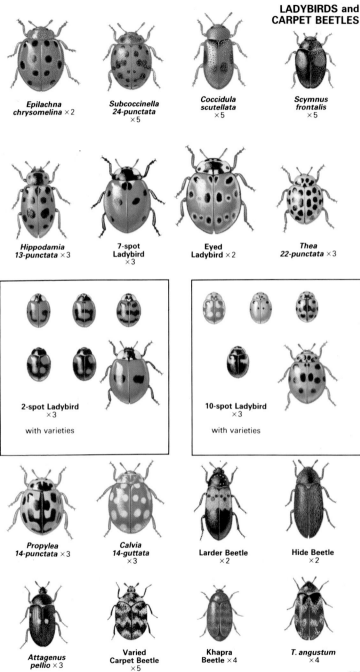

Epilachna chrysomelina ×2

Subcoccinella 24-punctata ×5

Coccidula scutellata ×5

Scymnus frontalis ×5

Hippodamia 13-punctata ×3

7-spot Ladybird ×3

Eyed Ladybird ×2

Thea 22-punctata ×3

2-spot Ladybird ×3

with varieties

10-spot Ladybird ×3

with varieties

Propylea 14-punctata ×3

Calvia 14-guttata ×3

Larder Beetle ×2

Hide Beetle ×2

Attagenus pellio ×3

Varied Carpet Beetle ×5

Khapra Beetle ×4

T. angustum ×4

Ptinus fur Ptinidae. One of the 'spider beetles', so called for the rounded bodies of many of the females: sexes differ markedly in shape. Colour and pattern vary. Scavenges and breeds in dry organic matter indoors and out, often damaging museum specimens and other stored materials.

▲ **Furniture Beetle** *Anobium punctatum* Anobiidae. Dark brown to yellowish and very downy. Antennae with unusual and very characteristic club. Abundant indoors and out, 5–7. Larva is the woodworm, tunnelling in dead coniferous and broad-leaved timber and causing serious damage. Escape holes of adults 1.5–2 mm across.

▲ **Death-watch Beetle** *Xestobium rufovillosum*. Hairy and, as in all the family, the head is more or less hidden from above. Breeds in old trees and building timbers – usually oak and other hardwoods, especially where damp. Tunnelling larvae cause immense damage to old buildings, but less common than furniture beetle. Adults appear in spring and make tapping noises to attract mates. Exit holes 3–4 mm across.

▲ ***Ptilinus pectinicornis***. Antennae are simply toothed in female. 5–8, often indoors. Breeds in dry deciduous timber.

▲ **Lesser Grain Borer** *Rhizopertha dominica* Bostrychidae. Pronotum forms hood over head. Antennae with 3-segmented club. Adult and larva feed on grain of various kinds. Commonly infests granaries and flour mills.

▲ ***Lyctus linearis*** Lyctidae. One of the powder post beetles. Antennae with 2-segmented club. Breeds in old deciduous timbers, indoors and out, and reduces them to a very fine dust. 4–7.

▲ **Cadelle** *Tenebroides mauritanicus* Trogossitidae. Dark brown to black. Found mainly in food stores and bakeries, where adult and larva prey on other insects. Sometimes out of doors, under loose bark, in warmer areas.

△ ***Lymexylon navale*** Lymexylidae. Soft, furry elytra. Female slightly larger and lacks feathery maxillary palps. 5–8, around dead and dying deciduous trees in which it breeds. Occasionally damages oak timbers. S & C.

△ ***Hylecoetus dermestoides***. Only male has feathery palps. 5–6, around dead and dying trees, usually deciduous. Like previous species, larva has horny spine at end.

▲ **Saw-toothed Grain Beetle** *Oryzaephilus surinamensis* Silvanidae. 6 blunt teeth on each side of thorax. Usually in grain stores and warehouses, feeding on larvae of other insects, including the grain weevils.

▲ ***Glischrochilus 4-punctatus*** Nitidulidae. Smooth and shiny: hind edge of thorax narrower than elytra. 3–11. Around conifers. Breeds under bark and in bark beetle galleries. ▲ *G. hortensis* is stouter, sides of thorax more or less continuous with elytra. 5 tarsal segments. Feeds on oozing sap and over-ripe fruit. 5–10.

▲ **Raspberry Beetle** *Byturus tomentosus* Byturidae. Clothed with fine hair. 5–7, gnawing raspberry buds and laying eggs in them. Larvae feed in the growing fruit.

▲ ***Mycetophagus 4-pustulatus*** Mycetophagidae. Superficially like *Glischrochilus* but flatter: 3 or 4 tarsal segments: pronotum semicircular. 4–9, usually on bracket fungi on deciduous trees: occasionally on dung.

▲ ***Gnatocerus cornutus*** Tenebrionidae. Female lacks horns, which are outgrowths from jaws. In grain stores, flour mills, etc. Feeds on flour. Also under loose bark.

▲ **Confused Flour Beetle** *Tribolium confusum*. Confined to flour mills, granaries, and food stores. Feeds on flour and other cereal products.

▲ **Mealworm Beetle** *Tenebrio molitor*. Seen mainly in granaries etc, where it damages grain and cereal products. Larva (p. 295) is the mealworm, widely sold in pet shops. Occasionally out of doors, usually under bark, in summer. Flightless, like most members of the family, with elytra fused together.

△ ***Diaperis boleti***. Shiny black with yellow or orange markings. Strongly domed. Feeds on fungi, mainly in woodland.

▲ **Churchyard Beetle** *Blaps mucronata*. A flightless, ground-living beetle of caves, cellars, stables, and other damp, dark places. Strongly nocturnal, like most members of the family. Scavenges on vegetable matter. Emits foul smell when alarmed.

Churchyard Beetle × 1.5

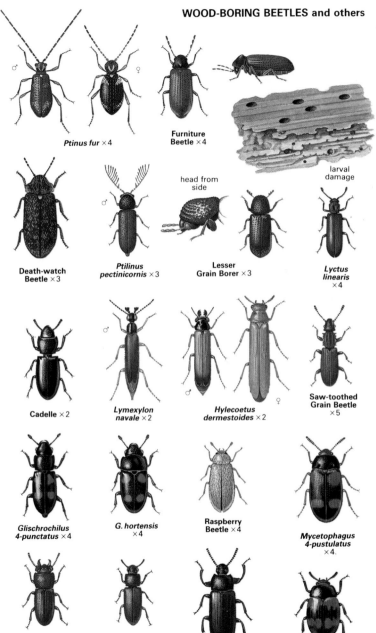

Ptinus fur × 4

Furniture Beetle × 4

larval damage

Death-watch Beetle × 3

Ptilinus pectinicornis × 3

head from side

Lesser Grain Borer × 3

Lyctus linearis × 4

Cadelle × 2

Lymexylon navale × 2

Hylecoetus dermestoides × 2

Saw-toothed Grain Beetle × 5

Glischrochilus 4-punctatus × 4

G. hortensis × 4

Raspberry Beetle × 4

Mycetophagus 4-pustulatus × 4.

Gnatocerus cornutus × 4

Confused Flour Beetle × 4

Mealworm Beetle × 1.5

Diaperis boleti × 1.5

275

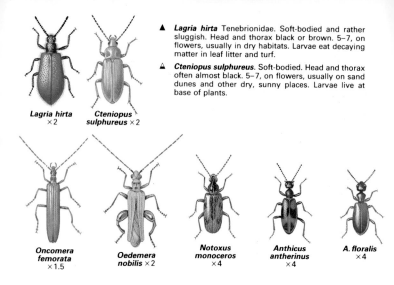

Lagria hirta Tenebrionidae. Soft-bodied and rather sluggish. Head and thorax black or brown. 5–7, on flowers, usually in dry habitats. Larvae eat decaying matter in leaf litter and turf. ▲

Cteniopus sulphureus. Soft-bodied. Head and thorax often almost black. 5–7, on flowers, usually on sand dunes and other dry, sunny places. Larvae live at base of plants. ▲

Lagria hirta
×2

Cteniopus sulphureus ×2

Oncomera femorata
×1.5

Oedemera nobilis ×2

Notoxus monoceros
×4

Anthicus antherinus
×4

A. floralis
×4

▲ **Oncomera femorata** Oedemeridae. Elytra and body soft. Pollen-feeding on various shrubs, including ivy, 4–10. Larvae in decaying wood. S & C.

▲ **Oedemera nobilis.** Female is thinner and lacks swollen hind femora. Elytra pointed and gaping. Pollen-feeding; common on flowers 4–8.

△ **Notoxus monoceros** Anthicidae. An agile, ant-like beetle with thoracic horn projecting over head. Elytra often black with just a pale triangle at tip. Among debris and turf on sandy ground: often on flowers.

△ **Anthicus antherinus.** Very agile. Usually on compost heaps and other vegetable debris or manure heaps. 5–10. ▲ **A. floralis** is very ant-like. Whole body often dark. In manure and vegetable refuse. 5–10.

Notoxus

△s **Spanish Fly** *Lytta vesicatoria* Meloidae. One of the blister beetles, so called because they emit a blistering fluid when alarmed. Mousy smell. 5–8, chewing leaves of various trees. Larvae live in solitary bee nests. S & C.

△ **Meloe variegatus.** One of the oil beetles, releasing a smelly, oily fluid when alarmed. Flightless, with short elytra overlapping at front. 4–7, in grassy places, chewing leaves of various plants. Larva in nests of solitary bees. S & C. ▲ **M. proscarabaeus** is bluish-black and, like all oil beetles, very variable in size. Male has kinked antennae. 4–7. △ **M. violaceus** is similar but more finely punctured on head and thorax. Habits are like those of *M. variegatus*.

Mylabris polymorpha. Pale markings vary in shape and may be orange or yellow. On flowers in sunny places, feeding on pollen. 6–9. Larvae parasitise grasshopper eggs. S.

Spanish Fly
×1.25

Meloe variegatus ×1.25
♀

M. proscarabaeus
×1.25
♀

Mylabris polymorpha ×1.25

LONGHORN BEETLES Cerambycidae A family of more than 20,000 beetles, mostly with very long antennae arising from prominent tubercles. Antennae usually longer in male than female. Body usually distinctly elongate and often rather flattened. Elytra may be much broader than thorax. Tarsi appear to have only 4 segments, with 3rd segment bilobed and almost completely enclosing the small 4th segment. Tarsal segments much broader in male than in female. Many species are very colourful, often with marked differences between the sexes, but there are also many sombre species. Most species are fully winged and fly, by night or by day, with a ghostly rising and falling motion. A few are fast and noisy. They feed on flowers – particularly the pollen – and leaves, although some species take little food in the adult state. Many can stridulate loudly by rubbing the thoracic plates together. They do this mainly when they are alarmed.

The larvae are almost all wood-feeders, attacking both living and dead timber. Several species cause severe damage to forest areas. They are usually pale-coloured, elongate, and slightly flattened – especially those species that live just under the bark. The jaws are powerful, but legs are very short or absent. Wood is not a very nutritious food, and larval life is consequently rather long – usually two or three years, and sometimes much longer in dry, seasoned timber. Pupation takes place in an enlarged feeding tunnel or in a chamber hollowed out just under the bark. The larvae often go on growing after their trees have been felled and used for building, and with today's worldwide trade in timber the adults often emerge far from their native homes.

Several hundred species of longhorns live in Europe, with about 70 species native to Britain. Most live in the woodlands. Their habits are all rather similar and only minimal descriptions of the species are given in the following pages. The habitats given are essentially those of the larvae.

A typical longhorn larva showing the tapering body and very short legs.

▲ *Prionus coriarius*. One of Europe's stoutest longhorns. Larvae in tree roots. 6–9.

♀

Ergates faber. Thorax spiny-edged: males thorax has two large spots. Larvae in stumps in old pine woods. 7–9. S & C: mainly eastern.

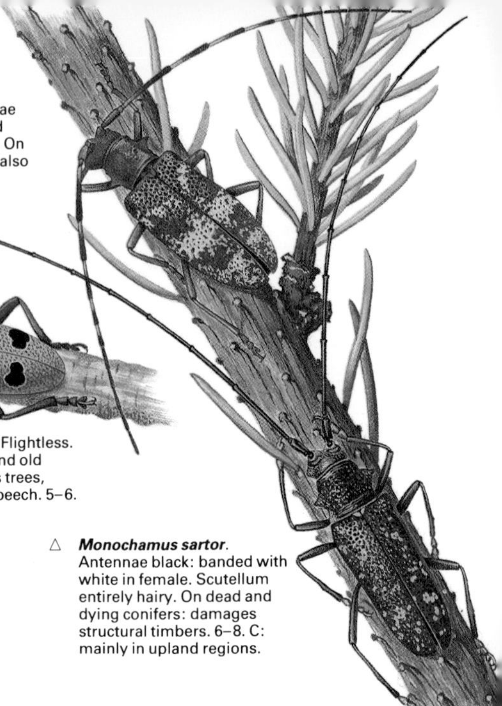

Monochamus galloprovincialis. Antennae reddish-brown. U-shaped hairy patch on scutellum. On pines. 6–9. Mainly S, but also plantations in C.

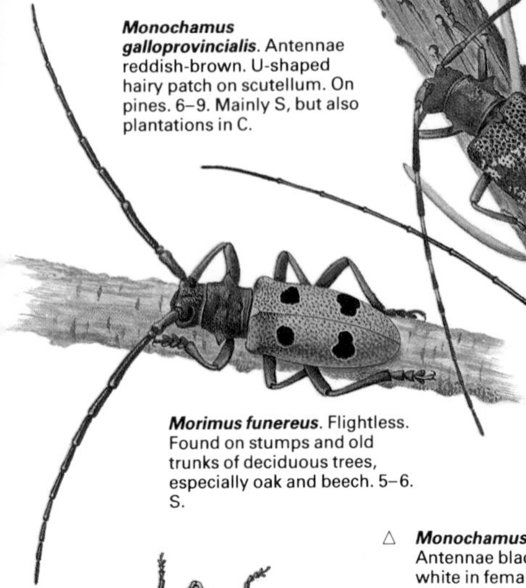

Morimus funereus. Flightless. Found on stumps and old trunks of deciduous trees, especially oak and beech. 5–6. S.

△ ***Monochamus sartor.*** Antennae black: banded with white in female. Scutellum entirely hairy. On dead and dying conifers: damages structural timbers. 6–8. C: mainly in upland regions.

×1.5

▲ **Musk Beetle** *Aromia moschata.* Sometimes coppery or blue. Emits musk-like secretion. Deciduous trees, especially willows. 6–8.

△ ***Saperda carcharias.*** Roots, trunks, and branches of young poplars: often a pest. 7–9.

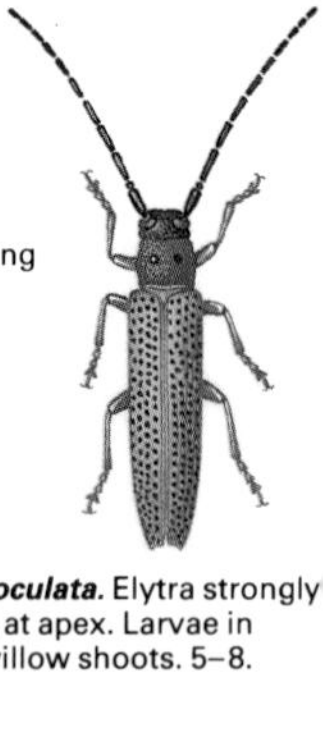

△ ***Oberea oculata.*** Elytra strongly concave at apex. Larvae in young willow shoots. 5–8.

△ ***Lamia textor.*** A lethargic species found around sallows and poplars: a pest of osier beds. 5–10.

▲ **House Longhorn** *Hylotrupes bajulus.* A pest of dry coniferous timber: often destroys telegraph poles and house timbers. 6–8.

278

▲ **Wasp Beetle** *Clytus arietis*. A superb wasp mimic, scuttling over tree trunks in sunshine with antennae waving. Common in gardens and hedgerows. 5–7. Larvae in fence posts and other dead deciduous timber.

△ *Plagionotus arcuatus*. Sides of thorax strongly rounded. On dead oaks and beeches in sunshine. 5–7. Often breeds in structural timbers.

Chlorophorus varius. Sun-loving: often on flowers, especially umbellifers. Breeds in various deciduous timbers, including vines. 6–7. Mainly southern.

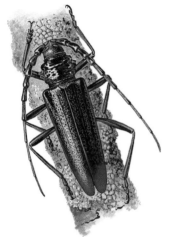

Cerambyx cerdo. One of Europe's largest beetles. Flies around oaks in evening. 6–8. Larvae damage standing oak timber. S & C.

×1.25

▲ *Strangalia maculata*. Elytra strongly tapered. One of several similar species: pattern varies but antennae yellow at base. On flowers. 6–8. Larvae in rotting deciduous tree stumps.

×1.25

△ *Phymatodes testaceus*. Head may be black and elytra bluish. 6–8: often swarms at dusk. Dead and dying deciduous trees.

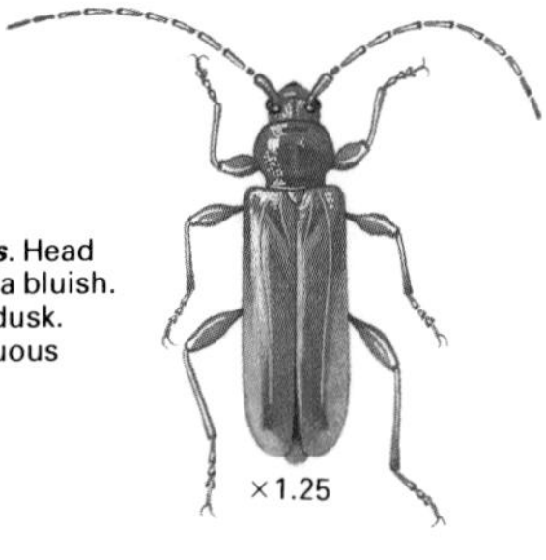

△ *Agapanthea villosoviridescens*. On flowers in hedges and damp places. 5–7. Breeds in stems of thistles and other herbaceous plants. N & C.

×1.25

279

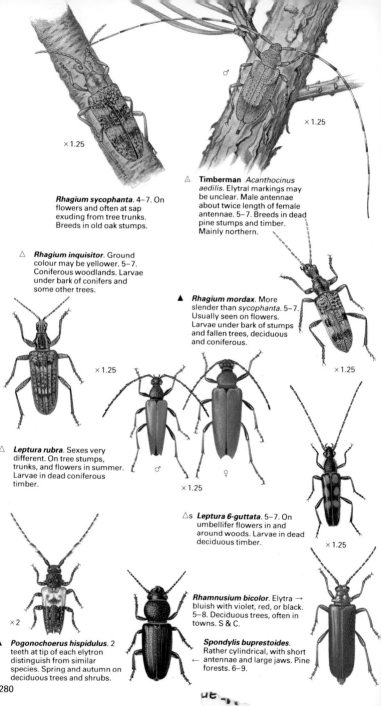

×1.25

×1.25

Rhagium sycophanta. 4–7. On flowers and often at sap exuding from tree trunks. Breeds in old oak stumps.

△ ***Rhagium inquisitor***. Ground colour may be yellower. 5–7. Coniferous woodlands. Larvae under bark of conifers and some other trees.

△ **Timberman** *Acanthocinus aedilis*. Elytral markings may be unclear. Male antennae about twice length of female antennae. 5–7. Breeds in dead pine stumps and timber. Mainly northern.

▲ ***Rhagium mordax***. More slender than *sycophanta*. 5–7. Usually seen on flowers. Larvae under bark of stumps and fallen trees, deciduous and coniferous.

×1.25

×1.25

△ ***Leptura rubra***. Sexes very different. On tree stumps, trunks, and flowers in summer. Larvae in dead coniferous timber.

♂   ♀

×1.25

△s ***Leptura 6-guttata***. 5–7. On umbellifer flowers in and around woods. Larvae in dead deciduous timber.

×1.25

×2

▲ ***Pogonochoerus hispidulus***. 2 teeth at tip of each elytron distinguish from similar species. Spring and autumn on deciduous trees and shrubs.

Rhamnusium bicolor. Elytra → bluish with violet, red, or black. 5–8. Deciduous trees, often in towns. S & C.

Spondylis buprestoides. Rather cylindrical, with short ← antennae and large jaws. Pine forests. 6–9.

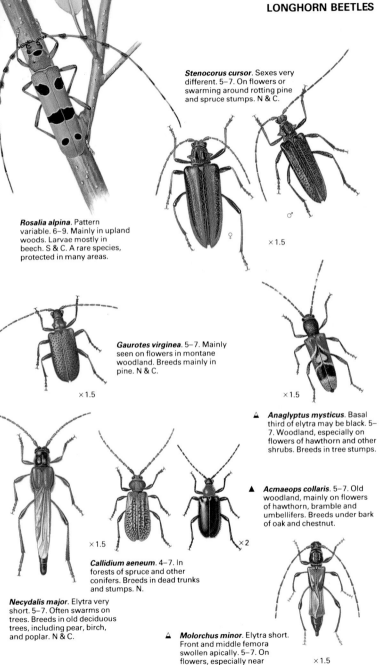

Stenocorus cursor. Sexes very different. 5–7. On flowers or swarming around rotting pine and spruce stumps. N & C.

♀

♂

×1.5

Rosalia alpina. Pattern variable. 6–9. Mainly in upland woods. Larvae mostly in beech. S & C. A rare species, protected in many areas.

Gaurotes virginea. 5–7. Mainly seen on flowers in montane woodland. Breeds mainly in pine. N & C.

×1.5

×1.5

▲ **Anaglyptus mysticus**. Basal third of elytra may be black. 5–7. Woodland, especially on flowers of hawthorn and other shrubs. Breeds in tree stumps.

▲ **Acmaeops collaris**. 5–7. Old woodland, mainly on flowers of hawthorn, bramble and umbellifers. Breeds under bark of oak and chestnut.

×1.5

×2

Callidium aeneum. 4–7. In forests of spruce and other conifers. Breeds in dead trunks and stumps. N.

Necydalis major. Elytra very short. 5–7. Often swarms on trees. Breeds in old deciduous trees, including pear, birch, and poplar. N & C.

▲ **Molorchus minor**. Elytra short. Front and middle femora swollen apically. 5–7. On flowers, especially near conifers. Breeds in stumps.

×1.5

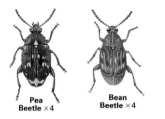

Pea
Beetle ×4

Bean
Beetle ×4

▲ **Pea Beetle** *Bruchus pisorum* Bruchidae. One of several similar beetles. A serious pest of peas. Legless grubs develop in growing pods. Adults emerge in spring and commonly sunbathe on walls.

▲ **Bean Beetle** *Acanthoscelides obtectus*. Like *Bruchus* but pronotum distinctly triangular. Hind femur has 3 teeth. A pest of beans, breeding in stored seeds and in growing crops.

LEAF BEETLES Chrysomelidae

A family of over 25,000 species, almost all leaf-eaters. Often brightly coloured and mostly with smooth, rounded outlines. Tarsi appear 4-segmented, but actually have 5 segments: 4th is minute and concealed in expanded 3rd segment. Some species might be confused with ladybirds (p. 270) but latter have only three visible tarsal segments. Larvae soft and slug-like.

▲ *Donacia vulgaris*. Elytra green or coppery with red or blue central area. On bur-reed 5–8. Larvae live in stems. One of several similar species on water plants.

▲ *Oulema melanopus*. Head and elytra blue or black. Abundant in grass and sometimes a minor cereal pest. 4–7, often sunning itself on walls.

△ *Asparagus Beetle Crioceris asparagi*. A pest of asparagus, adults and larvae chewing feathery leaves. 5–8, hibernating as adult. S & C.

△ *Lilioceris lilii*. 4–8, on various members of lily family, including garden varieties. A pest in the south. S & C.

△ *Clytra 4-punctata*. 5–8, on vegetation near wood ant nests. Scatters eggs on nest: larvae, protected by soil and excrement, eat scraps in the chambers and galleries.

▲ *Cryptocephalus hypochaeridis*. One of a large genus of very metallic beetles, commonly seen on flowers, especially hawkweeds and other yellow composites, in summer.

C. sericeus is golden green to bluish or purplish green. 4–7, in grassland, especially on yellow umbellifers. S & C.

C. bipunctata occurs mainly on hazel, birch, and oak. 4–7.

▲ *Bloody-nosed Beetle Timarcha tenebricosa*. Strongly domed and flightless, with elytra fused together. One of the largest leaf beetles. Named for habit of exuding a drop of red blood from mouth when alarmed – this frightens birds. 4–8, in grassy places, walking slowly over turf or bare ground. Feeds on bedstraw. S & C.

▲ *Chrysolina polita*. Common on herbage of river banks and other damp places all summer. Especially on mints. *C. grossa* of Mediterranean area is larger, with metallic blue thorax.

△s *C. menthastri* is one of our most brilliant leaf beetles, found on mints and other labiates in damp places. 5–9. S & C.

△s *C. cerealis* is usually metallic green with blue and red bands, but colour varies. Dry, sandy places, usually on wild thyme, throughout summer. S & C.

C. geminata is bronzy green or blue, sometimes all black. On St John's-wort (*Hypericum* spp) throughout summer. N & C.

▲ *Gastrophysa viridula*. Usually golden green; sometimes bluish. 5–8, on docks and related plants, normally on edges of ponds and streams.

△ *Colorado Beetle Leptinotarsa decemlineata*. A notorious potato pest, originally from N. America. Larva (p. 295) and adult both destroy leaves, and also feed on tomato, nightshades, and related plants. 4–9. Widely distributed in S & C: notify police if seen in B.

▲ *Chrysomela populi*. Pronotum dark green or bronze or almost black. Elytra orange to bright red, often with dark spots. On sallows and poplars, 4–9.

C. 20-punctata has 10 irregular black marks on each elytron. 4–8, usually near water and normally on willows. C.

▲ *Phytodecta viminalis*. Shiny rusty brown: black marks variable and sometimes absent, but usually a black band or heart-shaped mark at rear of pronotum. 5–8, mainly on willows. N & C.

▲ *Lochmaea caprea*. Locally abundant on sallows in fens and other damp places: also on birch. 4–9. ▲ *L. crataegi* is redder and occurs on hawthorn.

Leaf beetle tarsus showing the very small 4th segment almost enclosed in 3rd segment.

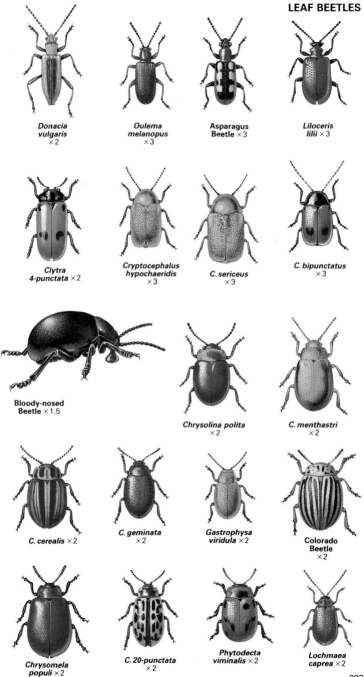

*Donacia
vulgaris*
×2

*Oulema
melanopus*
×3

Asparagus
Beetle ×3

*Liloceris
lilii* ×3

*Clytra
4-punctata* ×2

*Cryptocephalus
hypochaeridis*
×3

C. sericeus
×3

C. bipunctatus
×3

Bloody-nosed
Beetle ×1.5

Chrysolina polita
×2

C. menthastri
×2

C. cerealis ×2

C. geminata
×2

*Gastrophysa
viridula* ×2

Colorado
Beetle
×2

*Chrysomela
populi* ×2

C. 20-punctata
×2

*Phytodecta
viminalis* ×2

*Lochmaea
caprea* ×2

283

▲ **Galerucella lineola**. A rather sombre, hairy beetle with pubescence lying parallel to suture. Often abundant on willows 3–9, feeding on flowers and leaves. Several similar species on willows and water plants.

▲ **Galeruca tanaceti**. Shiny black. Elytra distinctly wider at hind end, especially in female, where abdomen may protrude beyond elytra. Roadsides and other grassy places, often quite dry, feeding on yarrow and other composites. 4–9.

▲ **Luperus longicornis**. Male is more parallel-sided, with antennae much longer than body. On trees in damp places. All summer.

▲ **Pyrrhalta viburni**. Very like *G. lineola*, but pubescence runs at right angles to suture. On wayfaring tree throughout summer, often reducing leaves to skeletons.

▲ **Phyllodecta vitellinae**. Golden green; sometimes bluish or coppery. On poplars and willows, especially osiers, spring to summer. Hibernates under bark.

△ **Phyllobrotica 4-maculata**. 5–8, usually on skullcap and other damp places.

▲ **Turnip Flea** *Phyllotreta nemorum*. One of the flea beetles – jumping species with enlarged hind femora. Like many other flea beetles, it is a pest of brassicas, including turnips. Adults feed mainly on seedlings, leaving them riddled with holes. Larvae tunnel in leaves and become adult in autumn. Adult flea beetles hibernate and re-appear in spring to feed and lay eggs.

▲ **P. nigripes** larvae feed on roots, but adult habits are like those of *nemorum*.

Psylliodes chrysocephala. Another troublesome flea beetle, with hind femora very large. Elytra sometimes yellowish brown. Larva live in stems and mid-ribs of brassicas, especially cauliflower. Adults nibble flowers and leaves.

▲ **Potato Flea Beetle** *P. affinis* is common on nightshades and is sometimes a pest of potatoes (rarely a problem in B). Adults nibble leaves, while larvae tunnel in roots.

Green Tortoise Beetle *Cassida viridis*. Pronotum and elytra extend well beyond body and beetle is very hard to see when they are pulled tightly down against the leaf. Hind angles of pronotum rounded (angled in *C. rubiginosa*). 6–9, usually in damp places and resting on leaves of mint and other labiates. Larva (p. 295) camouflages itself with excrement.

▲ **C. sanguinolenta** occurs on thistles and yarrow in grassland in summer. There are several similar species.

WEEVILS

WEEVILS A very large group, with a world total of over 40,000 species arranged in several families. Most weevils have a prominent snout (the rostrum), with jaws at the end and elbowed antennae normally attached about half way along. Many are clothed with scales and many are flightless, often with elytra fused together. Almost all are vegetarians throughout their lives. Larvae are usually legless and usually live inside their food plants: many live in seeds.

▲ **Brachytarsus nebulosus** Anthribidae. Similar to *Bruchus* (p. 282), with short snout although elytra cover abdomen. On hazel and various other trees. 5–7. Larvae have legs and feed on various bugs, including scale insects.

▲ **Rhynchites aequatus**. On hawthorn, spring to autumn. Female rostrum much longer than head and thorax together: male rostrum about as long as head and thorax together.

▲ **R. auratus** ranges from brassy green to purple. On blackthorn 5–7. Larva in kernel of fruit.

△ **Byctiscus populi**. Female lacks spines on front of thorax. On aspen. 6–9. Female rolls leaf around eggs. ▲ **B. betulae** is similar but has metallic legs. On various trees. Both species often blue or violet.

▲ **Apoderus coryli**. Head narrows at rear, forming distinct neck. 5–7, mainly on hazel. Larva feeds in rolled-up leaf.

▲ **Attelabus nitens**. Like *Apoderus* but head not narrowed at back. 5–7, on young oaks. Larva feeds in rolled leaf.

▲ **Apion miniatum** Apionidae. One of several similar species in this large genus. All are small, with characteristically pointed fronts. On docks, especially in damp habitats. 5–8.

▲ **A. pomonae**. Rather downy. Elytra sometimes greenish blue. Legs black. On vetches. 5–8.

Tortoise beetle camouflaged on leaf.

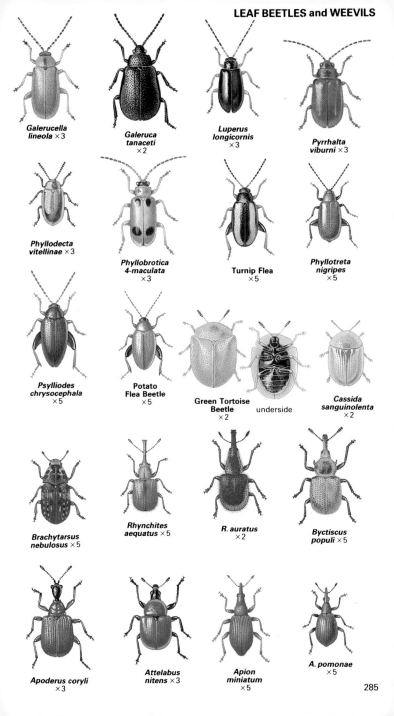

*Galerucella
lineola* ×3

*Galeruca
tanaceti*
×2

*Luperus
longicornis*
×3

*Pyrrhalta
viburni* ×3

*Phyllodecta
vitellinae* ×3

*Phyllobrotica
4-maculata*
×3

Turnip Flea
×5

*Phyllotreta
nigripes*
×5

*Psylliodes
chrysocephala*
×5

**Potato
Flea Beetle**
×5

**Green Tortoise
Beetle**
×2

underside

*Cassida
sanguinolenta*
×2

*Brachytarsus
nebulosus* ×5

*Rhynchites
aequatus* ×5

R. auratus
×2

*Byctiscus
populi* ×5

Apoderus coryli
×3

*Attelabus
nitens* ×3

*Apion
miniatum*
×5

A. pomonae
×5

▲ *Otiorhynchus clavipes* Curculionidae. One of our largest weevils, with very long antennae. Distinguished from *Liparus* and some other similar weevils by short rostrum with antennae attached to the upper surface instead of the side. Pale markings due to clusters of hairs, which often rub off with age. On hawthorn and other rosaceous trees and in dense grass tufts in summer. Several similar species.

▲ *Phyllobius pomaceus*. One of several similar species clothed with golden-green or bluish green scales: scales easily rub off and older specimens may be bald and black. Front femora toothed. Abundant on nettles 4–9.

▲ *Polydrusus tereticollis*. 4–6, in oak, aspen, and alder coppice. Elytra with alternating bands of bronze and paler brassy scales. This genus can usually be distinguished from *Phyllobius* because femora are usually untoothed.

P. picus Patches of pale scales often absent in older specimens. On birch, oak, and beech in summer. S & C.

▲ *P. sericeus* is very shiny. 4–7 on deciduous trees, especially birch.

▲ **Pea Weevil** *Sitona lineatus*. Prominent eyes and striped elytra. Abundant on peas, clovers, and other legumes in autumn and spring: hibernates as adult. Nibbles leaf margins, leaving them with frilly edges. Larva feeds in root nodules. A serious pest of peas in some years. Several similar species.

△ *Lixus paraplecticus*. Elytra dark, clothed with yellow scales. On stems of various umbellifers in damp places in autumn and spring: hiberates as adult. S & C.

▲ *Cionus hortulanus*. Grey or greenish grey, with shiny rostrum. On dark mullein, 6–9. Larva feeds externally, surrounded by gelatinous secretion. S & C. One of several similar species.

▲ **Pine Weevil** *Hylobius abietis*. Pubescent patches usually pale but may be deep chestnut: legs black or deep red: femora toothed. A serious pest of pine and spruce, damaging young shoots by chewing bark and stopping growth. Larvae develop in old stumps. Adult all year, but hibernates and seen mainly 4–10.

H. piceus, usually a little larger, is associated mainly with larch. N & C.

Liparus glabrirostris. Superficially like *Hylobius*, but plumper and elytra clearly rounded at front without 'shoulders'. Rather shiny. On umbellifers, butterbur, and other waterside plants in upland regions in spring and summer. C.

▲ *L. coronatus* is smaller, often without yellow scales on elytra. In turf and other low-growing vegetation in spring and early summer. Larvae in roots, including cultivated carrot.

▲ *Pissodes pini*. Similar to *Hylobius* but more slender, with a relatively longer rostrum and antennae inserted further back. Femora not toothed. On pine and spruce, mostly in upland forests but lower down in north. Hibernates as adult. Larva develops in living or dead timber.

▲ *Cryptorhynchus lapathi*. Pale scales are white or yellowish. On willows, poplars, birches, and alders in spring and summer. Larvae develop in timber and may kill branches and small trees.

△ **Apple Blossom Weevil** *Anthonomus pomorum*. On apple and pear blossom in spring. Eggs are laid in buds, which swell up but do not open as larva develops inside. Buds eventually fall.

▲ **Grain Weevil** *Sitophilus granarius*. Chestnut brown or black: elytra shiny. All year in granaries and similar places, breeding in stored grain of all kinds.

▲ *Notaris bimaculatus*. Striped pubescence often less obvious in older specimens. On waterside vegetation, including sallows and sedges, in spring. Several similar species.

△ *Dorytomus longimanus*. Male has extremely long front legs. Both sexes with very long, shiny black rostrum. 4–9, on poplars. Larvae in catkins and young shoots.

▲ *Curculio nucum*. Female uses her long rostrum to gnaw into young hazel nuts. She then lays an egg there and larva feeds on développing kernel. The grub remains n the nest until it falls in the autumn and then chews its way out and burrows into the soil to pupate. Rostrum is shorter in males, and the antennae are attached nearer to the tip. Adult 4–7, often visiting hawthorn flowers for pollen and nectar. ▲ *C. villosus* is black with scanty grey scales and a red antennal scrape. It is found on oaks during the summer, its grubs developing in the acorns. ▲ *C. salicivorus* is black with a scaly white covering. Abundant on willows throughout the summer. It is only 2.5 mm long.

C. elephas has longer and straighter rostrum. Breeds in oak and sweet chestnut fruit. 6–9. S & C. (mainly south).

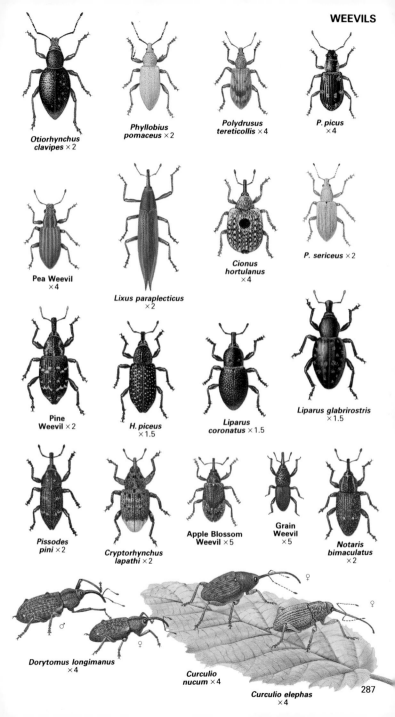

Otiorhynchus clavipes ×2

Phyllobius pomaceus ×2

Polydrusus tereticollis ×4

P. picus ×4

Pea Weevil ×4

Lixus paraplecticus ×2

Cionus hortulanus ×4

P. sericeus ×2

Pine Weevil ×2

H. piceus ×1.5

Liparus coronatus ×1.5

Liparus glabrirostris ×1.5

Pissodes pini ×2

Cryptorhynchus lapathi ×2

Apple Blossom Weevil ×5

Grain Weevil ×5

Notaris bimaculatus ×2

Dorytomus longimanus ×4

Curculio nucum ×4

Curculio elephas ×4

287

BARK BEETLES Scolytidae Cylindrical beetles, related to weevils but with almost no rostrum. Head almost hidden from above. Antennae distinctly elbowed. Elytra usually concave at hind end and used as shovels when excavating. Adults normally mate in a chamber under the bark of the host tree, and female then excavates one or more galleries in which she lays her eggs. The larvae then make their own tunnels just under the bark and produce characteristic patterns (right) as they leave the main galleries and chew their way through the nutritious tissues. After pupation, adults emerge through small holes in the bark. A few species live deeper in the wood.

△ ***Xyleborus dryographus***. Dark orange to chestnut. Male has a pit at front of pronotum and is more pointed in front. Adults and larvae bore deeply into timber – mainly oak and chestnut – and feed on fungi which grow on tunnel walls. S & C.

△ ***Pityogenes chalcographus***. Deep brown to black, with 3 teeth on each side of elytral hollow. Mainly on spruce, often swarming round trees 5–6. Sometimes a second generation late summer. Female makes radiating galleries from nuptial chamber, and larvae tunnel at right angles from them. △ ***P. bidentatus***. Only the male has 2 downward-pointing teeth on each side of elytral hollow. On pine and spruce.

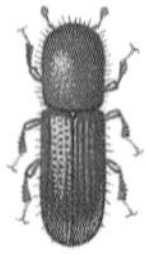

Xyleborus dryographus × 6

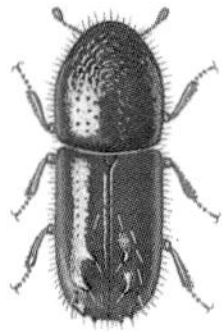

Pityogenes chalcographus × 6

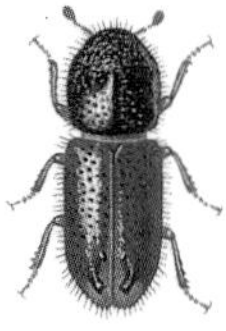

P. bidentatus × 6

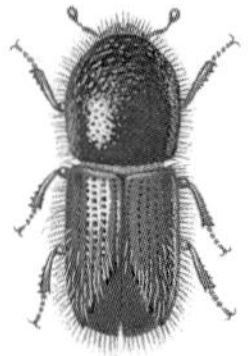

Ips typographus × 5

△ ***Ips typographus***. Very hairy and much larger than *Pityogenes*. Elytral pit with 3 teeth on each side. 5–7. Breeds in spruce, with 2 vertical egg galleries made by 2 females mated to one male.

△ **Pine-shoot Beetle** *Tomicus piniperda* chestnut to black. Mainly on pine, in stumps and fallen trunks. Main gallery vertical, with pairing chamber at base. Adults hibernate: active mainly in spring. △n ***T. minor*** is similar, but galleries like *Leperisinus*. N & C.

Pine-shoot Beetle × 4

Ash Bark Beetle × 4

Elm Bark Beetle × 4

Pinhole Borer × 4

▲ **Ash Bark Beetle** *Leperisinus varius* Black, with irregular pattern of scales. 4–10, in 2 generations. Usually in diseased or fallen trunks and branches of ash. Main galleries horizontal, with 2 more or less equal arms.

▲ **Elm Bark Beetle** *Scolytus scolytus* Notorious carrier of Dutch Elm Disease, adults carrying spores from tunnels and infecting new trees as they chew young shoots. 5–9. Egg gallery vertical and quite short; larval galleries irregular.

────────────

△ **Pinhole Borer** *Platypus cylindrus* Platypodidae. Very cylindrical. 6–7, producing characteristically splintery debris when tunnelling before egg-laying. Usually in oak, larvae tunnelling deeply into standing trunks or unseasoned logs. S & C.

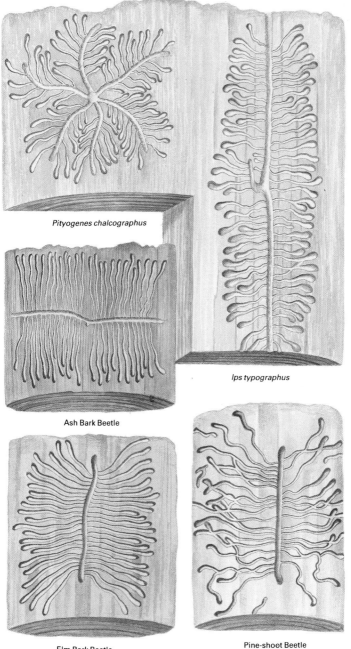

Pityogenes chalcographus

Ips typographus

Ash Bark Beetle

Elm Bark Beetle

Pine-shoot Beetle

Dytiscus renewing air supply

Family Dytiscidae A large family, related to the ground beetles (p. 256) although much modified for life in water. The head is sunk partly back into the thorax and the whole outline is smoothly rounded, while the hind legs are usually broad and flat and fringed with hairs for efficient swimming. Males of many species have swollen front tarsi, with which they grip females during mating. The beetles renew their air-supplies by coming to the surface tail-first. They nearly all fly well. Most can be found throughout the year, although they may hibernate in the coldest months. Adults and larvae are all fiercely carnivorous.

▲ **Great Diving Beetle** *Dytiscus marginalis*. Reddish brown with a deep green sheen, although latter disappears after death. Male elytra very smooth: those of female usually dull and ribbed. Pronotum has yellow border all round. Weedy ponds and other still waters: often very common. Larva (p. 297) and adult both attack frogs and newts as well as fishes, tadpoles, and various invertebrates. *D. latissimus* is larger and blacker, with elytra expanded sideways. Prefers large lakes. N & C.

　　Cybister laterimarginalis. Resembles *D. marginalis* but pronotum has yellow only at the sides. 3–7, in still and running water in lowlands. Not in far north.

▲ *Acilius sulcatus*. Elytra shiny in male: ribbed in female, with dense hair between ridges. Black pattern on elytra often indistinct. Ponds and other still or slow-moving water.

▲ *Platambus maculatus*. Readily identified by its pattern, although this does vary slightly. 5–10. Occurs in some well-aerated lakes, but mainly in running water – from fast-flowing mountain streams to weedy rivers and even brackish stretches: prefers stony or sandy bottoms. Absent from far south.

△s *Noterus clavicornis*. Yellowish brown to brick-coloured. Very convex and, unlike most dytiscids, narrower at the back than the front. Antennae dilated, especially in male. 3–10, in densely vegetated ponds and lakes. Widely distributed, but local. Often placed in a separate family – the Noteridae.

▲ *Potamonectes depressus*. Clothed with short hair. Yellow deepens with age. Relative amounts of black and yellow on elytra vary, some beetles being largely black and others largely yellow. Elytra toothed near apex. Essentially a bottom-dwelling species, with legs less modified for swimming than in most other dytiscids. Lakes and rivers with gravelly beds.

▲ *Laccophilus minutus*. Rather flat, with distinctly lobed hind tarsi. Elytra sometimes quite green and frequently decorated with pale spots. Ponds and ditches.

▲ *Hygrotus versicolor*. Relatively large eyes, together with the characteristic elytral pattern, distinguish this from several closely related species. Very common in lakes, canals, and slow-flowing rivers.

▲ *Hydroporus palustris*. One of several closely related species, but usually distinguished quite easily by the yellow or orange borders of elytra. The rest of the elytral pattern varies and may be absent. Very common in all kinds of still water, including mountain tarns.

▲ *Ilybius fenestratus*. One of several very similar species with unequal claws on hind feet. Most are black or bronze, but *fenestratus* has a distinctly reddish tinge above and a red underside. 4–10, in ponds and lakes: less often in slow-moving streams. Larva (p. 297) is typical of many dytiscids in shape. N & C.

▲ *Colymbetes fuscus*. Distinguished by its narrow shape (relative to *Dytiscus*) and by the yellow margins to elytra and thorax. Often with a green iridescence. Abundant in weedy and muddy ponds and ditches.

▲ *Agabus bipustulatus*. Antennae and front legs reddish brown: rest of body black, with a faint shine in male but dull in female. Claws on hind feet equal. In standing water of all kinds and often abundant. Flies very readily and not uncommon at lights at night. There are several similar species, but most are smaller.

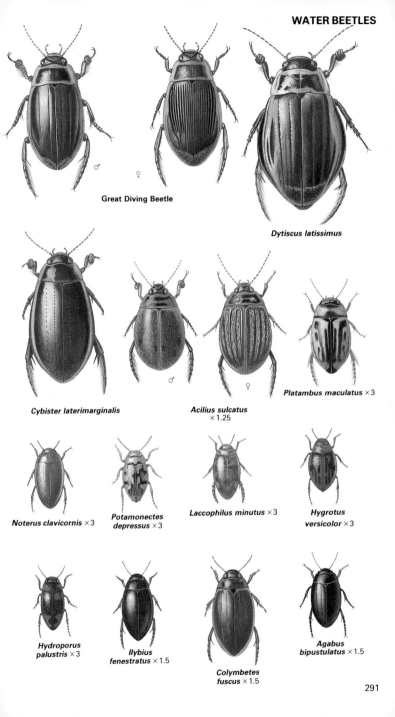

WATER BEETLES

Great Diving Beetle

♂ ♀

Dytiscus latissimus

Cybister laterimarginalis

♂ ♀

Acilius sulcatus ×1.25

Platambus maculatus ×3

Noterus clavicornis ×3

Potamonectes depressus ×3

Laccophilus minutus ×3

Hygrotus versicolor ×3

Hydroporus palustris ×3

Ilybius fenestratus ×1.5

Colymbetes fuscus ×1.5

Agabus bipustulatus ×1.5

291

▲ **Haliplus fulvus** Haliplidae. Very convex, with rows of elongate punctures on elytra. Hind coxae very big. A poor swimmer, with hind tarsi not broad. Crawls on plants and stones in weedy pools and streams, browsing on algae. Larva (p. 297) has long 'tail'.

⚠ **Screech Beetle** *Hygrobia herrmanni* Hygrobiidae. Very convex, with large eyes. Legs hairy, but not broad. Squeaks when alarmed by rubbing tip of abdomen against elytra. Adult and larva (p. 297) feed on invertebrates in muddy ponds. S & C.

▲ **Whirligig Beetle** *Gyrinus natator* Gyrinidae. One of several similar species whirling round and round on surface of still and slow-moving water, often in large groups: dive when alarmed. Middle and hind legs very short and oar-like. Each eye in 2 parts, one looking down into water and one looking across surface. Larva (p. 297) and adult both predatory, feeding largely on mosquito larvae. Adults hibernate.

Great Silver Beetle
renewing air supply

▲ **Hairy Whirligig** *Orectochilus villosus*. Antennae, legs, and underside of body orange. Upper surface hairy. Nocturnal, but otherwise like *Gyrinus*.

Family Hydrophilidae This family contains both aquatic and terrestrial species (see p. 260). Palps are long and act as antennae: true antennae short and clubbed. Aquatic species usually omnivorous scavengers in still and slow-moving water. They are poor swimmers, with legs little modified, and crawl over submerged vegetation. There is an air reservoir under elytra and another enclosed by hairs on underside of abdomen: underside of body thus looks silvery in water. Air supply is replenished by coming up head-first and breaking surface with one of the antennae. Larvae nearly all carnivorous. Most species are adult all year, although they may hibernate.

⚠ **Great Silver Beetle** *Hydrophilus piceus*. One of Europe's largest beetles. Shiny above, with a greenish sheen in life: very silvery below when in the water. A sharp spine under thorax. A better swimmer than most hydrophilids. Scavenges on plant debris and also eats water snails. Still water with much weed and mud. Widespread, but becoming rare through loss of habitat. Larva, p. 297.

▲ **Laccobius sinuatus**. Readily identified by convex shape and thoracic pattern, although elytra are often very pale. Long hairs on middle and hind tarsi. Mainly in small, slow-flowing streams: sometimes in ponds and brackish pools. Several similar species.

△ **Spercheus emarginatus**. Brick-coloured or yellowish brown: strongly domed. Carnivorous. Among roots and debris in muddy water.

▲ **Helophorus aquaticus**. Easily recognised by 5 ridges on thorax: several related species are similar, but smaller. Very hairy beneath. Mainly in still water, including ditches and brackish pools: often amongst debris at water's edge.

▲ **Enochrus testaceus**. Pronotum and elytra yellow to brick red: head black, although may be yellow in front of eyes. 2nd segment of palp dark. Still and slow-moving water: often in debris at water's edge. Larvae are caterpillar-like.

▲ **Hydrochus elongatus**. Protruding eyes and large pronotal pits distinguish this genus, of which *elongatus* is largest species. Head and pronotum black or green: elytra usually very dark: occasionally green. Weedy still water. Mainly in spring.

⚠ **Hydrochara caraboides**. Very like *Hydrophilus* in shape and habits, but no more than half its size. Still water.

▲ **Hydrobius fuscipes**. Shiny black elytra, often with blue or green iridescence in life. Legs long and rust-coloured. Hind femora hairy. Abundant in still water and detritus. Larva, p. 297.

▲ **Dryops auriculatus** Dryopidae. Densely hairy. Antennae very short and stout. In and around ponds and streams, gripping debris and plants with strong claws.

▲ **Heterocerus flexuosus** Heteroceridae. Very hairy. Heavily spined front legs used to excavate tunnels in mud or sand in and around ponds and streams. Flies readily at night. There are several similar species, all scavengers.

▲ **Elmis aenea** Elmidae. Cannot swim and lives among stones, moss, and algae – usually in fast-flowing water. Grips with strong claws. Vegetarian. The insect uses plastron respiration (p. 255) and does not have to surface for air.

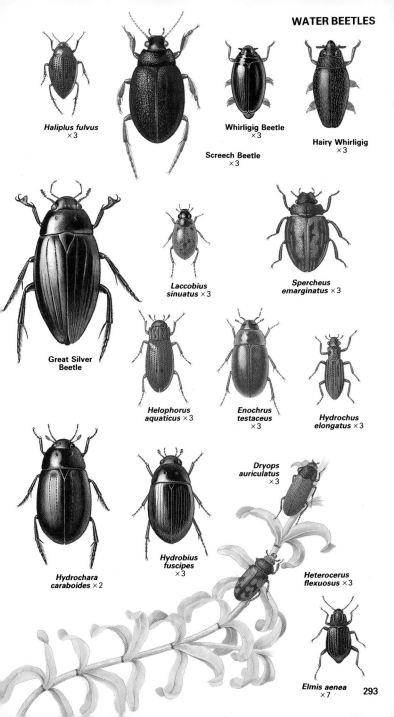

WATER BEETLES

Haliplus fulvus
×3

Whirligig Beetle
×3

Hairy Whirligig
×3

Screech Beetle
×3

Laccobius sinuatus ×3

Spercheus emarginatus ×3

Great Silver Beetle

Helophorus aquaticus ×3

Enochrus testaceus ×3

Hydrochus elongatus ×3

Dryops auriculatus ×3

Hydrochara caraboides ×2

Hydrobius fuscipes ×3

Heterocerus flexuosus ×3

Elmis aenea ×7

293

TERRESTRIAL LARVAE

Insects with a complete metamorphosis (p. 8) are markedly different in the young and adult stages. The young are always wingless and often feed on totally different foods from the adults. They are called larvae and a selection is illustrated here to show the wide variation in form. Page numbers refer to adult insects. Fly larvae (Diptera) are always legless, but nevertheless display an immense range of form (see also p. 191). Most Hymenoptera larvae are legless, because they are generally completely surrounded by food and do not need to move (see p. 218). The larvae (caterpillars) of butterflies and moths are illustrated on pages 112 to 181. Sawfly larvae often resemble them but have more than five pairs of prolegs on the hind part of the body. Some aquatic larvae are illustrated on the next two pages.

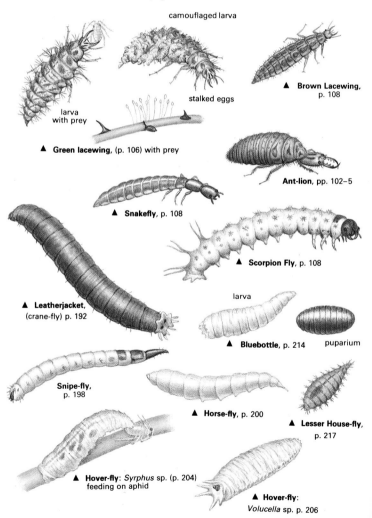

camouflaged larva

▲ **Brown Lacewing,** p. 108

stalked eggs

larva with prey

▲ **Green lacewing,** (p. 106) with prey

Ant-lion, pp. 102–5

▲ **Snakefly,** p. 108

▲ **Scorpion Fly,** p. 108

larva

▲ **Leatherjacket,** (crane-fly) p. 192

▲ **Bluebottle,** p. 214   puparium

Snipe-fly, p. 198

▲ **Horse-fly,** p. 200

▲ **Lesser House-fly,** p. 217

▲ **Hover-fly:** *Syrphus* sp. (p. 204) feeding on aphid

▲ **Hover-fly:** *Volucella* sp. p. 206

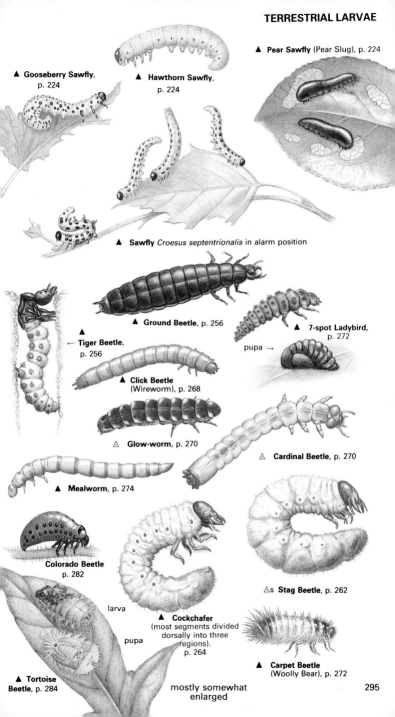

▲ **Pear Sawfly** (Pear Slug), p. 224

▲ **Gooseberry Sawfly**, p. 224

▲ **Hawthorn Sawfly**, p. 224

▲ **Sawfly** *Croesus septentrionalis* in alarm position

▲ **Ground Beetle**, p. 256

▲ **7-spot Ladybird**, p. 272

pupa →

▲ ← **Tiger Beetle**, p. 256

▲ **Click Beetle** (Wireworm), p. 268

△ **Glow-worm**, p. 270

△ **Cardinal Beetle**, p. 270

▲ **Mealworm**, p. 274

Colorado Beetle p. 282

larva

△s **Stag Beetle**, p. 262

▲ **Cockchafer** (most segments divided dorsally into three regions). p. 264

pupa

▲ **Carpet Beetle** (Woolly Bear), p. 272

▲ **Tortoise Beetle**, p. 284

mostly somewhat enlarged

AQUATIC NYMPHS and LARVAE

Many insects spend their early lives in fresh water and their adult lives in the air. Mayflies, dragonflies, and stoneflies are familiar examples. They all exhibit partial metamorphosis and their young stages, known as nymphs, show some similarity with the adult form despite living in water. A range of their forms is shown below. Mosquitoes and many other flies also grow up in the water, but these insects have a complete metamorphosis and their young, known as larvae, are totally unlike the adults. Some of their larval forms are shown on these pages. Caddis flies have a similar life history and their larvae are illustrated on pages 184 to 189. Water beetles remain in the water throughout their lives but, having a complete metamorphosis, their larvae are still very different from the adults. A selection of water beetle larvae is shown on the opposite page.

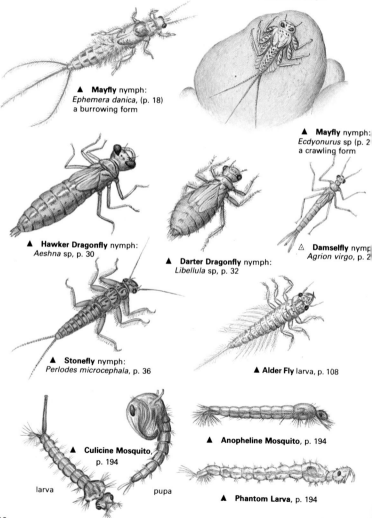

▲ **Mayfly** nymph:
Ephemera danica, (p. 18)
a burrowing form

▲ **Mayfly** nymph:
Ecdyonurus sp (p. 2
a crawling form

▲ **Hawker Dragonfly** nymph:
Aeshna sp, p. 30

▲ **Darter Dragonfly** nymph:
Libellula sp, p. 32

△ **Damselfly** nymph
Agrion virgo, p. 2

▲ **Stonefly** nymph:
Perlodes microcephala, p. 36

▲ **Alder Fly** larva, p. 108

▲ **Culicine Mosquito**,
p. 194

larva   pupa

▲ **Anopheline Mosquito**, p. 194

▲ **Phantom Larva**, p. 194

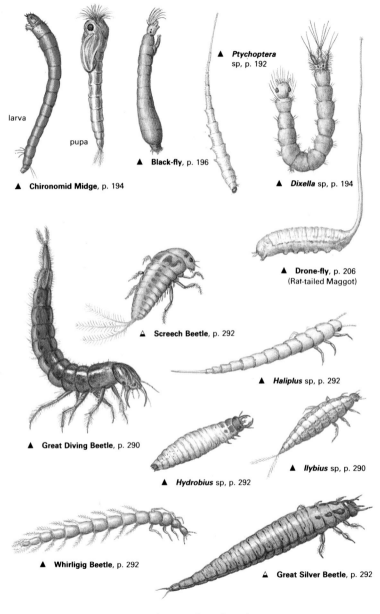

larva

pupa

▲ **Chironomid Midge**, p. 194

▲ **Black-fly**, p. 196

▲ ***Ptychoptera*** sp, p. 192

▲ ***Dixella*** sp, p. 194

▲ **Drone-fly**, p. 206 (Rat-tailed Maggot)

△ **Screech Beetle**, p. 292

▲ ***Haliplus*** sp, p. 292

▲ **Great Diving Beetle**, p. 290

▲ ***Hydrobius*** sp, p. 292

▲ ***Ilybius*** sp, p. 290

▲ **Whirligig Beetle**, p. 292

△ **Great Silver Beetle**, p. 292

mostly somewhat enlarged

The other arthropods

The insects form just one class, albeit a very large one, of the immense animal group known as the arthropods, all of which have jointed limbs. Examples of some of these other classes are illustrated on this and following pages to show how they differ from the insects, with which they are very often confused.

CENTIPEDES Class Chilopda Elongate, predatory arthropods with just one pair of legs to each body segment: hind pair of legs long and sensory. A pair of poison claws surround the head, but no British species is dangerous to man. **Haplophilus**lives among leaf litter, and **Necrophloeophagus** lives in the soil. **Cryptops hortensis** occurs under bark and stones, as do **Lithobius variegatus** and **L. forficatus** – both with 15 pairs of legs. The long-legged and very fast **Scutigera coleoptrata** lives mainly on walls, often indoors. **Scutigerella immaculata** is like a very small centipede, but it is a vegetarian and belongs to a group known as the symphylans. It is often a pest in greenhouses.

▲ *Haplophilus subterraneus*× 3. 77–83 pairs of legs

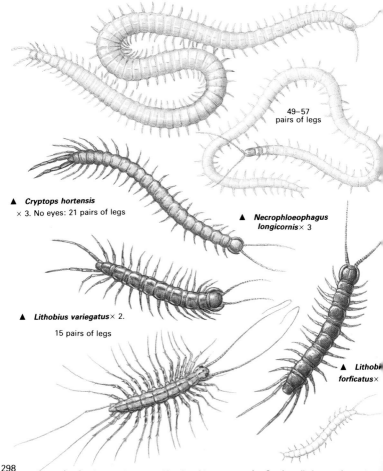

49–57 pairs of legs

▲ *Cryptops hortensis*
× 3. No eyes: 21 pairs of legs

▲ *Necrophloeophagus longicornis*× 3

▲ *Lithobius variegatus*× 2.
15 pairs of legs

▲ *Lithobi forficatus*×

△s *Scutigera coleoptrata* 15 pairs of legs

▲ *Scutigerella immaculata* × 4

Centipedes and millipedes are sometimes collectively known as myriapods (= many feet), although they are not closely related.

Scolopendra cingulatus, the largest European centipede, is found in scrubby habitats around the Mediterranean. Its bite is painful and potentially dangerous. Yellowish brown to olive green.

MILLIPEDES Class Diplopoda   Generally elongate arthropods with two pairs of legs on each body segment. Relatively slow-moving and feeding on living and dead plant matter. Body segments essentially circular in cross section, but flat-backed millipedes, such as ***Polydesmus***, appear flat because segments have flat extensions on upper surface. ***Polymicrodon polydesmoides*** and ***Oxidus gracilis*** have similar extensions, but upper surface remains domed. Millipedes are most common in leaf litter and other decaying vegetation, but ***Tachypodoiulus niger***, one of several very similar species that coil up like watch springs when alarmed, often climbs trees to browse on mosses and algae. ***Blaniulus guttulatus***, known as the Spotted Snake Millipede, lives mainly in cultivated soil and is a pest of potatoes. (See also p. 300).

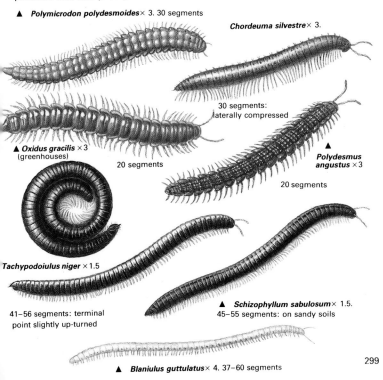

▲ ***Polymicrodon polydesmoides*** × 3. 30 segments

Chordeuma silvestre × 3.

30 segments: laterally compressed

▲ **Oxidus gracilis** × 3 (greenhouses)

20 segments

▲ ***Polydesmus angustus*** × 3

20 segments

Tachypodoiulus niger × 1.5

41–56 segments: terminal point slightly up-turned

▲ ***Schizophyllum sabulosum*** × 1.5. 45–55 segments: on sandy soils

▲ ***Blaniulus guttulatus*** × 4. 37–60 segments

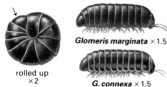

Glomeris marginata Glomeridae. One of the pill millipedes – short, stout species which can roll into a ball. In leaf litter and debris. Glossier than Pill Woodlouse (below) and with many more legs.

G. connexa is one of several red-spotted species commonly found under stones on the continent.

Glomeris marginata ×1.5

rolled up ×2

G. connexa ×1.5

WOODLICE Land-living crustaceans of the order Isopoda. 7 pairs of walking legs. Although terrestrial, most still require damp habitats. Most live as scavengers amongst decaying vegetation. About 30 species are native in B. *Oniscus asellus*, *Porcellio scaber*, and *Philoscia muscorum* are all common in gardens. *Ligia oceanica* lives on the sea shore. *Armadillidium vulgare* is the Pill Woodlouse, found in slightly drier places. When rolled up it is distinguished from the Pill Millipede by the numerous small plates of the hind end.

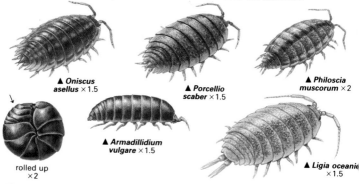

▲ *Oniscus asellus* ×1.5

▲ *Porcellio scaber* ×1.5

▲ *Philoscia muscorum* ×2

rolled up ×2

▲ *Armadillidium vulgare* ×1.5

▲ *Ligia oceanic* ×1.5

The Arachnids.

This group of arthropods, which includes the spiders and scorpions and their relatives, are the most frequently confused with the insects, but they are readily distinguished by having 4 pairs of legs. They never have wings and their bodies are never clearly divided into three regions.

FALSE SCORPIONS Order Pseudoscorpiones Mostly minute predatory arachnids with poison claws. *Garypus beauvoisi* is one of the largest and lives on seashore in S. Others, generally very much smaller (perhaps only 2 mm long) live in leaf litter and even in buildings - often among books where they feed on booklice (p. 98). 25 species occur in B.

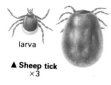

Garypus beauvoisi ×3

TICKS and MITES Order Acarina A very heterogeneous group of arachnids, mostly very small and globular and with relatively short legs. **Sheep Tick** *Ixodes ricinus* lives in grassy places and feeds on many mammals: young will attach themselves to and take blood from man. Mites are vegetarian, carnivorous, parasitic, or scavenging. The carnivorous **Velvet Mite** *Eutrombidium rostratus* is often common on garden paths in spring. **Red Spider Mite** *Panonychus ulmi* is a serious pest of fruit trees. *Hydrachna globosus* is one of many very similar water mites, feeding on other tiny aquatic animals.

larva

▲ Sheep tick ×3

▲ **Velvet Mite** ×3

▲ **Red Spider Mite** ×6

▲ **Water Mite** ×3

SCORPIONS Order Scorpiones Arachnids with large claws (pedipalps) and a slender tail tipped with a sting. Nocturnal predators. Mostly tropical, but a few species in southern Europe. ***Euscorpius flavicaudis*** lives in cracks in walls and buildings, protruding claws at night to catch passing insects. Harmless to man. S & C: established in some dockland areas of B. ***Buthus occitanus*** lives under stones. Its sting is painful and can be dangerous to infants. S.

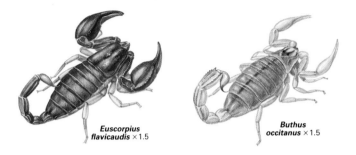

Euscorpius flavicaudis × 1.5

Buthus occitanus × 1.5

HARVESTMEN Order Opiliones Arachnids resembling spiders, but body undivided and 2nd pair of legs the longest. No venom and no silk. Generally mature in late summer – hence the name. Mainly nocturnal, feeding on a wide range of other small animals, both living and dead. 23 species live in B. ***Leiobunum rotundum*** is abundant everywhere, often resting on walls and tree trunks by day. ***Phalangium opilio*** has a pure white underside and male has horned chelicerae: in dense vegetation. ***Nemastoma bimaculatum***, like other short-legged species, lives on the ground.

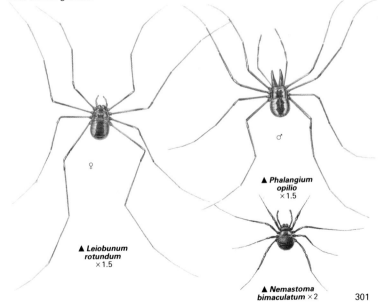

▲ *Phalangium opilio* ×1.5

▲ *Leiobunum rotundum* ×1.5

▲ *Nemastoma bimaculatum* ×2

SPIDERS

The spiders (Order Araneae) are certainly the most familiar of arachnids (p. 300) and, with the possible exception of the mites, they are the largest group. The body is in two parts – the relatively hard cephalothorax at the front and the softer abdomen behind – and this distinguishes them from the harvestmen (p. 300). The dorsal surface of the cephalothorax is called the carapace. The 1st pair of legs are the longest. There are no antennae, although a pair of palps at the front of the cephalothorax act like antennae and could be mistaken for them. Male spiders have clubbed palps which they use in courtship and mating. There are usually eight simple eyes, not necessarily all the same size, arranged in various patterns on the front of the cephalothorax. Some spiders have only six eyes.

Spiders are all predatory creatures and many spin elaborate silken snares to trap insects. The most familiar of these snares are the orb-webs (see below), but there are many other designs. Several different kinds of silk are produced in glands that fill much of the spider's body. The threads are extruded from the hind end through three pairs of spinnerets. These are usually very small, but in some spiders they protrude well beyond the tip of the abdomen. The silk is used for wrapping eggs, making shelters and life-lines, and for wrapping prey, as well as for making webs. But not all spiders actually make snares: many actually go hunting, while others merely lie in wait and leap on passing prey. The spider's weaponry consists of a pair of poison fangs called chelicerae, which are hinged just under the front of the carapace. The prey is usually stabbed just behind the head, where the nerves are concentrated, and it is quickly paralysed by the venom. It may then be wrapped in silk before being drained of its body fluids. Digestive juices are pumped into the victim to liquefy the tissues, for the spider can ingest only liquid food. Several spiders in southern Europe can give painful and potentially dangerous bites, but none of the British species is in any way dangerous.

ORB-WEB SPIDERS Argiopidae The spiders in this large family spin more or less circular webs. The orb is built in a framework, whose shape depends on the available supports. Most of the webs are slung in bushes, but walls and fences are equally acceptable. The orb consists of a number of radii on which are laid sticky spiral threads. The droplets of gum which provide the stickiness show up well on misty or frosty mornings. Waxy hairs on its feet prevent the spider from becoming trapped itself, but insects are quickly snared. Some spider species spin a non-sticky central platform, and some also produce a stabilimentum – an area of additional silk along certain radii (below) which may be concerned with strengthening the web. While waiting for prey to arrive, the spiders usually retreat to a shelter a short way from the web, but they remain in contact via a signal thread. Some spiders wait in the centre of the web. Males are usually much smaller than females and have to approach very carefully during courtship to avoid being eaten. Most species pass the winter in the egg stage and mature in late summer. This is when their webs are at their largest and most obvious.

Web of *Araneus*

Web of *Argiope* showing stabilimentum

WEB-SPINNING SPIDERS

▲ **Garden Spider** *Araneus diadematus*. Easily recognised by the white abdominal cross, which gives it its alternative name of cross spider. Abundant in gardens, on fences, and in hedgerows. Generally rests under a nearby leaf.

Garden Spider ×1.5

▲ *A. quadratus* has an extremely rounded abdomen, ranging from deep green to brick red but always with 4 prominent pale spots. Especially common on heathland.

▲ *Araniella cucurbitina* is one of the smallest orb-web spiders. Has a bright red spot under tip of abdomen. Often spins its web across a single leaf. Abundant in a wide range of trees and bushes.

△s *Argiope bruennichi*. Yellow or cream with black lines. Carapace distinctly silvery. Male is extremely small – about 4 mm long and only ⅓ of female's length. Web (opposite) has a vertical stabilimentum. Common in bushes and long grass in S & C. *A. lobata* is an unmistakable spider of southern Europe, spinning a web like that of *bruennichi* in shrubs and dense herbage.

▲ *Zygiella x-notata*. Abdomen with leaf-like pattern edged with pink. Web has 2 empty sectors near top. Very common around window frames and on garden sheds. Closely related species on bushes.

Araneus quadratus ×1.5

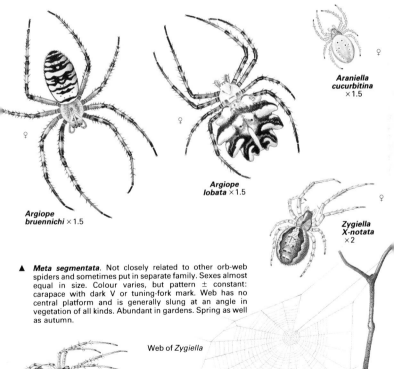

Araniella cucurbitina ×1.5

Argiope bruennichi ×1.5

Argiope lobata ×1.5

Zygiella X-notata ×2

▲ *Meta segmentata*. Not closely related to other orb-web spiders and sometimes put in separate family. Sexes almost equal in size. Colour varies, but pattern ± constant: carapace with dark V or tuning-fork mark. Web has no central platform and is generally slung at an angle in vegetation of all kinds. Abundant in gardens. Spring as well as autumn.

Web of *Zygiella*

Meta segmentata ×2

▲ **Amaurobius similis** Amaurobiidae. Makes lace-like webs on old walls and fences, wherever there is a small crevice into which it can retreat. Web bluish when fresh, but usually greyish and rather scruffy: not remade regularly like orb-webs and new silk is added somewhat haphazardly. ▲ **A. fenestralis** is similar but slightly smaller and more boldly marked. It likes slightly damper habitats than *similis*: common on tree trunks. ▲ **A. ferox** is slightly larger than *A. similis* and almost black, although a faint skull-and-crossbones pattern can usually be seen on the abdomen. It likes much damper places than its 2 relatives and can usually be found lurking under logs and stones and in damp outbuildings.

△ **Pholcus phalangioides** Pholcidae. Commonly known as daddy-long-legs spider: easily identified by very long legs and cylindrical body. Hangs from flimsy web in buildings. Insects flying into web are secured by more silk thrown over them by legs. Also eats other spiders. Vibrates web rapidly when alarmed. S & C.

▲ **Linyphia triangularis** Linyphiidae. Male abdomen uniformly brownish. Dome-shaped sheet-web abundant in hedgerows and bushes in autumn: spider hangs upside-down from lower surface. Irregular scaffolding threads above sheet impede insects, which fall on to sheet and are caught before they can escape: sheet not sticky. There are several similar species. ▲ **L. montana** is equally common, but has plainer and darker abdomen. Its webs sags to form hammock. The money spiders, which make small sheet webs in the grass, also belong to this large family.

?△ **Eresus niger** Eresidae. Female larger than male and velvety black all over. Body very broad at front. She makes burrow with a silk awning over it and a flimsy web on surrounding ground. Adult male, quite unmistakable, wanders freely over ground. Heathland slopes in S & C: probably extinct in B.

▲ **Segestria senoculata** Dysderidae. 6 eyes. Hides in crevices in walls and bark, with a dozen or so silken trip-wires radiating from its silk-lined retreat. Male has relatively longer legs. One of several similar species.

Steatodea paykulliana Theridiidae. Carapace dark brown to black. Male much more slender, with white stripe at front of abdomen and pale chevrons down the middle: legs banded brown and black. Lurks under stones in summer. Female bite said to be poisonous to humans. S & C (southern).

▲ **Enoplognatha ovata** Red stripes often absent, but top of abdomen may also be entirely red. Abundant on nettles and other dense vegetation in summer. Female rolls leaves and deposits bluish green egg cocoon among them. Web is flimsy 3-dimensional trellis, sticky on outside. 5–9.

▲ **Theridion sisyphium** Readily identified by attractive pattern. Spins 3-dimensional web in hedges and bushes: particularly fond of gorse. The web is like flimsy scaffolding, with interlocking horizontal and vertical threads. Central area is sticky and traps small flying insects. The spider makes a thimble-like shelter in upper part of web, using silk and plant fragments. Female rears her brood here and feeds them when they are very young – puncturing the prey so that they can suck up the fluids, or actually regurgitating fluids for them. 5–9.

▲ **Tegenaria gigantea** Agelenidae. One of the house spiders, of which several similar species can be found in houses and other buildings, especially in autumn when males run about in search of mates. Females adult all year and much plumper than males. Triangular sheet-web spun in neglected corners, with tubular retreat at apex. Abundant in sheds and other out-buildings and also out of doors. The females can survive for several years and can exist for several months in houses without either food or drink.

△ **Agelena labyrinthica**. Makes a conspicuous sheet-web among grasses and low shrubs. Sheet leads into tubular retreat from which the spider rushes when food arrives. Web not sticky, but surface covered with a network of trip-wires, like *Tegenaria* web, and insects find escape difficult. 7–8, mainly on heathland.

▲ **Water Spider** *Argyroneta aquatica*. The only truly aquatic spider. Constructs a bell-shaped web under water and fills it with air bubbles. Lives in this air-filled web by day and hunts in the water at night: will also dart out to catch passing insects by day. Air supply periodically renewed by bringing fresh bubbles from the surface. Male often larger than female. Still and slow-moving water.

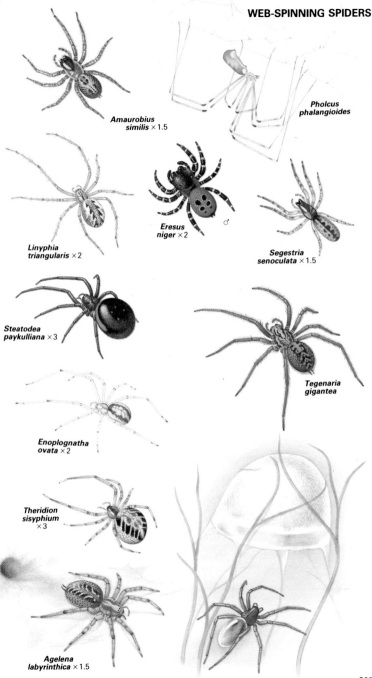

Amaurobius similis ×1.5

Pholcus phalangioides

Linyphia triangularis ×2

Eresus niger ×2 ♂

Segestria senoculata ×1.5

Steatodea paykulliana ×3

Tegenaria gigantea

Enoplognatha ovata ×2

Theridion sisyphium ×3

Agelena labyrinthica ×1.5

Water Spider ×1.5

▲ **Pisaura mirabilis** Pisauridae. Hunts in nettle-beds and other dense vegetation. Sunbathes on leaves with front two legs of each side extending forward and very close together. Male markings stronger. Female carries egg cocoon in fangs. When eggs are about to hatch she attaches cocoon to vegetation, spins a silken tent over it, and stands guard until youngsters disperse. 5–7.

△ **Dolomedes fimbriatus**. 5–8 in swamps and around margins of still water. Often sits on a floating leaf with front legs resting on water surface to pick up vibrations, and then darts over surface to capture insects. Submerges when alarmed.

▲ **Drassodes lapidosus** Gnaphosidae. Spinnerets prominent. A nocturnal hunter spending daytime in silken chamber under stones etc. Prey includes other spiders and is rapidly bound with broad bands of silk. There are several similar species.

▲ **Pardosa amentata** Lycosidae. One of the wolf spiders, hunting prey on the ground and low vegetation. Male uses clubbed palps to signal to female with a kind of semaphore. She carries her wide-seamed egg cocoon attached to spinnerets. Young ride on her back for a few days after hatching. Sunny places with some moisture and shelter: enjoys sunbathing on stones. 4–9. Often abundant in gardens. There are several similar species.

Lycosa narbonensis. A large wolf spider and one of the true tarantulas. Lives in a burrow and races out to capture passing insects. Its bite is painful to humans but not usually dangerous. Mediterranean.

▲ **Dysdera crocata** Dysderidae. 6 eyes. Carapace without central depression. Abdomen grey or white. A nocturnal hunter with huge fangs used to capture woodlice. Spends daytime under stones and debris: fond of compost heaps, where finds both warmth and woodlice. 5–9. ▲ **D. erythrina** is very similar but slightly smaller.

CRAB SPIDERS Thomisidae
These are spiders which lie in wait in flowers and elsewhere and pounce when prey arrives. 1st two pairs of legs longer than others: a crab-like sideways walk. Most are beautifully camouflaged to hide from prey.

▲ **Xysticus cristatus**. Commonest of several similar species. 4–9 in low herbage.

△ **Misumena vatia**. Female pale green, white, or yellow: sometimes with thin red lines on abdomen. Male very much smaller than female. 5–7. Usually on flowers.

△ **Diaea dorsata**. Female carapace bright green in life, but fades after death. Male has reddish brown carapace and yellowish legs with brown rings. 5–7 in trees and bushes, especially box. 5–7.

Heriaeus hirtus. Unusual among crab spiders in being hairy. Male abdomen pale yellow. Both sexes may have red streak along top of abdomen. Lurks among hairy plants 5–7. S & C (southern).

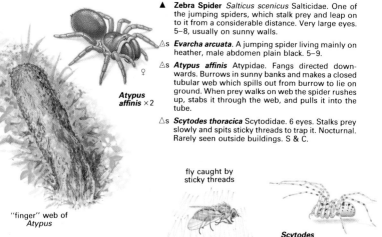

▲ **Zebra Spider** *Salticus scenicus* Salticidae. One of the jumping spiders, which stalk prey and leap on to it from a considerable distance. Very large eyes. 5–8, usually on sunny walls.

△s **Evarcha arcuata**. A jumping spider living mainly on heather, male abdomen plain black. 5–9.

△s **Atypus affinis** Atypidae. Fangs directed downwards. Burrows in sunny banks and makes a closed tubular web which spills out from burrow to lie on ground. When prey walks on web the spider rushes up, stabs it through the web, and pulls it into the tube.

△s **Scytodes thoracica** Scytodidae. 6 eyes. Stalks prey slowly and spits sticky threads to trap it. Nocturnal. Rarely seen outside buildings. S & C.

♀

Atypus affinis × 2

"finger" web of *Atypus*

fly caught by sticky threads

Scytodes thoracica × 2

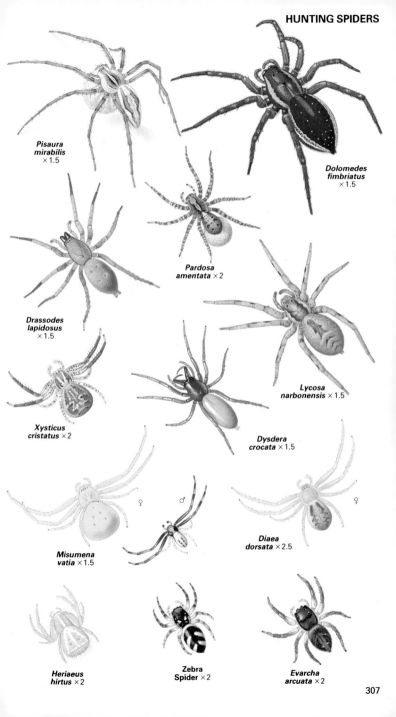

Pisaura mirabilis ×1.5

Dolomedes fimbriatus ×1.5

Pardosa amentata ×2

Drassodes lapidosus ×1.5

Lycosa narbonensis ×1.5

Xysticus cristatus ×2

Dysdera crocata ×1.5

♀ ♂

Misumena vatia ×1.5

♀

Diaea dorsata ×2.5

Heriaeus hirtus ×2

Zebra Spider ×2

Evarcha arcuata ×2

Glossary

Abdomen   Hindmost of the 3 main divisions of the insect body, p. 6

Alula   Conspicuous lobe of the wing membrane in certain files, p. 190

Anal   (1) Concerning the anus or hind end of the abdomen. (2) Concerning the hindmost region of the wing

Antennae   The 'feelers' – the pair of sensory organs on the head, p. 5

Antenodal veins   Small cross veins at the front of dragonfly wings, p. 22

Apical   At or concerning the apex of any organ

Appendage   Any limb or other organ attached to the body by a joint

Apterous   Wingless

Apterygote   Any primitive wingless insect, p. 16

Arista   A bristle-like branch from the antenna in certain flies,

Basitarsus   1st segment of tarsus (foot): usually the largest

Brachypterous   Short-winged

Calypter   A flap-like outgrowth from the thorax of certain flies, p. 190

Campodeiform (larva)   Flattened and elongated, with well developed legs and antennae. Typified by lacewing larva, p. 294

Caste   Any of the 3 or more distinct forms in the colony of a social insect, p. 218

Caudal   Concerning the tail or the rear end

Cell   An area of wing bounded by veins, p. 7

Cerci   The paired appendages, often threadlike, at the tip of the abdomen in many insects, p. 16

Cheek   (= Gena)

Claspers   (1) Last pair of legs of a caterpillar. (2) Modified cerci (q.v.), used by males of some insects to grasp females during mating, p. 48

Clavus   Part of the forewing in heteropteran bugs, p. 70

Clypeus   Lower part of the insect face, just above the mouthparts, p. 5

Corbicula   Pollen basket on the hind leg of many bees, p. 248

Corium   Main part of the forewing of heteropteran bugs, p. 70

Cornicle   One of the paired tubular outgrowths from the aphid abdomen, p. 94

Costa   A long vein, usually forming the front margin of the wing

Coxa   Basal segment of the insect leg, p. 6

Cross Vein   Any short vein linking two neighbouring longitudinal veins, p. 7

Cubitus   One of the major longitudinal wing veins, p. 7

Cuneus   Part of the forewing of certain heteropteran bugs, p. 70

Discal cell   A large or prominent cell near the middle of the wing, p. 7

Distal   Concerning that part of an appendage furthest from the body

Ecdysis   The skin-changing process, p. 8

Ectoparasite   A parasite (q.v.) living on the outside of its host

Elbowed (antenna)   With 1st segment (scape) longer than the rest and with a distinct angle between 1st and 2nd segments, p. 234

Elytron   Tough forewing of a beetle or earwig

Emarginate   Distinctly notched or indented

Embolium   A narrow strip along the front edge of the forewing in certain heteropteran bugs, p. 70

Endoparasite   A parasite (q.v.) living inside its host's body

Endopterygote   Any insect with complete metamorphosis, p. 8

Epiproct   Central 'tail' of bristletails, p. 16 and mayflies, p. 18

Eruciform (larva)   Caterpillar-like

Exopterygote   Any insect with partial metamorphosis (p. 8), with the wings developing gradually on the outside of the body

Femur   3rd and often the largest segment of the insect leg, p. 6

Filiform (antenna)   Threadlike

Flagellum   That part of the antenna beyond the 2nd segment, p. 5

Frenulum   Bristle or group of bristles linking fore and hind wings in moths, p. 110

Frons   Upper part of the insect face, between and below the antennae, p. 5

Gall   Abnormal growth of a plant caued by insects of other organisms in the tissues, p. 226

Gaster   Main part of the hymenopteran abdomen, p. 220

Gena   That area of the insect head below and behind the eye, p. 5

Geniculate   (= Elbowed)

Genitalia   Copulatory organs

Genus   A group of closely related species, all sharing the same first name. (Plural *genera*)

Glabrous   Hairless

Haltere   Modified hind wing in true flies, p. 190

Hemelytron   Forewing of heteropteran bugs, p. 70

Hemimetabolous   Having an incomplete metamorphosis

Holometabolous Having a complete metamorphosis

Humeral Vein A small cross vein near the base of the wing, p. 7

Imago The adult

Instar The stage of development between any two moults, p. 8

Intercalary Vein A longitudinal vein running in from the wing margin but not directly connected to any major vein, p. 20

Larva Young stage of an insect with complete metamorphosis, p. 8

Macropterous Fully winged

Mandible The jaw

Marginal cell Any cell bordering the front margin of the wing

Media A longitudinal vein near the middle of the wing in most insects

Mesothorax 2nd of the 3 thoracic segments

Metamorphosis Change from young to adult form, p. 8

Metatarsus (= Basitarsus)

Metathorax 3rd of the 3 thoracic segments

Micropterous With very small wings

Moniliform (antenna) Composed of bead-like segments

Moulting (= Ecdysis)

Mouthparts Collective name for the feeding appendages around the mouth, p. 5

Nodus A short cross vein in the dragonfly wing, p. 22

Nymph Young stage of an insect with incomplete metamorphosis, p. 8

Ocellus A simple kind of eye, p. 5

Ootheca Egg case of mantids and cockroaches, p. 60–2

Ovipositor Egg-laying tool

Palp A small, sensory leg-like extension of the mouthparts, p. 5

Parasite An organism spending part or all of its life on or in another species (the host), taking food from it but giving nothing in return

Parthenogenesis Virgin birth

Pectinate (antenna) Comb-like, p. 271

Pedicel (1) 2nd segment of the antenna, p. 5 (2) The waist of an ant, p. 234

Petiole The narrow part (waist) of the hymenopteran abdomen, p. 220

Plumose (antenna) Feathery

Probosis Any feeding apparatus used for sucking up fluids

Proleg Any of the stumpy legs on the hind part of a caterpillar, p. 111

Pronotum Upper surface of 1st thoracic segment, p. 6

Propodeum 1st abdominal segment of bees, wasps, etc., p. 220

Prothorax 1st of the 3 thoracic segments, p. 6

Proximal Concerning the basal part of an appendage nearest to the body

Pterostigma (1) A small coloured area near the wingtip of many insects, p. 23. (2) A prominent cell in the psocid wing, p. 98

Puparium Barrel-like pupal case of many flies, p. 190

Quadrilateral An important cell in the damselfly wing, p. 22

Radial sector Posterior of the 2 main branches of the radius vein, p. 7

Radius A major longitudinal wing vein, p. 7

Rostrum A beak or snout, especially in bugs, p. 70 and weevils, pp. 284–6

Scape 1st segment of the antenna, p. 5

Scutellum Large, often triangular plate extending back from the top of the mesothorax, pp. 70, 190

Spur A large and often movable spine on the legs of many insects, p. 183

Stigma (= Pterostigma)

Subcosta The longitudinal vein just behind the front margin of the wing, p. 7

Tarsus The insect foot, p. 6

Tegmen Leathery forewing of grasshoppers, cockroaches, and related insects

Tegula A small lobe or scale overlying the base of the forewing, p. 218

Thoracic Squama (= Calypter)

Thorax Middle of the 3 main body sections, carrying the legs and wings

Tibia One of the segments of the insect leg, p. 6

Triangle An important region near the base of the dragonfly wing, p. 22

Trochanter One of the segments of the insect leg, p. 6

Tympanum Ear drum of various insects, p. 48

Vertex Top of the head, between and behind the eyes, p. 5

Vestigial Poorly developed or degenerate

Index of English Names

Index of Genera and Species

Acknowledgments

The author is extremely grateful to all the numerous friends and colleagues who have generously helped with their answers to questions and expert criticism – particularly to the following: Dr P. C. Barnard, Mr S. J. Brooks, Mr P. S. Broomfield, Mr D. J. Carter, Mr B. H. Cogan, Mr M. C. Day, Mr G. R. Else, Mr P. D. Hillyard, Mrs J. A. Marshall, Mr R. D. Pope, Mr J. Quinlan, Dr D. R. Ragge, Mr W. J. Reynolds, Mr C. R. Vardy, Dr. I. H. H. Yarrow.

He also thanks the Trustees and staff of the British Museum (Natural History) for making specimens available for study and painting, and is also very grateful in this respect to Mr B. R. Baker and Mr C. Sizer of Reading Museum and Art Gallery and to Mr M. Scoble of the Hope Department of Entomology at Oxford.

Most of all, we are grateful to our artists. Principally, **Denys Ovenden** contributed the whole initial design, all the line-drawings, his imaginative advice throughout, and painted the Odonata, Orthoptera, Hemiptera, the bees and many of the minor groups; **Richard Lewington** the Lepidoptera, Coleoptera and much of the Hymenoptera; and **Stephen Falk** (while still a student at London University) the Diptera. **Réné Préchac** painted the Trichoptera, **Anthony Hopkins** the wasps, and **John Wilkinson** the plates of stoneflies, larvae and myriapods. Such fine work in turn demanded exceptional care from both colour reproducers and printers, which we greatly appreciate.